THE STRUCTURE OF RESURRECTION BELIEF

The Structure of Resurrection Belief

PETER CARNLEY

CLARENDON PRESS · OXFORD

Oxford University Press, Walton Street, Oxford OX2 6DP
Oxford New York Toronto
Delhi Bombay Calcutta Madras Karachi
Kuala Lumpur Singapore Hong Kong Tokyo
Nairobi Dar es Salaam Cape Town
Melbourne Auckland Madrid
and associated companies in
Berlin Ibadan

Oxford is a trade mark of Oxford University Press

Published in the United States
by Oxford University Press Inc., New York

British Library Cataloguing in Publication Data
Data available

Library of Congress Cataloging in Publication Data
Carnley, Peter.
The structure of resurrection belief.
Bibliography: p.
Includes index.
1. Jesus Christ—Resurrection. 2. Resurrection—
History of doctrines—20th Century. I. Title.
BT481.C37 1987 232'.5 86–18203
ISBN 0–19–826756–8

Printed in Great Britain
on acid-free paper by
Bookcraft (Bath) Ltd.,
Midsomer Norton, Avon

FOR ANN

It is foolish to sigh and complain about mankind's disbelief if one cannot furnish men with the persuasive evidence that the matter demands, based on a healthy reason.

HERMANN SAMUEL REIMARUS.

PREFACE

THIS book should have been completed by the end of 1980. The initial work on the manuscript was done in Cambridge during the first half of that year whilst I was on study leave which I had accrued as Warden of St John's College within the University of Queensland.

Unfortunately, Australian universities were at that time under governmental pressure to restrict study leave entitlements: it was a privilege, we were told, rather than a right. In this unsympathetic environment, my lecturing commitments in the Department of Studies in Religion in the University of Queensland were deemed not to permit an extended absence. Indeed, my study leave 'entitlement' entirely evaporated.

Then, at the end of 1980, I was quite unexpectedly elected to be Archbishop of Perth and Metropolitan of the Anglican Province of Western Australia. This put an end to my hope of completing the manuscript, for the need to learn the new tasks of episcopal ministry following my consecration on 26th May 1981 and the obligation to get to know literally thousands of new faces in a lively and adventurous diocese, left no time at all for writing.

However, after three very full years, I was indebted to the good people of Perth for tolerating my absence from the diocese from May to July 1984. This gave me the long-waited opportunity to tie off the threads of this book.

I am very grateful to all those who so generously accommodated me and provided hospitality and care during my absence from home in 1984. Especially I wish to record my thanks to Dean James Fenhagen and the Trustees of the General Theological Seminary in New York, not only for providing accommodation for the six weeks I spent at the Seminary, but for the honour of the award of the honorary degree of Doctor of Divinity, which was conferred upon me by the Seminary at its Commencement Ceremony on the 16th May 1984. This was a very happy and memorable occasion. I am also very grateful to my good friend, Alan Jones, who was at that time the Stephen F. Bayne Professor of Ascetical Theology and Director of the Centre for Christian Spirituality at the Seminary, and to his secretary, Sherri McNeeley, for so kindly organizing my Manhattan programme in such a way as to leave time for writing and for the checking of references.

Very importantly, I wish to express my gratitude to the Master and Fellows of St John's College, Cambridge, who, since my time as a research student (1967–9) and later as a Research Fellow (1971–2), have so generously extended the hospitality of the College to me by providing rooms and dining rights and the congenial support of an academical community. Without the month of quietness in July 1984 in B5 of the Cripps Building at St John's, with its splendid view of the Cam and its proximity to the University Library, the project would not have been completed.

Given that it is now likely that this book will be read outside narrowly academical circles, I have attempted, at the risk of some repetition, to unpack my meaning so as to make it a little more accessible to people for whom the general approach and level of treatment is more detailed than that to which they may be accustomed. I am aware, nevertheless, that it is not an easy or 'popular' book.

The only part of it to have been given a public airing was an early draft of Chapter IV. This was first read at a seminar at the University of Nottingham in 1980 and again, at around the same time, at the 412th Meeting of the Lightfoot Society in Durham. I am most appreciative to Richard McKinney and his wife, Margie, who were then at Nottingham and to Stephen Sykes and his wife, Joy, for their kind hospitality at Durham.

Students and old boys of St John's Theological College, Morpeth, New South Wales, where my mind was first opened to the scientific study of theology, will also recognize a few echoes of lectures which were delivered at the College in the course of the 1983 reunion. I am grateful to George Garnsey, the College Warden, for inviting me back for this hilarious occasion.

Pam Penman, is to be thanked for her quiet dedication to the production of a fair copy of the manuscript from bits and pieces which arrived through the post from various parts of the globe. John Kollosche facilitated the safe transmission of manuscripts and proofs from Perth to Oxford and Susan Maushart helped compile the Index. I thank them both. Robin Denniston and staff members of the Oxford University Press have been patiently helpful in the preparation and copy editing of the manuscript and in the painstaking work of final production. On the other hand, I am grateful to Maurice Wiles, who read the manuscript, for responding so positively to it, and for encouraging its publication in the first place.

Finally, my dear wife, Ann, who has lived with me, along with the regular distraction of the Resurrection of Christ and its historical and theological problems, for most of our married life, and my children, Benedict and Sarah, deserve a particular word of gratitude. My time overseas in 1984 necessitated our separation for ten weeks. I thank them for so willingly agreeing to that. Certainly, without the support of my wife, Ann, the task of completing this book would probably have been deferred in favour of any one of a hundred other things. To her I dedicate the finished product; it certainly would not have come to be without her sustained and loving encouragement.

In and through all this I have glimpsed something of the Spirit which in faith I recognize as the gracious presence of the raised Christ himself; he in all of us, and we in him. I am grateful to my family and all my friends; whether consciously Christian, or unwitting, they have been the mediators of the revelation of the Spirit of Christ in their lives and it is marvellous in my eyes.

Archbishop's House, Perth   †PETER PERTH
July 1985

CONTENTS

Contents   xiii

I

The Resurrection and Contemporary Theology

Resurrection and Incarnation

THEOLOGY, like most other man-made things, is subject to fashion. One only has to reflect upon the history of theology over the course of our own century in order to be able to distinguish the remnant survival of nineteenth-century liberal protestant theology from the dialectical theology which very self-consciously challenged it in the first decades of this century; then came the Biblical Theology movement in the period immediately following the Second World War, with its eirenic desire to enter the mind of the first-century Christians through a study of the distinctive meanings of key terms in their vocabulary. This enterprise was in turn rudely disturbed by theology's brief flirtation with modern secularism in the 'Death of God' debate of the late 1960s, which, if nothing else, reminded us of the folly of seeking to live our Christian lives in the intellectual world of the first century. After the Second Vatican Council ecclesiology held pride of place until the human deprivation of the world's hungry and socially marginalized people shamed the Church out of its pre-occupation with its own self-understanding and prompted it to make a spirited theological response to human need in the form of the liberation theology and political theology of more recent times.

Because theology is a co-operative enterprise it is necessarily subject to fashion and changes of fashion. Theologians are stimulated and challenged by one another's ideas and prompted to articulate new theological insights as they correct the flaws they see in one another's work or otherwise build upon what others have done. In this way the Church is gradually led into all truth, even if there is at times a little kicking and screaming or if the process of debate is sometimes strained and painful or over-sensationalized by the media, which still regard doctrinal controversy as an eminently newsworthy matter. Generally speaking it is a good and hopeful thing that theology is not practised in a self-contained retreat, remote from the life of the Church at large and that parish clergy and laity take an interest in what is being said by their academic theologians. Even if it is not always fully understood or the subtleties of debate are sometimes unappreciated, this is better than a patronizing attempt to keep people in the dark for fear of 'disturbing them with new ideas'. Indeed, theologians have a responsibility to keep the Church abreast of new theological trends and developments; this is especially so if there are good grounds for thinking that received opinions are in urgent need of revision.

In recent years the interest of theologians has been directed with more than usual excitement to the discussion of the doctrine of the person and work of Christ. Indeed, this is one of the most absorbing concerns of current theology and there is little sign yet that the point of resolution is near or that the debate is running out of steam. Christology is still very much in the theological air, precisely because a technical interest in the question of the definition of the person of Jesus has become a matter of sporadic controversy, which has broken out in the media and thus in full public view.[1]

The most recent phase of the discussion of the correct or most satisfactory means of conceiving of the way in which humanity and divinity come together in the person of Jesus Christ may be reckoned to date from the publication in Britain of the controversial volume of essays entitled *The Myth of God Incarnate*, in July 1977.[2]

[1] The cyclone of controversy surrounding the consecration of the Revd Professor David Jenkins as Bishop of Durham in July 1984, following remarks he made on British television concerning the Virgin Birth and the necessity of belief in a physical resurrection, is a good example of what I mean. The wide media coverage given to the examination of the Christology of Edward Schillebeeckx by the Vatican's Sacred Congregation for the Doctrine of the Faith during 1980 is an alternative example.

[2] J. Hick (ed.), *The Myth of God Incarnate*; see also M. Green (ed.), *The Truth of God Incarnate*; Don Cupitt, *The Debate About Christ*; A. E. Harvey (ed.), *God Incarnate: Story and Belief*. See also C. F. D. Moule, *The Origin of Christology*.

Another important stimulus to Christological reflection was the publication in English of Edward Schillebeeckx's *Jesus* in 1979 and *Christ* in English translation in 1980. These works had appeared in Holland in 1974 and 1977 respectively. Something of the controversy surrounding the publication of Schillebeeckx's books may be seen in the journalistic account of his harassment at the hands of the Roman magisterium in Peter Hebblethwaite, *A New Inquisition?*, and Schillebeeckx's own apologia *Interim Report on the Books Jesus and Christ.*

The discussion concerning the viability of expressing Christ's divinity in terms of the conception of the 'incarnation of God', which followed immediately upon the publication of that volume, was conducted within remarkably narrow limits. These were imposed by an original agenda of a well-defined and specific kind which the contributors to the volume adopted as the programmatic outline of their work: the debate had to do with the coherence or otherwise of what, for better or worse, was called 'the traditional way' in which Christians have understood and expressed their apprehension of the uniqueness of Christ's person. This means that, by and large, the ensuing debate focused on the nature of his inner make-up or essential constitution. The chief issue was whether Jesus is best understood quite simply as being identical with God despite the human, finite form in which he was known on this earth, or whether it makes more contemporary sense to see him as a man expressing the image of God in unique degree. Is he God-made-Man or a representative man, mediating the divine saving activity of God to other men in a uniquely poignant and non-repeatable way?

Either way, those on both sides of the debate became involved in a somewhat airborne discussion of the idea of the incarnation. Apart from the clarification of difficulties attaching to the use of the controversial term 'myth', a great deal of the energy that was expended in the course of the debate therefore had to do with the clarification of the precise meaning of the term 'incarnation'. Professor Maurice Wiles, in an early review of the debate,[3] recognized that this is a very slippery concept which calls for careful definition. Does it necessarily imply the pre-existence of Christ as a heavenly and eternal 'centre of personality', or 'I-centre' as Karl Rahner puts it,[4] or can an understanding of the incarnation of God be worked out in terms of the embodiment of divine purpose and activity in the life of one whose centre of personality remains unequivocally human? Does the concept of incarnation entail that Jesus is a divine being, different from us *in kind*, or is he essentially one of us, a human being used by God in such a way that an eternal and pre-existing divine purpose and activity can be said to have been brought into clear focus and defined in and through his historical life, thus

[3] 'A Survey of Issues in the Myth Debate' in *Incarnation and Myth*, ed. M. Goulder, pp. 1–12.

[4] K. Rahner, 'Current Problems in Christology' in *Theological Investigations*, Vol. 1, pp. 149–200.

making him different from others but only *in degree*? A third possibility, barely touched upon in the course of the debate, is that both these ways of explaining Christ's divinity may be accorded the status of models, which together may help to reduce something of the incomprehensibility of the divine mystery in Christ, but neither of which is to be given the status of an exact description.

In any event, it was not Jesus' divinity, uniqueness, and ultimate religious significance that was at issue, so much as the precise manner in which his divinity may best be expressed. I think we must say that the issue remains unresolved.

Whatever the eventual outcome of this debate, it has to do with the Christian understanding of the *person* of Christ. What is at stake in terms of doctrine is the question of exactly what is to be believed about him, his nature and personal identity.

The liveliness and intensity of this debate, concentrated as it has been upon this narrowly defined agenda, should not blind us, however, to the fact that the reasons for Christian commitment to Christ are not exhaustively expressed in statements of belief about his unique inner make-up and the religious significance of it. Despite the contemporary pre-occupation with the question of the best way to express an understanding of the nature of his person, the doctrine of the incarnation may not be quite fundamental or even central to the Christian understanding of things. Indeed, some critics of the essays in *The Myth of God Incarnate* pointed out at the time of its publication that the very narrowness of fundamental approach adopted by the authors was not so much evidence of the virtue of intellectual self-discipline as a basic defect in their work. There is a need, for example, to approach an understanding of the incarnation with an eye to the wider question of the relationship between the doctrine of the incarnation and other fundamental Christian beliefs that are perhaps less central but no less important to the Christian understanding of the relation of God and Man. The doctrine of the *work* of Christ, the atonement, for instance, has been held to be of importance to a correct understanding of Christ's person: whatever way the inner constitution of his person is explained, it must be of such a kind that it can account for the Christian experience of reconciliation with God. The doctrine of the incarnation of God in Christ clearly has something to do with the more broad question of the way God and humanity in general 'come together'. In other words, the moral and religious consequences of abandoning the idea of 'incarnation' may be a very relevant theological consideration.[5] Alternatively, and working from the opposite perspective, an appreciation of the nexus between Christology and Soteriology may help us to see that reflection upon the Christian experience of reconciliation with God may be the only satisfactory way to an adequate understanding of Christ's person; Soteriology is the way to Christology.

More importantly for our present purposes, some of the critics of the original essays in *The Myth of God Incarnate* pointed to the authors' almost complete lack of interest in the doctrine of the resurrection of Christ. This, once again, is an aspect of the work of Christ, or to put it more properly, the work of God in Christ, which may bear directly upon an understanding of who he was. Indeed, some reviewers not only expressed their regret that the authors had not taken sufficient account of the resurrection, but even went on to suggest that many of the basic deficiencies that they found in the final outcome could have been avoided if the resurrection of Christ had been taken more seriously.

John Austin Baker, for example, noted with some consternation that in treating the sources of incarnational belief less than two pages were given to a consideration of the resurrection[6] and complained that, in view of the importance of the Easter faith to the interpretation of Jesus in the New Testament Church, the whole of one major essay ought to have been devoted to it. By leaving the resurrection of Christ out of account the contributors to *The Myth* certainly made their task easier but, says Baker, 'they also made the finished product superficial and very much less helpful to the debate they desire than it might have been'.[7]

Apart from pointing to the dangers involved in isolating one aspect of Christian doctrine from others, this highlights the potential importance of the doctrine of the resurrection, in particular to the Christian understanding of other matters, including Christ's person. Certainly, the resurrection of Christ is an issue of quite

---

[5] See Brian Hebblethwaite, 'The Moral and Religious Value of the Incarnation', *Incarnation and Myth*, pp. 87–100.

[6] J. A. Baker, Review of *The Myth of God Incarnate*, JTS, 29 (1978), p. 293. See also the review of John Coventry 'The Myth and the Method' in *Theology*, lxxxi (1978), pp. 252–61.

[7] Ibid., p. 297.

fundamental importance to Christology. It ought not to be left out of account.

Despite the fact that the authors of *The Myth* paid the subject of the resurrection of Christ very scant attention, most contemporary New Testament scholars have been anxious to affirm that the resurrection is not just a loosely connected appendage to a set of beliefs that might be formulated concerning Jesus' nature and identity as the Christ of God. The datum for faith in Christ is not just the historical life of Jesus from his birth to his crucifixion. Even if some inkling of his divine significance was arrived at during his lifetime, it was shattered by his premature and devastating death. Genuine Christian faith is a post-Easter phenomenon, and the presentation of his life and death in the gospels is made in the retrospective light of it.[8] Indeed, it was primitive resurrection faith which initiated the various attempts of the early Church to express its understanding of the uniqueness of Jesus' person. What had happened to Jesus, what God had done to and for him and, indeed, for the world, preceded talk of who he was and how it was that the divine was united to the human in him.

It can be cogently argued that the formulation of the original theological assessment of the person of Jesus and the use of the various messianic titles such as Lord, Messiah, Son of God, to designate something of his distinctive role in the processes of human redemption, comes at the end rather than at the beginning of the set of beliefs that centre upon him. The affirmation of belief in Christ's resurrection and in Christ as the raised, exalted Lord of the Christian community, was indisputably the point of origin of the efflorescence of the original Christological assessment of Jesus' function and identity. Indeed, in the recent climate of preoccupation with the formulation of the doctrine of incarnation, we have to remind ourselves that, prior to all the Christological talk *about Jesus*, which eventually resulted at Chalcedon with the definition of the incarnation of God in Christ in terms of one person with two natures, there were Christian men and women whose fundamental affirmation of belief seems to have centred almost exclusively upon his resurrection from the dead. Indeed, amongst the first generation of Christians there may have been little or no interest in the question of the nature of his being or inner identity at all. Rather, early

[8] G. Bornkamm, *Jesus of Nazareth*, p. 181.

Christian faith and practice seems to have focused upon the affirmation of the resurrection of Christ and upon what could be expected to happen in the imminent future of the world as a consequence of it. I think for example of the primitive declarations of faith in the sermons now found in the early chapters of the book of Acts in which it is argued, on the basis of the resurrection belief, that Jesus had been designated or made 'Lord' and 'Christ' (Acts 3: 12–21; 2: 22–36). These early Christological titles drew their meaning not only from their former use in Jewish religious and prophetic traditions (as is now regularly said in Christological discussion) but also from the actual Easter experience which grounded the affirmation that Jesus had been raised. It was as a consequence of the resurrection that Jesus could be understood as one who exercised a continuing sovereignty or lordship over his people by virtue of which the use of such a title as 'Lord' became appropriate.

On the other hand, belief in Jesus' continuing heavenly life and exalted status as the raised Lord meant that he could be expected in the imminent future to return from the radical hiddenness of heaven in a messianic role to dispense divine judgement and deliverance. He could thus be called 'Christ' or 'Messiah.' Whatever inherited meanings attached to these Christological titles, the early resurrection experience brought them to the lips of the first Christians, charged them with new significance, and gave them their distinctively Christian colouring. In other words, it was not just that the resurrection operated as a neutral trigger and stimulus that prompted the early Christians to begin to interpret Jesus christologically with inherited titles; rather, belief in his continuing heavenly and exalted status entailed that he was understood to exercise the role of Lord and Messiah in a divinely transcendent way and this to some extent redefined the actual meaning of these inherited titles. Too much contemporary Christology concentrates on the historical analysis of the inherited meaning of the titles and too little on the question of the impact of the concrete experience of the resurrection on the titles and their meaning.

I stress this because it has been fashionable, particularly in Anglican theology since the mid-nineteenth century, to regard the incarnation as the central affirmation of Christian belief, in the light of which other elements within the edifice of Christian doctrine may be understood. Under the influence of the pioneering work of

Charles Gore and others, for example,[9] the so-called 'incarnational principle' has been utilized to express an understanding of God, the atonement, the Church, and the sacraments. The seriousness with which the contemporary debate about the concept of incarnation has been prosecuted has inevitably tended to reinforce the centrality of incarnational doctrine in the Anglican tradition. Some contributors to the recent debate about the incarnation of God, have even defended its centrality in quite unequivocal terms. Professor Stephen Sykes has argued, for example, that 'incarnational theology' is 'the foundation of theology'.[10] For him, the incarnation is to be understood as the central element in a story which is fundamental to the life of the Church in the sense that the Church is said to be 'constituted around the story'. By the constant rehearsal of the story in which the incarnation of God in Christ is the central event, the story itself becomes woven into the liturgy and life of the community, which would not exist without it. The incarnation is foundational to the Church in so far as it is a key element in this story around which the Church gathers.

Whilst this seems true enough, it has a negative implication as far as the resurrection and its importance is concerned. From this incarnational perspective the resurrection of Christ takes a secondary and subsidiary place. It becomes little more than the final episode and climax of the story. But the resurrection is much more fundamental than that. If anything it is the resurrection which is the foundation of the Church, its worship and its theology, for the Church gathers not just around the rehearsal of the story of the incarnation of God, but around the perceived presence of the raised Christ *himself*. What provides us with the really crucial, controlling category for Christian theology, is the idea of the *Christus praesens*. Resurrection theology is in turn the foundation of all theology in the sense that secondary affirmations of belief are drawn from it concerning Christ's messianic role and divine status. Eventually this leads on to incarnational talk of God's sending of his Son into the world.

Apart from the logical priority of resurrection talk over incarnation talk, the resurrection has a temporal priority in the evolution of faith. The experience of the presence of the raised Christ, indeed,

---

[9] See the essays in *Lux Mundi*, ed. Charles Gore, especially the contribution by R. C. Moberly, 'The Incarnation as the Basis of Dogma', pp. 215–72.

[10] *Incarnation and Myth*, pp. 115–27.

marks the historical beginning of the telling of the Christian story. Moreover, from the perspective of resurrection belief it was affirmed that Jesus was present in the Christian community through the medium of his continuing Spirit, the concrete inner substance of the corporate fellowship. The continuing experience of the Spirit of Christ in the life of the Church, is in turn the ground of its forward-looking hope for the future manifestation of the Raised One in all the world. This means, as Walter Künneth has correctly put it, that the Resurrection '*is the primal datum of theology*'.[11]

Whether belief in the resurrection can act as a salve to soothe away all the difficulties that have emerged concerning the doctrine of the incarnation is another matter. Both John Baker and John Coventry, whilst bewailing the fact that the essayists of *The Myth of God Incarnate* did not place the doctrine of the incarnation in a broader context and omitted particularly to relate it to the resurrection, have themselves failed to say clearly what they mean by 'the resurrection' nor shown how it might purge defective christology from error. In other words, it is one thing to call attention to the absence of any sustained or controlling reference to the resurrection; it is another matter to trace the logical route from affirmations of belief in the resurrection of Christ to a theologically adequate and acceptably coherent understanding of his personal being and identity.

On the other hand, the theology of the resurrection is hardly the most straightforward and uncomplicated of theological topics. As we shall see in subsequent chapters of this book, a theology of the resurrection has to pick its way through a minefield of problems of a historical, theological, and epistemological kind, and even the most introductory reading of theologies of the resurrection that have appeared over the last generation, let alone over the last one hundred years, will amply demonstrate the irreconcilably diverse and confused nature of Christian thought on the subject. As one contemporary theologian has said, 'it is a source of no small embarrassment to Christian theology that our accumulated efforts remind one of nothing so much as the tower of Babel'.[12]

Certainly, Christians cannot simply assume that they know what they mean by 'the resurrection of Christ'. If anything, it must be

---

[11] W. Künneth, *The Theology of the Resurrection*, p. 294.
[12] R. R. Bater, 'Towards a More Biblical View of the Resurrection', *Interpretation*, 23 (1969), p. 49.

admitted that the event of the resurrection of Christ is as obscure and impenetrable as the understanding of the nature of his person.

Those who have pointed to the folly of attempting to express the nature of Jesus' unique identity without first treating the resurrection are almost certainly on the right track, but given the current state of resurrection studies, we may not be able to move very far along it. Leslie Houlden, for example, is perfectly aware of this sorry state of theological affairs and is therefore sceptical about the capacity of the doctrine of the resurrection to illuminate anything. The hope of elucidating the doctrine of incarnation 'by setting it alongside of another area which is equally problematic makes only for deeper darkness'.[13] This points to the regrettable fact that, though utterly central to the entire Christian dispensation, the doctrine of the resurrection of Christ suffers from a remarkable under-systematization which leaves it less than clear. This means that whilst the contemporary Christological debate has focused attention almost exclusively on the question of the continuing viability of the doctrine of the incarnation, it is just as important, if not more so, to raise the question of the viability or otherwise of the traditional belief in the resurrection of Christ, upon which all Christological talk ultimately depends.[14]

Theological diversity

In 1945 Michael Ramsey noted that apart from the third century when gnosticism stirred up a hornet's nest of controversy concerning the bodily resurrection, surprisingly little energy has been directed towards the theology of the resurrection.[15] This neglect may possibly be traced to the fact that for centuries the resurrection

---

[13] L. Houlden, 'A Wider Framework' in *Incarnation and Myth*, pp. 106–7.

[14] Cf. J. Moltmann, *The Theology of Hope*, p. 165: 'Christianity stands or falls with the reality of the raising of Jesus from the dead by God. In the New Testament there is no faith that does not start a priori with the resurrection of Jesus.'

[15] Michael Ramsey, *The Resurrection of Christ*, pp. 115 f., says: 'There has yet to be written a great book telling of what the resurrection has meant in the thought, doctrine and worship of Christians down the ages'. See C. F. Evans's response to this in *Resurrection and the New Testament*, p. 5 and R. C. Ware, 'The Resurrection of Jesus I', *Heythrop Journal*, 16, (1975), p. 22. As Ware notes, the exception to the historical tendency to neglect the theology of the resurrection is the Eastern Orthodox Church and its concentration of attention on worship in relation to the Easter Jesus. 'It is to this hiatus in Christian consciousness and theological reflection, exacerbated by the radical new conditions and presuppositions of the modern world-view, that the resurrection debate of recent decades has addressed itself.' (p. 24.)

has been handled with a deceptively unambiguous matter-of-factness. However, since the Enlightenment and the rise of modern historical consciousness and the development of the most sophisticated critical-scientific techniques of historical enquiry, this central tenet of the Christian confession has been cast in an uncomfortably problematic light.

Certainly, during the two hundred years since the publication by Lessing of the infamous Wolfenbüttel *Fragments* of Hermann Samuel Reimarus (between 1774 and 1778) theologians have come to an unparalleled array of radically different understandings of what is involved in resurrection faith. The emergence of a wide variety of conflicting views concerning the nature of the resurrection of Christ is accompanied by a corresponding diversity of views concerning the mode of its apprehension in human consciousness. These diverse views range from the traditional belief in the resurrection of Christ as an objective historical event, accessible to the historical reason, to the view of Reimarus himself, that the occurrence of the resurrection is actually to be denied on the basis of the many discrepancies in the records that are exposed by a critical-historical examination of the texts.[16] This in turn allows for the Easter faith to be explained as a kind of after-effect of Jesus' historical life, from birth to death, and nothing more.

Whilst the Church for eighteen centuries admittedly perceived something of the diversity in the New Testament Easter tradition, this diversity was entertained within a generally admitted base-line consensus about the fundamental understanding of the resurrection as, at the very least, an objective event. As a result of this basic consensus it could unequivocally be affirmed by believers that Jesus was certainly raised from the dead. This at least was thought to be fact.

In the last two hundred years, however, this has become problematical to many, not only outside the Church but also within it. As a consequence we can now quite seriously ask whether the resurrection is properly understood as a post-mortem event, subsequent to the crucifixion of Jesus, or is it better understood merely as religiously significant myth which in fact frees us from the embarrassment of having to speak of it as an actual happening? After all, the resurrection could be understood as a symbolic or mythical way of

---

[16] H. S. Reimarus, *Fragments*, pp. 197–200.

affirming some general truth of a moral or religious kind: is the story of the resurrection anything more than a graphic way of affirming the truth that 'death does not have the final say' or that 'the innocent sufferer will be vindicated' and that 'God's justice will ultimately prevail over the unrighteousness of men'?

In contemporary theology it is therefore possible to find a spectrum of views, ranging from belief in the resurrection of Christ as a historical event of the past, to talk of it as little more than a religiously useful story, or myth. This is not to mention a very significant number of theologians who are content to treat the resurrection with a degree of ambivalence or lack of candour which makes it somewhat difficult to discern any clear outline of the exact position that they espouse!

Broadly speaking, contemporary views about the resurrection fall into three main groupings. First, there are those who hold what may for the sake of convenience be called the 'traditional' view that the resurrection of Christ was a historical event of the past to which people have access primarily by the exercise of historical reason. It is true that few have held that historical research can actually prove the occurrence, but many at least contend that a rational consideration of the evidence leads in the direction of the truth of the traditional Christian claim. The belief that Jesus was raised from the dead has been said to be supported by evidence that is as good as one can ever expect historical research to find, even if it does not prove its point with absolute certainty. Reason is, in this way, a support to faith which becomes a commitment of the will where reason leaves off. The historical evidence of the empty tomb and the alleged appearances are therefore 'signs' of the truth of resurrecion belief even if they do not constitute a watertight case. This is the classical Thomist view which still lives on amongst contemporary theologians as well as amongst a great majority of Christian people. It is the 'commonsense' view of things.

Second, there are those who are far more pessimistic about the role of human reason and who doubt its ability to ground and support faith. Some, indeed, deny quite categorically that human reason has a part to play in the structure of resurrection belief at all and have developed theologies in which the principle that the findings of critical-historical research have no place in the structure of belief is carried through as a methodological programme. These usually affirm that faith is a gift from God, quite unrelated to the

exercise of critical-historical techniques and the drawing of inferences from evidence. Faith is therefore said to stand on its own feet,
making its own *sui generis* claims and refusing to respond to those
who call for the tabling of its credentials: God cannot be put to the
test.

Amongst this group there are those, represented pre-eminently in
the twentieth century by Karl Barth, who hold that the resurrection
can and even must be understood in objective terms as an event of
the past, even if as an event of an extraordinary kind, which does
not yield to the techniques of critical historical enquiry. Then there
are others, amongst whom the chief protagonist is Rudolf Bultmann, who hold that the Easter faith of the disciples is primarily a
subjective response to the Easter kerygma with no clearly objective
content. In this case the resurrection is not to be spoken of or described as an event of the objective order. It can only be spoken of in
the most equivocal sense as the event in which the disciples came to
faith in response to the address of the raised Christ who is said to be
'present to the believer' in so far as his address is heard in the
church's ministry of proclamation. It is not to be talked about as an
objective occurrence by employing one's discursive reason, but the
living Word of the raised Christ is to be responded to in an individual decision of will.

Third, there are those, particularly in more recent years, who
insist that the Easter faith of Christians is nothing more than a
response based upon the historical life of Jesus from his birth to his
death and not on any post-mortem occurrence at all, irrespective of
whether that occurrence is established or supported by historical
evidence, or whether it is an occurrence of an altogether different
kind that is accessible only to faith in independence of reason. I shall
call this the modern reductionist view. In this category we may
place those who, since Reimarus and the work of the nineteenth-
century theologian D. F. Strauss, have held that the primitive Christian claim that Jesus was the Messiah was simply a judgement based
upon the historical life of Jesus from his birth to his death alone.
The datum for faith is thus the historical life and death and not a
post-mortem event after the crucifixion of Jesus. In the case of D. F.
Strauss, the so-called event in which early Christians claimed to see
the raised Jesus is to be understood in terms of a 'subjective vision'
or, as we would today call it, a 'hallucination' of a purely psychological kind, rather than something actually and objectively seen.

Some might wish to argue that Rudolf Bultmann should be placed alongside Strauss in this category, since he allegedly denies the historical reality and objectivity of the resurrection. In so far as he speaks of the coming to faith as itself the Easter event, rather than of an event involving Jesus to which faith is a response, his understanding of things might well be called reductionist. I am inclined not to place him in this category, however, for there are other important respects in which his views differ radically from those which are certainly to be discussed under this head. For example, even though Bultmann denies that faith is based upon a post-mortem occurrence involving the perception of the objective presence of Jesus, it is at least said to be precipitated in the period after the crucifixion of Jesus *by something*. In his case it is the church's proclamation of the saving significance of the cross rather than an appearance of Jesus that precipitates faith, but Bultmann at least describes the ensuing experience of faith as an experience of encounter with Christ 'present in the kerygma'. Those who are more clearly to be termed 'reductionist' have no need to speak of the 'presence of Christ' in the period after the crucifixion at all. Such talk can be set aside as positively misleading.

Given this somewhat bewildering diversity of view concerning what happened at the first Easter and how the resurrection faith of Christians is to be understood, it might be thought that all that is needed to rectify the situation is to beat a hasty retreat 'back to the Bible'. All that the systematic theologian need do is to harmonize and develop a basically simple and clear understanding of things that are already found within the pages of the New Testament. Unfortunately, over the last generation the possibility of doing this has entirely evaporated.

During the period of the ascendancy of the Biblical Theology movement, particularly in the years immediately following the end of the Second World War, the environment was much more congenial. In that period, the prevailing *Tendenz* amongst biblical theologians was to seek a harmony of theological opinion within the admitted variety of the New Testament writings. It was quite innocently assumed that it was possible to establish a kind of common theological denominator, at least on essential doctrinal issues, which could be regarded as *the* New Testament view of this or that subject. The pages of the New Testament were therefore understood to be capable of supplying the systematic theologian with materials of a partially systematized kind; his task was simply to extend a system that was believed to be already there at hand. *The* New Testament doctrine of God or of Christ or of the Holy Spirit, or *the* New Testament understanding of the church or of Christian ethics, thus became the solid ground upon which the contemporary systematician could build his doctrinal edifice or moral theology or whatever.

Implicit within this approach to theology was the assumption that all canonical writers of the New Testament said basically more or less the same thing, or at least complementary things about the same subject, which could be harmonized into a single coherent doctrinal view. Such an assumption easily insinuated itself into the theological mind with the support of a background belief in the unifying impact of the mind of God himself, inspiring the individual human authors of the biblical books to write down roughly the same theological thing, despite their individual idiosyncrasies, which were assumed to introduce only very superficial discrepancies of opinion.

More recently, however, it has become clear that more serious account must be taken of the variety of theological opinion generated by the various New Testament writers. The efflorescence of redaction criticism amongst the present generation of New Testament scholars has had the effect of clarifying and highlighting the individuality of the gospel writers as they edited the traditions which they received in the interests of communicating to their own particular time and circumstance. The mind of Paul and other authors of epistles is different again. If a belief in biblical inspiration is to survive at all, it is now more likely to be understood in terms of the creative inspiration of each individual author as he grappled to answer essentially new questions and meet the changing needs and unique demands of his own particular situation in life, which also contributed to the distinctive character of his work.

The methodological implications of this quite new state of biblical affairs for systematic theology are quite momentous. It is now clear that the variety of theological views found within the pages of the New Testament on this or that matter may not even be complementary, let alone basically identical. On the contrary, they may be in logical competition with one another. This stands as a warning against any attempt to impose an awkward doctrinal harmony upon the New Testament. Theological homogenization of the biblical texts is today frowned upon, for the isolation of a single, coherent, doctrinal pattern from within it may be a logical impossibilty. Ernst Käsemann has pointed out, for example, that the Reformers' appeal to Scripture as the ground of doctrinal unity in the church and as the court of appeal for settling doctrinal disputes, must now contend with real possibility that the lack of New Testament uniformity actually constitutes the ground of diversity in the contemporary church.[17] The New Testament is the source of doctrinal differences, rather than a ready means of resolving differences. The canon of the New Testament imposes limits upon the number of things that can be said on the basis of it, but within the embrace of the wide variety of permissions that it does allow, there are often logically incompatible views. Sometimes they do not go very well together. Unfortunately, whilst the Reformers confidently believed that the Bible could stand in judgement on doctrinal development, as the canon of what was to be believed, they overestimated its ability to settle doctrinal differences. Contemporary biblical scholarship has led us all into an entirely new arena where we must play a game of a new kind, sometimes with rules that are yet only partially formulated. Even if systematic theologians have yet to come to terms in a creative way with the critical results of present-day exegesis, it is clear that a return to a pre-critical era is entirely impossible. The future of systematic theology and indeed the future health of faith and life in the church will not be well served if theologians react to the bewildering results of modern exegesis by an ostrich-like burying of their heads in the sand.

The very central question of the nature of faith in the resurrection of Christ is certainly not immune from this problem. Over the last generation, New Testament scholars have devoted a great deal of energy to a critical-historical analysis of the resurrection traditions in the New Testament. Because the method has tended to be analytic rather than synthetic, the final position of rest tends almost inevitably to be characterized by a complete lack of system in which differences in the traditions protrude themselves at the expense of any underlying unity. Recent historical studies of the resurrection traditions in the New Testament have, as a consequence, been inclined to argue that the diversity of view found there forces us to accept the impossibility of harmonizing the tradition into one clear

---

[17] E. Käsemann, 'The Canon of the New Testament and the Unity of the Church', in *Essays on New Testament Themes*, pp. 95–107.

overall view.[18] Indeed, Christopher Evans concludes his excellent redactional study of the resurrection traditions by affirming that 'it is not simply difficult to harmonize these traditions, but quite impossible'.[19]

Amongst the more glaring inconsistencies in the Easter traditions, we may note for example, that the earliest resurrection tradition, which is preserved by Paul in 1 Cor. 15: 3–8, contains no explicit mention of the empty tomb and Paul nowhere else alludes to it in his epistles, whilst it is clearly central to the traditions found in the gospels. The list of witnesses in the chronological order given by Paul can be made to harmonize with the detailed accounts of actual appearances in the gospels only at one or two points: the gospels mention that women were prominent amongst the first witnesses to the resurrection; Paul does not mention them in his list of witnesses at all. Moreover, Paul's list suggests that Peter was the first to experience the presence of the raised Jesus, rather than Mary Magdalene, as in the gospel account of the appearance at the site of the tomb. But even amongst the gospels there are variant traditions: Mark and Matthew suggest that Galilee was the scene of the first appearances; Luke deliberately relocates all the first appearances in Jerusalem. In order to do this, he has to re-write the angel's words in Mark 16: 7: 'Go into Galilee, there you will see him', to read: 'Remember how he said when he was in Galilee' that he would 'on the third day rise' (Luke 24: 5–7; cf. Matt. 28: 7). John's Gospel narrates an appearance at Jerusalem (John 20) and then an appearance by the lake in Galilee (John 21), but the surprise of the disciples on seeing the raised Christ on this latter occasion suggests it is the first appearance they have witnessed. Matthew has the raised Christ appear 'from heaven' from the first as one whom God has already exalted (Matt. 28: 18–20); Luke separates the first appearances on earth from the exaltation to heaven by a period of forty days. During this period Jesus is said to eat and drink and come and

[18] See, for example, the conclusions of C. F. Evans in *Resurrection and the New Testament* and of Reginald H. Fuller, *The Formation of the Resurrection Narratives*; Willie Marxsen, *The Resurrection of Jesus of Nazareth* and C. F. D. Moule (ed.), *The Significance of the Message of the Resurrection for Faith in Jesus Christ*; Norman Perrin, *The Resurrection Narratives*.

[19] C. F. Evans, op. cit., p. 128. E. Brunner, *Dogmatics*, Vol. II, p. 369, concludes that the 'sources contradict one another, and only a "harmonizing" process which is not too much concerned about truth, could patch up a fairly connected account of the events'.

go, walk and talk (Luke 24: 15 ff.); he blesses and breaks bread
(Luke 24: 30). Furthermore, he is not only seen; he invites disciples
to touch him as proof that he is not a ghost but has 'flesh and bones'
(Luke 24: 39). He is often in their company and shows himself alive
'by many proofs' (Acts 1: 3 f.). Finally, at the end of the period he is
removed from their presence by a physical, spatial ascension (Acts
1: 9). In Matthew 28 the raised Christ clearly enjoys a heavenly
status and authority and there is no suggestion at all that a future
ascension into heaven is necessary. This suggests that, as Matthew
received the tradition, the first appearances seem to have involved
the manifestation of the raised and exalted Christ 'from heaven', as
it were. Luke, in contrast to Matthew, so presents the Easter
appearances as to give the impression that Jesus' body is concrete
and material, yet to be glorified in the ascension, which is post-
poned for forty days. In John a similar materializing tendency is
clear: Jesus is presented as lighting a charcoal fire on which to cook
fish in Chapter 21; he breathes on the disciples in Chapter 20; and in
the Doubting Thomas story he extends the invitation to touch his
side (John 20: 27). On the other hand, the suggestion of the tangibility of Jesus' resurrection body is also expressed by Matthew in his
account of the meeting of the raised Christ with the women near the
empty tomb, where they are said to have held on to his feet (Matt.
28: 9) despite his own tradition of an appearance to the gathered
disciples 'from heaven', which was ambiguous enough to allow
room for doubt (Matt. 28: 17).

The discrepancies that are only too apparent in a surface reading
of the texts mean, quite simply, that it cannot be assumed that the
various New Testament writers are rightly treated when they are
thought to have preserved a set of more or less contemporaneous
and complementary but independent reports of the one event, similar to the several reports of the witnesses of a road accident, each of
whom describes what happened in a slightly different, but essentially congruent way. Attempts to piece the fragments of the resurrection tradition together, in the manner of the pieces of a jigsaw, so
as to produce a single harmonious picture of what is understood to
have constituted the Easter event, must be ruled out of court at the
outset as a fundamentally mistaken enterprise.[20]

[20] The classic mistake of this kind is F. Morison's *Who Moved the Stone?*.
  The same tendency is present in David Holloway's singularly unhelpful *Where
Did Jesus Go?* More recently John Wenham has followed the same procedure in

Indeed, when it is clearly understood that the evangelists were redactors of a tradition which they received, it is entailed that the stories as we now have them bear the fingerprints of their handling: those who in many and varied ways have taken them and adapted them for their own particular purposes, have imposed their own theological design on the original traditions. In order to uncover the original nucleus of tradition the historian must therefore peel away the various layers which have in the course of transmission developed around it. For example, in John 20 there is clear evidence of the conflation of an original empty tomb tradition involving Mary Magdalene in the Garden (1; 11–18) with another tradition involving Peter and the disciple whom Jesus loved (2–10). The latter are suddenly inserted into the story which originally involved Mary Magdalene alone, and just as suddenly drop out of it. In this interpolated section of the narrative there is no reference to Mary Magdalene at all. It is as though the original story is snipped in half to allow the story of Peter and the other disciple to be inserted into it in a typical scissors and paste exercise. Behind this Johannine tradition, there seems to be an empty tomb tradition involving Mary Magdalene in or near Jerusalem, and an appearances tradition involving Peter and the other disciples to whom Jesus appeared, almost certainly in Galilee. Whilst these two traditions seem to have been independent of one another, John 20 represents the editorial conflation of the two.

Unless one seeks to penetrate behind the developed tradition to its more original nucleus in this way, one is left with a range of conflicting stories that defy harmonization.

Given the complexity of this undertaking, however, most theologians have preferred to take a somewhat safer course. In practice, the question of 'what happened' tends to be forsaken as a fruitless pursuit for which we do not have sufficient evidence; or else the tools of critical historical research are deemed to be inadequate to handle it. Instead the theological centre of interest is deflected to the

Easter Enigma. Wenham's entirely pre-scientific and uncritical method of 'harmonistic exegesis' is employed to give credence to a surface reading of the traditions, even to the point of providing surface maps and diagrams showing the disciples' movements over the days of Jesus' death, burial, and the location of the appearances! One only has to count the number of times this author has to resort to the words 'presumably' or 'probably' in his re-construction of the 'probable course of events' to perceive that the book is a somewhat fanciful one which goes well beyond the evidence and thus falls under the judgement of the author's own dictum that 'forced harmonizing is worthless' (p. 128).

question of what the Easter faith meant to Paul and to those who wrote the gospels. Since the sources do not readily yield historical information about the Easter event itself and the original experience of it, interest turns to what the sources convey about the meaning of the resurrection (whatever it was) and the implications of resurrection faith (whatever it involves) for the life of the Church today. The structure of Easter faith as such is left untouched. Consequently, whilst most studies of the resurrection over the last generation have attempted to handle it in a past-centred way and have therefore become pre-occupied with the problem of the historicity of the resurrection tradition, the apparent impossibility of harmonizing the sources has led most recent scholars to conclude that the only really secure historical results have to do with the way Easter faith was understood and expounded by the redactors of the tradition themselves. How Matthew, Mark, Luke and John handled the resurrection and interpreted its theological significance for the church of their day is known with a fair degree of certainty. Thus, Christopher Evans concludes that 'whatever the Easter event was, it must be supposed to be of such a kind as to be responsible for the production of these traditions as its deposit at whatever remove'.[21] But 'whatever it was' is somewhat obscured from view by the combined effect of the several redactional treatments.

Since the rise of redaction criticism there has therefore been a tendency, first, to rest content with the recognition of the diversity of the gospel traditions and, second, to develop a sensitivity for hearing what theological meaning and significance individual redactors were seeking to communicate through their particular treatments of the story. This means that during the last decade we have been tutored in the acceptance of the unharmonizable nature of the various traditions from the point of view of historicity and, because we have become attuned to the 'redactional frequency' with which the story now resonates, we have become accustomed to hear what each individual evangelist has wanted to transmit concerning the nature of faith in the Lordship of Jesus and what it entails for the life and mission of the church.[22] This has meant that most scholars have

---

[21] C. F. Evans, op. cit., p. 130. Cf. pp. 113 ff. and p. 148.
[22] See R. C. Ware, op. cit., p. 174: 'the artless indifference with which the New Testament writers allowed these discrepancies to stand teaches us that resurrection faith is not a matter of believing in the historical accuracy of the gospel stories, but of believing the central proclamation which these stories enshrine.'

stopped their enquiry at what John Alsup has termed the 'redactional wall'[23] without seeking to penetrate beyond it to piece together the history of the traditions or to attempt a systematic reconstruction of the nature of the *experience* of Easter faith. Instead, they have concentrated on the meaning of the primitive experience for the life of the post-Easter community or on the articulation of the theological implications of Easter for the church today in the context of the world and its problems. There is a sense in which what the original Easter experience *was* tends to recede from view behind talk about its theological meaning and significance, as each individual evangelist understood it and expressed it in his particular presentation of the Easter story.

The fact that recent exegetical work has tended to underline the apparent diversity both of detail and theological view contained in the sources seems to make the diversity of modern theologies of the resurrection quite unavoidable. Certainly, this welter of diverse and fundamentally disharmonious views about the resurrection means that we must acknowledge that the present state of theological affairs is very bewildering indeed for the contemporary Christian, to say nothing of the large company of bemused spectators outside of the church who must often wonder what this key element of the Christian faith is really all about.

Given that modern secularism is the product of a complex association of historical forces, it is probably not accidental that the contemporary abandonment of belief by large numbers of people has coincided with the internal disintegration of the former underlying theological consensus. It could be argued, for example, that the parlous condition of much contemporary church life may in no small part be caused by the preacher's enforced hesitancy in declaring exactly what may be believed within a wide range of possible alternatives. The contemporary Christian often seems to be left juggling a variety of different theological options, upon which he may draw from day to day, according to whim or the demands of circumstance. Whilst it can be argued that a certain degree of theological diversity can be tolerated and even welcomed as an enrichment of intellectual life, pluriformity of belief, if left in an utterly disordered state, seems inevitably to lead us to a debilitating lack of

[23] John E. Alsup, *The Post-Resurrection Appearance Stories of the Gospel Tradition: A History-of-Tradition Analysis with Text-Synopsis*, p. 146.

clarity. This can only hinder the Christian proclamation through want of a cutting edge, or worse, it may degenerate utterly into doctrinal confusion of a kind that leads Christians themselves to have to confess that they no longer really know what they believe. The nineteenth-century question, 'What is the essence of Christianity?', is as poignant today as ever it was.

It is true, of course, that the Christian virtue of humility, coupled with the mysterious transcendence of God, dictates that Christians must not behave in the world as though they know everything and have nothing to learn. However, the church's contemporary inability to articulate its Easter faith in a coherent and compelling way suggests that it has nothing to teach! Factors of this kind point to a prima facie need for some kind of systematized and coherent presentation of Christian belief in the resurrection of Jesus. But, this means that we have a considerable problem of a historical and theological kind to seek to reduce to as much coherence as possible.

Where to from here?

The systematic theologian must, of course, be scrupulously honest; he dares not fudge the biblical evidence in order to defend a rough and ready harmony of the Easter traditions in the throughly reprehensible way that modern fundamentalist and conservatively minded apologists tend to do. And yet theologians surely need not resort to such a wholly abstract and altogether too complicated understanding of the Easter experience as to remove it from the comprehension of those who comprise the majority of the community of faith. It should be possible to approach the resurrection from the point of view of ordinary language and ordinary perception, without generating an esoteric vocabulary of highly technical terms or defining the Easter experience in such a rarefied way as to deny access to it to all but those acquainted with the most up-to-date existentialist theory.[24]

There are three possibilities which I wish to pursue and, indeed, try to hold together in this book in an attempt to bring the multiplicity of specific New Testament assertions about resurrection faith together within the framework of a single systematic perspective.

---

[24] Pinchas Lapide, *Auferstehung: ein Jüdisches Glaubenserlebnis*. Though a Jewish New Testament scholar, Lapide accepts the resurrection, but is critical of the 'far too abstract and learned' account of the matter of some Christian exegetes; for example W. Marxsen. See p. 77.

First, it may be methodologically helpful to register some dis-satisfaction with a purely redactional interest which comes to rest in the early resurrection theology—the meaning for the life of the church of the Easter event, whatever it was and however it was experienced. To define Matthew's image of the raised Jesus and what he understands the resurrection to mean for the church in terms of world-wide mission, or Luke's image of the raised Christ as Sovereign Lord of the continuing life and work of the church, or John's image of the raised Christ as one who sends his people just as he was sent by the Father, is not unhelpful. But we need to try to penetrate behind the redactional ikonastasis upon which these doc-trinally didactic images are hung to grasp the structure of the experi-ence of Easter faith itself. We may attempt this by seeking to uncover the more primitive experience behind the developed redac-tional presentations in a history-of-traditions study of the narra-tives[25] and especially by taking what Paul has to say concerning his experience of the Spirit of Christ seriously as a datum of Easter faith. Whilst the experience of the Spirit is regularly spoken of as a consequence of Easter, its relevance to an understanding of the structure of Easter faith itself is only rarely, if ever, examined. It may be that a consideration of the experience of the Spirit of Christ and of the question of how it was identified *as* the Spirit of Christ should come before or at least alongside a consideration of the appearance narratives, rather than simply as something that follows on as a secondary and contingent matter. This will involve us in a systematic reversal of the Lucan dogmatic scheme, in which Easter and Pentecost are separated, in favour of an earlier model found in Paul and John, which very closely associates the raised Christ and Spirit.[26]

Second, we may find it helpful to recognize the limitations of the critical historical method normally used in the exegetical work of redactional criticism. It may be that 'whatever the Easter event was' eludes a redactional-critical study of the narratives precisely because the Easter reality is not amenable to treatment purely by the

---

[25] John E. Alsup, op. cit., has attempted to do this with considerable success.

[26] Note that Karl Barth can say that Resurrection, Pentecost and the Parousia are only different forms of the one event. *Church Dogmatics*, (subsequently referred to as *CD*) IV/3, p. 293. Whilst, from the point of view of the timelessness of eternity, one can see what Barth means, from the point of view of those of us who exist within time and space it is true only of Easter and Pentecost. We await the Parousia.

scientific methods of historical research of the kind that such a study necessarily relies upon. It may be that the reality of the raised Christ must be approached with additional conceptual tools and from a different perspective or set of perspectives. This is because the multidimensional richness of the Easter event, its uniqueness and transcendence, will simply not permit it to be handled with critical-historical methods alone. Indeed, as critical-historical research spreads its net around the raised Christ to capture and 'have' him, he, passing through the midst of it all, will 'go his way'. The transcendence of the Raised One is not amenable to such man-handling. He, after all, is the Sovereign Lord of the human race and not vice versa: he possesses us and not we him. As a consequence, we shall, if we are to do justice to the transcendental aspect of the Easter event, need to interpret it with an alternative heuristic model and with conceptual tools more appropriate to its 'heavenly' or eschatological nature. From one point of view the resurrection appears as a historical event which invites treatment with normal tools of critical-historical research; from another it appears as an other-wordly event, defiantly awesome and inscrutable.

As one goes behind the tendency of the gospel of John and of the much later gospel of Luke, to present the raised Christ in a somewhat mundane or materially restored way, one inevitably begins to speak about a more exalted and genuinely transcendent original form of Easter appearance 'from heaven'. One then begins to appreciate something of the radical uniqueness of the object with which faith has to do. All the indications point to the truth that the object of Easter faith, the raised Christ, was not just a restored Jesus but Jesus *the Lord*. Indeed, even the most conservative treatments of the tradition now seem prepared to concede this.[27] The raised Christ was revealed rather than simply inspected or viewed, and revealed precisely in some transformed and glorified mode, so as to allow him to be experienced as *God*.[28] As a result of the resurrection in

[27] For example, David Holloway, op. cit., pp. 28–30. The distinction between resurrection and restoration or resuscitation is reflected in the German, which employs *Auferstehung* for the resurrection of Jesus and *Erweckung* for re-awakening of the kind experienced by Lazarus. Any adequate theology of the resurrection must take account of this distinction, otherwise God's raising of Jesus at Easter will be reduced to the naturalistic dimensions of a mere release from the tomb.

[28] Note that in the Matthean appearance story the immediate response of those who come to faith is worship. (Matt. 28: 17); in the story of the coming to faith of Thomas he declares 'My Lord and my God!' (John 20: 28.)

the tomb, Jesus must not be thought to re-appear in much the way that a damaged antique chair might be restored and re-presented for sale. The resurrection is not just a matter of an emotionally moving 'flickering of the eyelids' signifying 'business as usual'.[29] At the resurrection the raised Christ 'goes to God', as Karl Barth put it sixty years ago,[30] and enters upon a mode of existence of a radically transformed kind. Precisely because he is to be thought of as an eschatological and heavenly reality he is to be understood as one who is revealed 'from heaven' as it were. His appearance is by definition unique. It is impossible to locate it and hold it within a field of like historical occurrences.

For this reason attempts to handle the resurrection purely as a historical event are destined to appear pathetically inadequate; the raised Jesus, precisely because he is *raised*, is no longer available for handling simply by the normal methods of historical and scientific enquiry appropriate to the understanding of historical and natural occurrences of this world. Rather, because of this eschatological uniqueness, we must begin to speak theologically and not just historically. Our theological language will not just be designed to unpack the meaning of Easter faith for the continuing life of the church in worship and mission, but will attempt to describe the structure of faith itself and what it apprehends. In this case, as in the case of theological language generally, various images and models of the resurrection will need to be called into service, each with its own method of approach and, of course, each with its own limitations. On one hand we may attempt to handle the resurrection as a historical event, but this will need to be balanced (rather than replaced) by an attempt to handle it from quite a different perspective as an 'eschatological' and 'heavenly' event, unlike rather than like the usual happenings of history. These different model approaches are in one sense antithetical to each other in their difference, but our

---

[29] A point graphically made by Edouard Le Roy, *Dogme et critique.*

[30] Karl Barth, *The Resurrection of the Dead.* See also Xavier Léon-Dufour, *Resurrection of Jesus and the Message of Easter*, p. 45: 'It is only the exaltation which gives the resurrection of Jesus its full meaning.' Also Karl Rahner in his article on 'Resurrection of Christ' in *Sacramentum Mundi*, Vol. V, p. 324, insists that 'the Resurrection is essentially other than the return of a dead man to his previous biological life, to space and time . . . hence it is not in any way an ordinary object of experience, which could be subsumed under the common conditions and possibilities of experience. It is an "experience" *sui generis* which, if possible at all, grasps in fact the definite transformation of the historically knowable.'

task will be so to integrate their respective insights as to the nature of the Easter experience that we may begin to form some inkling of its structure. By trying to hold various models together we shall see that each goes some way towards reducing the Easter mystery to a measure of comprehension by illuminating a different aspect of it, whilst the Easter reality transcends them all.[31]

Third, it is important for systematic theology to remember that, because the resurrection of Jesus involves not only his 'going to God' but his living presence with his people 'till the close of the age' (Matt. 28: 20), faith in principle has access to an object of present experience from the point of view of those of us who live in the temporal framework of history. This means that the structure of *our* experience of faith and what is both presupposed and implied by our claims to know the presence of Christ is not an irrelevant theological datum.

Most recent studies of the resurrection have been past-centred studies of a heavily exegetical kind. Because the resurrection is said to have occurred at a datable time and place this is a wholly legitimate enterprise. The verbal deposit left by the first witnesses must be studied historically. This is, however, only one avenue of approach to the problem of reducing the mystery of Easter to some humanly comprehensible form. In addition we must tackle the epistemological and systematic issues relating to the structure of faith as we experience it in the present. Because there are certain logical implications of any claim to perceive and recognize, it may be that if we concentrate not on the historical question of 'what happened' so much as upon what is logically entailed by our own present-day claims to recognize the raised Christ as also Jesus of Nazareth, we may be able to 'fill in' some of the gaps in our understanding of the structure of the original Easter experience.

One must keep an eye to the historical question, but systematic theology may be able to illuminate it from the perspective of the present and in the light of an understanding of what is involved today in the structure of resurrection belief. It may be that our

---

[31] A similar approach to the resurrection has been suggested by B. Klappert, in *Diskussion um Kreuz und Auferstehung.* See G. O'Collins, *What are they Saying About the Resurrection?*, p. 7 f. and R. C. Ware, op. cit., p 27. Ware speaks of the need of a pluriformity of interpretative models even though the Easter event transcends them all 'in its concrete reality'. Klappert also speaks of the integration of aspects: *'eines aspektivischen Ineinanders', Die Auferweckung des Gekreuzigten,* p. 285.

experience may illuminate the nature of the faith of the first believers, just as their experience and the vocabulary they developed to handle it certainly helps us to understand ours. Apart from an exegetical concern with the meaning of the scriptural texts, we must therefore give equal weight to a systematic enquiry into the epistemological questions relating to the structure of the knowing of the presence of the raised Christ in our own living contact with sacred reality. After all, the object of our faith is the raised Christ *himself*, not the experience of the first Christians. An over-preoccupation with the biblical texts can at best lead simply to the conviction 'that it happened'. Then the believer, as one committed to this propositional attitude (usually with insufficient evidence to back it) is abandoned to imagine the presence of Christ above or alongside of him or her. Without an epistemology of faith there is no alternative. I call this the 'fallacy of retrospectivity'. My suspicion is that this leads to a form of pious fervour which suppresses a troublesome deeper agnosticism or latent doubt, because it does not really get beyond the believer's own imagined picture of the raised Christ, constructed out of the raw materials of the images of scripture. In such an understanding of the response of faith the only cognitive element is a presumed knowledge about the Easter Jesus as he is reported to have been; there is no present knowing of the raised Christ. Prayer and worship are dutiful consequences of belief, not responses to his perceived presence. Given this cognitive deficit, the believer naturally becomes threatened and disturbed when modern redactional studies uncover the diversities and discrepancies of the biblical traditions, for this seems to pull the rug from under his or her feet: the redaction critic in this case will, more often than not, find himself bearing the projected hostility of the believer's own 'shadow side' of suppressed doubt.

An apologetic of an anxiously defensive kind, which seems to result almost inevitably from an exclusively past-centred preoccupation with an historical model of the resurrection, is clearly inadequate. For this reason, fundamentalist writers and ultra-conservative popularizers of the Easter faith do the church no lasting service by nervously seeking to defend a superficial harmony of the gospel narratives. Despite some short-term benefit in the form of ease of communication in practical evangelism, in the long term this will be found to be an inadequate distortion of faith and a potentially disastrous factor for the future of Christian life in the modern world. This is precisely because it is entirely devoid of an epistemology of faith which is capable of illuminating how it is that the contemporary believer may claim to know the actuality of the present Christ.

In addition to the use of different conceptual models in order to try to get at what the resurrection of Jesus was, what is required is a holding together of various historical and theological approaches to it as a *past event* along with an approach to the Easter Christ as a *present* datum of faith and Christian experience. This means that we shall need to work, not just with historical and theological models in order to approach the resurrection as an event of the past, but with an epistemological model for understanding the means of apprehending the reality of the raised Christ in the present. Indeed, we shall need to move backwards and forwards from the one to the other. We shall therefore pursue a systematic rather than an exegetical line of questioning as we seek to bring together in a single view the life, death, resurrection, and continuing presence of Jesus Christ.

Before we attempt that, we must consider some of the more noteworthy theological treatments of the resurrection of Christ that have been offered to the church in the recent past. We shall begin by examining some of the diverse theologies of the resurrection that have been developed over the last one hundred and fifty years or so, for even if they appear to be irreconcilable and even if we find none of them quite adequate, there are elements of truth to be found in all of them. By attending to them we shall be able to learn a great deal about the structure of belief from different perspectives and at the same time avoid innocently repeated error. Only then shall we be in a position to articulate an understanding of the structure of resurrection belief for our time.

II

The Resurrection as a Historical Event

The Event and its Dogmatic Significance

FOR many centuries the accepted and, indeed, quite unchallenged way of understanding the resurrection of Jesus, on one hand, and the way in which it is appropriated in human consciousness on the other, was to regard it as a historical event. If it was something more than a historical event, it certainly was nothing less. Even today it is usually assumed by the average man or woman in the pew that talk of the resurrection of Christ refers to an event of the past of which people come to know through a reading of the testimony of the original eye-witnesses. This is generally thought to be a reasonably uncomplicated procedure.

At first a claimed knowledge of the resurrection as an event which had occurred at one time in the human past was understood to have been transmitted from generation to generation as an item of authoritative biblical tradition whose acceptance was urged on the basis of the trustworthiness and sincerity of the apostolic witnesses who stood at the head of its impeccable ancestry. In the more recent scientific environment of the last two hundred years, which has witnessed the rise of critical-historical enquiry, the Church's belief in the resurrection of Jesus has been more clearly seen to be not so much a matter of passively 'receiving' a traditional testimony as of drawing a rational inference after first submitting the evidence of the earliest witnesses to the scrutiny of careful testing. The traditions have been regularly cross-examined, not only to ascertain the trustworthiness and sincerity of the first witnesses, but with an eye to determining the likelihood or otherwise of their being the victims of sincere delusion: it is always possible that the original Christians were innocent and honest victims of error and the scientific historian's task is to seek to determine where truth lies.

Regardless of whether one relied on an authoritatively backed, transmitted tradition or a more scientifically based reconstruction, supported by evidence and rational inference from it, the assertion that the resurrection of Jesus was a historical event of the past has been offered to men and women as the distinctive substance of Christian belief. This belief has, therefore, almost inevitably been understood as a propositional attitude of assent in which the truth of the assertion *that* the resurrection of Jesus did occur is acknowledged and then acted upon in terms of trust and obedience and the enthusiastic acceptance of the continuing lordship and sovereignty of the raised One. Already in the New Testament Paul seems to be conceiving of Easter faith in terms of this attitude of trust and obedience based upon a propositional assent when he says in Romans 10: 9 that 'if you confess with your lips that Jesus is Lord and believe in your heart that God raised him from the dead, you will be saved'.

This is not to suggest that assent to the occurrence of the resurrection has ever been a perfectly straightforward and easy matter. As early as the second-century critic of Christianity, Celsus, we have explicit evidence that the question of whether Jesus had really been raised from the dead was being asked. But there is evidence already in the New Testament itself that the very first Christians also had to defend their Easter faith in the face of incredulity. Indeed, apart from having to contend with the disbelief of others, there is evidence to suggest that they had to work through their own incredulity: to the apostles, the women's report of the empty tomb is said to have seemed an idle tale and they did not believe them (Luke 24: 11). In the appearance narrated by Matthew in the closing chapter of his gospel, when Jesus appeared to the assembled disciples on a mountain in Galilee, some are explicitly said to have doubted that Jesus had actually appeared at all (Matt. 28: 17) and in the story of the appearance to Thomas doubt, of course, is the central theme (John 20: 24–8). C. H. Dodd has observed that, because of its uncomplimentary overtones as far as apostolic reputations were concerned, this element of initial doubt and incredulity which is a regular feature of the otherwise diverse resurrection traditions, can hardly have been purposely or consciously added to the tradition in the course of its later transmission.[1] Even the first disciples seem to have had difficulty accepting the resurrection and sub-

---

[1] In 'The Appearances of the Risen Christ: An Essay in Form-Criticism of the Gospels' in *Studies in the Gospels*, p. 12.

sequently had to bear the embarrassment of what St Luke called
their own 'slowness of heart to believe' (Luke 24: 25).

Because the alleged return from the dead of a human person is, on
any reckoning, a very remarkable thing indeed, and because the evidence which grounds the assertion of its occurrence in the specific
case of Jesus of Nazareth is, at best, fragmentary and ambiguous, if
not actually contradictory in some of its more detailed aspects,
Christian theologians have inherited the task of defending the
Church's resurrection belief in the face of doubt and incredulity.
This is not to mention the more hostile criticism of those who, having heard the Easter story, remain utterly sceptical of its truth. The
Easter faith of Christians has always had to struggle for life in a
tough environment of nagging doubt mixed with open antagonism.
There has never been a time when the fact of the resurrection was
uncritically accepted as a matter of course so that theologians had
little more to do than to explain facets of its theological significance
to docile believers. Moreover, the earliest traditions themselves disclose hints of misunderstanding concerning the precise content of
what was to be believed about the resurrection of Jesus, so that from
the start the resurrection had to be defended against misunderstanding as much as against rank disbelief and the hostile attack of non-
believers. Paul, for example, in his defence of resurrection belief in 1
Cor.15 does not contend with sceptics outside of the Christian fold
but with gnosticizing Christians within, who had begun to interpret
their resurrection belief in such a way as to empty it of any future
reference or external significance by containing it within the present
inner experience of the believer. In addition to Paul's intramural
defence of resurrection belief there are, in the gospel traditions,
hints that the original reception of the Easter proclamation went on
in an atmosphere of contentiousness in which it was necessary to
engage in sustained defensive argument. In Matthew's gospel, for
example, there is the suggestion that the charge that Jesus' body
had been stolen from the tomb was countered by a tradition that
soldiers had been stationed at the tomb to prevent this.

As a consequence of all this, the remnants of the primitive Easter
proclamation come to us not just as a fusion of 'fact and interpretation' in the sense of uncontentious historical fact plus debatable
theological evaluation and speculation, as has often been said by
twentieth-century theologians, but in the form of an amalgam of
assertions of alleged historical fact mixed with apologetic and

defensive argument designed to secure the very historicity of the alleged facts themselves. It was not just that the resurrection of Jesus had to be interpreted so that its theological significance was fully understood. Rather, the fact of its very occurrence had first to be established and vigorously defended.

As a general rule, the theological defenders of the Easter faith have, at least until very recently, done their work in the belief that they possessed a reasonably clear idea of what it was they were defending. Admittedly, they have been ready to concede that they had to do with a divine mystery which transcended human capacities of understanding and they may well have been the first to allow that they could not pretend to plumb its depths or fully explain it to others. Nevertheless, they have been nonchalantly inclined to assume, notwithstanding its profound dimensions, that what they were defending was simply the contention that the resurrection of Jesus was a historical event which had actually occurred in the past. Even if it was understood as a divinely willed and miraculous event of the most extraordinary, impressive, and unique kind, it was nevertheless understood as an event which could be said to have occurred at a particular point in time and at a given place. Its occurrence at an approximately datable instant three days after Jesus' crucifixion and burial at a geographical location in or near Jerusalem entailed that the category of 'historical event' inevitably suggested itself as the natural and appropriate means of handling it.

Moreover, this fundamental contention that the resurrection of Christ was a historical event has regularly been common ground, at least until the twentieth century, between the champions of resurrection belief and their adversaries. They may have come to antithetical conclusions about the historicity or otherwise of the event, but at least they could engage in argument on the basis of a commonly-held view of the substance of the basic issue. Whilst the theologian took up the challenge to explain and defend the propriety and reasonableness of the Church's resurrection belief in the face of the sceptic's doubt and criticism, both theologian and sceptic were agreed that they were arguing about the occurrence or otherwise of a historical event which could be pinned down both temporally and geographically, just like any other historical event. The resurrection apologetic from as far back as we can see, including those hints and glimpses of it that can now be discerned behind the New Testament documents themselves, was concerned with the question of whether or not the resurrection of Jesus had actually happened.

The twentieth-century debate about the resurrection, as we shall see in subsequent chapters, has taken a somewhat different and novel turn. Contemporary theologians have been very largely concerned with the question of whether the category of 'historical event' can simply be assumed to be the best or most appropriate category that can be found for handling the resurrection of Jesus. Indeed, the question that faces us today is not just the question of truth, concerning whether it did or did not occur, so much as the prior question of meaning. What kind of phenomenon was the resurrection of Jesus and how is it best conceived and talked about? As we shall see, many contemporary theologians have raised doubts as to whether the category of 'historical event' can be appropriately used with respect to the resurrection of Jesus without emasculating it to the point of destroying it. Some have categorically denied the propriety of approaching the resurrection on the basis of the methodological presupposition that it is rightly talked about as a historical event. As a consequence they have been obliged to offer alternative and radically different ways of looking at it. We shall examine the most important of them in subsequent chapters.

In this chapter we shall confine our attention to a discussion of the structure of resurrection belief of the traditional kind in which the use of the category of 'historical event' is accepted or defended as appropriate to the handling of the resurrection of Jesus and, indeed, in which the chief apologetic concern has been to demonstrate the occurrence of this alleged event. This means we shall therefore avoid any a priori assumption that the resurrection of Jesus is inappropriately approached through the category of 'historical event' in order to ascertain how far this particular approach will take us.

To this end we shall take, as paradigm examples of this approach to the structure of resurrection belief, the work of the nineteenth-century Anglican theologian, B. F. Westcott and the more recent work of the German theologian Wolfhart Pannenberg who, in our own time, has no less vehemently than Westcott defended an understanding of the resurrection as a historical event.

The one hundred years which separate the publication of Westcott's *The Gospel of the Resurrection* (1866) from Pannenberg's *Grundzüge der Christologie* (1964) are densely populated with other examples which might have served our purposes just as well. However, it is more convenient, and certainly more manageable, to focus on a couple of paradigm cases, rather than compile a catalogue of essentially similar views. Moreover, these two theological giants suggest themselves because between them they raise all the relevant issues. In addition, they have the merit of providing us with relatively cogent and sophisticated statements of the position which we are to examine. For this reason, they can justifiably be numbered amongst the more weighty and impressive of available specimens.

Apart from their shared methodological standpoint, both Westcott and Pannenberg wrote for remarkably similar audiences. Westcott who, before becoming Bishop of Durham, was Regius Professor of Divinity at Cambridge, addressed his words to Christians of wavering faith and non-Christian sceptics. More specifically, he spoke to those who by the mid-nineteenth century had begun to dismiss the very possibility of a resurrection from the dead in the course of embracing an aggressively scientific and positivistic turn of mind of the kind that is now commonplace in the modern world. The theological scene in England at the time was reeling under the impact of the publication of Darwin's *Origin of the Species* (1859) and the sustained and logically stringent critique of religion of John Stuart Mill. But the scientific positivism of Auguste Comte with its concentration of attention on the methods of careful observation and the faithful reporting of hard fact was also perceived by Westcott to be troublesome from the point of view of traditional Christian belief. Westcott was very self-consciously aware that he stood on the brink of the flowering of the scientific method and discerned that the only acceptable means of defending the resurrection was to espouse that method enthusiastically himself. Indeed, he was confident in his belief that there is no 'fundamental antagonism between the Positive method and Christianity'.[2] On the other hand, the theological world was beginning to grapple with those within its own ranks who were prepared to retreat into the safety of Jesus' ethical teaching and to soft-pedal the supernatural and miraculous. In Germany David Strauss had, as early as 1835, suggested somewhat notoriously that the number of things that were to be believed about Jesus could be dramatically reduced by

[2] B. F. Westcott, *The Gospel of the Resurrection*, Appendix I, 'Aspects of Positivism in Relation to Christianity', p. 250.

off-loading belief in his resurrection, where the resurrection is understood as an objective event.[3] Instead, he offered the explanation that has since become known as 'the subjective vision hypothesis', which seeks to explain the resurrection appearances in terms of the disciples' psychological disturbance. This view was reaffirmed in 1864 when he published *A New Life of Jesus*, the English edition of which appeared in 1865, the year before Westcott's own book.[4] Though Westcott does not explicitly grapple with Strauss's arguments, his spirited defence of a more positive and realistic view of the resurrection may be understood as a direct reaction to Strauss as certainly as it was a response to the pervading rationalism and scientific positivism of the day.

Wolfhart Pannenberg, on the other hand, has written for the twentieth-century equivalents of those scientifically-minded positivists outside of the Church with whom Westcott felt it necessary to begin to grapple. In addition, Pannenberg has endeavoured to respond to a growing and more vocal band of theologians within the community of faith who have been prepared to dispense with talk of the resurrection as a historical event in which Jesus is said objectively to be restored to life. More particularly, Pannenberg has been constrained to defend the historicity of the resurrection in the face of a weighty body of contemporary theological opinion associated with the eminent personages of Karl Barth and Rudolf Bultmann who, in different ways, have called in question the appropriateness of using the category of historical event at all in explaining the nature and meaning of faith in the resurrection of Jesus. It is against this background that Pannenberg vigorously contends that 'Whether or not Jesus was raised from the dead is a historical question insofar as it is an enquiry into what did or did not happen at a certain time'.[5]

Though separated in time, as well as in terms of national background and denominational persuasion, both Westcott and Pannenberg are clear in their own minds about the matter in hand: for them

---

[3] David Strauss, *The Life of Jesus Critically Examined*, pp. 735ff.

[4] W. R. Cassels, who published *Supernatural Religion, An Enquiry into the Reality of Divine Revelation*, Vols. I, II, and III without revealing his own identity, notoriously and somewhat sensationally promoted views very similar to Strauss. Westcott responded to this work in an article entitled 'The Resurrection of Christ— A New Revelation', in *Contemporary Review* (Nov. 1877), pp. 1070–87.

[5] W. Pannenberg in *New Frontiers in Theology* Vol. III, *Theology as History*, p. 128.

the resurrection is to be understood as a historical event and vigorously defended as such. Moreover, they are agreed that, precisely
because of its nature as a historical event, the resurrection is rightly
handled with the methodological tools appropriate to the handling
of other events of the human past—the techniques of scientific, critical-historical research.

The vehemence and vigour with which Westcott and Pannenberg
have defended the historical actuality of the resurrection can be
understood, not only in the light of the background of alternative
views against which they have worked, but as a function of the dogmatic significance that they deem it to have. This is something that
they also share in general terms with most other theologians who
approach the resurrection as a historical event. Most theologians
who are anxious to defend an understanding of the resurrection as
an event of past history, are motivated by a desire to secure its
unequivocal reality and objectivity as something to which the man
or woman of faith responds. It is an event which, precisely for this
reason, can therefore claim to provide a firm historical basis for the
development of Christian doctrine, particularly Christological doctrine, as well as a secure foundation for the whole of Christian life,
worship and practice. Westcott thus argued that the resurrection is
to be understood as a historical event whose 'objectivity is essential
to its significance'.[6] Its significance, as he understood it, was precisely that it was a key factor in securing Christianity's unique place
amongst the religions of the world as a 'historical religion'. In other
words, its historical objectivity was deemed to be significant
because it secured the very uniqueness of the Christian religion as a
religion involving more than an abstract set of doctrines or ethical
teachings, more than a philosophy of life.

The claim that Christianity is 'a historical religion' meant more to
Westcott than simply believing that its founder was an actual historical person. He clearly discerned that as much could be said of
Muhammadanism and Buddhism whose founders were no less real,
historical people, than Jesus. Christianity's unique claim to be a historical religion meant that it was not just a body of teaching or system of beliefs, such as might be taught by its founder, but a religion
whose teaching 'is conveyed in facts'.[7] What Jesus' followers pro-

[6] *The Gospel of the Resurrection*, p. 4.
[7] 'The Resurrection of Christ—A New Revelation', op. cit., p. 1083.

claimed was not his teaching so much as his person and the facts of his death and resurrection which illuminated 'the mysteries of being'. Thus, the person and what befell him constituted the historical foundation of Christianity; Christian doctrine is the progressive elucidation of it.

On this reckoning, the resurrection of Jesus could be said to conform to the principle of Comtean positivism which 'decides nothing prior to observation'.[8] At the same time it could be held that it gave faith 'a firm standing ground in history',[9] where faith was understood as the assent to the truth of certain doctrinal beliefs centring on Jesus' divine status and Messianic identity. If the occurrence of the resurrection could be demonstrated historically, then there was little room left to doubt the theological claim that such an occurrence must have been the work of God himself and that this in turn vouched for the truth of the Christological claim that Jesus was the Messiah. The dogmatic significance of the resurrection was that it provided a clear and objective demonstration of what had been ambiguous and only faintly perceived during Jesus' lifetime—his Messianic identity, which had been rendered problematic by his humiliating death on the cross. Westcott therefore argued that from the standpoint of the Easter experience a flood of light illuminated the historical life of Jesus.[10] Indeed, he contended that 'the Apostolic view of the nature of Christ is deduced from His rising again'.[11]

The dogmatic significance of the resurrection, therefore, is that it is the clue to the true nature of the identity of Jesus, 'the historic seal of the Incarnation,'[12] and this meant that a demonstration of the historicity of the event became absolutely vital for the subsequent development of doctrine.

This claim implies that the resurrection of Jesus must be an event of such a kind that it is capable of making Jesus' true, hidden identity unambiguously clear. If the 'facts of the Faith precede the dogmas',[13] as Westcott put it, then it is imperative for the survival and development of doctrine that the occurrence of the event should be

---

[8] *The Gospel of the Resurrection*, Appendix I, p. 251.
[9] Ibid., p. 10.
[10] Ibid., p. 123: 'a flood of light is seen to have been poured on all which they had regarded before with silent and hesitating wonder.'
[11] Ibid., p. 109.
[12] Ibid., p 174. See also p. 175: 'After the Resurrection . . . they saw in Christ a Saviour of boundless power.'
[13] 'The Resurrection of Christ—A New Revelation', p. 1084.

established as securely as possible, otherwise the entire edifice of Christian doctrine would inevitably begin to sway and totter on a patently insecure foundation. In defending the historicity of the resurrection Westcott was therefore doing more than just commending one of a number of articles of Christian belief; he was defensively arguing for the basic security of the whole.

Pannenberg likewise recognizes that the historical question of the resurrection becomes decisive when its significance for the confession of the incarnation is clearly perceived.[14] For him the event of the resurrection is dogmatically significant because it provides the historical basis for the perception of Christ's divinity or of 'God's revelation in him'.[15] The words and deeds of Jesus as he was in his historical life from birth to death are not unimportant for Christology, but the unity of Jesus with God is said to be substantiated not by appeal to his pre-resurrection ministry but only by his resurrection from the dead. In other words, information about the historical Jesus, his teaching and deeds, might be deemed to be a necessary datum for Christology, but alone it would be insufficient. Pannenberg thus sees the importance for faith of a return to historiographical fact of the kind promoted by the so-called 'new quest of the historical Jesus' of the last generation,[16] but he stands apart from those whose historiographical interests stopped short of a treatment of the resurrection of Jesus as a historical event. For Pannenberg the datum for Christology is not exhausted simply by the words and acts of Jesus from birth to death on the cross. Rather, the resurrection of Jesus is to be regarded as a 'proof and endorsement' of Jesus' claims, for the whole ministry of Jesus remained dependent upon the future authentication of his claim to authority, upon a confirmation which Jesus himself was unable to provide, precisely

---

[14] 'Dogmatische Erwägungen zur Auferstehung Jesu', *Kerygma und Dogma*, 14 (1968), p. 105–8. Cf. E. Frank Tupper, *The Theology of Wolfhart Pannenberg*, p. 147.

[15] *Jesus—God and Man*, p. 108.

[16] Following the publication by Ernst Käsemann of '*Das Problem des historischen Jesus*', *ZTK*, 51 (1954), pp. 125–53, English trans. in *Essays on New Testament Themes*, pp. 15–47. See also Gerhard Ebeling 'The Significance of the Critical Historical Method for Church and Theology in Protestantism' in *Word and Faith*, pp. 18–61, (an article which first apeared in *ZTK*, 47 (1950), pp. 1–46); E. Fuchs, *Zur Frage nach dem historischen Jesus*, pp. 143–67 (first published in *ZTK*, 53 (1956), pp. 210–19) English trans. 'The Quest of the Historical Jesus' in *Studies of the Historical Jesus*, pp. 11–31; Günther Bornkamm, *Jesus of Nazareth*.

because what was needed was a legitimation of his own personal identity.

Given that Pannenberg's emphasis on the authentication or legitimation of Jesus' claims reflects a characteristically twentieth-century interest in the future-centred, eschatological orientation of Jesus' earthly ministry, he nevertheless repeats the essential points of the approach to faith exhibited a century ago by Westcott. The resurrection of Jesus is seen as a historical event which legitimates and confirms the implicit and explicit claims of the historical Jesus to enjoy a unique relationship of unity with God. The resurrection, in other words, is the clue to a correct understanding of his person; it is the way in which the claims of Jesus were ratified at a specific point in time by God.[17] The resurrection is therefore a quite fundamental historical datum for Christology. Moreover, given its dogmatic importance, the demonstration of its historicity becomes vital to the entire edifice of Christian doctrine.

The Event: Its Constituent Parts

Before we begin to assess the arguments that have been adduced in support of the historicity of the resurrection of Jesus, we should note that there has rarely been any suggestion that the actual resurrection of Jesus was witnessed by anybody. The resurrection, according to the New Testament evidence, occurred in the solitariness and silence of the tomb or 'in the silence of God' as Ignatius of Antioch so aptly put it.[18]

Any historical evidence that may be summoned to support the conclusion that Jesus was raised by God inside the tomb must be constituted by the subsequent emptiness of the tomb and by the alleged re-appearance of Jesus after his death outside the tomb. Only the apocryphal gospel of Peter dares to describe the actual raising of Jesus and his emergence from the tomb. This means that the occurrence of the actual event of the resurrection had originally to be inferred by the first witnesses from the available evidence, just as today it must be inferred by processes of rational argument from their reported testimony. A statement asserting the occurrence of the resurrection is therefore an inference that was originally drawn from statements describing phenomena of experience. It is now

---

[17] *Jesus—God and Man*, p. 67–8.
[18] Eph 19: 1.

inferred from the testimony in which that phenomena is described. Both Westcott and Pannenberg are perfectly aware of this distinction.[19]

By way of additional clarification we can say that this entails that the event which is usually referred to as 'the resurrection of Jesus' is a complexity comprising a number of distinguishable constituent parts. First there are those elements of it which can be said to have involved direct human experience—the alleged discovery of the empty tomb and the appearances of Jesus outside of the tomb. Then there are other elements which were not directly experienced and which therefore have to be inferred on the basis of these experiences—the raising of Jesus by God inside of the tomb and his continuing life with God 'between' and after the several appearances. In so far as resurrection belief is a propositional attitude of assent to the truth of the assertion that Jesus was raised from the dead by God, it implicitly involves assent to the logically prior truth of the assertion that the grave was found empty and that Jesus appeared to certain witnesses.

Though Westcott distinguishes the unwitnessed event of the raising of Jesus inside of the tomb from what was subsequently witnessed outside of the tomb, he does not always maintain this distinction with clarity. For example, in his concern to establish the objective reality of the resurrection of Jesus, he was led to argue that the 'Death, the Burial and the Resurrection of Christ claim to be facts exactly in the same sense'[20] and that the resurrection must be true 'in the same sense in which the Passion is true'.[21] Strictly speaking this does not preserve the distinction that whilst the death and burial could have been observed by anybody in the vicinity at the time, the resurrection inside of the tomb was not available to observation by anyone. What Westcott means, however, is that, had a witness been present inside the tomb the resurrection would have been as objectively real as the burial and also that the human experi-

[19] See B. F. Westcott, 'The Resurrection of Christ—A New Revelation', p. 1076 where he speaks of the event of the resurrection as 'an inference from the records' and p. 1080 where he argues that the contention of the author of *Supernatural Religion* (Vol. III, pp. 449 and 549) that 'there was no eye-witness of the Resurrection' is in no way a difficulty for faith and may be accepted. See W. Pannenberg, 'Dogmatische Erwägungen zur Auferstehung Jesu', *Kerygma und Dogma*, 14 (1968), p. 112 for the same point.

[20] B. F. Westcott, *The Gospel of the Resurrection*, p. 3.

[21] Ibid., p. 5.

ences upon which the assertion of the occurrence of the resurrection is based (the empty tomb and the appearances) were also as real as the human experience of the passion and death of Jesus. On this ground Westcott argued that the resurrection is 'a fact of the same order as the Burial of the Lord'.[22]

This means that, in this approach to Easter faith, the resurrection inevitably tends to be assimilated to other events of the historical life of Jesus, from his birth through to his death and burial. All were in principle observable by witnesses and therefore appropriate subjects for verbal reports or testimony. We can say, therefore, that the type of evidence used for inferring the occurrence of the resurrection is the same as that used to establish any other historical occurrence—a war, the birth of a famous person, the erection of a building or, in the course of the life of Jesus, his walking and talking with his friends and then his death on the cross or his burial. Thus, he says 'the direct evidence for the event is exactly the same kind which we have for other events in the Life of Christ'.[23] It was precisely for this reason that Westcott believed that the resurrection of Jesus could be understood as an event that could be handled with the methods and techniques of scientific historiography. Just as, when we are speaking of the burial of Jesus, we are speaking of an event which at the time of its occurrence was perceivable and, indeed, perceived in so far as it presented itself 'to the senses' of the observer, so the resurrection of Jesus was an empirical event of the objective order, at least to the extent that it was also apprehended through the deliverances of sense. The resurrection of Jesus, though inferred to have occurred inside the tomb, was not just 'an abstract article of belief' because it was grounded in the sensory experiences of seeing the empty tomb and meeting with the raised Jesus. It was therefore for Westcott 'a sensible ground of hope'.[24]

One implication of the contention that the apprehension of the event of the resurrection is through sense experience is that the resurrection offers a foundation for faith 'external to the believer'.[25] It also entails that when the occurrence of the resurrection is

[22] Ibid., p. 4.
[23] Ibid., p. 135.
[24] Ibid., p. 6. Elsewhere Westcott speaks of the ascension of Jesus as a 'sensible sign' of his withdrawal to exalted status. See 'The Resurrection of Christ—A New Revelation', p. 1076.
[25] Ibid., p. 10.

affirmed, an assertion is made in straightforward, literal language of the kind that is used to assert the occurrence of any other objective or outwardly experienced event of the past.[26] Even so, Westcott was clear that the literal nature of the assertion of the historicity of the resurrection of Jesus does not mean that every detail of the apostolic testimony is to be accepted as literal fact. The description of the apostolic witnesses, he says, can be compared with the description of the tumult of a battle 'where fictitious or unreal details convey a relatively true idea of the whole'.[27] Whilst it is impossible to record or even apprehend all that goes to make up a complicated and changing scene, 'the genius of an artist may be able to convey to others the reality which he has himself grasped through representative incidents moulded to his purpose'.[28] Westcott thus hinted that the same may be true 'with the details of the Resurrection'.

On the other hand, given that the human experiences which provided the ground of the belief that Jesus had been raised were perceptual experiences and, therefore, in principle as clear and distinct as the observation of Jesus' burial, the actual nature of the risen life of Christ is admitted to be hidden. Writing in the aftermath of H. L. Mansell's Bampton Lectures *On the Limits of Religious Thought*, Westcott appreciated something of the limitations of human knowledge and conceded that the supernatural nature of the resurrection as an event in which Christ's body was transformed and in which he entered a heavenly life means that human beings this side of the grave can only *imagine* what it might now be like. This in turn means that the heavenly existence of the raised Christ can only be conceived in metaphorical terms, for we are obliged to rely on our fundamental experience in this world for the basic images: 'We can form no clear positive conception which is not shaped by the present laws of thought . . .'.[29]

Because the resurrection of Jesus was not merely 'the continua-

---

[26] Ibid., p. 135. The literalness of language asserting the occurrence of the resurrection as a historical event continues to be stressed by many modern thinkers. See for example Stephen Neill in *The Interpretation of the New Testament*, p. 234, where he speaks of Jesus being 'raised from the dead, literally and in the completeness of his manhood'.

[27] Ibid., p. 5.

[28] Ibid.

[29] Ibid., p. 164.

tion of the present life' but a life transfigured and glorified, it is a life 'which we can regard at present only under signs and figures'.[30] Here Westcott apprehends that the language which is used to describe the heavenly and transformed life of the raised Christ can only be analogical or metaphorical. It can be imaginatively conceived by using images drawn from this world but 'stretched' to suggest at least something of the heavenly reality. Nevertheless, the historical fact of the resurrection itself, as distinct from the continuing heavenly life that resulted from it, can be literally asserted, even if the details of Jesus' continuing heavenly existence are hidden from our eyes. This is precisely because of what was humanly and unambiguously experienced. Moreover, Westcott contended that this human experience was of the same order as the experience of seeing Christ die or seeing his body being laid in the tomb.

Pannenberg's position is once again quite parallel to Westcott's at this particular point. The resurrection, he argues, was originally appropriated in human consciousness, not in some esoteric and unaccountably mysterious way, but 'through the eyes' of the natural man, at least in so far as the empty tomb, and even Jesus' appearances, were outwardly perceived by men.[31] The actual resurrection inside the tomb was not perceived by anybody, nor is the continuing heavenly existence of Jesus (apart from his sporadic and limited appearances) available to human scrutiny. This means also that Pannenberg recognizes that the language in which it is claimed that Jesus rose from the dead is metaphorical. He notes, for example, that the resurrection event can be compared with a waking from sleep. Pannenberg appreciates that metaphors are unavoidable in view of the fact that the resurrection inside the tomb and the continuing life of the raised Jesus both lie beyond ordinary experience and can therefore only be piously imagined on analogy with more mundane day-to-day experiences. In so far as the historian seeks to establish the historicity of the resurrection, this means that he can be quite positive about the fact that an event occurred, as a result of which it is possible to claim that Jesus 'lives', but he is not able to say in precise or detailed terms what his 'life' beyond death is actually like. The historian, says Pannenberg, has sufficient evidence

---

[30] Ibid.
[31] W. Pannenberg, 'Dogmatische Erwägungen zur Auferstehung Jesu', *Kerygma und Dogma*, 14 (1968), p. 110.

to affirm the literal fact that 'an event has happened' even if its more detailed qualities 'evade his judgment'.[32] The appearances, which were apprehended in experiences of space and time, allow a statement asserting the occurrence of the resurrection of Jesus inside the tomb to be inferred. This means that the occurrence of the resurrection can be fixed temporally and spatially as a historical event by the evidence of the empty tomb and the appearances, yet they provide insufficient information to admit a knowledge of the 'wider course of the event, in so far as it concerns Jesus himself' which 'remains unknown'.[33]

The historical inference to a statement asserting the occurrence of this partly elusive event of the resurrection is drawn from what is said to have been concrete and clear in apostolic experience—the sight of the empty tomb and the appearances of the raised Christ. These sub-events, as it were, constitute the event of the resurrection in so far as it was humanly experienced. As 'what was seen' they open the resurrection to historical enquiry and examination, for it is 'what was seen' that the early witnesses reported and passed on. This is what we now have as the only historical evidence available to us in the written traditions of the New Testament.

The Historical Evidence: The Empty Tomb

It is already clear that the traditional material which constitutes the basic evidence of 'what was seen' and from which it is inferred that Jesus was raised by God inside the tomb and that he now lives eternally 'with God' separates into the two strands—the empty tomb story and the cycle of stories in which the appearances of the raised Jesus are asserted or narrated.

These two strands of tradition appear to have originated independently and to have been combined only in the course of the later editing of the material. Their independent origin becomes apparent when it is observed that the traditions of the appearances favour Galilee as the location of the first appearances and Peter as the person to whom Jesus first appeared,[34] whilst the empty tomb story must necessarily have had a Jerusalem origin with Mary Magdalene

---

[32] Ibid., p. 112.
[33] Ibid.
[34] Mark 16: 7; Matt. 28: 16–20; John 21. For the primacy of Peter in the succession of Easter experiences see Paul in 1 Cor. 15: 5 and Luke 24: 34.

as the first to discover it, without the presence of the other male disciples to whom Jesus appeared in Galilee.[35] In Luke it is possible to detect a distinct tendency, for theological reasons, to dissociate the first appearance from Galilee and to bring those who witnessed them to Jerusalem.[36] Originally, however, we seem to have two separate traditions: a Galilee tradition of appearances and a Jerusalem tradition of the discovery of the empty tomb.[37]

In view of the fact that these two traditions appear to have had independent origins we may justifiably deal with them separately. We shall turn to the Jerusalem tradition of the discovery of the empty tomb first.

Curiously, when Westcott comes to discuss what he calls the 'specific evidence of the resurrection' he makes very little of the empty tomb story at all. He states that the 'sepulchre in which the Lord had been laid was found empty'[38] and contends that 'this fact seems to be beyond all doubt and is one where misconception was impossible'. However, whilst accepting the historicity of the empty tomb in these unequivocal terms, he clearly gives primacy to the tradition of the appearances, particularly the Pauline tradition where in 1 Cor. 15 the appearances of the raised Christ to Peter and the twelve, over 500 brethren at once, James and the apostles and finally to Paul himself, are listed without any explicit mention of the empty tomb story. Westcott, following this Pauline emphasis, likewise stresses the historical importance of the appearances tradition and omits to labour the point about the discovery of the tomb.

Pannenberg, however, makes a good deal more of the evidence of the tomb's being found empty and of its essential historicity. He

---

[35] Mary Magdalene is the only name common to all the empty tomb traditions.

[36] In Luke 24: 6–7 the words of the angel at the tomb are deliberately changed from 'Go into Galilee, there you will see him' to 'Remember how he told you (before the crucifixion) when he was in Galilee, that the Son of Man must be delivered up . . . and on the third day rise.' It has already been noted that there is clear evidence of the editorial work of uniting the two separate traditions in John 20 where John quite clearly interrupts the story of Mary at the tomb to introduce Peter and 'the disciple whom Jesus loved'. They then disappear as abruptly as they are introduced to the scene—a clear sign of interpolation. See Chapter 1, p. 19 above.

[37] The separate origin and nature of the traditions is very adequately discussed by C. F. Evans in *Resurrection and the New Testament*, and Reginald H. Fuller, *The Formation of the Resurrection Narratives*.

[38] *The Gospel of the Resurrection*, p. 114.

does not canvass all the arguments that are now available or even the most telling arguments, so we shall have to help his argument along by fattening it up where its thinness begins to show if we are to examine the strongest possible case for its alleged historicity.

The story of the empty tomb occurs in all four gospels (Mark 16: 1–8; Matt. 28; Luke 24; and John 20) but in each case with marked divergences in matters of detail.[39] Of these four accounts Pannenberg is prepared, with most contemporary opinion, to accept the priority of Mark 16: 1–8 and to explain the discrepancies in Matthew and Luke as kerygmatic and apologetic expansions of the Marcan original, though it should be noted that some writers now favour the primitiveness of the Johannine version.[40]

In any event the basic story is the same in all four versions and we can bypass the discussion of the discrepancies in the various accounts and the factors responsible for the formation of the different traditions, in order to tackle the more pressing issue from a dogmatic point of view: the place of the kernel of the bare fact of the discovery of the tomb by the women in the structure of subsequent resurrection belief.

It is sometimes said, however, that the appearance of discrepancies in the various accounts of the discovery of the empty tomb itself constitutes positive evidence of fundamental historicity. In other words, it is sometimes argued that the barometer of confidence rises as we note that the various traditions lack any evidence of false harmonization. The presence of discrepancies means that deliberate fabrication and collusion is ruled out in a way that it would not be if there were no discrepancies at all.[41] However,

---

[39] For a discussion of the traditions and a comparison of the different accounts see C. F. Evans, *Resurrection and the New Testament*, or Reginald H. Fuller, *The Foundation of the Resurrection Narratives*. Also Jean Delorme, 'Résurrection et Tombeau de Jésus: Marc 16, 1–8 dans la tradition évangélique' in *La Résurrection du Christ et l'exégèse moderne, Lectio Divina*, 50, pp. 105–53.

[40] See P. Benoit, 'Marie-Madeleine et les disciples au tombeau selon John 20: 1–18' in W. Eltester (ed.), *Judentum, Urchristentum, Kirche, Festschrift für J. Jeremias*, *BZNW*, 26 (1964), pp. 141–52. J. Jeremias himself follows Benoit in holding that John's version of the empty tomb story is earlier than Mark. See *New Testament Theology*, Part 1, pp. 300–5: 'the latest literary text has preserved the earliest form of the tradition'. Whether John's gospel is the latest is however an open question, given the clear lateness of Luke.

[41] See J. A. T. Robinson, 'Resurrection in the New Testament', *IDB*, IV, p. 46 for an expression of this view.

whilst there is no evidence of deliberate fabrication of the kind that would be suggested by a suspicious harmonization of detail, it cannot be argued that contradictions in detail actually stand as a positive sign of the historicity of the empty tomb story. The presence of discrepancies might be a sign of historicity if we had four clearly independent but slightly different versions of the story, if only for the reason that four witnesses are better than one. But, of course, it is now impossible to argue that what we have in the four gospel accounts of the empty tomb are four contemporaneous but independent accounts of the one event. Modern redactional studies of the traditions account for the discrepancies as literary developments at the hand of later redactors of what was originally one report of the empty tomb by one witness, Mary Magdalene, or one discovery of the tomb by Mary and companions, if indeed she was not alone. There is no suggestion that the tomb was discovered by different witnesses on four different occasions, so it is in fact impossible to argue that the discrepancies were introduced by different witnesses of the one event; rather, they can be explained as four different redactions for apologetic and kerygmatic reasons of a single story originating from one source. We are thus dealing, not with the testimony of four witnesses which might be held to be corroboratively inter-supportive and trustworthy, precisely because of the absence of signs of collusion, but basically one testimony which has undergone development in the course of transmission. The presence of discrepancies is therefore irrelevant with respect to the question of the truth or otherwise of the original kernel of the tradition.

In this respect the story of the empty tomb differs from the evidence of the appearances which were claimed to be numerous, temporally and geographically dispersed and given to a variety of different witnesses from Peter through to Paul. By contrast the empty tomb story has a single toehold in the tradition. Our question is: is the testimony of the discovery of the empty tomb reliable enough for us to be able to use it to ground the inference (1) that Jesus was raised by God inside the tomb and (2) that he went to an exalted life 'at the right hand of God' (to use one of the metaphors that were used to picture his ultimate destination)? Can we be confident enough about the historicity of the discovery of the empty tomb to continue to make a fundamental and indispensable place for it in the structure of resurrection belief?

This is, of course, a much-debated question which has produced a voluminous literature in recent years.[42] Those who doubt the historicity of the original empty tomb tradition and who are inclined to dispense with its necessity to the make-up of Easter faith, contend that even the earliest version of it is legendary and that it is to be understood as the product of faith rather than a basic ingredient in the origin of faith. This view has in recent times been most notably promoted by Rudolf Bultmann who argues that the empty tomb is an 'apologetic legend' which sets out to prove the resurrection in an original *Sitz im Leben* of hostility to an already existing Easter belief.[43] Though this is now identified as a typically Bultmannian position it has in fact had a long currency right through the twentieth century.[44] Indeed the variety of the background of those holding this view is only matched by the variety of the explanations offered to account for the secondary nature and alleged lateness of the tradition. Some argue, with Bultmann, that the story of the empty tomb is only meaningful for faith when it is interpreted with

---

[42] On the question of the historicity of the story of the empty tomb see H. von Campenhausen 'The Events of Easter and the Empty Tomb' in *Tradition and Life in the Church*, pp. 42–89; W. Nauck, 'Die Bedeutung des leeren Grabes für den Glauben an den Auferstandenen', *ZNW*, 47 (1956), pp. 243–67; M. Hengel, 'Maria Magdalena und die Frauen als Zeugen' *Abraham unser Vater: Festschrift für O. Michel*, hrsg. O. Betz, M. Hengel and P. Schmidt, pp. 253ff; J. Jeremias, *New Testament Theology*, Part 1, pp. 300–5; C. F. Evans, *Resurrection and the New Testament*, Ch. II; Reginald H. Fuller, *The Formation of the Resurrection Narratives*, Ch. III; E. L. Bode, *The First Easter Morning: the Gospel Accounts of the Women's Visit to the Tomb of Jesus*, *Analecta Biblica*, 45; G. Vermes, *Jesus the Jew*, pp. 39ff.; W. Pannenberg, *Jesus—God and Man*, pp. 100–6; J. C. O'Neill, 'On The Resurrection as an Historical Question' in *Christ Faith and History*, ed. S. W. Sykes and J. P. Clayton, pp. 205–19.

[43] Rudolf Bultmann, *The History of the Synoptic Tradition*, p. 287–90.

[44] See A. Loisy, *L'évangile selon Marc*, pp. 481–2, where it is argued that the story of the empty tomb was a late invention to support a faith long since acquired on other grounds; also Charles Guignebert, *Jesus*, trans. S. H. Hooke. p. 496 and pp. 499–500, where it is argued that the tomb is a secondary tradition. Similarly E. Meyer, *Ursprung und Anfänge des Christentums*, Vol. 1: *Die Evangelien*, p. 18, sees the empty tomb as secondary and the beginning of *Mythenbildung*. Selby McCasland, *The Resurrection of Jesus*, pp. 175–6, suggests a number of contributory influences to the development of the empty tomb legend including visionary experiences of the disciples, the drawing of inferences from an existing faith and syncretism of motifs from pagan cults. More recent adherents of the view that it is legendary and late include Hans-Werner Bartsch, *Das Auferstehungszeugnis*, p. 22; H. Schlette, *Epiphanie als Geschichte: ein Versuch*, p. 68; L. Geering, *Resurrection: A Symbol of Hope*; H. Grass, *Ostergeschehen und Osterberichte*, 2nd edn., pp. 138–86; G. W. H. Lampe, *The Resurrection*, says: 'I regard the story of the empty tomb as myth rather than literal history, and profoundly significant as myth'. It is not a literal report of historical fact but a 'mythical description of what we mean by the Resurrection', (p. 40).

the words of the resurrection kerygma, which are put into the mouth of the angel, 'He is risen!', and that the story is itself merely one of a number of optional and passing forms in which the resurrection was preached. Given the existing Pharisaic belief not only in angels but in the resurrection of the end-time in terms of a physical or mundane restoration to life, the empty tomb story is, in this view, nothing more than an accommodation of the Easter kerygma to pre-existing thought-forms. On the other hand, the fact that Paul, the most prolific of early Christian writers, fails so much as to mention it, leads Bultmann to the view that it is not essential, but a secondary way of proclaiming the Easter message, to which Christians were unavoidably but, from a modern point of view, unhelpfully driven, by apologetic pressures.[45]

Others, notably H. Grass, are inclined to argue that the empty tomb tradition can be explained as a development which went hand in hand with the tendency which we see increasing in the later gospels, particularly Luke and John, to stress the corporeality of the appearances of Jesus.[46] Alternatively it can be argued that the point of the empty tomb story is to counter a gnostic and Docetic tendency to 'spiritualize' and de-historicize the resurrection, such as we see Paul grappling with already at Corinth in the middle of the first century.

Yet others argue in quite the opposite direction. Neill Q. Hamilton contends that the empty tomb story, in the earliest form in which we have it, is a creation of Mark himself in the interests of answering what was held to be an undesirable tendency to stress the corporeality of the resurrection appearance. The story, he says, is meant to suggest not a resurrection of Jesus in the sense of a restoration to this life but a translation of Jesus out of this world, the emphasis lying on the words 'he is gone, he is not here'.[47]

Whilst these, mainly Protestant, explanations of the origin of the tomb tradition focus attention on kerygmatic elements in the story, as indications of the fact that it was generated and used in the course of the preaching of the Easter message, a series of modern Roman

---

[45] R. Bultmann, *The History of the Synoptic Tradition*, p. 290.

[46] H. Grass, *Ostergeschehen und Osterberichte*, pp. 23, 173, 183–4.

[47] See N. Q. Hamilton 'Resurrection Tradition and the Composition of Mark', *JBL*, 84 (1965), pp. 415–21 and *Jesus for a No-God World*, pp. 6off.; E. Bickermann, 'Das leere Grab', *ZNW*, 23 (1924), pp. 281–92; M. Goguel, *La foi à la résurrection de Jésus dans la christianisme primitif*, pp. 213–33; T. J. Weeden, *Mark—Traditions in Conflict*, pp. 106 ff.

Catholic studies has discerned what are held to be echoes of ancient
liturgical practices in the story. These are said to suggest an original
liturgical context rather than simply one of preaching. Ludger
Schenke has noted, for example, the reference to sunrise in Mark 16:
2 as a time appropriate to worship and also the credal character of
Mark 16: 6; J. Kremer interprets the angel's words, 'see the place
where they have lain him' as a cultic reference to the grave.[48] On the
basis of these factors, it has been argued that the story arose as an
aetiological legend stimulated by an Easter liturgy, which may have
taken place annually at each Easter celebration. This explanation of
the story has to overcome a natural Jewish revulsion from tombs as
unclean places (Num. 19: 18; cf. Matt. 23: 27) and begs the question
as to why women should feature so prominently in a story developed out of liturgical practices. For this reason it may be somewhat
fanciful.[49] In any case, this assessment of the empty tomb tradition
leaves the question of the original historicity unresolved. Those
who have championed the liturgical explanation of the origin of the
story have been inclined to argue that the story of the original discovery of the tomb was liturgically rehearsed annually each Easter
at the actual site of the tomb. Thus the legendary story of the first
discovery might be late, but the actual emptiness of the tomb which
gave rise to the story could nevertheless be an original datum of
Christian faith and practice. It is hard to see, however, how this can
be anything more than conjecture. Against this, the story of the discovery of the empty tomb could have been developed in the course
of explicating an Easter ceremony which was carried on in complete
independence of the actual tomb in Jerusalem.

Another, slightly more secure argument contends that the story
of the empty tomb itself contains not only hints of the use to which
it was later put, but a direct acknowledgement of its own secondary
and late origin in so far as the women at the tomb are said in the

[48] L. Schenke, *Auferstehungsverkündigung und leeres Grab*; J. Kremer, *Die
Osterbotschaft der vier Evangelien*. The idea of the liturgical context of the origin of
the empty tomb story was anticipated by Gottfried Schille in 'Das Leiden des Herrn:
Die evangelische Passionstradition und ihr "Sitz im Leben" ', *ZTK*, 52 (1955),
pp. 161–205, pp. 195–9; and W. Nauck, 'Die Bedeutung des leeren Grabes für den
Glauben an den Auferstandenen', *ZNW*, 47 (1956), pp. 243–67.

[49] This theory is followed by G. O' Collins, *The Easter Jesus*, pp. 41f, though E.
L. Bode regards it as 'a most imaginative conjecture lacking solid foundation'. See
*The First Easter Morning: the Gospel Accounts of the Women's Visit to the Tomb of
Jesus*.

Marcan version to have disobeyed the command of the angel or at
least to have delayed in carrying it out, for it is said that 'they told
nobody' (Mark 16: 8). This verse is held to be an indicator of the
fact that the story only came to light relatively late in the history of
Christian origins, the delay being explained by the women's original
silence.[50]

All these arguments for the lateness of the story fall short of
proof. They all work to a similar pattern in so far as they suggest
plausible reasons for regarding the story as the product of faith
rather than as an original historical datum of faith. In each case a
theological, kerygmatic, apologetic or liturgical motive for generating the story is produced on the basis of alleged echoes of its original use in the received text. But, given that these factors may be
hints that the story was put to a kerygmatic and apologetic or liturgical use, this does not mean that the story is entirely accounted
for by reference to these elements, or that the original kernel of the
story is necessarily to be explained in any of these ways. The use of
an angel to perform the function of a preacher or lector in church
does not mean that what he is given to interpret is not based on fact.
The fact that the story was put to a later kerygmatic, apologetic or
liturgical use, that can now be detected in the texts, leaves the question of the origin of the core story open.

Certainly the historicity of the empty tomb tradition is not without its defenders. There is a strong and, indeed, popular body of
contemporary opinion which holds that the story of the empty
tomb is not the product of faith and proclamation or liturgy but the
sine qua non of the original proclamation. On one hand it is argued,
for example, by J. D. G. Dunn, that the primitive Christians could
not have from the beginning come to faith and confidently proclaimed the Easter kerygma, without the story of the empty tomb
being an integral part of it. Thus, he argues that the essential historicity of the empty tomb story is vouchsafed by the fact that without
the empty tomb it is questionable whether the disciples would have
interpreted their experience of 'appearance' in terms of the resurrec-

---

[50] This view is very widely held. See J. Wellhausen, *Das Evangelium Marci*,
p. 136; V. Taylor, *The Life and Ministry of Jesus*, p. 223; H. Grass, *Ostergeschehen
und Osterberichte*, pp. 22f; G. Bornkamm, *Jesus of Nazareth*, p. 183. G. W. H.
Lampe in *The Resurrection*, p. 48, accepts it without argument: 'The fact that the
women do not pass the message on may suggest that the evangelist, or his source,
knew that the story of the tomb and the angel was not part of the original Easter proclamation and had only developed at a relatively late stage in the tradition.'

tion of Jesus.[51] In other words, he seems to suggest that the experiences of the appearance of Jesus were too vague and imprecise to ground the firm conviction that Jesus was risen without the clarifying evidence of the empty tomb. This means that it did not just become necessary to tell the story of the empty tomb in order to communicate to others, but that the first disciples themselves needed the story in order to come to a clear resurrection belief in the first place. The empty tomb story, he says, is necessary if the 'then current thought about the resurrection' was to be satisfied.[52] Thus, even if we can today envisage, with Bultmann and many others, the possibility of an Easter belief which does not include a reference to the empy tomb, it would be anachronistic to attribute such an understanding to the first Christians, whose presupposition of bodily restoration necessitates or implies the telling of the tomb story.

On this reckoning it would have to be argued that Paul, who does not explicitly mention the empty tomb, implies as much. However, the contention that primitive Easter faith originally required the inclusion of belief in an empty tomb cannot be asserted with absolute confidence. When Paul, for example, declared that Jesus had died and was buried, the mention of the burial in 1 Cor. 15: 4 is usually interpreted to underscore the finality of the death, rather than to imply that he was raised from the grave in such a way as to leave it empty.[53] Von Campenhausen admits that his own original intention to argue for Paul's acquaintance with the empty tomb story, was rendered impossible by Grass[54] who cogently demonstrated that such a conclusion is not unassailable, for in view of 2 Cor. 5: 1, and despite Rom. 8: 11, it is conceivable that Paul did not hold that there was a re-animation of the dead body of Jesus, and so had no need to postulate an 'emptying' of the tomb. On the contrary, Paul's declaration that 'flesh and blood cannot inherit the Kingdom of God', with its implicit suggestion that the living cannot escape the transformative impact of death and bodily decay, could be said to have the force of positively excluding the possibility of

---

[51] J. D. G. Dunn, *Jesus and the Spirit*, p. 120

[52] Ibid., p. 119.

[53] See C. F. Evans, *Resurrection and the New Testament*, p. 75. For the argument in favour of the Pauline belief in the empty tomb see G. Stählin, 'On the Third Day', *Interpretation*, 10 (1956), p. 282f.

[54] H. von Campenhausen, op. cit., pp. 54f and n.52 and 53; cf. H. Grass, op. cit., pp. 146 ff.

admitting the empty tomb story to his own latent but unexpressed understanding of the resurrection of Christ.[55] In other words, not only does Paul not mention the empty tomb, but the way in which he speaks of the resurrection may not even logically imply it. The fact that Paul does not reckon it important enough to mention explicitly and the likelihood that Paul's words about the resurrection do not even imply a knowledge of it, means that the story of the empty tomb must be held to be secondary to faith.

Moreover, contrary to J. D. G. Dunn, it is not at all certain that a mundane restoration of flesh and bones, such as is implied by the empty tomb, would have been a logically necessary part of all expressions of resurrection belief at the time. Even if, as seems undeniable, the Rabbis interpreted Ps. 16: 9–10 as a reference to resurrection in terms of the preservation of the flesh beyond death, others seem to have held to a much more 'spiritual' understanding of things, reminiscent of the view of the Apocalypse of Baruch: 49–51.[56] Paul himself with his talk of 'the spiritual body' may well fall into this category. The fact that Paul was a Pharisee cannot be used to bolster the belief that even after his Christian conversion he must have shared the detailed pharisaic belief in the restoration of the mundane flesh and bones without first considering the question of the relation of the newly emerged Christian belief generally to antecedent pharisaic views. We must contend with the very real possibility that the early understanding of the resurrection of Jesus may have entailed the revision of some aspects of the former pharisaic beliefs. After all, why should the resurrection of Jesus conform in every respect with pharisaic conceptions and hopes? Given that the early conviction that Jesus was the Messiah involved a revision of the precise nature of the messiahship he embodied and the abandonment of this-worldly views of contemporary messianic belief, it is also conceivable that the primitive belief in the resurrection of Jesus called for a revision of what in precise and detailed terms had

[55] Ibid., p. 54, n.52.
[56] See H. L. Strack and P. Billerbeck, *Kommentar zum Neuen Testament aus Talmud und Midrasch*, Vol. II, p. 618. Also C. F. D. Moule 'St. Paul and Dualism: The Pauline Conception of the Resurrection' in *NTS*, 12 (1965–6), pp. 106–23. A. E. Harvey, *Jesus and the Constraints of History*, pp. 150f., draws attention to the fact that few scholars have faced the fact that Josephus, when describing the beliefs of the Pharisees, unmistakably suggests a doctrine of transmigration of souls as one of a variety of ways of expressing the hope of survival beyond death found in Jewish writing of the Hellenistic and Roman periods.

been envisaged in the prevailing mentality of the Pharisees. It is therefore somewhat difficult to insist that the story of the empty tomb must be original to faith because it is an unavoidable presupposition of any primitive proclamation of Easter faith, as though the resurrection of Jesus had to conform to pre-existing pharisaic beliefs in every detail. Rather, by its very uniqueness, it may have called for revision and refinement of some aspects of pharisaic pre-conceptions. This means that the argument in favour of the historicity of the empty tomb story on the grounds that it would have been a *sine qua non* of any Easter proclamation fails as a conclusive argument. Indeed, it begs all the important questions.

When we come to Pannenberg's own defence of the historicity of the empty tomb we find that the same difficulties render his argument weak and unconvincing. Pannenberg is persuaded by an argument of Paul Althaus in which it is held that the empty tomb story is a *sine qua non* for the success of the early proclamation, on the ground that the continuing ability of Christians to assent to the truth of the Easter proclamation depended precisely on the inability of their Jewish opponents to produce the grave with the body of Jesus still in it. In other words, the historicity of the empty tomb is not said to be given credence because the disciples could not have originally believed without it, or because they could not have even conceived of the resurrection of Jesus without it, but because they could not have continued to believe without it. Given the negative and hostile responses they encountered amongst their Jewish adversaries, it would have been only too easy to silence the new and troublesome sect simply by producing Jesus' body. In other words, Pannenberg argues, it is not so much that the historicity of the empty tomb is logically necessary to the primitive Christian conception of the resurrection, but that it is practically necessary for the continued assent to the validity of Easter claims. Pannenberg is impressed by Althaus's reasoning: The resurrection kerygma 'could not have been maintained in Jerusalem for a single day, for a single hour', says Althaus, 'if the emptiness of the tomb had not been established as a fact for all concerned'.[57] This means that, if the resurrection was proclaimed immediately after Jesus' death in Jerusalem, the place of his execution and of his grave, then the 'situation

---

[57] P. Althaus, *Die Wahrheit des kirchlichen Osterglaubens: Einspruch gegen E. Hirsch*, p. 22 f.

demands that within the circle of the first community one had a reliable testimony for the fact that the grave had been found empty'.[58]

Apart from this argument's reliance on the presupposition that the early proclamation cannot be conceived, except anachronistically, without implicit acceptance of the empty tomb, it relies on the additional pre-supposition that the proclamation of the Easter message in Jerusalem 'not long after Jesus' death' was in fact soon enough after his death to allow for the possibility of finding and positively identifying a tomb as the one in which Jesus' body had been placed. It would also have had to be soon enough to allow for the positive identification of a body as certainly that of the dead Jesus. Even if the content of the early proclamation was of such a kind that the production of the body in the tomb would have been an ultimately devastating factor, the success of the early proclamation may possibly have been guaranteed by the fact that, by the time the Easter message got from Galilee to Jerusalem, the exact location of the tomb could not be traced. The gospel assurance that the women noted the place of burial may well represent an apologetic answer to the Jewish charge that they had perhaps gone to the wrong tomb, rather than a factual report of their original observant attention to detail and tenacious memory.[59]

These arguments which seek to defend the basic historicity of the empty tomb story on the ground that it was the *sine qua non* of the success of the proclamation of the Easter kerygma therefore fall short of proof.

A more convincing argument, which Pannenberg summons to defend the historicity of the empty tomb story, rests on the absence

---

[58] Ibid., p. 25. Pannenberg follows this argument in *Jesus—God and Man*, p. 100; K. Lehmann, *Auferweckt am dritten Tag nach der Schrift*, agrees with the Althaus/Pannenberg argument that it would have been impossible to preach the resurrection in Jerusalem without secure evidence of the emptiness of the tomb.

[59] This is a possibility forcefully canvassed by R. R. Bater, 'Towards a More Biblical View of the Resurrection', *Interpretation*, 23 (1969), pp. 47–65. The view that the body was stolen has been put by D. Whitaker, 'What Happened to the Body of Jesus?', *Expository Times*, 81 (1970), pp. 307–11, whilst the view that the women possibly went to the wrong grave was seriously entertained by Kirsopp Lake, *The Historical Evidence for the Resurrection of Jesus Christ*, pp. 68–9 and pp. 250–2 and P. Gardner-Smith, *The Narratives of the Resurrection: A Critical Study*. That this was early raised in anti-Christian polemic is said to be indicated by apologetic references to the fact that the women could not have been mistaken in Mark 15: 47, Matt. 27: 61 and Luke 23: 55. See G. Vermes, *Jesus the Jew*, pp. 39–41.

of any Jewish anti-Christian polemic in which it was confidently and forcefully held that the tomb of Jesus *had* been found not to be empty but rather to contain the decomposing body of Jesus. There is no evidence, says Pannenberg, that the emptiness of the tomb was ever disputed even by the opponents of Christianity.[60] The absence of any claim to have discovered the tomb with the body of Jesus in it, amounts to evidence that its emptiness was accepted. In other words, the Jewish polemic accepted the tomb's emptiness, and never tried to argue that the tomb was still the repository of Jesus' corpse; instead an admitted emptiness was explained in other ways. For example, it was held that the body had been stolen or that the women had mistakenly gone to the wrong tomb, or even that the body had been deliberately removed by Joseph of Arimathaea for personal reasons or by the Jewish authorities to prevent the grave becoming a focus for continuing dissension.

The absence of any Jewish polemic in which it was held that the grave was found not to be empty but, contrary to the alleged early Christian preaching, to contain the corpse of Jesus, could however also be explained if the location of the tomb had long since been forgotten or if it was never really known to the Jewish authorities, thus preventing the possibility of settling the issue either way. If the precise location of Jesus' grave could not be determined, or if the body of Jesus could not be positively identified by the time the Christian preaching reached Jerusalem, there would have been no alternative for Jewish polemicists than to concede the possibility of the bare fact of the grave's emptiness and then go on to point out that, in any event, the emptiness of a grave, even if it could be demonstrated, would not prove anything more than that the body had been stolen or deliberately removed by the followers of Jesus themselves.

Amongst the explanations found in later Jewish polemic of how the grave came to be empty, the most frequent is that 'Judah the gardener', who had foreseen the possibility of deception, removed the body himself in order that, after the Christian declaration that Jesus had been raised, he could produce it. The body is in fact said to have

---

[60] See *Jesus—God and Man*, p. 101. Von Campenhausen makes the same point. See also J. C. O'Neill, 'On the Resurrection as an Historical Question' in *Christ Faith and History*, ed. S. W. Sykes and J. P. Clayton, p. 209: 'We have no evidence, apart from late Jewish stories, that any attempt was made to produce the body of Jesus. All traditions, whether Christian or non-Christian, agree that Jesus' tomb was empty'.

been dragged through the streets to refute Christian claims.[61] Whilst this is a late tradition there is an earlier hint of it in Tertullian who gibed that the gardener took the body 'so that the crowd of visitors should not damage his lettuces'.[62] The earlier existence of a story of the kind may of course have been the cause of the Christian reply in the form of Matthew's account of the military guard at the tomb, which has the effect of rendering such a story impossible.[63] In the face of this, Pannenberg's contention that no Jewish polemic seems to have existed which held that the tomb was found to contain the body of Jesus seems somewhat hollow. There are hints that a polemic relating to the finding and taking of the body did exist and that is was used against the early Christians.[64]

On the other hand, whilst there may not be any evidence of Jewish polemic to the effect that the grave was examined after the first reports of the resurrection and found still to contain the body of Jesus, there is nothing in the continuing Christian tradition to suggest that the Christians were able repeatedly to return to the tomb to confirm the women's story either. Either way we are arguing from silence and it has to be conceded that the arguments of both sides are consonant with an inability to find the grave in order to verify its emptiness or otherwise.

Furthermore, the absence of early Jewish polemic in which it was held that the grave was not empty is once again explicable if the story of the empty tomb was not in fact a clear and quite definite part of the original Easter kerygma. If the resurrection was understood in such a way as not necessarily to imply that the tomb was vacated 'without remainder', as it were, then it is unlikely that any

---

[61] H. von Campenhausen, 'The Events of Easter and the Empty Tomb', p. 67, cites S. Kraus, *Das Leben Jesu nach jüdischen Quellen* (1902), especially pp. 170ff., cf. pp. 59, 107ff., 126f.

[62] Tertullian, *De Spectaculis*, 30. von Campenhausen is therefore prepared to admit that the core story about the gardener removing the body is old. See 'The Events of Easter and the Empty Tomb', p. 67.

[63] C. F. Evans discusses the apologetic purpose behind the Matthean tradition of the placing of the soldiers at the tomb in *Resurrection and the New Testament*, pp. 81–2. For the view that the disciples were not deceivers but victims of deception see Joseph Klausner, *Jesus of Nazareth, His Life, Times, and Teaching*, p. 357: 'We must assume that the owner of the tomb, Joseph of Arimathaea, thought it unfitting that one who had been crucified should remain in his own ancestral tomb . . . Joseph of Arimathaea, therefore, secretly removed the body at the close of Sabbath and buried it in an unknown grave.'

[64] See W. Pannenberg, *Jesus—God and Man*, pp. 101ff.; also Eugène Mangenot, *La Résurrection de Jésus*, pp. 223–40.

polemic would bother to argue about the presence of Jesus' corpse in the grave. That would be a somewhat irrelevant concern. It may have been that the emptiness or otherwise of the tomb was not originally a contentious issue precisely because the primitive faith, being based on other evidence, such as the visions of the raised Jesus, did not necessarily imply the emptiness of the tomb. In this case the emptiness or otherwise of the tomb was not an immediate issue. The emphasis of 1 Cor. 15 in which the empty tomb is not so much as mentioned in consonant with this. In other words the early Christians may have conceived of the raised Jesus in a less material way, as a 'spiritual body' which was *exchanged* for the old physical body, to use Paul's image (2 Cor. 5: 1). In this case, whether or not physical remains were left behind in the grave would be irrelevant. We cannot assume what needs to be proved.

The same holds good in the case of the further suggestion of J. D. G. Dunn that the historicity of the tomb is to be accepted in view of the fact that 'we find no trace of any interest in the place of Jesus' burial within earliest Christianity' which he says is 'a surprising fact if Jesus' tomb had remained undisturbed or if his body had been removed and buried elsewhere, but not if the tomb was found empty'.[65] I must confess that I do not understand this argument which suggests that the grave in which Jesus had been laid would have been interesting to Christians had Jesus' body been found in it, but of no continuing interest even as the site of the resurrection, if it was found empty! Apart from the fact that a lack of early interest in the site of the tomb would also be congruent with the thesis that by the time the kerygma reached Jerusalem the site of the tomb could not be located, the pious interest in the alleged site of the Holy Sepulchre in our own day seems to render such an argument completely impotent.

Pannenberg is content to rely on arguments such as those we have been discussing to secure the historicity of the tomb story. All of them centre on the nature of the early Christian kerygma and the necessary conditions for its successful proclamation. None of these arguments, however, is capable of dimissing the alternative possibility that the story was generated by faith for a kerygmatic, apologetic, or perhaps even liturgical reason.

[65] J. D. G. Dunn, *Jesus and the Spirit*, op. cit., p. 120.

However, there is one further argument which Pannenberg passes over but which von Campenhausen, Pannenberg's former teacher at Heidelberg, clearly believes to be a telling piece of evidence and which may bolster Pannenberg's case. Von Campenhausen argues that one of the most important arguments in favour of the primitiveness and essential historicity of the empty tomb tradition is constituted by the undisputed fact that women rather than men feature in it as witnesses. Since women were not qualified to supply reliable testimony at Jewish law, any invented story, whether for kerygmatic, apologetic, or liturgical purposes, and whether early or late, would have furnished the scene at the tomb with male witnesses whose testimony would have been held to be beyond dispute.[66] In view of the force of this argument, it is surprising that Pannenberg does not refer to it. This prompts us to ask why?

Though Pannenberg accepts the argument of his former teacher concerning the historicity of the empty tomb, he differs from him in one respect. Von Campenhausen argues that the discovery of the empty tomb is early relative to the appearances in Galilee, which he believes were subsequent to it. Indeed, he contends that the disciples went to Galilee in expectation of apearances precisely as a result of the discovery of the empty tomb. However, Pannenberg sees, for one thing, that this sequence of events would create the right psychological conditions of expectation and enthusiasm for the disciples to have hallucinatory experiences in Galilee. It thus plays right into the hands of Strauss's subjective vision hypothesis. Pannenberg is naturally anxious to avoid this possibility. On the other hand, the actual textual evidence of 1 Cor. 15, as we have already noted, seems to favour the contention that the appearances traditions were primary and originally independent of the empty tomb tradition. Pannenberg holds to this view and appreciates that the independent discovery of the tomb in Jerusalem by the women complements the

---

[66] See H. von Campenhausen, op. cit., p. 75; P. Seidensticker, *Die Auferstehung Jesu in der Botschaft der Evangelisten*, p. 90; For the argument that the sex of the first witnesses is a case in favour of historicity see C. Masson, 'Le tombeau vide: essai sur la formation d'une tradition', *Revue de théologie et de philosophie*, NS, 32 (1944), pp. 161–74; J. Jeremias, *Jerusalem in the Time of Jesus*, pp. 374f.; A. A. Trites, *The New Testament Concept of Witness*, pp. 54–5 and 234. The relevant evidence will be found in *M. Shebu* IV.I, *Siphre Deut.* 19.17, 190; b.B.K. 88a. It was concluded from Genesis 18: 15 that women were liars. *Ant* 4: 219: 'Let not the testimony of women be admitted because of the levity and boldness of their sex'. See also Mishnah, *Rosh Hashanah* 1–8, *Shebu ʿoth* 30a.

Galilee experiences of the disciples and so strengthens the case for the historicity of the resurrection as a total event.

If the appearances have priority, however, this weakens the force of the argument concerning the inclusion of women witnesses in the empty tomb story. For if the disciples had fled to Galilee where they claimed to have had experiences of the raised Lord, then any subsequently generated story of the empty tomb would have no alternative than to draw upon the women as witnesses. If it was already known that the disciples had left Jerusalem and that they had experienced the appearance of the raised Jesus in Galilee they cannot have been the first to discover the empty tomb. In addition, there was an existing tradition that only the women were in the close vicinity of the crucifixion and that they alone participated in the burial. This would dictate that only the women, therefore, despite their unfortunate incompetence at law to supply evidence of the highest calibre, could really be called into the empty tomb story. Thus, despite its current vogue, the argument that the story of the tomb cannot have been a later invention or a way of proclaiming the resurrection in an apologetic situation, because of the inclusion of women, is not unassailable.[67]

Von Campenhausen believes that, when we test what is capable of being tested, the story of the empty tomb and its early discovery remains unshaken and that 'there is much that tells in its favour, and nothing definite or significant against it'. He therefore concludes that it is 'probably historical'.[68] In the final analysis, however, he finds it more prudent to admit that there is no argument for the historicity of the tomb that is 'unconditionally conclusive'.[69] Certainly, the contemporary study of the empty tomb traditions hardly warrants Westcott's confidence that the fact of the emptiness of the tomb 'seems to be beyond all doubt, and is one where misconception was impossible'.[70] For, try as we may, and with all the positive good will in the world, we simply do not have sufficient evidence to say for certain whether the tomb is a very primitive story whose kernel is factual, or whether in fact it is a later development, the pro-

---

[67] E. L. Bode, *The First Easter Morning: the Gospel Accounts of the Women's Visit to the Tomb of Jesus*, ranks the argument about the presence of women as the most telling point in favour of the historicity of the empty tomb. See pp. 177–8.

[68] 'The Events of Easter and the Empty Tomb', p. 77.

[69] Cf. H. Grass, op. cit., p. 183.

[70] *The Gospel of the Resurrection*, p. 114.

duct of faith, given a particular set of theoretical presuppositions about what might necessarily be involved in resurrection belief.

Given the meagreness of the evidence it is difficult to see that the logical shortfall can be overcome by purely rational argument, using only the critical techniques of scientific historiography.

But, even if we for the moment take an optimistic view of the evidence, and give the tomb story the benefit of the doubt, its capacity to ground the conclusion that because it was found empty Jesus must have been raised from the dead is, to say the least, somewhat problematic. In other words, the inference from 'what was seen' to the conclusion that Jesus must have been raised from the dead does not follow with logical necessity. Even if the historicity of the story of the arrival of the women at an empty tomb were to be conceded, as it was in later Jewish polemic, it is possible to explain it in a variety of other ways, which is precisely why the Jews are able comfortably to remain Jews to this day!

We should note from all this that the ambiguity of the evidence has to be overcome at two levels. This is not always brought to the surface in discussions of the usefulness or otherwise of the empty tomb story. First, the ambiguity of the evidence concerning the bare occurrence of the event of finding the tomb empty has to be overcome. We cannot assume the historicity of the tradition, as in the case of Westcott; Pannenberg's own attempts to prove it do not succeed. Second, once the bare historicity of the emptiness of the tomb is said to be secured, the ambiguity of its *meaning* has still to be overcome so that it is interpreted as evidence of nothing else except the resurrection. The best we can do is conclude that the assertion of the resurrection of Jesus is one possible interpretation of the available evidence. The story is a sign, which alerts us to the possibility that Jesus was raised. Certainly, when we raise the question 'what does the empty tomb actually prove?' even if its historicity were secured, and what role did it play in the structure of primitive resurrection belief, we have a second evidential shortfall to overcome before we can reach the positive conclusion that Jesus certainly rose from the dead.

We must therefore conclude that there is insufficient evidence to deny categorically that the tomb was found empty, but insufficient also to prove beyond all doubt that it was found empty. Certainly, there is insufficient evidence to prove that the emptiness of the tomb can have resulted only from the raising of Jesus by God. At best the story of the empty tomb can continue to raise the possibility of the resurrection in our minds and offer itself for our puzzlement. We may therefore choose to outline a systematic understanding of the nature of Easter faith in which there is no real call for it to do more than this.

However, what is clear, and what can be admitted on all sides is that, regardless of the outcome of the examination of the empty tomb tradition, it certainly does not constitute all of what was alleged to have been seen. Indeed, it only really becomes significant for faith in the resurrection of Jesus in the light of the apparently independent tradition of the appearances, to which we must now turn.[71]

The Historical Evidence: The Appearances

In the case of the tradition of the appearances, the question of whether it is an early or late tradition and whether it is an integral element in the earliest proclamation or otherwise does not arise. In this respect the evidence of the appearances is quite different from that relating to the empty tomb for there is little doubt that the appearances of the raised Christ constituted part of the Easter proclamation from the start. Not only do the Easter appearances assume a centrality in the gospel narratives, where they have the effect of relegating the empty tomb tradition to a secondary or preliminary role; in the earliest proclamation of which we have any knowledge in 1 Cor. 15: 3–8, the central importance of the appearances is stressed whilst the tomb is not explicitly mentioned at all.

Both Westcott and Pannenberg cite the primitiveness of the appearances tradition as it is found in this passage of 1 Corinthians as positive evidence of its authenticity. With respect to the fact of primitiveness itself they are certainly on very solid ground. When St Paul wrote this letter in AD 55 or 56 he reminded the Corinthians of the content of the gospel which he had originally preached to them on his first visit to their city. At the same time he disclosed that what he had preached then had in turn been at an even earlier time handed on to him, a fact which is corroborated by the appearance of un-Pauline language in this passage. Paul lists those to whom Jesus had appeared in chronological order, beginning with the first appearance to Peter and ending with the appearance which he him-

---

[71] This is openly admitted even by von Campenhausen, op. cit., p. 73.

self witnessed on the Damascus Road. This sequence is corroborated, at least with respect to the priority of Peter, in Luke 24: 34 and in John 20: 6, where Peter, whilst being outrun, enters the tomb first.

In recent years New Testament scholars have devoted a considerable amount of energy to the analysis of the apparent primitiveness of the resurrection proclamation as it is presented in 1 Cor. 15: 3–8. J. Jeremias has even attempted to demonstrate echoes of an earlier Aramaic original behind the Greek form that we now have. This is disputed by Conzelmann, but either way an early dating and the apparent legitimacy of its claim to be the oldest and most reliable account of the rise of the Easter faith is rarely disputed.[72]

This is the correct point of insertion in the New Testament for an understanding of the resurrection, for whatever importance is placed on the empty tomb tradition, it is the appearances that are central and vital to the primitive Easter faith. Thus, despite his concentration of attention upon the tradition of the empty tomb, even von Campenhausen acknowledges that 1 Cor. 15: 3–8 is the oldest and most reliable account that we have of what the disciples experienced at Easter: 'This is universally admitted. Any investigation of the subject must start with this'.[73]

Even if the appearance narratives in the later gospels have a strong legendary and apologetic character which marks them as 'late' relative to the origin of faith, this cannot be said of this outline of the kerygma recorded by Paul. This makes it difficult to argue that the

---

[72] On the date and place of origin of this early formula see J. Jeremias, *The Eucharistic Words of Jesus*, pp. 101–5; Hans Conzelmann, 'On the Analysis of the Confessional Formula in 1 Corinthians 15: 3–5', *Interpretation*, 20 (1966), pp. 15–25 (originally in *Evangelische Theologie*, 25 (1965), pp. 1–11); and J. Jeremias, 'Artikelloses Χριστός', ZNW, 57, pp. 211–15 and 60, pp. 214–19. That 1 Cor. 15: 3–8 is the correct point of insertion into the New Testament for an understanding of the resurrection is accepted by most contemporary writers; see especially C. F. Evans, *Resurrection and the New Testament*, Reginald H. Fuller, *The Formation of the Resurrection Narratives*, and essays by Willi Marxsen, Ulrich Wilckens, Gerhard Delling, and Hans-Georg Geyer in C. F. D. Moule (ed.), *The Significance of the Message of the Resurrection for Faith in Jesus Christ*. As we shall see in Chapter V, however, this is to some degree disputed by E. Schillebeeckx who argues that the early proclamation asserted that Jesus had been exalted to heaven, whence he would return at the Parousia, without any initial reliance on Easter appearances.

[73] H. von Campenhausen, op. cit., p. 43. See also W. Pannenberg, *Jesus—God and Man*, p. 89: 'The historical question of the appearances of the resurrected Lord is concentrated completely in the Pauline report, 1 Cor. 15: 1–11.'

proclamation of the fact of the appearances was a late or legendary development, the product of faith rather than the ground of it. Pannenberg, like Westcott, is therefore also impressed by the age of the tradition of appearances used by Paul. In view of the antiquity of this tradition and the proximity of Paul himself to the events which he reports, the historicity of the accounts of the appearances as against free invention in the course of later legendary development is said to have 'good historical foundation'.[74]

It seems clear enough that, on the basis of these alleged experiences, the disciples were convinced that they had seen the raised Christ. Whether the disciples did in fact see him, rather than experience some kind of psychogenic hallucination which deceived them is another matter, for any attempt to prove the resurrection on the basis of the evidence of the appearances must now grapple with the contention of D. F. Strauss, that they were nothing more than psychologically induced 'subjective visions'. The historical question therefore centres not upon the apparent primitiveness of the appearances tradition, which can be readily admitted to be early, but upon the historical reliability and accuracy of the reports of the alleged appearances.

Before we even attempt to assess the reliability of these reports we need to come to some clarity of understanding concerning the nature of the purported occurrence. For Westcott and others in the nineteenth century who assumed that the historical method was the appropriate means of coming to a knowledge of the resurrection, the question of the meaning of the early testimony seems to have been deceptively clear. Westcott believed that the gospel narratives of the appearances could be employed to reconstruct a picture of what occurred and thus to throw light on the detailed nature of the experiences which are simply listed by Paul in 1 Cor. 15: 3–8. This meant that it was assumed that a straightforward visual experience was what Paul had in mind. In addition, the intellectual environment confirmed Westcott in his view of the concrete, visual nature of the appearances. The scientific preoccupation of the time with accuracy of observation had an aesthetic counterpart in the inclination of the age for realism. In literature and art, for example, a premium was placed on reproducing the evidence of visual experience in the form of the faithful and sincere reportage of facts. The

[74] W. Pannenberg, op. cit., p. 91.

scientific quest for hard fact also had its historiographical expression in the nineteenth-century preoccupation with the reporting of exactly what happened in the past—*wie es eigentlich gewesen* (as it actually happened), as Leopold von Ranke, the father of the modern critical-scientific study of history, put it. Amongst theologians this scientific and historical realism was amply expressed by Westcott in so far as he placed supreme confidence in direct observation. His repeated emphasis on the value of sensory perception is expressed in the belief that nothing can be more certain 'than an immediate intuition'.[75] In so far as the theologian worked with the tools of critical-historical research, he naturally believed he was in the business of reconstructing and reporting what had originally been perceived through sense experience.

We have already noted that this led him in his theology of the resurrection to speak of 'what was seen' (the appearances of the raised Jesus no less than the empty tomb) as evidence which could be literally described, just as appropriately as the burial of Jesus or any other event in the life of Jesus. Thus, whilst Westcott admitted that we really have very little idea of the nature of the resurrected life, and that it is 'vain for us to speculate on the nature of the transformed human Body'[76] which we conceive only under 'signs and figures',[77] his initial methodological presupposition that the appearances of the raised Jesus constituted an experienced historical event, meant that he assumed that he was able to talk about and describe them just as legitimately as the first Christians did when they reported them. Moreover, his emphasis on the reality of the object seen and its apprehension through sense experience led to the inevitable conclusion that it must be possible to talk about it in straightforward literal discourse. It is not just that at the resurrection Jesus had disappeared. He was not therefore hidden and so the object only of imagination. Westcott's reiterated claim is that Jesus was seen and that therefore he was the object not of pious imagination but of actual observation and description. And whilst he admits that some of the details that arose in the reporting of the appearances

---

[75] *The Gospel of the Resurrection*, p. 14. He is using the word 'intuition' in Kant's sense of 'sensory experience' or 'the deliverances of sense'.
[76] Ibid., p. 163–4
[77] Ibid., p. 164.

may not be factual, he was clearly anxious to urge that the general picture may certainly be accepted.

Even so, in *The Gospel of the Resurrection* Westcott did not himself spell out exactly what it was that was seen. He was more interested to move on to urge that the conclusion that Jesus must have been raised is validly drawn. In effect this meant that, though he was prepared to admit that some details of the appearances stories may not be quite factual, the historicity of the basic nucleus had to be defended. His contention was that the general impression that the narratives give is beyond dispute. If he was somewhat reticent about spelling out the detailed implications of his view that the appearances were occurrences of similar kind to the burial, in so far as they could be described, he at least did not cease from stressing the objectivity and observability of the appearances of Jesus. He is content to bring the Pauline tradition in which the appearances are baldly affirmed into loose synthetic association with the tradition of the empty tomb and the gospel stories of the appearances. In the absence of any further descriptive detail the reader is left with the impression that the gospel stories of the appearances, though not necessarily accurate in every detail, are reliable enough in general terms and that what happened was more rather than less like the reports that have come down to us in the gospel narratives.

This was made more explicit in 1881 when he published his *The Revelation of the Risen Lord*, as 'An Introduction or A Supplement to *The Gospel of the Resurrection*'. No longer is he so concerned to prove the occurrence of the resurrection; that is now presupposed as a fact. He is more interested in an analysis of the 'signs' which the raised and exalted Christ allegedly gave of his continuing heavenly existence and their continuing revelatory significance. Yet, his commitment to the historical method remained. He assumed that the first appearances which were granted to the disciples of Jesus were apprehended through sense impressions, primarily of sight and hearing.

It seems that Westcott understood the 'sensible signs' constituted by the appearances as accommodations to the needs and mental capacities of those to whom they were made known.[78] The disciples

---

[78] *The Revelation of the Risen Lord*, p. 6.

could therefore describe them in the reports which we now have in the gospels. This in turn meant that the contemporary historian could examine the reports of these alleged appearances and write a 'history of the Manifestation of the Risen Christ'.[79] In practice this means that the more detailed and graphic accounts of the appearances in Luke and John condition the less detailed and less concrete resurrection manifestations reported elsewhere in the gospels and the bare, unadorned credal statements found in the epistles. The end result is that a fuzzy harmony is achieved. Whilst some details still need to be brought into sharp focus and some details seem difficult to harmonize completely with others, the general picture of what happened at Easter remains. Only with such a picture, be it ever so puzzling and incomplete, can the attempt to handle the appearances as datable historical events of the past proceed at all, for one must have some conception of what it is that one is trying to prove before proceeding to try to demonstrate that it did in fact occur.

The one hundred years of biblical research since Westcott have rendered this relatively straightforward understanding of the appearances rather problematic from a historical point of view. The first difficulty of which we are now aware is that such an understanding of the appearances can operate only by taking a very synthetic view of the traditions. What is understood to have been seen outside the tomb in the days after Easter is reconstructed by harmonizing the traditions into one overall picture. However, as we have already noted,[80] the tendency of biblical theologians right up to the last generation to draw together the various elements found within the pages of the New Testament into one harmonious view of what happened at Easter and on subsequent days is today rejected as no longer possible. One of the most conclusive results of contemporary redactional studies of the New Testament traditions of the appearances, no less than of the empty tomb, is that an original nucleus of tradition has been developed during the course of its transmission and that the resulting diversity can be explained by reference to apologetic motives and concerns along the way; the modification of the tradition is an inevitable by-product of the attempt to communicate and defend resurrection belief in different

---

[79] Ibid., p. 4.
[80] Chapter 1, pp. 16ff. above.

contexts to different people with different preconceptions and concerns. All this conditions what is said. The diversity of the resulting traditions cannot just be added together to form one synthetic account of what is supposed to have happened at the first Easter so that all the historian need do is turn his attention to the question of truth—to determine whether it is possible to prove that the sum of what is reported in the New Testament sources did happen or not. The systematic theologian cannot proceed on this assumption without putting on blinkers which exclude the most firm results of his contemporary colleagues in New Testament studies.

In this respect we have the advantage of knowing much more about the traditions than Westcott, but this brings with it a problem of which Westcott did not even dream. Today it is commonplace to distinguish the original proclamation of the resurrection from the later narratives of the resurrection appearances. These later narratives represent the particular form the proclamation took on in the course of its transmission and it is undeniable that they tend to present the raised Christ in increasingly concrete and positive language. Later embroidering results in the more materializing and concrete stories of Luke and John. However, once the concrete, materializing tendencies of the appearance stories of Luke and John are accounted for as apologetic developments rather than reports of original fact, the outlines of the original fact begin to become imprecise and elusive. When we set aside these positive narrative descriptions, we find it more difficult to express exactly what it is that we are talking about. If we cannot say what it was that they originally claimed to have experienced and what the broad contours of it were like, how can we proceed to try to demonstrate that it actually occurred? More importantly, if we cannot say what it was, how can we judge whether or not the early disciples were justified in so far as they identified what they claimed to encounter as the appearance of *Jesus*? In other words we come face to face with the 'redactional ikonastasis' and the elusiveness of the original Easter experiences behind it. This then raises in an acute and pressing form, the contention usually associated with the name of D. F. Strauss, that the original experiences may have been nothing more than 'subjective visions'.

Since Strauss articulated his famous 'subjective vision hypothesis', this kind of explanation has repeatedly been offered as an adequate historical account of the origin of the primitive faith and mission.[81] Pannenberg appreciates the need to rebut the charge that the visions were merely psychogenic or subjective phenomena. Even so, Pannenberg is himself prepared to speak of the first appearances in terms of the category of 'visions' on the ground that the phenomena were not open to public scrutiny: 'Any event of this sort', he says, 'must be designated as a vision. If someone sees something that others present are not able to see, then it involves a vision.'[82] In view of the fact that the alleged visions of Bernadette Soubirous at Lourdes on 11 February 1858 and following days also seem to have been witnessed by her without anything being seen by others who accompanied her, this raises the possibility that the primitive Easter experiences and the phenomenon of Lourdes, were all of the same visionary kind. However, Pannenberg is not willing to allow that the Easter visions were indistinguishable from any other reported visions from the history of Christian piety, or from the religious traditions of other world religions for that matter. Inevitably he is therefore obliged to argue that there are visions and visions. Some are apparently to be understood as being psychologically induced by an excess of religious enthusiasm. The original vision of the raised Christ, however, is said to be of a more fundamental kind. There is a suggestion of such a distinction where Paul distinguishes the seeing of the raised Christ on the road to Damascus which he regarded as foundational to his faith and his subsequent experiences of visions and revelations of the Lord (2 Cor. 12: 1) which were not similarly determinative or significant. Westcott makes the same point. The initial 'objective and outward' appearance which grounds the conviction of faith is contrasted with ecstatic visions and revelations of 2 Cor. 12: 1 ff., which left room for doubt.

Pannenberg goes on to contend that the early Christians must have had criteria for distinguishing between 'ecstatic visionary experiences' and 'the fundamental encounters with the resurrected

---

[81] It was forcefully argued in England in Westcott's day by W. R. Cassels in his anonymously published *Supernatural Religion*, Vol. III, pp. 426ff. and by R. W. Macan in *The Resurrection of Jesus Christ*. More recently it has been revived by H. M. Teeple in 'The Historical Beginnings of the Resurrection Faith' in *Studies in the New Testament and Early Christian Literature*, ed. D. E. Aune, pp. 107–20. Don Cupitt is clearly drawn towards the same explanation in *Christ and the Hiddenness of God*, Chapter 10 and in 'The Resurrection: A Disagreement: A Correspondence with C. F. D. Moule' in *Explorations in Theology*, 6, pp. 27–41.

[82] W. Pannenberg, *Jesus—God and Man*, p. 93. See H. Grass, op. cit., p. 229.

Lord'.[83] His point seems to be that the appearances of Jesus should not be understood as purely subjective visions in view of the fact that the disciples themselves made a clear distinction between visions which were fundamental for faith and later visions and revelations of the Lord which were of an ecstatic and less fundamental, perhaps even subjective kind. Such a distinction is implied in so far as the early Christians themselves distinguished visions that were foundational for faith and visions which may well have been produced by faith.

He admits, however, that the question of the nature of the criteria for making such a distinction is difficult for us to determine. Certainly, the historian cannot test the validity of the distinction if he does not know what the criteria are. Nevertheless, Pannenberg goes on to argue that the visions of the first disciples are unlikely to have been of a purely psychogenic kind. His argument against the 'subjective vision' hypothesis of Strauss and others who have followed in his footsteps, comes down to two basic points. First, he says that there is no evidence to substantiate the occurrence of the kind of psychological pre-conditions which would *explain* the visions as subjective hallucinations. The same point was made by Westcott.[84] This is largely an argument from silence, for we do not have the evidence to demonstrate precisely what the psychological condition of the first believers was. Second, Pannenberg argues that the number and temporal dispersion of the experiences also argues for their authenticity. Westcott once again makes the same point about the reliability of the reports of visions because of the number of those who had the experiences and the temporal and geographical dispersion of them.[85]

The contention that the visions cannot have been subjective or psychologically induced visions therefore assumes that the necessary and appropriate conditions of enthusiasm and excitement could only have been sustained for a brief period, but in the case of the Easter tradition visions are reported over a longer period.

Unfortunately, this does not dispose of the 'subjective vision

---

[83] Ibid., p. 94.

[84] *The Revelation of the Risen Lord*, p. x: 'There was no enthusiastic hope to create visions'.

[85] *The Gospel of the Resurrection*, p. 114: 'the manifestations of the Risen Saviour were widely extended both as to persons and as to time'. Cf. also p. 115 where he refers to 'the length of time during which the appearances of the Lord were continued'.

hypothesis'. Most of those who have argued for the subjective nature of the visions contend that psychological disturbance induced by the guilt of having deserted Jesus sufficiently accounts for them. The presence of the guilt is hinted at in the New Testament traditions at least in the case of Peter, whose denial of Jesus (Mark 14: 66–72) may have had psychological repercussions, and Paul, whose persecution of Christians may have been a contributing factor to his experiences (Acts 26: 9–11). The fact of the temporal dispersion of the experiences might count against the possibility of the visions being caused by brief mass hysteria following close upon Jesus' death, but not if, in the passage of time, nagging guilt was a basic contributing factor. Pannenberg's dismissal of the subjective vision theory on the ground that there is no historical evidence of the existence of the right conditions for such an occurrence is therefore a little too cavalier. Certainly he fails to convince us that he has finally put the subjective vision theory to rest.

But, even if the 'subjective vision' hypothesis could be dispatched by historical methods, as Pannenberg attempts to do, we are still left at something of a loss concerning what an 'objective vision' of the raised Christ, as distinct from a 'subjective vision', would be like. As an experience available to some and not to others it becomes tantalizingly elusive and ambiguous. Indeed, precisely what it was that the disciples claimed originally to have experienced, apart from the fact that they believed they could legitimately identify it as 'Jesus', is not at all clear. It is at this point that any attempt to establish the historicity of the resurrection as an event of the past begins to run into substantial difficulties. Unanswered questions of meaning frustrate any speedy attempt to move directly to tackle the question of the truth of the appearance traditions: How are we to prove 'that it occurred' if we have little understanding of 'what it was'?

The historian, far from assembling evidence with which he is able to demonstrate the objective occurrence of the resurrection, finds himself grappling with the prior and puzzling question of what exactly it was that the primitive Christians were trying to describe. Only when he has solved the question of meaning can he proceed to seek to determine whether they were being truthful or dishonest, or honest but mistaken and deluded.

It should be said that the modern tendency amongst New Testament scholars to reduce the importance of the concrete, material and tangible nature of the raised Christ, and the straightforwardly visual nature of the Easter experience, is not motivated by a liberalizing attempt to make belief easier for contemporary people by accommodating it to intellectual norms of modern culture. If anything the whole thing is made harder, for an understanding of things in straightforward visual terms at least has the virtue of being clear. Christian faith becomes if anything more complicated, just as soon as it is seen that the manner in which Jesus appeared is no longer exactly as it is presented in a surface reading of the texts, particularly the developed traditions of Luke and John. On the other hand, it can be appreciated that the contemporary task is to try to penetrate behind the traditions in order to reconstruct the nature of the original experiences of the raised Christ, rather than just synthesize the texts more or less as they are. We shall ourselves seek to go behind the traditions to discern something of the nature of 'what was seen' in Chapter VI. For the moment I must simply raise the question of what this difficulty implies for the attempt to handle the resurrection as a straightforward historical event. For, given that the results of contemporary historical criticism were not available to Westcott, he was nonchalantly able to harmonize the traditions into an overall view of what was seen, and this was precisely what allowed him to handle the evidence of the resurrection as historical evidence. He assumed that an appearance of Jesus was clear and distinct enough to be classified as visual evidence, similar to that which might be used to establish the occurrence of any other observed fact. But once the concrete, clearly visual nature of the appearances is called in question and the appearances are spoken of in visionary rather than visual terms, the appropriateness of the historical method for handling the resurrection purely as an observed event of the past becomes somewhat problematic.

Dogmatic Difficulties

This historical difficulty did not even occur to Westcott. Nevertheless, he did come to discern that there were problems in his own basic approach to the resurrection from a dogmatic point of view.

So long as it is argued in the manner of Westcott that the appearances constituted evidence for Jesus' resurrection that is of a similar kind to the evidence for asserting his burial, it can be argued that both occurrences can be appropriately handled using the methods of critical-historical research. However, this basic methodological commitment inevitably entails that the resurrection begins to be assimilated to purely natural events in the life of Jesus. This may be dogmatically disastrous, for to assimilate the appearance of Jesus to observable events in his life and to his death and burial means that justice can hardly be done to its absolute uniqueness and to its transcendent revelatory nature.

The creeping awareness of this dogmatic difficulty can be discerned as a conditioning factor in Westcott's work. It is true that Westcott always held the resurrection to be a supernatural event, discontinuous with the normal chain of cause and effect, because it was said to be the result of a miraculous, direct intervention of God in the historical process. Nevertheless, the event itself, given its supernatural divine cause, is treated, in so far as it was humanly experienced, as though it were an occurrence of the natural order, to be perceived in exactly the same way as any natural occurrence. The presupposition that it could be handled with the methods of critical-historical research entailed that its outlines could be reconstructed and its bare occurrence, as distinct from its divine cause, could be demonstrated by citing the relevant evidence. This evidence is understood to be similar in kind to the evidence which might be summoned to demonstrate the occurrence of any other event in time. It is precisely because of this that Westcott was able to say that the apprehension of the appearances of Jesus was based in sensory experience. In so far as the resurrection is assimilated to the ordinary, natural events of history in this way, it follows that it was an event that could be described in literal or prosaic language, as indeed Westcott explicitly says.[86]

However, the inevitable consequence of approaching the understanding of the resurrection from this starting-point and of following such methods as these, is that the resurrection of Jesus tends to be 'naturalized' in such a way that its ultimate theological significance becomes somewhat problematic. For a start, Westcott himself saw that by assimilating the appearance of the raised Jesus to his burial there was a danger of confusing the resurrection of Jesus with the kind of happening narrated in the story of the raising of Lazarus. We might add that there was a danger of assimilating it to the raising of the daughter of Jairus and the son of the widow of Nain, as well as Lazarus (Mark 5: 21–43; Luke 7: 11–17; John 11), not to mention countless other reported resuscitations of a miraculous

[86] Ibid., p. 135.

kind from ancient religious literature. But, the resurrection of Jesus is not to be assimilated to a mere bodily resuscitation. Rather, the resurrection of Jesus is 'essentially unique'; it marks an entry into the eternal or 'heavenly' life of God, a going from 'seen into the unseen'. As was noted in the previous chapter, far from being just an emotionally-moving 'quivering of the eyelids' or a restoration to life in this world, the resurrection of Jesus speaks of a transformation, an 'entry into glory' (Luke 24: 26) not a temporary return to mortal condition. As St Paul has it, 'Christ being raised from the dead will never die again' (Rom. 6: 9).[87]

The resurrection is not the resumption of the old life, but the beginning of the new creation. In view of this strand of New Testament reflection upon the nature of the resurrection, Westcott argued[88] that it is a complete misunderstanding persistently to represent the Resurrection of Christ 'as one of many raisings from the dead'.[89] He therefore became critical of 'popular conceptions of a carnal Resurrection'.[90]

Long before Westcott, Thomas Aquinas appreciated the same difficulty. He saw that there was a clear difference between what he called the 'genuine and perfect resurrection of Christ' and the imperfect type of resurrection of those reported to have been restored to life under the ordinary conditions of space and time. By contrast with these imperfect resurrections, Christ's perfect resurrection excluded the possibility of ever dying again. Moreover, it involved a transformation and glorification.[91] Westcott's position is exactly the same, yet his approach to an understanding of the resurrection via the methods of critical historical research which inevitably assimilate it to other events of the mundane order, tends to strip it of its transcendent and heavenly qualities.

If anything, today we are even more sensitive to the transcendental aspect of the resurrection than either Aquinas or Westcott were. We now appreciate that it was as a result of the resurrection that the early Christians claimed, not that their former master had been

---

[87] See Rom. 7: 24; 6: 9–11; Rev. 1: 17–18; Acts 13: 34. Cf. Gregory of Nyssa, 'First Sermon on the Resurrection', *Patrologia Graeca* 46, Col. 615–28 where he calls on his hearers to appreciate the *mystery* of the resurrection.

[88] In 'The Resurrection of Christ: A New Revelation', *Contemporary Review* (Nov. 1877).

[89] Ibid., p. 1074.

[90] Ibid., p. 1075.

[91] *Summa Theologicae*, 3a, Q. 53, art. 3.

restored to them, but rather that they now experienced him as their divinely exalted Lord. The emergence of Christological talk in which Jesus came to be seen not only as their old master restored but as *Lord* and *Messiah*, and ultimately as *Son of God* and the *Word Incarnate*, is the direct result of the Easter experience of Jesus, precisely now as the exalted one: what was at best ambiguous and indistinct in the time before Easter now became, in the light of the Easter experience, clear and distinct. Jesus had been exalted to God's right hand, there to reign with 'his enemies as his footstool'. All this characteristically post-Easter Christian talk is hardly congruent with a mere resuscitation of Jesus. The concept of resurrection, by contrast, implies exaltation and transformation: to be raised from the dead is necessarily also to be exalted.[92] This means that the resurrection of Jesus is quite misconceived when it is understood in such a way as to imply a return to earthly life.

Whilst Westcott's theological sympathies led him to take account of the transcendental qualities of the raised Christ, his entire historical method tended to pull his account of the resurrection in a more mundane direction. In his later work on the resurrection his earlier position therefore tended to be modified in so far as he began to stop comparing the appearances with the burial. At the same time he began to stress the heavenly and revelatory nature of the Easter event which marked it as essentially dissimilar from ordinary historical events. In his article 'The Resurrection of Christ: A New Revelation' (1877) he emphasized that, whilst the evangelists write 'as if they were dealing with ordinary phenomena',[93] the essentially novel elements of the resurrection as a 'new revelation' had to be noted. The raised Jesus who appeared at Easter was not 'of earth only', otherwise 'it might be possible, perhaps, to imagine how any single observer might have ascertained the fact by outward observation'.[94] But 'no external tests could have established what is of the essence of the fact' for an integral part of resurrection belief is that Jesus was transformed so that he now belonged to heaven. The appearances are now said to be sensible signs of his heavenly existence, just as the ascension is a 'sensible sign' of his going to heaven.[95] In *The Revelation of the Risen Lord*, as the title suggests, the

---

[92] See Luke 24: 26; Phil. 2: 8–11; Mark 14: 62, Rom. 8: 34; Acts 2: 32–33.
[93] Op. cit., p. 1079.
[94] Ibid., p. 1077.
[95] Ibid., p. 1076.

same preoccupations are evident. The heavenly and revelatory nature of the appearances is stressed so that the ascension can now be said only to ratify and present in a final form the lessons of the forty days.[96] It is therefore perfectly clear that Westcott became acutely aware of the theological inadequacy of placing an over-emphasis on the unambiguous visibility and tangibility of the raised Christ. Such an approach over-naturalized him so that he belonged rather more to earth than to heaven.

What Westcott did not see so clearly was that this is a fundamental problem for any systematic theology of the resurrection which seeks to approach it as a historical event. Indeed, it is a problem for which answers have been sought ever since Luke's systematic attempt to resolve it in the New Testament itself. Once the resurrection is treated, as in Luke, in a way which tends to assimilate it to any occurrence in history and to speak of the appearances in a very concrete, materializing way, it is necessary to introduce a further mechanism in order to de-historize and transform Jesus into the eternal, exalted and omnipresent Lord of the Christian community. Indeed, after narrating a series of very material or concrete appearances of Jesus, as though he had merely been resuscitated and restored to the conditions of this world for forty days, Luke does precisely this: he ends the time in which Jesus seems to experience the normal bodily need to eat and drink by having Jesus exalted to heaven. In order that the raised Jesus might be lifted on to a divinely exalted plane an ascension has to be effected so that Jesus can then be understood to be forever exalted 'at the right hand of the Father'. This is a quite necessary episode if the raised Christ is not to become a theologically useless curiosity of this world.

Whilst this Lucan schema was acceptable enough to Westcott as a report of what actually happened, we now appreciate that a dichotomy between resurrection and exaltation is peculiar to Luke and is almost certainly his own creation. Elsewhere in the New Testament the exaltation of Jesus is seen as but one facet of the resurrected life.[97] In some New Testament texts, on the other hand, the exaltation can be spoken of without any explicit mention of the motif of resurrection whatsoever. This is the case, for example, in the pre-Pauline hymn to Christ in Philippians 2: 9 and in the Epistle to the

[96] *The Revelation of the Risen Lord*, p. 8.
[97] See Rom. 1: 3f.; 10: 9; 1 Thess. 1: 10; Eph. 1: 20–21; 1 Pet. 1: 21; 3: 22. See also Phil. 2: 8ff.; Col. 1: 18; Heb. 1: 3–5.

Hebrews.[98] Indeed, even in Luke with his own distinctive dogmatic viewpoint there are surviving remnants of the alternative view in which resurrection and exaltation are assimilated.[99]

If originally the resurrection of Jesus and the ascension with its associated ideas of the glorification and transformation of Jesus were different ways of speaking about the one event by focusing on different aspects of it, then it would be methodologically disastrous to revert to a Lucan but pre-critical position by treating the raising of Jesus as a restoration to the conditions of life in this world simply in order to allow it to be handled more or less along with any other event in history.

Westcott saw that for dogmatic reasons the resurrection of Christ could not be represented in such a way as to suggest that it involved nothing else than a restoration of Jesus to the conditions of life in this world. What he did not appreciate was that his original commitment to treating the resurrection exclusively by the historical method tended inexorably to lead him towards this kind of picture of what happened. An unresolved tension therefore remained in his later work, his theological insights pulling against the implications of the historical method.

On the other hand, Westcott began to see that the approach to the resurrection as a historical event distorts not only the way in which the resurrection of Jesus is actually understood in the New Testament, but the way in which the New Testament speaks of the appropriation of the resurrection of Jesus in human consciousness. Any attempt of the kind Westcott originally pursued, to handle the resurrection appearances simply as historical evidence of similar kind to the evidence of burial, inevitably tends to suggest that anybody who chanced to be in the vicinity at the time could have observed an appearance, given a basic inclination to attend to it. Once it is seen that there is a distinction to be drawn between faith and sight, it can be appreciated that an over-readiness to present the appearances as quasi material, visible phenomena that were accessible to anybody, tends to eliminate the nature of faith as an apprehension attained by some and not by just everybody possessing the natural endowment of eyesight.

Westcott was probably not aware that in stressing the heavenly

[98] This finds an echo in Eph. 4: 8ff.; 1 Tim. 3: 16; Heb. 12: 2; 1 Pet. 1: 11.
[99] See Luke 24: 26 and 23: 42f.; Acts 2: 32f., 13: 33f.

nature of the raised Christ and the utter uniqueness of the resurrection, over against stories of mere resuscitations or restorations to life in this world, he was in fact pulling the mat from under his former argument that the resurrection was a historical event, similar to the burial or any other natural event in Jesus' life, and like them historical precisely because it was observable. If the appearances constituted evidence of similar genre to the burial then it seems to be unavoidably implied that the risen Lord might have been observed even by somebody who was not a believer. The raised Christ's leaving of the tomb might well have been observed with a clarity similar to that experienced when his body was observed being carried into it. For example, the soldiers who, in Matthew's version of the empty tomb story, were said to have been appointed to guard the tomb against the possibility of the illicit removal of the body, might well have been witnesses of it. It is even implied by such an understanding of the appearances tradition that had the techniques of modern photography been available at the time, not only the empty tomb but the consequent physical apearances of Jesus could have been photographed. For just as the human experience of these things was via the senses, the eye, optic nerve, and brain, so whatever was seen could in principle have been caught for posterity by lens, shutter, and film. Only the modernity of the arrival of the camera made this impossible in the first century. This means that in the absence of a photographic record of the appearances we must be content with the verbal descriptions of the apostolic witnesses. The dogmatic implication of this is that, even though the evidence we have is fragmentary, the resurrection is presented as though it were a historical event which in principle could have been observed by anybody and which could have been reported in greater detail and clarity, given a little more human industry and ingenuity at the time and an eye to satisfying a future thirst for facts.

The difficulty that such a view must face, from the point of view of the New Testament evidence of the way in which the appearances were appropriated in human consciousness, is that relatively few people apprehended the presence of the raised Christ and these were for the most part those who had formerly been Jesus' disciples.[100]

---

[100] A point stressed by W. Marxsen, 'The Resurrection of Jesus as a Historical and Theological Problem', op. cit., p. 36

The raised Jesus was apparently not seen by Caiaphas or Pilate or the Jewish crowd. Thus, whilst the burial or the empty tomb may well have been observed by anybody, the appearance of the raised Jesus was not in similar manner available to the scrutiny of all comers. Indeed, in Acts Luke says quite explicitly that Jesus appeared not to all the people but to those 'who were chosen by God as witnesses' (Acts 10: 40–1). This seems to make the clear point that the raised Christ was not observed openly by everybody or just anybody. Moreover, Luke suggests that in the case of Paul even those who were travelling with him did not see what he saw (Acts 9: 7; Cf. Acts 22: 9). However, this not only now brings up questions concerning the congruence of the appearances tradition with the empty tomb tradition, but also moves the 'seeing of the raised Christ' away from any similarity with the observance of the burial. Suddenly the appearances become quite unlike the death and burial. Westcott therefore came to say that, whilst the burial could have in principle been observed by anybody, the resurrection was an event of a different kind, precisely because it was not in principle available to everybody. But if likeness to the burial is one reason for handling the appearances as historical events with the tools of critical-historical research as Westcott originally thought, then lack of similarity with the burial seems to dictate that we must begin to question whether the appearances are rightly treated with the tools of critical-historical research at all.

To add to our difficulties, apart from the fact that the appearances were seen by some and not others, even those who claimed to see were not universally clear and unequivocal about what it was that they perceived. Indeed, as we have seen, C. H. Dodd in his form-critical study of the appearances traditions drew attention to the recurring theme of doubt and ambiguity that is so much a part of them.[101] But if the appearances of Jesus were not open to every-

---

[101] C. H. Dodd, 'The Appearances of the Risen Christ: An Essay in Form-Criticism of the Gospel' in *Studies in the Gospels, Essays in Memory of R. H. Lightfoot*, pp. 9–35; F. W. Beare, 'Sayings of the Risen Jesus in the Synoptic Tradition: An Inquiry into their Origin and Significance' in *Christian History and Interpretation: Studies Presented to John Knox*, p. 164, notes, in the case of the manifestation of the risen Jesus in Matthew 28, 'the strange note that it was not of the kind to *compel* faith'.

body, and if they were ambiguous even to those who claimed to have witnessed them, so that their occurrence could not be verified by those who were living at the time, then any attempt to verify them at a distance of twenty centuries by critical-historical research seems doomed to failure.[102]

Thus, the attempt to treat the original appearances as observable phenomena to which we can gain access by using the techniques of historical research, is seriously called in question. It seems that any attempt to handle the appearances of Jesus with these categories and methods alone is apt to reduce the Easter reality so that it becomes unrecognizable as the resurrection. Instead it leads us in the direction of a mundane restoration and thus distorts our understanding of what the resurrection originally was. Even if it is unanimously agreed that the resurrection did not just involve a resuscitation of a corpse such as is constantly implied by approaches of this kind, the use of the historical method tends to draw the understanding of the nature of the resurrection back to this kind of view because it inevitably tends to empty the concept of the resurrection of Jesus of its heavenly and divine dimension as a revelation of the Glory of God. Rather, it is relentlessly made to conform to the proportions of the mundane. So long as a clear distinction between appearances and the exaltation of Jesus is maintained, on the Lucan pattern, this is possible. But when the Lucan separation of resurrection and ascension is seen to be theologically motivated and somewhat artificial, and when we appreciate that in the original traditions, from the moment of resurrection Jesus was also in some sense exalted, the purely historical nature of the event of the appearances begins to become problematic. So long as this event is naturalized so that it can be talked about as though it were as clear and distinct as the burial, it, like the burial, can be handled as a historical event. It can be described and verified by recourse to and testing of the testimony. But as soon as we begin to talk of transformation to divine status, the resurrection begins to become so unlike the burial that the ability of historical methods of enquiry

---

[102] See R. R. Bater, 'Towards a More Biblical View of the Resurrection', *Interpretation*, 23 (1969), p. 60: 'If there was that much ambiguity about the resurrection of Jesus for the eyewitnesses, on whose testimony all the succeeding ages must depend, do not the efforts twenty centuries later to establish it as a demonstrable and unambiguous fact take on a certain comical effect?'

to handle it, without reducing it and severely distorting it, becomes problematic.

The Problem of Meaning

It seems clear enough that if we do not treat the appearing of the raised Christ as being essentially similar to the burial, but stress instead its uniqueness, and if at the same time we judge the concrete images offered by Luke and John to be developments of the original proclamation, then the character of the resurrection event becomes so elusive that we have difficulty in saying what we mean by the term. Like Jacob at the Jabbok, we find that what we are wrestling with slips out of our clutches. This already began to loom as a problem, even for Westcott, but during the course of the century since he wrote *The Gospel of the Resurrection*, it has become even more accentuated. This is amply demonstrated by examining Pannenberg's approach to the problem.

Pannenberg, writing in the light of the last hundred years of historical and theological reflection upon the Easter tradition, clearly wishes to avoid the suggestion of a mundane restoration that could have been observed by just anybody. As we have already seen, it is precisely for this reason that he has seen the need to speak of the appearances in terms of 'visions'.

But once we acknowledge, as we must now do, that the stories of the visions were 'thickened up' in the course of their use in an apologetic context, exactly what comprised the original 'visionary' nucleus recedes from view. If we have no clear conception of what the experience was, how can the historian even begin to prove that it occurred? How can he be sure that it was not a subjective hallucination?

Even though the appearance of Jesus is said to be an 'objective vision' Pannenberg apparently does not have access to any descriptive details of its outline characteristics or any clear criteria for distinguishing an allegedly 'objective vision' of the first Easter from subsequent 'subjective visions'. He cannot describe the nature of the vision. In other words he has extreme difficulty in saying what he means. Rather, he says that whatever it was that the first disciples experienced, they were sure that *Jesus* had been raised and that this anticipated the eschatological restoration of all the righteous at the Last Judgement. Astonishingly, he then says, presumably because of the imprecise nature of the Easter experiences, that the Resurrection

was 'an event that is expressible *only* in the language of the eschatological expectation'.[103]

Now it is important to be aware of some linguistic sleight of hand
that begins to operate at this point. Pannenberg has already argued
that the resurrection of Jesus as distinct from the visionary appearances can only be spoken of in metaphorical terms because what
went on in the tomb and the details of the continuing heavenly life
of Christ are hidden from our scrutiny.[104] These things were not
directly observed, but only inferred from the evidence of the
appearances; we can only imagine them. But, now, the visionary
appearances have become so elusive that they too can only be
imagined and spoken of by resorting to the metaphorical language
which speaks of the heavenly existence and future eschatological
disclosure of the raised Lord! Surely, however, the appearing Jesus
of Easter, precisely because of this fact of his alleged *appearing*, is
not hidden from view. Pannenberg should be able to tell us something about what the appearance was like, even if he cannot tell us
what the hidden, heavenly life of the raised one is like. But Pannenberg does not distinguish these two elements in the Easter event, the
observed and the hidden, at this point. We must endeavour to be
more precise than he has been in order to get the matter clear.

The Easter event is in fact a complexity in which there are at least
two elements. The first is the alleged seeing of the raised Jesus, an
experience determined by what was disclosed. But this is only the
tip of the iceberg, as it were, from which we infer the continuing
hidden reality of the heavenly Jesus, as he is in himself. And we
must be clear that this heavenly reality is hidden whilst the appearances on earth were necessarily 'seen' or experienced. Pannenberg
says that the heavenly life can only be imagined, but the appearances
having been experienced, should in principle be describable. However, he then says that the appearance of Jesus was 'a completely
alien reality' because it was the apprehension of the glorified, tran-
formed Jesus, which could appropriately be described only in concepts that properly belong to the heavenly, eschatological future. In
other words the mysterious experience of appearance and vision is

[103] *Jesus—God and Man*, p. 98. Also 'Did Jesus Really Rise from the Dead?', *Dialog*, 4 (1965), p. 135: the resurrection experience is said to be so unique 'that we have
no other name for this than the metaphorical expression of the apocalyptical expectation'.
[104] See p. 43 above.

spoken of in the metaphorical language which is said properly to relate to what is not directly experienced—the ascended life of Jesus at 'God's right hand'. Theological language appropriate to this hidden reality is then employed to describe the appearances, in a thoroughly circular manner. There is no account of the appearances to justify and ground such imaginative and metaphorical language except talk of an 'objective vision' and we do not really know what that was like. In other words, Pannenberg's argument is that in so far as Jesus appeared to the disciples, they had an experience to which they could only refer by speaking of the inference that was drawn from it—that in the silence and hiddenness of the tomb Jesus had been raised from the dead to God's right hand in heaven. This consequence may only be spoken of in more concrete form in terms of metaphor, because the transformed and glorified Christ is hidden. The experience in history, the appearance, which touched off the drawing of the inference to a metaphorical statement asserting its consequence, cannot be described other than as 'an objective vision', and the first apostles are said to have spoken of it only in terms of the consequence that was inferred on the basis of it!

This means that the more precise nature of the appearances and of the object apprehended in these experiences, disappears from view. We are therefore in the awkward position of having to try to envisage the appearance from the assertion of its consequence. But the appearance is said to be a historical occurrence in space and time and the heavenly life that is inferred from it as its consequence is said to be vague because it is heavenly! How can the appearance be the ground and basis of an inference to a statement asserting the occurrence of the resurrection and ascension if we are not sure what the appearance was?

It does not help when the language of 'resurrection to God's right hand' is used to refer to it, for that does not describe an appearance, but only what can be inferred to have occurred on the basis of it. The vision or appearance becomes a mysterious, alien something, 'an objective vision' which is said to ground the inference 'that Jesus was raised' and also the affirmation 'that Jesus had gone to heaven from whence he will return'. But then these same phrases are said to be the only way of describing or referring to the appearances!

It is clear from much of what Pannenberg says that the appearances are the strictly historical aspects of the event, for they belonged in space and time. These appearances provide the historical evidence for the assertion of the occurrence of the resurrection of Jesus. The actual resurrection is not so clearly a historical event for it is not experienced. It is also a going from history to heaven. Jesus, says Pannenberg, 'departs from our world'. In the metaphorical language of theology we imagine him 'sitting at the right hand of God' in his eternal majesty. Since historical enquiry investigates occurrences of this world, the heavenly life of the raised Son seems to be removed from its field of investigation. It is neither in space nor time. It is a reality which should be described theologically rather than historically. This conclusion seems to be reinforced by Pannenberg's insistence that the Easter Christ is only appropriately spoken of in metaphor because he is hidden. Yet the historian *qua* historian is said by Pannenberg to be competent to assert the occurrence of the resurrection—not just the occurrence of visionary experiences. Indeed, the assertion of the resurrection is said to be the *only* way he has of handling the appearances. The assertion of a heavenly eschatological event thus becomes the *only* way of explaining the historical. This gravely confuses the matter concerning the need of a historical basis of dogmatic utterances. We now find that a dogmatic, theological utterance is the only way of referring to the alleged historical experience, which indeed is said to be describable in 'no other way'.

The result is that it is not just what occurred inside the tomb, or the continuing heavenly life of the exalted Christ, that is hidden from us; what actually occurred outside the tomb is equally hidden from us. If an apologetic motive is behind the gradual materializing processes which we detect, for example in Luke and John, so that the tendency seems to have been to make the appearances or visions more concrete than they originally were, then exactly what they originally were recedes from view in a way that raises very serious questions as to the adequacy of historical research for handling the matter.

Moreover, it is pertinent to ask how it is that the alleged historical experience which grounds the inference to the dogmatic or theological statement 'that Jesus was raised from the dead', is itself only describable in the language of its dogmatic or theological consequence.

This becomes very embarrassing from a dogmatic point of view for those intent upon proving the occurrence of the resurrection by using historical-critical methods. Once it is remembered that this, now somewhat ambiguous and elusive, reality was not only what justified talking of the resurrection as a historical event in the first place, but what grounded the inference to the assertion of Jesus' resurrection inside of the tomb and of his continuing exalted life in heaven, we seem not only to be unable to prove that the empty tomb and observable appearances occurred, we do not really have tools adequate for assessing what the reports of the appearances were really all about.

At this point it is pertinent to note the dogmatic importance with which the resurrection is endowed in the broader sweep of Pannenberg's theology. For if the resurrection experience ratifies and confirms what was only ambiguously and uncertainly revealed in the events of Jesus' historical life, then it must be an event of quite decisive clarity and force. But how can it confer clarity and force, when it is itself so unclear? How can it provide the historical basis for dogmatic construction when its own historicity is so questionable? Clearly the resurrection is not the historically demonstrable ground for faith, where faith is understood as assent to a set of doctrinal propositions which draw out its theological, revelatory, and soteriological significance. Rather, the resurrection is itself the *object* of faith, a tantalizing mystery, a puzzle perpetually demanding attention.

Pannenberg is in the unenviable position of being more certain of the conclusion 'that Jesus was raised' than of the evidence on which it was based! As soon as the evidence is made more clear so that it *can* be handled with the techniques of critical-historical enquiry it becomes theologically suspect. As Westcott found, such an approach suggests a resuscitation to this life, and as such is positively misleading. The inevitable 'naturalization' of the Easter Jesus that ensues when the resurrection is handled in this way tends to suggest a restoration of Jesus to the conditions of life in this world. Both Westcott and Pannenberg are aware of this and to some extent seek to ward off its effect upon their theology by stressing the otherness and uniqueness of the raised Christ. But this has the effect of undermining their original presuppositions by suggesting that the resurrection is so radically different from ordinary events that it may not be susceptible of simple treatment by the methods of scientific historiography after all.

However, whilst Westcott and Pannenberg are at least aware that their basic methodological commitment draws them in this dangerous direction, others have not been so perceptive and have in fact ended disastrously. Merrill C. Tenney, to take just one representative example from the self-conscious school of contemporary North American neo-evangelical theology, quickly slips into the inevitable and unhappy dilemma that awaits those who wish to pursue this course. Having expressed a firm resolve to defend the resurrection of Jesus as an event 'as factual as the discovery of America by Columbus in 1492',[105] Tenney naturally begins to talk in very matter of fact terms of Jesus having been revived and released from the tomb on the first day of the week and even of the resurrection as 'the resuscitation of a corpse'.[106] Jesus' resuscitated 'material body' is said to be both visible and tangible. Thus 'in the post-resurrection hours' the apostles are understood really to have seen and heard 'a tangible person who had returned from death'.[107] In the same volume Clark H. Pinnock promotes the same general view by insisting that the symmetrical construction of Paul's words in 1 Cor. 15: 3–5 implies that precisely the same body that was buried re-emerged: 'the *same* body is meant'. Thus, in their fervent attempt to defend the resurrection as an objective historical event, the resurrection of Jesus is emptied of any element of exaltation which in theological terms is so essential to it. Instead it is reduced to the dimensions of a mere bodily restoration or revival, which could have been observed by anybody present. Indeed, the language that is used to speak of what happened at the resurrection conjures up the graphic imagery of the apocryphal gospel of Peter where the emergence of the revived Jesus from the tomb is described, complete with two angels assisting him as he walked.[108] Tenney condemns 'the grotesque features of this spurious work' which are notably absent from the canonical writings. The gospel narratives in turn are commended for their restraint in refraining from describing the method of the resurrection, and for simply emphasizing the bald fact. However, without an alternative reconstruction of the appearance of Jesus we have no real notion of what the fact was. On the other hand, what is implied by Tenney's own language about the nature of the event? Tenney's account of what happened can hardly

---

[105] Merrill C. Tenney, 'The Historicity of the Resurrection' in *Jesus of Nazareth: Saviour and Lord*, ed. Carl Henry, p. 135.

[106] Ibid., p. 136.

[107] Ibid., p. 142.

[108] *The Gospel of Peter*, Ch. 10.

be heard without leading the imagination directly to the kind of scene that the gospel of Peter so graphically provides. So long as the pure historicity of the resurrection is emphasized such an unfortunate outcome can hardly be avoided.

The Question of Truth

For all their insistence on the need to ground theological reflection and dogma on a solid basis of historical fact, established by critical-historical research on the evidence, both Westcott and Pannenberg in the final analysis turn to theology and dogma in order to commend resurrection belief as a reasonable commitment. In other words, far from being a secondary consideration, theology and dogma are called into service, not just in order to try to elucidate the meaning of what is said to have happened, but to try to prove the question of historicity.

Westcott believed that his historical investigation into the Easter traditions proved the historicity of the resurrection with a fair degree of certainty. Indeed, he asks if the explanation that Jesus rose from the dead is anything more than the adequate conclusion to account for the evidence. As a general rule theologians in the late nineteenth and early twentieth century not only assumed that they were clear about what they understood the appearance of the raised Christ to be, they themselves tended to be far more sanguine about the conclusiveness of their investigations than the actual evidence warrants. We have already noted that Westcott completed his examination of the empty tomb traditions by declaring that 'this fact seems to be beyond all doubt', and that it was 'one where misconception was impossible'. After considering Paul's appeal to his own experience and to the experience of the apostles as evidence 'for the certainty of its literal accomplishment'[109] he concluded triumphantly that 'taking all the evidence together, it is not too much to say that there is no single historic incident better or more variously supported than the Resurrection of Christ'.[110] Whether such confidence in the capacity of the evidence to lead the reason to this conclusion is justified is another matter.

We have already seen that the attempt to handle the resurrection as a historical event encounters the problem of the meaning of the

---

[109] *The Gospel of the Resurrection*, p. 114 and 135.
[110] Ibid., p. 137.

testimony preserved in the texts. We need to penetrate through the texts to the nature of the alleged event that gave rise to them. Before any attempt is made to demonstrate the truth claims of the early affirmations of faith, we need to have some reasonably clear idea of what it is we are trying to prove. In the light of this, Westcott's conviction that the evidence is adequate enough to lead almost with logical necessity to the conclusion that Jesus did rise from the dead, seems a somewhat over-optimistic position. Like the original disciples we find ourselves 'puzzled to know what "resurrection from the dead" might mean' (Mark 9: 10). Westcott slides over this little difficulty with regard to meaning in order to move quickly on to the issue of validity. When we examine the logical route that Westcott took to reach the conclusion that the evidence was adequate to prove the occurrence of the resurrection we find that he commended belief in the truth of the historical evidence only by first attempting to justify belief in God, and by discussing the question of the resurrection in relation to a prior belief in God and the possibility of the occurrence of miracle. He then provides a context for a consideration of the occurrence of the resurrection by sketching the broad themes of what would be called today the history of salvation. The resurrection is said not to have occurred abruptly without any relation to past or future, but rather as 'climax of a long series of Divine dispensations' that will not appear incredible or even improbable 'to any one who believes in a Personal God'.[111] The resurrection, he says, may be seen to be the point towards which 'all former history converges as to a certain goal' and from which 'all subsequent history flows as from its life-giving spring'.[112] The weight of his argument concerning the occurrence of the resurrection therefore relies heavily on a prior assent to his broader theological interpretation of history. Indeed, a prior dogmatic commitment to a belief in the eschatological drawing near of God at particular points in history seems essential, for Westcott contended that 'the fact that Christ rose from the grave *and did not again die* . . . is to be taken in connexion with the whole course of human life, and with that instinct of immortality which from time to time makes itself felt with an overwhelming power. Its verification lies in its abiding harmony with all the progressive development of man

[111] Ibid., p. 135.
[112] Ibid., pp. 104–5.

and with each discovery which casts light upon his destiny.'¹¹³ It is only too clear that Westcott presupposes a substantial edifice of Christian dogma *before* he so much as broaches the question of 'the direct evidence for the Resurrection'.¹¹⁴ Thus, whilst the sub-title of his book, *The Gospel of the Resurrection*, is *Thoughts on its relation to reason and history*, it is clear that his thoughts are in fact related to faith and to a belief in revelation in history. The resurrection belief is defended from the point of view of a pre-existing faith which renders somewhat confused his initial declared intention to demonstrate the truth of the resurrection as a foundation for faith 'external to the believer' and to give faith 'a firm standing ground in history'.¹¹⁵

Moreover, this entails that Westcott has virtually abandoned his contention that faith is based on historically established fact, for the resurrection is now moved to the centre of things as the object of faith rather than the basis of faith. Indeed, as soon as the appearances tradition is intepreted in terms of 'objective signs' of the continuing presence of the raised Christ, the arena of faith has already been entered. One has to have faith in order to believe that an 'objective vision' was had of the raised and exalted Jesus from heaven and this can no longer purport to provide the historical ground of faith. In this case faith in God and in human immortality is appealed to in order to provide the ground of faith in the resurrection in the sense of the belief that Jesus was raised in the tomb and that he is now exalted in heaven. The assessment of the historical evidence by critical techniques of scientific historiography has been left far behind. At best the historian can say that there were men and women in the first century who earnestly believed that they had seen the raised Christ, but what was said to have been seen does not seem to conform to the pattern of events with which history normally deals. The historian cannot say that the raised Jesus was seen in a vision without himself becoming a man of faith. Nor can he account for the certainty with which the early Christians held to the conviction that they had seen Jesus. He must *qua* historian hold his peace.

¹¹³ Ibid., p. 17.
¹¹⁴ Ibid., p. 106.
¹¹⁵ Ibid., p. 10.

Sometimes the shortfall in the historical evidence is made up in the theology of Easter faith by enlisting the support of the Holy Spirit. The ability to overcome incredulity and doubt left by the failure of the evidence to establish its point with logical certainty is said to be given as a gift to selected individuals. Faith is thus the gift of the Holy Spirit, rather than a conclusion based upon evidence and using human reason alone. Pannenberg is reluctant to espouse this option. Pannenberg has spoken of this as a kind of 'gnostic knowledge of secrets', privately revealed to the elect in a hidden process that is beyond the scrutiny of reason.[116] In order to avoid this 'gnosticising' view of faith he is anxious that revelation should be available 'to anybody who has eyes to see'.[117] The resurrection as a consequence must be demonstrable to anybody who cares to follow the argument. It is remarkable that Pannenberg argues that faith as trust is not a blind risk but a commitment based upon a knowledge that is in principle available to all (to anybody 'who has eyes to see') and yet in so far as the appearances offered themselves for knowledge in the first century they are said to have been 'visions' available to some and not to others. In any event, Pannenberg is anxious that the conclusion that Jesus rose from the dead should follow as closely as possible from the evidence. It is the historical knowledge upon which faith as trust is firmly based. In some of his statements he suggests that it is the inevitable conclusion to be drawn from the evidence, and chastises H. Grass for suggesting that the evidence does not reach its goal and for saying that it must therefore be pronounced inconclusive: Grass is charged with slipping into the piety of affirming that 'it is God's will that no final proof is possible'.[118] To this Pannenberg snorts: 'How does Grass know God's will?' By contrast, he himself insists that a dispassionate treatment of the evidence, employing human reason and free of the arbitrary dogma that faith is independent of reason, can show that the evidence *does* arrive at a final result. He roundly declares that the only way of 'achieving at least approximate certainty with regard to the events of a past time is historical research',[119] for faith cannot override reason by asserting what reason has felt impossible to assert. History, not faith, establishes the factuality of the resur-

---

[116] W. Pannenberg (ed.), *Revelation as History*, p. 135.
[117] Ibid.
[118] H. Grass, op. cit., pp. 184ff.
[119] *Jesus—God and Man*, pp. 99–100.

rection. But then he adds the rider, 'to the extent that certainty can be attained at all about questions of this kind'.[120] Clearly, Pannenberg is somewhat undecided about the power of the evidence to secure the conclusion that the resurrection of Jesus did occur, whilst being anxious that the evidence should establish that result as securely as possible. Elsewhere he argues that in the absence of evidence to the contrary, the evidence adduced in support of the resurrection is sufficient to justify the Christian in accepting it. It may not be sufficient to prove the matter absolutely, but there is enough to justify acceptance so long as contrary evidence does not come to light. In this case he might be on safer ground if he resorted to talk of probabilities. Given the evidence, it might be argued that this is where the balance of probability lies. But, unfortunately, this will not be sufficient for Pannenberg's purposes.

We have noted that Pannenberg argues that faith is not a risk, but rather trust grounded in knowledge. This means he is anxious to justify a claim to knowledge in the case of the resurrection, and yet he cannot quite squeeze this result from the evidence. For one to claim to *know* that Jesus rose from the dead, one would need sufficient evidence to establish this fact with certainty since it would be logically improper to say 'I know that x but I am not certain that x'. Without evidential support of the required calibre, Pannenberg must content himself with talk of probabilities. But, in this case, he must in turn desist from speaking of historical 'knowledge' and speak rather of 'belief'.

On the other hand, there is a fundamental confusion in Pannenberg's theology at another level. Normally when he speaks of history he means not a special redemptive history known through faith, but universal history, known through the exercise of reason and the use of the historical method.[121] He insists that the historical knowledge arrived at by this method is logically prior to faith as trust: it is not at all necessary for one first to have faith in order to know the revelation of God in the history of Israel and Jesus Christ. Rather, true faith is first awakened through an impartial observation of the relevant events.[122] Yet, for all his emphasis both on the fact

---

[120] Ibid., p. 99.
[121] 'Did Jesus Really Rise from the Dead?', *Dialog*, 4 (1965), pp. 128–35.
[122] See *Revelation as History*, p. 136–7.

that faith cannot make certain what the historical evidence is itself
unable to establish, and on the impartial nature of the historical
judgement upon which faith is based, Pannenberg admits that the
resurrection of Jesus is not even highly probable, unless one first
believes in 'the resurrection of the dead' in general and in principle.[123] With this prior belief in the general resurrection of the
dead, the historical evidence becomes confirmatory and satisfactory
in the specific case of the resurrection of Jesus. In other words, Pannenberg, despite his emphasis on the role of human reason and his
repeated declaration that the resurrection of Jesus may be historically demonstrated, confesses at the end of the day that the evidence
is somewhat ambiguous and inconclusive and that originally it only
led to resurrection faith for those who entertained a *prior* apocalyptic belief in the future general resurrection of the dead. This means
that Pannenberg can only 'prove' the historicity of the resurrection
of Jesus by considering the Easter tradition of empty tomb and
appearances in the light of the eschatological hope of a general
resurrection of the dead. Despite his methodological commitment
to approaching the resurrection as a historical event via the methods
of critical historical research, he in the final analysis admits that it
must be understood as an eschatological event, to be apprehended
by being placed in the context of eschatology in the specific form of
apocalyptic expectation. Instead of faith (trust) and dogma being
based squarely upon knowledge arrived at by reason, the resurrection is placed in the context of eschatological faith. This entails that
the facts of history are approached from a particular perspective and
the partiality of faith in God.

   In order to believe in the resurrection of Jesus, we must accept the
broad contours of what Jesus himself accepted—the apocalyptic
belief in the End, the general resurrection of the dead, and final
Judgement. With this pre-understanding the early Christians interpreted their experience of the appearances as the 'resurrection' of
Jesus. It was not precisely what they expected, but what they
expected nevertheless provided the only concepts that were at hand
to describe what they experienced. Thus *faith* is needed *before* affirmation of the resurrection, in the specific case of Jesus, is possible.
But now the resurrection is hardly the historical foundation of faith;

[123] See *Jesus—God and Man*, pp. 81–2 and pp. 108–14.

it is a further extension of a pre-existing faith. The argument is from faith to faith and is thus circular. If Jesus' own beliefs, shared by the primitive disciples, are called on to interpret what subsequently happened, what happened is then said to clarify and confirm the same beliefs. In what sense, then, is the event of the resurrection the *basis* of faith, established independently of faith by 'impartial observation' of reason and the use of universally accepted canons of historical argument?

It is clear enough that Pannenberg is only able to 'prove' the occurrence of the resurrection of Jesus by arguing that the appearances could not be interpreted in any other way, given the early Christians' prior belief in the general resurrection of the dead. But it follows that we can affirm the occurrence of the resurrection today, only if we also entertain a prior belief of a similar kind. Pannenberg, therefore, contends that the apocalyptic hope of a future restoration to life beyond the grave is not just a piece of first-century mythology but that it expresses a constant human desire. Clearly, this seems to call for some general kind of *faith* as a presupposition of resurrection belief.[124]

---

[124] See W. Marxsen, 'The Resurrection of Jesus as a Historical and Theological Problem' in *The Significance of the Message of the Resurrection for Faith in Jesus Christ*, ed. C. F. D. Moule, for a related view. Marxsen also recognizes that the experience of the appearances was only interpreted in terms of the concept of resurrection because of a pre-existing apocalyptic belief in the resurrection of the dead at the end of the world. The difference between Marxsen and Pannenberg is that whereas Pannenberg argues that the broad outlines of an apocalyptic world view is perfectly legitimate, even for modern people to hold, Marxsen regards it as an expendable, optional extra which the contemporary believer can set aside, leaving the experience of the appearances to be interpreted other than in terms of resurrection. Marxsen agrees with Pannenberg that, beginning with the experience of what were claimed to be appearances of the raised Jesus, the early Christians, 'by a process of reflective interpretation, and against the background apocalyptic belief in the resurrection of the dead, arrived at the conclusion that Jesus had been raised' (p. 30). However, Marxsen differs from Pannenberg in so far as he says that this was only one interpretative theory, a secondary reflection based upon the primary experience of the appearances, using the apocalyptic concept of the 'resurrection of the dead'. This very concept, which Pannenberg regards as necessary and integral to a right understanding of the appearances, is for Marxsen a contingent, optional extra which might well be off-loaded. For whilst, with the help of the apocalyptic tradition, the early Christians came to the conclusion on the basis of their Easter experience that Jesus had been raised, they also used the same experience to ground talk of the future mission of the Church and the furtherance of Jesus' purposes. Marxsen argues that it is possible to speak of the appearances as the beginning point of the ongoing mission without necessarily drawing a reflective inference back to the interpretation which

This means that both Westcott and Pannenberg commend the evidence of the resurrection to reason but only by first placing it in the broader context of faith and dogma. There is a clear circularity in calling in faith to give credence to what is said to be the *ground* of faith. For all their protestations about the resurrection of Christ being an objective historical event whose occurrence can be demonstrated by historical research, thus to provide a firm basis for faith, both Westcott and Pannenberg, at the end of the day, allow dispassionate historical research to fade into the background whilst they resort to a set of dogmatic affirmations to provide a context within which the particularity of Easter faith may be accepted.

This means that quite serious difficulties emerge as an inevitable consequence of the methodological commitment to seek to handle the resurrection of Jesus purely as a historical event. Whilst the traditions suggest that there are respects in which the resurrection of Jesus resembles any other historical event of the natural order, there are clearly other respects in which the resurrection shows a marked resistance to such a treatment. The fact that the first experiences, which led to the conviction that Jesus had been raised from the dead and exalted to heaven, were experiences in space and time, speaks of a similarity with other events which are likewise experienced in space and time. But in so far as the resurrection of Jesus involves a going from time to eternity and a transformation and glorification of his body, appropriate to its new eschatological mode of existence, it is quite unlike any other event of history. This means that the category of 'historical event' can only be of limited use. The resurrection continually breaks free and mocks at human attempts to contain it in this simple category. This means, not only that the historicity of the resurrection cannot be proved in the way that any other event might in principle be proved to have occurred, but that we cannot even understand exactly what the resurrection was if we seek to deal with it only in terms of the category of 'historical event'.

asserted the resurrection of Jesus in the tomb. Indeed, *that* reflective interpretation is only possible for those who hold a prior apocalyptic conviction about the general resurrection of the dead, which is said not to be part of the mental furniture of the twentieth century. It is one interpretation amongst others. This means that 'the raising of Jesus is not the fundamental *datum* of Christianity' (p. 47); *a fortiori* the resurrection of Jesus is not a historical event. For a full discussion of Marxsen's views see Chapter IV below.

On the other hand, the idea that the resurrection can be approached as though it were a historical event is not entirely fruitless. The category of 'historical event' can be understood as providing one model for approaching the subject-matter. This approach may yield some insights of understanding, but like all models, it will lead to misunderstanding if its limitations are not clearly recognized. In order to appreciate its usefulness we must therefore also acknowledge its defects. This means that we must be open to the possibility that there may be other avenues of approach to an understanding of the resurrection which may illuminate aspects of the Easter mystery but which the category of 'historical event' fails to recognize.

III

The Resurrection as an Eschatological Event

The Resurrection and Salvation

WE come now to a consideration of views of the structure of resurrection belief of quite a different, even antithetical kind, from those of Westcott and Pannenberg. Instead of understanding resurrection faith as a judgement of religiously-minded men and women built upon what are held to be reasonably secure statements of historical fact asserting the resurrection of Jesus, a number of very influential twentieth-century theologians have spoken of faith as a judgement that is distinguished by the fact that it sees no need to rely on the conclusions of historiographical enquiry at all. In this case, the response of faith is not a decision to hold a particular interpretation of the available evidence to be the true historical interpretation, despite its admitted inconclusiveness from a strictly logical point of view. Faith is not a matter of coming to the conviction that Jesus did rise from the dead, even if the available evidence is insufficient to prove it. Nor is it the decision to regard the historical evidence adduced in support of the occurrence of the resurrection as 'good enough' to exclude rival explanations of the origin of Christian faith and mission. Rather, in this case faith becomes a commitment of obedience and trust in response to what is understood to be the call or Word of God. In this responsive decision the voluntaristic commitment in the face of risk is heightened and the need for rational or evidential supports of the kind that might be furnished by the critical-historical assessment of sources, is declared to be not only unnecessary but even wholly inappropriate. The effect of this is to maximize the voluntarism and to reduce the rational support to a minimum, or even to eliminate it altogether.

Amongst those whose views of what is involved in Easter faith fall within this type of approach are the two key theological figures of twentieth-century Protestant thought, Karl Barth and Rudolf

Bultmann. Together they provide us with classical statements of the understanding of things with which we are concerned, though, as we shall shortly see, they hold irreconcilable views with regard to the actual details of what is involved. The common ground between these Reformed theologians is that they outline an understanding of faith in which the Christian believer is said to know himself to be saved, almost at the same moment, as it were, that he acknowledges Jesus to be raised. Indeed, the experience of salvation is said by them to be an integral part of resurrection belief, rather than a secondary and contingent theological consequence that might or might not be based upon it. As a result they argue that it is just as inadmissible to think that the resurrection of Jesus could be established by just anybody, using the scientific techniques of modern historiography, as it would be to think that the first appearances could have been photographed by just anybody with a camera. Faith does not result from human activity of this kind, but rather, is a response to revelation and divine initiative. It is not that the impartial historian is able to turn his scientific procedures to the provision of a relatively neutral statement of fact concerning what may be understood to have happened, which the man or woman of faith might *then* appropriate in his or her experience of faith, repentance and salvation. Rather, the resurrection of Jesus can only be understood in the response of faith itself in which, at the same time, the believer subjectively knows himself to be saved. Assent to the resurrection and experience of salvation are inseparable.

This positive concern to outline an understanding of Easter faith which does justice to its soteriological aspect is often overlooked in theologies of the resurrection, as indeed it is even in many comparative discussions of the theologies of Barth and Bultmann. Commentators tend to dwell upon their theological differences rather than on what they hold in common, and thus concentrate attention on the discussion of the themes of hermeneutical procedure, the validity and scope of Bultmann's method of demythologizing and the appropriateness of interpreting the texts of the New Testament with categories drawn from the existentialist philosophy of the late 1920s.[1] However, their common commitment to the articulation of an understanding of the resurrection of Jesus that will do justice to

---

[1] See for example James D. Smart, *The Divided Mind of Modern Theology: Karl Barth and Rudolph Bultmann 1908–1933*.

its soteriological aspect cannot be underplayed if they are to be properly understood.

This emphasis which they share is also perfectly justified from a biblical point of view. It is certainly true, for example, that from an early time the resurrection of Jesus was understood to be a key factor in the primitive Christian experience of the forgiveness of sins and of reconciliation with God. Admittedly, in the history of Christian theology, soteriology has, generally speaking, been rooted in the story of the death of Christ upon the cross, rather than in his resurrection from the dead. This can be traced to its origin in biblical references to the death of Christ as a 'ransom for many' (Mark 10: 45) and to Paul's declaration in 1 Cor. 15: 3 that the death of Christ was 'for our sins, according to the scriptures'. But we must not lose sight of the fact that Paul also contends that, whilst Jesus was 'put to death for our trespasses' he was also 'raised for our justification' (Rom. 4: 25) and that in the same chapter of 1 Corinthians in which he declares that Christ's death was 'for our sins' he affirms also that 'if Christ has not been raised' then 'you are still in your sins' (1 Cor. 15: 17–18). A similar close association of the resurrection of Jesus with a soteriological implication is present also in 2 Cor. 5: 15: 'He died *for all*' and for their sake 'was raised.' Clearly, the resurrection of Jesus could be interpreted as a promise of the ultimate salvation of mankind. What God had done in and through him anticipated what God will do for us all. Indeed, the soteriological significance of Jesus' resurrection gives it its decisive theological importance.[2]

This same soteriological emphasis survives in the gospel narratives of the Easter appearances. John, for instance, records that the raised Jesus commissioned the gathered community with the words: 'If you forgive the sins of any they are forgiven; if you retain the sins of any, they are retained' (John 20: 22–3). It is not surprising also to find that, according to Luke, at Easter the disciples were commissioned to proclaim 'the forgiveness of sins' in the name of Jesus to all nations (Luke 24: 47). This suggests that the cross cannot be isolated from its context in the broader Easter event; in the

---

[2] Thomas Aquinas discerned this point in so far as he held that the passion of Christ affected our salvation 'by removing evils' and the resurrection did so 'as the beginning and exemplar of all good things'. *Summa Theologiae*, 3a, Q. 56. See G. O'-Collins, 'Thomas Aquinas and Christ's Resurrection', *Theological Studies*, 31 (1970), p. 517.

articulation of a doctrine of the atonement, belief in the resurrection, with its associated experience of the gracious, welcoming and forgiving presence of Jesus, reconciling men to himself and to one another, is also an important datum. As Bultmann rightly says, 'the cross and the resurrection form a single, indivisible cosmic event',[3] though, as we shall see, Bultmann put his own idiosyncratic interpretation on the nature of the connection between cross and resurrection.

By the same token Barth and Bultmann have drawn attention to the fact that our understanding of our own resurrection faith must itself take account of the soteriological implications of the resurrection of Jesus: an understanding of the resurrection of Jesus and a consciousness of salvation go hand in hand. This entails that the resurrection of Jesus is to be seen not just as an isolated event of the past but, at the same time, as the point of emergence into self-consciousness of the new humanity, the community of the redeemed. As Barth puts it: 'the miracle of God to Christ is immediately and simultaneously the miracle of God to us, and not the miracle about which it may, at any rate, still be asked: What has it to do with us?'[4]

A shared sympathy for the importance of the soteriological element in the make-up of resurrection faith entails that these two theologians also take seriously the fact that only a comparatively small band of witnesses came to faith in the resurrection of Jesus and these were originally the former disciples of Jesus who, as Luke says, had hoped for salvation through him (Luke 24: 21). And whilst others, like Paul, were soon drawn into the community, it was as true then as it is today that not everybody is able to come to the decision of faith. Thus, whilst historians operate with techniques which are in principle capable of convincing all those who care to attend to the steps of an argument, providing there is adequate evidence of sufficient quality to determine the matter, the resurrection of Jesus may be held to be an event of a kind which is not even in principle susceptible of satisfactory treatment by these methods. Even with the best evidence that one could desire, it seems

---

[3] R. Bultmann, *Kerygma and Myth*, ed. H.-W. Bartsch, Vol. I, p. 38. Bultmann never tires of emphasizing that the cross and resurrection are always closely associated in the New Testament. See W. Schmithals, *An Introduction to the Theology of Rudolph Bultmann*, Chapter 6: 'The Saving Event: Cross and Resurrection'.

[4] *The Resurrection of the Dead*, p. 159.

undeniable that the scientific historian cannot establish the historicity of the resurrection in so far as it is held to be the revelatory deed of God for man's salvation. Barth, for example, affirmed that, unlike the ordinary events which constitute the nexus of cause and effect that makes up human history, the resurrection of Jesus is a transcendent event, a miracle of God, which God performed in revealing himself to men for their salvation. Because this event occurred in time, there is a sense in which it can be called 'historical', but it is 'an historical, divine fact, which is only to be grasped in the category of revelation and in none other'.[5] Because it was in this regard so unlike the ordinary events of human causation, he spoke of the Easter event somewhat equivocally as a 'non-historical' happening.[6] By this he seems to have meant that the resurrection is essentially a supra-historical occurrence of eternity which only impinges on history where it is glimpsed in faith by time-bound, historically conditioned people. He thus argued in his famous commentary on Romans that 'the raising of Jesus from the dead is not an event in history elongated so as still to remain an event in the midst of other events. The resurrection is the non-historical relating of the whole historical life of Jesus to its origin in God.'[7] At Easter Jesus leaves the realm of human history to go to God.

From Barth's point of view the human perception of this transcendent event in which Jesus enters into the eternity of God is somewhat indifferent as to time and place. Given that humanly speaking it was *first perceived* outside of Jerusalem in AD 30, it may now be glimpsed equally well by us: 'Of what these eyes see it can really be equally well said that it was, is, and will be, never and nowhere, as that it was, is and will be always and everywhere possible.' Every epoch is a 'potential field of revelation and disclosure'.[8] Thus, the resurrection of Jesus is a transcendent event, which is available to men in time only in so far as it is revealed to them. Its historical rooting depends upon its being perceived from within time.[9] Inasmuch as Barth tended to speak of the resurrection of Jesus as a leaving of history, a going into eternity, its nature as a historical event became somewhat equivocal, and that is why he can

[5] Ibid., pp. 145–6.
[6] *The Epistle to the Romans*, p. 203.
[7] Ibid., p. 195.
[8] Ibid., p. 29.
[9] Ibid., p. 30.

speak of it as a non-historical event. It is only in so far as it was first perceived in time, outside of Jerusalem in AD 30, that he tends to speak of it as a historical occurrence at all. Moreover, it is grasped by men in faith as the promise of their own resurrection,[10] when at death they too will leave the world of time and enter into the eternity of God. Thus, the resurrection of Jesus which is announced in the kerygma is not a mere historical event of the mundane order which can be isolated in the past and talked about as though it were of a piece with any other event of human history. This is why it is comprehensible 'only as revelation'[11] and not as the mere 'continuation of human experiences'.[12]

Subsequently, in his *Church Dogmatics*, the first volume of which was published in 1932, Barth sought to clarify his meaning by distinguishing two different genres of historical events. Those which were clearly deeds of men, and which could be accounted for in terms of human causation, were to be called *Historie* and those which were more clearly revelatory events because they were directly caused by God, were to be termed *Geschichte*. Whilst the occurrence of events of the first kind could be described and explained by the scientific historian, those belonging to the category of *Geschichte* were said to be outside the historian's field of competence and were to be apprehended only by faith.[13] Having made this distinction Barth believed that the resurrection of Jesus is the principal event of the latter kind. The distinctive nature of the event of the resurrection means that 'as we pass from the story of the passion to, the story of Easter we are led into a historical sphere of a different kind'.[14] Thus, 'the death of Jesus Christ can certainly be thought of as history in the modern sense, but not the resurrection.'[15] This means that the resurrection is only really understood when it is seen to have been miraculously caused by God. It is an event in which God thus unequivocally shows his hand and it can only properly be talked about in a vocabulary which includes the word 'God' as one of its terms: This is the language of religious faith rather than of scientific, critical-historical enquiry. This means that

---

[10] *The Resurrection of the Dead*, p. 122.
[11] Ibid., p. 146.
[12] Ibid., p. 147.
[13] See *CD*, III/2, p. 446. Also III/1, p. 78 f.
[14] *CD*, IV/1, p. 334.
[15] Ibid., p. 336.

the resurrection of Jesus must be treated essentially as a revelatory event in so far as it is directly caused by God and as a soteriological event in so far as it is for men and women and their salvation. For this reason it cannot be appropriated in human consciousness by just anybody, but only by those to whom God reveals it as a saving deed. Precisely for this reason the resurrection of Jesus is not the kind of event that can be adequately handled using the normal methods of critical-historical research. The methods of critical-historical enquiry might be appropriate enough for dealing with ordinary or natural occurrences, even surprising or unexpected and novel ones, but the resurrection is not just a novel or unexpected ocurrence of the natural order. Rather, it must be received into human consciousness in a manner appropriate to the revelation of the transcendent and divine; that is to say, by faith. As Barth says, 'Because the resurrection takes place in the majesty and will and act of God, the knowledge of it cannot derive from the knowing man, but only from the one who is revealed in it.'[16] This goes some way towards explaining why faith is attained by some, whilst others do not comprehend at all and remain quite unmoved. At the same time, it explains why Barth believed that the resurrection of Jesus is not the kind of event that falls within the secular, scientific historian's field of competence.

Moreover, as a unique revelatory and salvific event it can also be described in a more inclusive term as an 'eschatological event' of the drawing near of God for the salvation of men and women. For this reason, what Barth called the 'non-historical event par excellence', in order to emphasize the uniqueness of the resurrection as a revelatory and saving event, Bultmann referred to as 'the eschatological event *par excellence*'.[17] Once conceived in this way the resurrection of Jesus was lifted out of the realm of modern critical-historical research and treated as a unique occurrence that could only be appropriated in human consciousness by faith.

However, whilst this emphasis on the theological considerations of revelation and salvation goes some way towards explaining why Barth and Bultmann felt that the resurrection of Jesus could not be dealt with by the methods of scientific historical enquiry, some other background considerations of a philosophical kind also con-

---

[16] *CD*, IV/2, p. 149.
[17] 'The New Testament and Mythology' in *Kerygma and Myth*, Vol. I, p. 41.

dition this point of view. These background considerations account to a large extent for the distinctive features of the work of Barth and Bultmann, and certainly cannot be overlooked, particularly if we are to appreciate something of the vehement confidence with which Barth and Bultmann prosecuted their particular approach to the understanding of Easter faith and their characterisitic ways of drawing out its implications. For their articulation of theologies of resurrection faith which are independent of any reliance on the findings of scientific historical enquiry was the climactic result of a broader tide of thought which began its surge late in the nineteenth century and which carried them along in its irresistible flow. This was the rise of a self-conscious disenchantment with the capacity of critical historical research to reach conclusions which would be secure and fixed enough to provide a basis for the commitment of faith, a tide of thought, indeed, to which Barth and Bultmann contributed, as much as it in turn conditioned their own thinking.

Historical Scepticism

The story of the historical background of the twentieth-century espousal of the dogma that faith must at all costs be independent of critical historical enquiry and in no way beholden to it, has been told many times and it is not my intention to rehearse it again here.[18] It is sufficient for our present purposes to note that the evaporation of confidence in historiography and the consequent theological flight from a reliance on the historiographical conclusions of the so-called 'professorial curia' to provide the basis of faith, may be understood as a negative reaction to the nineteenth century's concentration of attention upon the historical Jesus. This reaction was touched off at the turn of this century by the publication of Martin Kähler's *The So-Called Historical Jesus and the Historic, Biblical Christ.* Kähler drew a clear contrast between the historical Jesus, whom the scientific historians sought by critical analysis to discover behind the glorious garments of dogmatic interpretation with which he had been clothed even before the last words of the New Testament had been written, and the Christ of the Church's faith who was proclaimed precisely by holding statements of historical fact and of theological evaluation together in an indissoluble synthesis. At the same time Kähler pointed to the permanent insecurity and

---

[18] For example see Heinz Zahrnt, *The Historical Jesus, or The Question of God.*

relativity of all historical conclusions, a defect which seemed in principle to debar them from providing a *sturmfreies Gebiet*, or incontrovertible basis for faith.[19] If faith was an absolute and fixed commitment, it seemed impossible that it should rely on the findings of critical historical research, which were always subject to revision and change.

Shortly afterwards Albert Schweitzer published *The Quest of the Historical Jesus*, which graphically demonstrated that the nineteenth-century liberal protestant 'lives of Jesus' were of such fundamental variety that none of them could possibly be trusted to provide a sure basis for Christian commitment. The effect of this was to demonstrate Kähler's point concerning the permanent insecurity of historical judgements and to highlight the need for an understanding of faith which would be free of any reliance on statements of a historiographical kind.

In the first decades of this century, the growing disenchantment with the adequacy of the liberal theologians' 'lives of Jesus' eventually fused with a philosophical conviction that historiographical enquiry can never reach results of a permanent or fixed kind. Not only were biblical sources too fragmentary and too overladen with the dogmatic formulae of the early church to allow the plain facts about Jesus to be clearly seen; all historiographical judgements whatsoever were held to be inherently defective. The theologian, seeking a firm and incontrovertible basis for faith and a more secure foundation in fact for the articulation of doctrine, was in no worse position than any other historian working on any other segment of the past, but it was a position in which he could not rest without suggesting that Christian faith involved a mere tentative and provisional acceptance. Hence, Wilhelm Herrmann, who was subsequently to influence Bultmann, argued that: 'It is a fatal error to attempt to establish the basis of faith by means of historical investigation. The basis of faith must be something fixed; the results of historical study are continually changing.'[20]

Ironically, in the second decade of this century, the nails were thoroughly hammered into the coffin of the liberal protestant quest

[19] M. Kähler, *The So-Called Historical Jesus and the Historic, Biblical Christ*, pp. 103, 111.
[20] W. Herrmann, *The Communion of the Christian with God*, p. 76.

for an historical basis for faith by Ernst Troeltsch, whose own theology was shortly to be dismissed by Barth and Bultmann. They condemned the work of Troeltsch in the area of the history of religions as a typical expression of the nineteenth-century folly of attempting to reach God by human effort. Even so, in his writings in the area of the philosophy of history Troeltsch provided them with what was accepted at the time as a clear philosophical demonstration of the permanent insecurity of historical knowledge of the very kind that nineteenth-century theologians had come to depend upon.[21] In outlining the principles of historical criticism as he understood them, Troeltsch affirmed that judgements about the past cannot be classified simply as true and false, but must be seen to be capable of claiming only a greater or less degree of probability for, he asked, how can the historian claim certainty for his judgements in the face of the ever-present possibility of discoveries of new evidence? Is it not always possible that new evidence will come to light which will show that our present conclusions must be modified, or even abandoned as being quite erroneous? The inevitable conclusion seemed to be that the theoretical possibility of the future discovery of new evidence makes it impossible to claim absolute historical certainty in the present.

Troeltsch also urged that we must recognize the 'fundamental historizing of all our thoughts about man, his culture and values'[22] and admit that an appraisal of the past is always open to revision at the hands of men living in a future time with different values, interests and attitudes. He therefore emphasized that all the judgements the historian makes are conditioned by his own world-view. Indeed, the historian's understanding of history (*Geschichte*) and his world-view (*Weltanschauung*) are in tension and condition each other.[23] This means that one cannot be confident about the objectivity and security of one's own historical judgements. As Troeltsch says, not only the 'accession of new material' but 'the fresh sifting of facts by criticism, new ideas, and views in the linking of causes to historical aggregates—all of these call for ever new beginnings, and

---

[21] See Van A. Harvey, *The Historian and the Believer*, Chapter I, for an appraisal of Troeltsch's influence on dialectical theology. Dialectical theology in turn rendered his own theology obsolete and unfashionable.
[22] *Gesammelte Schriften*, III, p. 102.
[23] *Gesammelte Schriften*, III, p. 7.

lead to a revision of previous delineations'.[24] Besides the threat that a new discovery may come to light, there is always the possibility that somebody, dealing with the same evidence as is now possessed, may one day view it differently.

Unwittingly, Troeltsch was here providing fuel for his theological opponents by articulating a philosophical explanation of the relativism to which Kähler, Schweitzer, and Herrmann had pointed. Both Barth and Bultmann, the heirs of this historical scepticism and a succession of twentieth-century theologians after them, have recoiled from any reliance on historiographical conclusions as an ingredient of the structure of faith, precisely because the alleged permanent insecurity of such findings brands them as inappropriate for providing the basis of an absolute and irrevocable commitment.

The idea of the permanent insecurity of historical knowledge is expressed succinctly by Bultmann when he declares that in history 'there is nothing of absolute value; all values are relative. All thoughts and actions are determined by the place within history in which [Man] finds himself. Where this leads is obvious: the conception of truth is dissolved'.[25] This entailed that Bultmann felt that faith had little if any interest in the historical details of the life of Jesus, but it also meant that the resurrection of the raised Christ, which he admitted was quite central to faith, could not be approached with the tools of critical-historical enquiry either. If historical research, as Bultmann argued 'can never lead to any result which could serve as a basis for faith,'[26] then the resurrection of Jesus was *eo ipso* included: '*All its results have only relative validity*'. Bultmann therefore quite simply excludes as fundamentally mistaken, any interest in seeking to establish the rise of Easter faith historically, for that 'would be to tie our faith in the word of God to the results of historical research'.[27]

Barth, on the other hand, shared the same basic methodological

[24] E. Troeltsch, 'Historiography' in James Hastings (ed.), *Encyclopaedia of Religion and Ethics*, Vol. VI, pp. 716–23; especially pp. 719–20. See also W. Herrmann, *The Communion of the Christian with God*, p. 77: 'historical work is constantly constructing afresh, with every possible new modification, whatsoever results can be obtained from the records'.

[25] 'The Quest for Meaning in History', *Listener*, (1 Sept. 1955), p. 329. Cf. W. Herrmann, *The Communion of the Christian with God*, p. 77, where he speaks of the 'relative truth obtained by historical research'.

[26] *Faith and Understanding*, p. 30. Cf. *Essays Philosophical and Theological*, p. 18.

[27] 'The New Testament and Mythology' in *Kerygma and Myth*, Vol. I, p. 41.

standpoint. In his commentary on Romans he also argued that 'if the Resurrection be brought within the context of history, it must share in its obscurity and error and essential questionableness'.[28] The theological demand for an incontrovertible basis for faith, free of the alleged permanent insecurity of historical research, inevitably led to the articulation of an understanding of the structure of faith that was free-standing and utterly independent of critical-historical enquiry.

The theologies of the resurrection of Barth and Bultmann are permanent monuments of this flood of opinion. Clearly, it was not just because they saw the resurrection as a divinely caused event, designed to accomplish man's salvation, that they came to believe that the resurrection could not adequately be handled by the dispassionate methods of historical enquiry. The methods of historical enquiry also disqualified themselves from a claim to any part in the structure of resurrection belief because their inherent defects made them an inappropriate basis for a fixed and absolute commitment.

On the other hand, another important element in the background of this distinctively twentieth-century approach to resurrection belief comes from the tradition of post-Kantian Lutheranism in which human reason came to be distrusted as a human work and also from Calvinism which, as an implication of the doctrine of total depravity, regarded human reason as defective. In Reformed theology these contributory influences worked against any suggestion that divine truth might be achieved by the exercise of human reason or that it might be taken by force of human argument. A Calvinist lack of confidence in human reason was complemented by the post-Kantian Lutheran conviction that the exercise of reason was a human work, antithetical to faith.

Luther had resoundingly declared that 'justification is by faith alone' and not human effort. Kant on the other hand, had conclusively demonstrated the inability of reason to prove the existence of

---

[28] *The Epistle to the Romans*, p. 204. Emil Brunner also held that faith cannot be based on history only in the belief that history only ever deals in probabilities: 'Dependence on history as a science leads to a state of hopeless uncertainty. Therefore, when a thoughtful person refuses to build his relation to the eternal on anything so unsafe as historical science, he is acting rightly; for such building is indeed a glaring example of building one's house upon the sand'. E. Brunner, *The Mediator*, p. 156. This means that the attempt to know the facts of the past can never hope to achieve certainty: 'with regard to these facts there is only a relative certainty, that is (from the historical point of view) a mere probability.'

God. Hence his triumphant declaration 'I have abolished reason in order to make room for faith'. The synthesis of these intellectual forces led inevitably to a situation in which faith came to be treated as a response of the will to the revealed Word of God, a response that is in principle independent of and even antithetical to the exercise of reason, which in turn tended to be spurned as a human work. Indeed, the attempt to reach God by the exercise of reason came to be regarded as a futile, even sinful attempt on the part of man to achieve salvation rather than accept it as a revealed gift. Barth's critique of 'religion' as a sinful human attempt to reach God is to be read in this light.[29] But, precisely because the resurrection of Jesus was understood as a divine revelatory act designed to achieve salvation for man, it could not in principle be handled by the methods of scientific, critical-historical enquiry.

This meant that faith had therefore to be regarded as a 'risk' or 'venture', an absolute commitment of obedience and trust 'without assurances', as Bultmann never tires of saying.[30] Alternatively, and this is the more characteristic Barthian way of putting it, faith must be without evidential support of a historical kind because it is 'caused by God'.[31] Without the supports of historiographical argument faith becomes self-authenticating, by which Barth meant to affirm that 'revelation as revelation, can, of course, only be proved by revelation itself'.[32] It cannot be submitted to the scrutiny of judgement by human canons of assessment. That would amount almost to a sinful rebellion against God.[33]

The Easter Kerygma and Faith

Having excluded the conclusions of critical-historical enquiry from the structure of resurrection belief, Barth and Bultmann were

[29] *CD* I/2, pp. 280–361: 'Revelation of God as the Abolition of Religion'. For the critique of 'religion' in the beginning of dialectical theology see E. Brunner 'Die Grenzen der Humanität' (1922) in *Anfänge der dialektischen Theologie*, Vol. I, ed. J. Moltmann, pp. 269 f.; Friedrich Gogarten, 'Die religiöse Entscheidung' (1921), *Anfänge*, vol. II, pp. 124–5; Eduard Thurneysen, 'Offenbarung in Religionsgeschichte und Bibel' (1928), *Anfänge*, Vol. II, pp. 281 f.

[30] R. Bultmann understands justification by faith in this sense; see 'The Case for Demythologizing' in *Kerygma and Myth*, Vol. II, p. 191; also W. Schmithals, *An Introduction to the Theology of Rudolf Bultmann*, p. 144.

[31] *CD*, III/2, p. 445.

[32] *The Resurrection of the Dead*, p. 148.

[33] Ibid., p. 165: 'The Gospel of a risen Christ, so far as it is not fundamentally preached and accepted as God's word for all time, is flatly a rebellion against the truth of God.'

agreed that faith is precipitated by the hearing of the kerygma, but they began to part company when it came to defining the exact content of the kerygma. Barth contends that it was the proclamation of the kerygma of the resurrection 'upon which the Church was founded'[34] and that the resurrection gospel which constituted the substance of the primitive kerygma is precisely that which Paul summarizes in 1 Cor. 15: 3–8.[35] There is no question about the primitiveness of the material contained in this passage, but Barth insists that it is wrongly handled if it is understood as a proffer of evidence upon which the judgement of faith might be inferred by the historical reason. Thus, whereas Pannenberg argues that the intention of Paul in enumerating the names of those to whom Jesus had appeared was 'clearly to give proof by means of witnesses for the facticity of Jesus' resurrection',[36] Barth is just as forthright in declaring that verses 5–7 of 1 Cor. 15 'have nothing whatever to do with supplying a historical proof'.[37]

Barth's argument is that the only unadulterated and clear statement of historical fact in this summary of the kerygma is the assertion that Jesus was buried. The rest is heavily overladen with theological pre-occupations: Jesus' death is 'for our sins'; his resurrection is 'according to the scriptures'. Consequently, Barth's conclusion is that Paul's intention is not to provide evidence upon which a historical judgement might be inferred but simply to declare what God has done *for us and our salvation* and to call for a response of obedience and trust.

In so far as Paul refers at all to appearances and lists the names of those to whom Jesus first appeared, Barth argues that his intention is not to offer the alleged appearances as evidence upon which a belief in the resurrection might then be based, but to establish the continuity of his kerygma with that of the leaders of the primitive community and thus to secure his own authority of leadership. Thus he argues that Paul 'conjures up the cloud of witnesses *not* to confirm the fact of the resurrection of Jesus, not for that purpose at all, but to confirm that the foundation of the Church so far as the eye can see, can be traced back to nothing else than appearances of the risen Christ'.[38]

---

[34] *The Resurrection of the Dead*, pp. 119–20.
[35] Ibid., Ch. III, pp. 132 ff.
[36] *Jesus—God and Man*, p. 89. Cf. H. von Campenhausen, op. cit., p. 77.
[37] *The Resurrection of the Dead*, p. 150.
[38] Ibid. See also *CD*, IV/1, p. 335.

This concentration of attention on the *use* to which these early kerygmatic statements were put rather than simply on their content, originated with von Harnack who saw them as legitimating formulae, originally designed to secure the leadership of Peter and James, who are singled out for specific mention by name. Von Harnack, noting the symmetry between the claim of v. 5 that Jesus 'appeared to Peter and the twelve' and v. 7 where he is said to have 'appeared to James and the apostles', became convinced that he here detected evidence of an early rivalry or struggle for the leadership of the primitive community.[39] He therefore went on to argue that the evidence of the appearances was originally intended, not so much as evidence upon which faith could be based, but as a criterion to establish the official position of certain authoritative figures in the church, including, last of all, Paul himself. The appearances tradition of 1 Cor. 15 therefore has the nature of legitimating formulae rather than evidence upon which it was intended that the judgement of faith might be historically grounded.

Similarly, Barth says that Paul's intention is to secure the continuity of his proclamation with that of the primitive church and its early leaders and thus to establish his own credentials. The eye-witness testimony is to 'guarantee Paul's preaching, not the fact of the resurrection'. His purpose in citing the appearances in 1 Cor. 15 is precisely the same as in 1 Cor. 9: 1 where the appearance of Jesus is explicitly mentioned to legitimate his apostleship. This means that Barth holds that the appearances were understood to have initiated the kerygma, which can be traced back to them, and that through this kerygma, the Word of God precipitates faith. He therefore avoids rather than positively excludes the alternative possibility that

---

[39] A. von Harnack, *Die Verklärungsgeschichte Jesu, der Bericht des Paulus, I Kor 15. 3 ff und die beiden Christusvisionen des Petrus.* Since Barth, U. Wilckens has also followed von Harnack's view that in 1 Cor. 15 we have legitimating formulae. See *Die Missionsreden der Apostelgeschichte*, pp. 74 ff; Also his article 'Der Ursprung der Überlieferung der Erscheinungen des Auferstandenen', pp. 56–95, especially pp. 63–81 where it is said that the formulae of 1 Cor. 15 are legitimation formulae for the justification of the special authority of particular Christians who were honoured by an appearance. R. Pesch, 'Zur Entstehung des Glaubens an die Auferstehung Jesu. Ein Vorschlag zur Diskussion', *TQ*, 153 (1973), pp. 201–28, continues the work of U. Wilckens by contending that the manifestation accounts and formulae are legitimizing formulae. Pesch, in a manner reminiscent of W. Marxsen and E. Schillebeeckx tries to dispense with the 'occurrence' of seeing Jesus and finds the foundation for the resurrection faith in the eschatological claim of Jesus, which was interpreted after his death using the neo-Judaic concepts of ecstacy and resurrection.

the appearances were cited as historical evidence which precipitated
faith, and which provoked the kerygma in the sense of bearing witness by telling what happened to others in order in turn to convince
them.

This is the point, however, at which Barth and Bultmann begin to
part company. In his review of Barth's *The Resurrection of the
Dead* in 1925, Bultmann rejected Barth's explanation and accepted
that in 1 Cor. 15: 1–8 Paul was attempting to make belief in the
resurrection credible 'as an objective historical event'.[40] Why did
Paul mention that some of the 500 were still alive if he did not mean
to imply that they could still be cross-examined in order that the
reliability of what they reported might be tested? Bultmann therefore felt that Barth set out to explain away the manner in which 1
Cor. 15: 1–8 seems to be used by Paul to provide evidence for belief
in the resurrection. But so convinced is Bultmann of the validity of
his own basic methodological stance in insisting like Barth that faith
must be understood to be independent of critical-historical research
that he is prepared simply to dismiss this piece of Pauline pleading
as 'mistaken'. Bultmann is also inclined to dismiss Acts 17: 31 which
uses the resurrection as a historical proof in so far as it suggests that
God substantiated the claims of Jesus by raising him from the dead.
The Resurrection narratives, the legend of the empty tomb and the
reported appearances (as in Luke 24: 39–43) are dismissed in so far
as they attempt to report demonstrations of the physical reality of
the risen body. These passages are held to be unknown to Paul, and
therefore to be later accretions. They are somewhat incidental and
not the crux of the kerygma which precipitates faith as it is found
elsewhere in the New Testament. Likewise 1 Cor. 15 fails the rigor-
ous test of kerygmatic authenticity.[41] The true kernel of the pure
kerygma as a word of address from God calling men to have to do
with him, but free of apologetic appeals to evidence and to reason to
defend its credibility, is to be found elsewhere in the Pauline literature. In Bultmann's view 1 Cor. 15: 3–8 is not one of Paul's better
moments!

This Bultmannian method of picking and choosing was offensive

---

[40] R. Bultmann, 'Karl Barth, *The Resurrection of the Dead*', *Faith and Understanding*, pp. 83–4. See also 'Jesus Christ and Mythology', *Kerygma and Myth*, Vol.
I, p. 39; W. Schmithals, *An Introduction to the Theology of Rudolf Bultmann*,
p. 137.
[41] Ibid.

to Barth, who discerned too much of the self-confident liberalism of the nineteenth century in it. Barth argued that all parts of the scripture were important in communicating 'God's Word,' which is not to be identified with any one part over against another. Rather, the Word of God is said to be independent of all the words and at the same time expressed through all the words, as something which lies behind or above the text. For Barth the Word of God is heard as the meaning expressed through the whole of scripture: in other words, it preserves a certain independence from the words of scripture by hovering in a platonic way as the true or essential heart of meaning behind them all. He was therefore unwilling to set 1 Cor. 15: 3–8 aside as a fundamental Pauline mistake. Rather, he was anxious that it should not be, as he saw it, mistakenly interpreted as a proffer of historical evidence designed to support a rational inference to the assertion that Jesus was raised.[42]

The disagreement between Barth and Bultmann with respect to what constitutes the authentic proclamation, whether the Word of God is more closely identifiable with a segment of what was declared by early Christians and less so with others, or something equally communicable by all the words of scripture, widens into two irreconcilably opposed theologies of Easter faith. This, to a large extent, resolves into a debate about the extent to which the kerygma may be understood not only as a call to faith and obedience, but also to report an objective state of eschatological affairs in the process.

For Barth the resurrection kerygma is the announcement of a fact of the objective order, even if it is a transcendent or eschatological fact rather than a purely mundane, historical fact. The language of proclamation, if the whole of scripture is taken into account, asserts the occurrence of a fact concerning what God has brought to pass for Jesus, so that we are to believe 'with the New Testament' in the ontological reality of the risen Jesus Christ.[43] The resurrection of Jesus, though no ordinary event of human history, is nevertheless an event of the objective order.

Barth also contends that, even though faith in the occurrence of

---

[42] Bultmann agreed that the resurrection of Jesus cannot be a miraculous proof by which the sceptic might be compelled to believe in Christ; it is something which is *declared*, not something to be reproduced by historical research. In what manner it was to be declared is the point where Barth and Bultmann part company.

[43] *CD*, III/2, p. 443.

this event is precipitated by the continuing proclamation of the kerygma, rather than by the critical assessment of the evidence of witnesses and the drawing of a conclusion in the manner of a historical judgement, the origin of the original proclamation lies with the appearances. The Easter kerygma concerning Jesus 'springs from His historical manifestation'. For even though the resurrection of Jesus is a miraculous deed of God, which as such is beyond the scrutiny of critical historians, it occurs at a given place and is perceived by men and women in time. This means that, whilst Barth wishes to shun any attempt to prove the resurrection by historiographical argument, he nevertheless wishes the kerygma to be understood to proclaim an objective state of affairs of which people began to become conscious around AD 30 near Jerusalem.

Moreover, Barth tends to shift away from his original inclination to argue that the raised Jesus is momentarily glimpsed as eternity breaks into time in the hearing of the proclamation, which is thus equally available to all people regardless of the particular place in time that they might occupy. Rather, his increasingly non-critical and 'sympathetic' approach to scripture, which held that revelatory value is to be seen in all its parts, meant that weight eventually had to be given to the Lucan suggestion of a set of appearances of a unique kind in the period of the great forty days, which were unlike any subsequent appearances. These clear manifestations that are said to have occurred within the period of the forty days root the resurrection more securely into past time for, says Barth, Christ 'is no longer present and revealed' as 'he once was in the forty days'.[44]

Because these temporally and geographically locatable appearances are revelatory they still do not constitute the kind of event that can be established by historical research; nor can their occurrence be asserted in a factual statement, supported by historical evidence of the kind that the critical scientific historian would find convincing. Revelation is still inimical to historical research. Precisely because of its essential nature as an eschatological event, the resurrection of Jesus can only be announced in the kerygma and perceived by men and women of faith, who at the same time appreciate it as the ground and promise of their own resurrection. For, on the basis of their faith, they can begin to entertain the hope of seeing the raised Jesus revealed in the clarity of those to whom he appeared

[44] *CD*, IV/1, p. 319 f.

during the forty days. Thus, faith remains the grasping of the truth that the resurrection of Jesus is the basis of one's own salvation.

This means that on Barth's reckoning 'Jesus himself did rise again and appear to his disciples' whose eyes were opened to his presence by the Holy Spirit.[45] Their faith in turn 'was established, awakened and created by God in this objective encounter'. It is this objective, if divinely transcendent, event, that is triumphantly announced in the kerygma.

Bultmann's view of the resurrection, by contrast to this view held by Barth, is quite inimical to the idea that it was an 'event of the past' that can be declared in the kerygma to be an objective state of eschatological affairs. Bultmann agrees with Barth that the resurrection can only be understood once it is seen as a revelatory event with soteriological implications for the man who 'makes it his own'. But Barth's understanding of the kerygma in terms of objectifying or eschatological fact-reporting language seemed to Bultmann to imply that faith could override historiography to make assertions of fact where reason had no justifying grounds for doing so. Such an arbitrary and unjustified assertion, said Bultmann, amounts to a *sacrificium intellectus*.[46]

Some more recent scholars, following Barth, have spoken of faith in terms of an 'intuitive certainty' of an unconditional kind, which even 'involves the perception of historical facts'.[47] This suggests that the person of faith steps in to make assertions about occurrences of the past in situations where the scientific historian acknowledges that he does not have sufficient evidence to allow him to do so. Barth's insistence on doing this provides the grounds for Bultmann's repeated criticism of his work. Pannenberg agrees with Bultmann that 'the only method of achieving at least approximate certainty with regard to events of a past time is historical research'.[48] Where historical evidence fails faith cannot legitimately step in to make up the deficiency.[49]

This, to be quite fair to Barth, is not exactly what he is about, for

[45] *CD*, III/2, p. 445.

[46] R. Bultmann, 'The Problem of Hermenentics', in *Essays Philosophical and Theological*, p. 261.

[47] See P. Althaus, *Fact and Faith in the Kerygma Today*, p. 69 and W. Künneth, *Glauben an Jesus?*, p. 285.

[48] W. Pannenberg, *Jesus—God and Man*, p. 99.

[49] See also G. O'Collins, 'Karl Barth on Christ's Resurrection' in *Scottish Journal of Theology*, 26 (1973), pp. 85–99.

Barth is not holding that faith can go beyond the findings of the scientific historian by asserting the occurrence of an event in a situation where the scientific historian acknowledges a shortfall in the evidence. Rather, Barth never tires of affirming that the resurrection of Jesus is not an ordinary event of the mundane order; it is not the kind of event that the scientific historian *as* scientific historian can even begin to investigate. No amount of evidence could ever satisfy him of the occurrence of the resurrection. By its very nature as a transcendent eschatological event the resurrection is inaccessible in principle to historical verification. Faith does not therefore override the historical reason; rather, faith has to do with a reality with which the historical reason is not qualified to deal. Barth's point is that precisely because the resurrection of Jesus was an eschatological event directly caused by God it is outside the scientific historian's field of competence. It belongs to the realm of *Geschichte* not *Historie*. Nevertheless, men and women of faith to whom it is revealed and who appropriate it for their own salvation are able to speak of it in objectifying language and, to this extent at least, it may be said to be *like* events of ordinary history. What *Geschichte* and *Historie* have in common is that they both assert occurrences and Barth contends that it is pure superstition for Bultmann to say that the only occurrences that come to pass are those capable of proof by the scientific historian.[50] Both the divinely caused eschatological event glimpsed by people as it is revealed to them and the mundane humanly caused event which is proved by scientific historical research are actual occurrences for Barth.

Bultmann, on the other hand, wishes to insist that the absolute uniqueness of the eschatological event makes it so unlike ordinary historical events that it cannot properly be talked about as though it were, like them, an objective occurrence. Indeed, Bultmann is himself so anxious to ensure that the resurrection is not understood otherwise than as a revelatory and saving event, in which the believer knows himself to be saved, that the objective pole of the event, the raised Jesus himself, notoriously seems to dissolve away into unimportance. And this is the crux of Barth's critique of Bultmann's views. His chief charge is that Bultmann takes the soteriological aspect of the resurrection of Jesus so seriously that the resurrection of Jesus is dissolved into soteriology. This means that the raised Jesus disappears in talk of the believer's subjective experience of salvation.[51]

For Bultmann the experience of salvation is essentially the experience of knowing oneself to have made the transition from inauthentic to authentic existence; in more biblical language, it involves knowing oneself to have passed from a self-assertive and self-centred existence to a life of God-centred obedience. Faith is the subjective acknowledgement of the claim of God's sovereign will on one's life. Because the hearing of the kerygma is the trigger which effects this transition, Bultmann interprets the kerygma as a Word in which the hearer becomes aware of himself as a creature, addressed and called to obedience by God. It is a Word of address rather than a word of report in which objective information is communicated. The revelatory Word is heard as call but not as communication. As such it is itself the eschatological event of the drawing near of God to effect man's salvation, rather than being *about* such an event. This means, for Bultmann, that in so far as the raised Christ is revealed, he is known in the kerygma in a kind of inner audition, as the one who addresses or calls his followers to discipleship and obedience. And any attempt to convert the kerygma into objectifying language, so that it may be held to be *about* an objective event or an objective state of affairs, in the manner of Barth, is held to be quite misplaced. Thus Paul's attempt to talk *about* the resurrection as an event attested by the witnesses he lists in 1 Cor. 15: 3–8 may be judged to be quite mistaken. It is an example of a retreat into the mythological language of popular piety and quasi-superstition.

In so far as the New Testament proclamation speaks in an objectifying way *about* the resurrection of Jesus as an actual event, open to descriptive analysis, it becomes mythological, for it begins to speak of the revelatory, eschatological event in terms of images drawn from this world. It is precisely such language which makes the unique event of divine revelation appear as though it were just another, if rather unusual, event of the mundane order, a mere nature miracle. When the raised Jesus is spoken of in the gospel narratives of the appearances, for example, he is inevitably spoken of or pictured on analogy with his former earthly being; the reality of the

---

[51] See K. Barth 'Rudolf Bultmann—An Attempt to Understand Him' in *Kerygma and Myth*, Vol. II, p. 96.

resurrection is thus pictured as an extension of the realities of this world. It is as much a mistake to think of the resurrection in this descriptive, objectifying way as to seek to prove its objective occurrence by employing the methods of scientific historiography. Rather, in order that the kerygma might be heard in such a way that faith results, objectifying or mythological language of this kind has to be de-objectified, or demythologized. It must be proclaimed in such a way that it is heard once again as an address which plunges the hearer into a crisis of self-understanding. From this ensues the decision of faith and the transition from inauthentic existence to authentic existence is accomplished as the believer puts himself at the disposal of the Divine Will.

In Bultmann's understanding of things the Word of address cannot, then, be objectified in reflective understanding without losing its essential eschatological nature as a saving event. Thus, religious statements of address cannot become reflective theological statements without becoming mythological statements. This means that as soon as the resurrection of Christ is talked about, we inevitably enter the realm of mythology.

Whether Bultmann is able to sustain his methodological commitment to avoid all objectifying language is problematic. Don Cupitt has recently argued[52] that, in effect, Bultmann is whistling in the dark because religiously self-involving statements always entail theological statements. The confessional statement, 'I believe that God is good' entails the theological assertion 'that God is good'. Cupitt therefore contends that there is no logical escape from this and that it is quite arbitrary and obtuse to insist that religious declarations are possible whilst theological affirmations about what is so are not. However, Bultmann would reply to this that, in so far as theological assertions do seem logically to be entailed by confessional statements, and in so far as theologians are side-tracked into the analysing of them, this is a hindrance rather than a help to faith, which is triggered not by such objectifying, descriptive discourse, but by non-objectifying statements of address: Follow me!

Both at this point and in his analysis of the experience of salvation as essentially the experience of transition from inauthentic to authentic existence, we see Bultmann drawing upon the categories of existentialist philosophy. Man is able to hear the call to obedience

<hr />

[52] Don Cupitt, *Christ and the Hiddenness of God*, Ch. 2.

precisely because of a prior questioning of the meaning of existence which, Bultmann acknowledges, is legitimately raised by an existentialist analysis of the human condition. This has given the opening to his critics, including Barth amongst the most vehement of them, to argue that he has paid too much deference to the existentialism of the early Heidegger and has thus fallen victim to the error of liberalism by seeking to make the gospel conform to a fashion in philosophy. It is to make scripture speak to a set of presuppositions rather than to allow it freedom to speak its own message in its own way.[53]

Barth insists that the experience of salvation must not be clamped in an existentialist strait-jacket, in which there is an over-emphasis on human self-understanding and a corresponding lack of concern with the resurrection as an event in which something happened to Jesus. The language in which the resurrection of Jesus is declared and expressed is not mythological. At this point, and under the pressure of Bultmann's critique, there has been some development in Barth's thought.

Despite the later divergence in the theologies of Barth and Bultmann, the position of the early Barth is not all that far removed from the Bultmannian position. In his commentary on Romans, after stressing an understanding of the resurrection of Jesus as a removal from history to eternity rather than as a restoration to history that could, like ordinary history be talked *about*, Barth says that 'within history, Jesus as the Christ can be understood only as Problem and Myth'.[54]

In his later theology, however, Barth self-consciously avoided the more characteristic Bultmannian term 'myth'. Instead he spoke of 'legend and saga'. The precise difference between Barth's understanding of legend and saga and Bultmann's understanding of mythology is that legend and saga, as Barth himself says, is about 'a man of flesh and blood'. This only begs the question, for Bultmann himself would hardly have denied this. But Barth also wishes to insist not only that there is a kernel of fact in the legend and saga about Jesus, constituted by the historical actuality of his personal existence; there is a hard kernel of eschatological fact in the stories of Easter as well. Moreover, Barth insists that the entire corpus of legend and saga about Jesus is of importance. In a way that is very

[53] See K. Barth, 'Rudolf Bultmann—An Attempt to Understand Him' in *Kerygma and Myth*, Vol. II, pp. 113 ff.
[54] *The Epistle to the Romans*, p. 30.

reminiscent of the work of Martin Kähler, Barth affirms that it is the fusion of the kernel of fact with theological and dogmatic interpretation expressed in the kerygma through even legendary elements, that communicates the truth about Jesus and his resurrection, not the historical-critical attempt at dissection designed to separate historical fact from theological assessment and legendary factors.

This means that the real issue between Barth and Bultmann concerns the analysis of the religious language comprising the proclamation. Bultmann argues that if the statements of the kerygma are understood as assertions of objective fact, even lifted onto the divine and transcendent plane, they are really a hindrance to faith. For Barth the assertion of facts, in which the resurrection of Jesus is viewed as an objective event, is integral to faith and cannot be gainsaid or set aside. Barth's plea here, is once again for a 'sympathetic' approach to the text. Bultmann opts for a thoroughly critical analysis and a reinterpretation of it, involving its translation into existentialist categories.

In so far as Bultmann systematically refuses to speak of the resurrection of Jesus in terms of an objective state of affairs, he refuses to make claims as to what is so. Barth interprets him to mean not only that the raised Jesus cannot be talked about or that his resurrection cannot be properly known with the saving significance that is proper to it, if it is merely asserted to have occurred as an objective state of affairs, but that Bultmann abolishes the raised Christ as the objective term of faith. On Bultmann's view, says Barth, 'the Easter history is merely the first chapter in the history of faith, and the Easter time the first period of the age of faith', so that it is possible to say that 'Jesus himself had not risen'.[55] By contrast Barth is himself anxious to preserve the objectivity of the resurrection as something that happened to Jesus; it is not to be reduced just to the subjective experience of those who come to faith. On his reckoning Jesus himself did rise again and appear to his disciples.[56]

The question of the relation of faith and works also continues to trouble Barth. In so far as he understands Bultmann at all he says this is the point where he has to confess that he particularly fails to understand.[57] For talk of the transition from 'inauthentic to authentic existence' seems to Barth to speak of an 'act of man' rather than

[55] *CD*, III/2, p. 445.
[56] Ibid.
[57] *Kerygma and Myth*, Vol. II, p. 97.

an 'act of God'. In so far as Bultmann speaks of 'self-understanding' and refuses to talk about the resurrection of Jesus as though it were an objective occurrence, independent of the subjective experiences of the believer, he leaves himself open to this charge. Yet Bultmann never ceases to insist on the 'objective pole' in the occurrence of faith and vehemently argues that the coming to faith, the transition from inauthentic to authentic existence, is an 'act of God' which cannot be over-psychologized and turned into a purely human experience. Even if it cannot be objectified, the experience of God is one in which God is 'different from man' and 'confronts man'.[58] In so far as faith is the subjective response to an address, which is itself the perceived expression of divine sovereign will, faith has a cause outside of the believer; it is something that 'comes to him' rather than being self-generated. Barth, he says, quite misunderstands him in so far as he reduces his meaning to the 'psychology of religion'. Bultmann also speaks of 'the self-manifestation of the risen Lord, the act of God in which the redemptive event of the cross is completed' as though the resurrection were in fact distinguishable from and subsequent to the crucifixion.[59] Moreover, he goes on tacitly to abandon his principle that objectifying language about the raised Christ is ruled out of court, when he speaks of the presence of the raised Christ in the kerygma: 'Christ meets us in the preaching as the crucified and risen. He meets us in the word of preaching and nowhere else'.[60] He also says, in a somewhat unfortunate statement, that 'the Easter faith is faith in the Church as bearer of the kerygma. It is equally the faith that Jesus Christ is present in the kerygma'.[61] All these statements infer the reality and objectivity of the raised Christ as one who does encounter believers in the proclamation. At least to the extent that Bultmann speaks of Jesus 'present in the kerygma' he seems to have yielded to the temptation to engage in a brand of objectifying language. These statements could leave us with the impression that his meaning is that Jesus was actually raised by God and that the kerygma is simply the medium through which he manifests his presence and the only way in which he is

---

[58]   R. Bultmann, 'The Problem of Hermeneutics', *Essays Philosophical and Theological*, p. 259.
[59]   'Jesus Christ and Mythology', *Kerygma and Myth*, Vol. I, p. 42.
[60]   Ibid., p. 41.
[61]   'The Primitive Christian Kerygma and the Historical Jesus' in *The Historical Jesus and the Kerygmatic Christ*, p. 15.

legitimately known in his saving significance. In the next breath, however, all this appears to be nothing more than metaphorical talk, a manner of speaking. For in concentrating attention upon the soteriological aspect of the Easter experience he argues that in the moment of transition from inauthentic to authentic existence the believer comes to see himself in relation to the cross of Christ as one who is saved: *'faith in the resurrection is really the same thing as faith in the saving efficacy of the cross'.*[62]

This has led Barth and others to the view that for Bultmann faith is little more than a 'mere decision on our part' with no objective reference. Thus Hans-Georg Geyer contends that Bultmann 'speaks of the events of Easter only as the rise of faith in the saving efficacy of the cross of Jesus Christ'.[63] This is today the most widely accepted and popular interpretation of Bultmann's views.

According to Hans Küng, however, Bultmann in private conversation insisted that his contention that Jesus was present in the kerygma is liable to misunderstanding, the implication being that his meaning has been widely misunderstood.[64] Küng himself points out that it is a mistake to try to imagine the wholly different life of the raised Christ, for there is 'nothing to be depicted, imagined, objectified' and that 'the reality of the resurrection is therefore completely *intangible* and *unimaginable'.*[65] However, this does not mean that the reality of the raised Christ as an object of encounter is eliminated. 'Even according to Bultmann', he says, the contention that Jesus is present in the kerygma 'does not mean that Jesus lives because he is proclaimed: he is proclaimed because he lives'.[66] Perhaps Bultmann's own clearest statement of his position is as follows:

It is often said, most of the time in a criticism, that according to my interpretation of the kerygma Jesus had risen in the kerygma. I accept this

[62] *Kerygma and Myth*, Vol. I, p. 41. This view was seriously entertained but rejected by the nineteenth-century Oxford theologian R. W. Macan: 'it may be argued that the bodily Resurrection of Jesus—or more correctly speaking the belief in it—was the necessary vehicle for the faith in the efficacy of his death . . . ' *The Resurrection of Jesus Christ*, p. 5.
[63] H.-G. Geyer in C. F. D. Moule, (ed.), *The Significance of the Message of the Resurrection for Faith in Jesus Christ*, p. 119. See also G. W. H. Lampe, *The Resurrection*, p. 31, for a similar assessment of Bultmann's views.
[64] H. Küng, *On Being a Christian*, p. 352.
[65] Ibid., p. 350.
[66] Ibid., p. 352.

proposition. It is entirely correct, assuming that it is properly understood. It presupposes that the kerygma itself is an eschatological event, and it expresses the fact that Jesus is really present in the kerygma, that it is *his* word which involves the hearer in the kerygma. If that is the case, then all speculations concerning the modes of being of the risen Jesus, all the narratives of the empty tomb and all the Easter legends, whatever elements of historical facts they may contain, and as true as they may be in their symbolic form, are of no consequence. To believe in the Christ present in the kerygma is the meaning of the Easter faith.[67]

This seems to mean that the raised Christ is met as he addresses the believer and calls him to faith, but that his heavenly being and existence cannot be conceptualized or visualized without falling into mythological imagery. This imagery is not really helpful to faith, precisely because faith is not a response of assent to the truth of what is objectively imagined or described, but a response to the word of call and address as it is heard.

Given Küng's assurance that Bultmann verbally clarified his meaning in the direction of the assertion of the ontological reality of the raised Christ we must give him the benefit of the doubt, though the residual ambiguity of Bultmann's talk continues to puzzle many commentators. Hans-Georg Geyer, for example, says: 'the meaning of the statement which forms the limit of Bultmann's assertion remains hidden in an unresolved ambiguity'.[68] The ontological question concerning the being of the *Christus praesens* who is the basis of faith, thus remains troublesome, and Barth himself asks: 'Is it right to leave the cause of the transition so obscure and mysterious as Bultmann does?'[69]

But is Barth really in any better case? Despite his vehement insistence, against Bultmann, on the reality and objectivity of the resurrection of Jesus, Barth himself is hardly clear as to what this involved. Where his meaning is clear, his account is hardly satisfactory.

In *The Resurrection of the Dead*, in which he concentrated on the revelatory nature of the event and affirmed that it was equally avail-

[67] R. Bultmann, 'The Primitive Christian Kerygma and the Historical Jesus' in *The Historical Jesus and the Kerygmatic Christ*, p. 42.

[68] 'The Resurrection of Jesus Christ, A Survey of the Debate in Present Day Theology' in C. F. D. Moule, ed., *The Significance of the Message of the Resurrection for Faith in Jesus Christ*, p. 112.

[69] 'Rudolf Bultmann—An Attempt to Understand Him', *Kerygma and Myth*, Vol. II, p. 96.

able to all people in every age, because of the 'simultaneity' of eternity, Barth contended that the emptiness or otherwise of the tomb is immaterial to Easter Faith. It is the purely historical residue of the Easter event, a residue which shares in the obscurity and questionableness of the historical. Barth also saw clearly that even if historical research could demonstrate that the tomb was found empty it would not prove much: 'he might, in fact have been stolen, he might have only appeared to be dead'.[70] The tomb, he says, 'may prove to be a definitely closed *or* an open tomb; it is really a matter of indifference' to the understanding of faith.[71] As a consequence, it would clearly be improper to draw any conclusions with regard to the nature of the resurrection of Jesus from the residue it is said to have left in history. Rather, faith is a response to the manifestation of the presence of the raised Christ, not the empty tomb. But for all his insistence on the objectivity of the revelatory manifestation of the raised Christ, Barth in his early work tended to leave the details of this experience as undetermined and mysterious as it remains in Bultmann's theology.

All this changed in Barth's later theology.[72] In his *Church Dogmatics*, he says that the Easter event has what he calls a tiny 'historical' margin. This is the mark of the resurrection which is left in history, the empty tomb.[73] A closer reading of Barth to see what he now makes of the empty tomb story reveals that, whilst he says that the empty tomb story is not necessarily to be taken literally, it nevertheless constitutes an 'indispensable sign' which 'obviates all possible misunderstanding'.[74] It demonstrates that the existence of the risen Christ is not 'purely beyond' or 'inward'. It distinguishes the confession that 'Jesus lives' from a mere manner of speaking on the part of believers, who really mean to refer only to their own subjective experience of salvation. On the contrary, the empty tomb speaks of the ontological reality of the raised Christ: 'It is the negative presupposition of the concrete objectivity of his being'.[75] Whilst it is clear enough here that Barth is endeavouring to answer

---

[70] *The Resurrection of the Dead*, p. 143.

[71] Ibid., p. 142. See also *The Epistle to the Romans, op. cit.*, p. 204 where historical considerations such as the empty tomb are said to be 'irrelevant'.

[72] The point of transition from the 'early' to the 'late' Barth is usually held to be the publication of *Fides Quaerens Intellectum* in 1931.

[73] *CD*, III/2, p. 446.

[74] *CD*, III/2, p. 453.

[75] *CD*, IV/1, p. 341.

the alleged psychologism of Bultmann, this unfortunately suggests that Barth himself does wish to insist on the historicity of the empty tomb after all, for it can hardly play the role as a sign of the true nature of the resurrection and not to be taken literally. If there was no empty tomb in the literal sense it would clearly be a sign of a different kind; a tomb containing the body of Jesus would lead to a quite different understanding of resurrection belief. Barth thus displays a tendency to drift from his early talk of the 'indifference' of the empty tomb story to the necessity of it for communicating a right understanding of the objective, even corporeal status of the raised Christ.

On the other hand, there is a similar drift towards the corporeality of the raised Christ even in Barth's talk of the revelatory appearances. In his early work on the resurrection Barth argued that, because the appearances of Jesus are not really the subject-matter for the historian to analyse, but are 'comprehensible only as revelation' we must be aware that in that case they are 'not comprehensible at all'.[76] However, in *Church Dogmatics*, by continuing to refuse to submit the Easter narratives to critical historical analysis and by treating the whole of the scriptural tradition on an equal footing, Barth inadvertently communicates a positively misleading impression of what was originally involved in Easter faith. Even though he argues in a platonizing way that the true meaning of the kerygma, the Word of God, is somewhat detached from, behind or above the words of the text as we have it, his non-critical handling of the text can hardly avoid suggesting that what happened is more rather than less like what is narrated in a harmony of a surface or literary reading of the texts. This includes what can now be identified as the later or 'developed' strata of the New Testament traditions. Thus, the Lucan picture is given a prominence it would not normally these days be accorded by New Testament scholars, for Barth repeatedly refers to the foundational 'appearances of the forty days'. These appearances are then said to have been a clear manifestation of the risen Lord to the original disciples, who are said to have seen in a way that we shall only see at the eschaton. We see though a glass dimly; the disciples did not, for they enjoyed a face to face encounter of the kind that awaits the rest of us at the End-time. This can only give the impression that the original appearances

---

[76] *The Resurrection of the Dead*, p. 146.

were more or less in the nature of the material and concrete or visual kind that Luke himself assigns to the forty-day period. As a result, Barth speaks of the objective and corporeal nature of the appearances of Jesus, apparently taking the Johannine and Lucan accounts quite literally. He speaks of Christ being 'truly, corporeally risen, and as such appearing to his disciples'.[77] Indeed, he even speaks of the appearances in such a way that Christ can be said to eat with the twelve who are invited to touch his body:[78] the initial experience is said to involve 'a definite seeing with the eyes and hearing with the ears and handling with the hands, as the Easter stories say so unmistakably and emphatically . . . It involves real eating and drinking, speaking and answering, reasoning . . . and doubting and then, believing'.[79] How there could be any room for doubt in such a transparently clear experience is anybody's question. More importantly, whilst Barth had earlier distinguished the resurrection from the crucifixion as two different kinds of event, he now ends by saying that Jesus Christ is 'risen—bodily, visibly, audibly, perceptibly in the same concrete sense in which he died'.[80]

At the time he wrote his commentary on Romans, Barth held that, because the Resurrection is a transcendent event, which in essence lies beyond the scrutiny of historical investigation, what vestiges of it are left behind in history must leave it essentially incomprehensible and mysterious. For this reason it was argued that there is little point in submitting the appearance traditions that are now found in the New Testament to historical analysis. The event which lies behind them is too elusive to be captured by historical reason and for human reason to become infatuated with the sifting and analysis of the evidence is to plunge into the sinful pit of human striving, from which the gospel is precisely intended to liberate us. We must accept the basic affirmation that *God did* raise Jesus from the dead without allowing our reason to be deflected to the scientific pursuit of determining exactly what seems to have happened. Even to seek to discern developments and redactional accretions in the traditions is to set out on a fundamentally mistaken path. So long as Barth speaks of the resurrection as a transcendent event, a divinely caused eschatological going to the eternity of God, it can be appreciated

[77] *CD*, I/2, p. 114.
[78] *CD*, III/2, p. 448.
[79] *CD*, IV/2, p. 143.
[80] *CD*, IV/1, p. 351.

that the resurrection is not the kind of event that can be handled with the tools of critical-historical research. But as soon as Barth debars the use of critical-historical research even from analysis of the New Testament traditions concerning the experience of Jesus' appearance, and uncritically accepts them, so that the resurrected Jesus seems to remain *in time*, in a very concrete, material, tangible, and audible sense, then why the tradition cannot be treated by historical methods becomes a puzzle. After all, this is exactly the reason cited by Westcott for dealing with the resurrection as a historical event. If it is so concrete an event of time that it can be talked about in straightforward literal speech, why is that speech not subject to scientific historical investigation? Why speak of the apostolic perception, such as is here outlined, as 'faith'? Why is it not now 'sight' or 'touch' which abolishes the need of faith?

We see, therefore, that Barth disqualifies the resurrection from assessment by critical-historical research, because (*a*) it is caused by God and (*b*) it has salvific consequences (both of which are essentially assessments of faith). Not only this, but having rejected Bultmann's inclination to pick and choose, in favour of a more 'sympathetic' reception of the whole of scripture, he cannot bring critical-historical analysis to bear on scripture to discern earlier from later, original kernel of fact from dogmatically embroidered and developed redactional presentation. Instead, he accepts a purely literary reading of the scriptural testimony more or less whole.[81] Barth therefore leaves the object of faith undefined, but a purely literary reading of the stories can only give the impression that the Easter appearances were more rather than less as Luke and John portray them.

Barth is therefore in the unhappy position of affirming with vehemence that the resurrection happened 'once upon a time'[82] in the experience of the first disciples, and that during this time Jesus 'was among them as the Resurrected'.[83] This time is historically datable as 'the time of the forty days' and in later history the specific memory of this time is said to have been a living element of the relations enjoyed between Jesus and his disciples. And yet Barth is dis-

[81] For a very helpful account of Barth's use of 'story' and its place in a literary reading of the scriptural texts, see D. F. Ford, 'Barth's Interpretation of the Bible' in *Karl Barth—Studies of His Theological Methods*, pp. 53–87.
[82] *CD*, III/2, p. 442.
[83] Ibid.

inclined to investigate critically the question of the precise nature of Jesus' being among them by historical enquiry. He speaks of the tradition of the resurrection in terms of 'legend' and 'saga' without attempting to isolate the kernel of fact from the subsequent development that these terms suggest. He doggedly resists any pressure of contemporary theological fashion to engage in a critical-historical analysis of the New Testament traditions. This means that he leaves quite unresolved the issue of the original manner of Jesus' appearing. This in turn inevitably entails that the way in which the appearance of the raised Jesus was apprehended also remains very obscure.

Barth and Bultmann, thus, in different ways, agree to avoid using the early kerygma such as is now found in 1 Cor. 15: 3–8 as historical evidence from which the occurrence of the event as a revelatory and saving deed of God may be inferentially established, but the application of the same principle also entails that they both avoid employing, not only 1 Cor. 15 but the Easter narratives of the gospels as well, as historical evidence from which something of the nature of the original experiences might be reconstructed and described. This means that the historical method is rejected as a means not only of proving the occurrence of the resurrection, but even as a means of analysing the Easter traditions to try to discover what it is that the first disciples claimed to experience. Bultmann is quite simply not interested in objectifying language about 'what happened'; Barth is prepared to accept a harmony of the developed traditions and to defend the theological point they are intended to safeguard, without seeking to probe behind them to the original truth concerning the nature of the experience that first gave rise to them. In both cases, the residual question of 'what happened' remains unanswered. Bultmann is more concerned that the traditions be 'demythologized' in the course of the proclamation so that they are heard as address; Barth is concerned that they are heard whole and in every part as an address which at the same time reports an objective event, and with this end in view, even the most developed New Testament traditions continue to have a positive voice.

On the other hand, the methodological presuppositions which are shared by Barth and Bultmann make it almost impossible for them to resolve the impasse that has developed between them. Instead of appealing to the concept of mystery, Barth came to accept a somewhat naive and uncritical, one might almost say crudely realist, portrayal of the appearances in material, bodily terms. His only defence is that the Word is not quite equivalent to a surface reading of the words, but lies 'behind' them and that the Holy Spirit's task is to illuminate the meaning so that the believer comes to a right understanding of them. That Easter involved an objective appearance of Jesus is asserted by Barth because this is what rings out from scripture as he hears it, with the illuminating help of the Holy Spirit. Yet Bultmann insists that, as he hears the kerygma, he is called to decision and moved to faith by the Holy Spirit, but nothing rings out from scripture *about* an object of faith over against him. He just hears a call to obedience.

Barth and Bultmann cannot settle their differences by engaging in an exegetical argument about passages of scripture relevant to the resurrection for that would lead back too closely to a historiographical analysis. Rather, the argument between them tends to come down to the rather airborne issue of the way in which the concept of the Word of God is to be dogmatically understood, Barth insisting that one must be free to hear it 'in any way' that it chooses to make itself known and without presuppositions, whilst Bultmann insists that it is to be heard exclusively in terms of self-understanding using existentialist categories. Barth's case would be the stronger if in fact he were not so confident that his hearing of the kerygma as a message with the objective content that God raised Jesus, were the only true way of hearing. For he can hardly argue that God must have the freedom to speak concerning the nature of the resurrection in the way he chooses, and then insist that his own way of hearing and interpreting is the only valid way and that Bultmann is necessarily wrong about it.

Certainly, pending the illumination of the Holy Spirit, and without a historical analysis of the Easter traditions, we are left somewhat in the dark as to what it was that led the disciples to begin the Easter proclamation. Barth and Bultmann cannot really tell us, for even as men of faith, they have to admit that it remains mysterious: only the Holy Spirit can illuminate us. How can we know that the truth as we perceive it bears the authorization of the Holy Spirit? To argue that the word is self-authenticating does not explain anything for the assurance that we shall know the truth as truth when it comes to us rings a little hollow when two theologians claim that what is heard as the alleged self-authenticating revelation in their own case, is entirely different.

In this situation of impasse Barth and Bultmann have no alternative but to charge each other with arbitrariness. Bultmann says that Barth's insistence on the resurrection of Jesus as an objective occurrence is a matter of 'arbitrary assertions'.[84] Barth on the other hand accuses Bultmann of arbitrarily choosing to hear the kerygma in only one way and to interpret it only in existentialist categories. He thus points to the 'extreme arbitrariness' of Bultmann's account of how the kerygma is to be interpreted.[85]

The impasse into which we are led by Barth and Bultmann raises doubts as to whether the initial point of entry to the discussion of the nature of resurrection belief is either valid or satisfactory. The systemic exclusion of critical-historical enquiry in favour of a free-standing, independent faith, as a response to grace and which is alleged to be inimical to critical-historical investigation, may be appropriate in so far as the question of the divine cause and soteriological effect of the resurrection is concerned. But it is equally inappropriate to use the methods of critical-historical research on the traditions to try to determine what the primitive Easter experience was claimed to be? The question of what the resurrection experience was like is logically distinct from the questions of whether it was God who caused it and what it achieved for man's salvation. Given that the scientific historian cannot without faith enter upon an answer to these latter two questions, it is not equally clear that faith is a prerequisite in order to understand the claims of the early Christians and to try to interpret what they were talking about. A sifting of earlier from later traditions and the isolating of the primitive Easter claims from later redactional embroidering and legendary material, in order to reach back to the nature of the original Easter experience and the first understandings of the object experienced, seem not only valid but essential. This possibility is tacitly dismissed as irrelevant to faith by Barth and Bultmann, for even here we cannot escape from the force of their methodological commitment to the principle that historical judgements are always defective and of no real use to faith.

Barth's and Bultmann's methodological commitment to the exclusion of historiographical judgements from the structure of belief on the ground that they are disqualified in principle has led them to go

---

[84] R. Bultmann, *Essays Philosophical and Theological*, p. 261.
[85] *Kerygma and Myth*, Vol. II, p. 117.

beyond both the contention that the historian cannot explain the resurrection as the product of divine causation and the contention that the secular historian cannot explain the significance of the resurrection in soteriological terms. Their uncompromising and thoroughgoing commitment to the exclusion of historiographical judgements from the make-up of belief also leads them beyond the contention that the occurrence of the resurrection cannot be proved by purely historical arguments from the available evidence. It leads them to reject a historiographical analysis of the early witness and thus to reject any attempt to reconstruct the nature of the original Easter experience and to express something of the peceived nature of the object of faith in so far as the early witnesses attempted to describe it. Bultmann rejects *all* attempts at description on the ground that objectifying discourse is in principle illegitimate. Even primitive talk about an object of faith is myth, to be demythologized rather than historically analysed in quest of the most primitive kernel. But Barth also refuses to use historiographical techniques to sift through the early witness in order to separate what seems to be the earliest and most reliable account of what happened from later developments of the tradition. Somehow he thinks the Holy Spirit can bypass this sifting so that each individual believer 'gets the intended message' as to the general nature of the event.

Whilst we can agree that the secular historian cannot *explain the divine cause or the salvific repercussions* of the resurrection in terms of theological categories, and may not be able to prove its occurrence, it is not so clear why the historian is likewise disqualified from a descriptive analysis of the primitive witness in his attempt to come to the clearest possible understanding of the nature of the early experience. Something at least may surely be said of the nature of what it was that was claimed to have been experienced. Only a prior methodological commitment to the systematic exclusion of historiographical judgements and a belief that an account of faith must be constructed that will be entirely independent of historiographical judgements can explain this. This is a presupposition that both Barth and Bultmann bring to the scriptural text and impose upon it rather than something that arises from it. This might be acceptable if it were a presupposition that could be rationally justified, but I shall argue below that it is not.

For the present, it is sufficient to note that both Barth and Bultmann have paid insufficient attention to the different kinds of judgements that fall within the compass of the historical method. There is a range of different kinds of judgements that a historian might make in relation to the resurrection of Jesus. He or she might seek

(a) to prove that it was alleged to be an event having a particular nature;

(b) to prove that it was constituted by alleged experiences of one specific kind rather than another;

(c) to prove the occurrence of the event;

(d) to prove that it was an event that was caused by God;

(e) to prove that it was an event having soteriological repercussions.

We might agree that, in the case of the resurrection, a secular historian, by definition, could not, on the basis of the available evidence have success with (d) and (e), on the ground that faith is presupposed by such talk. In the case of (c) we might agree that the evidence is not sufficient to prove the occurrence of the resurrection, particularly in the face of the fragmentary and inconclusive nature of the evidence itself and the usual sequence of events in which dead men normally do not rise. But even before we seek to establish the truth or otherwise of the claim that it occurred, we are logically obliged to know what 'it' was and it is here that the methods of the historian may not be either in principle illegitimate or entirely inadequate. It is not self-evident that the historian can in principle have no success in relation to (a) and (b). If this is so, it seems arbitrary to exclude the findings of the historian in so far as he seeks to provide answers to questions concerning the nature of the original Easter experiences.

Even if the presence of the raised Christ was revealed to the primitive disciples by God, there is no reason why the historian should not seek to understand something of the nature of what it was that they claimed to have revealed to them, even if they claimed that the experience was of no common or garden event but of an extraordinary event that transcended their power to describe by anything but the most stammering attempts at communication. In so far as they talked about it, their words should admit of some meaning being communicated. In seeking to understand their meaning the historian will inevitably take the first step in the transition from historian to theologian, but even in so far as he has to this extent become theologian he employs techniques of a historical-critical kind that are equally valid for use with respect to religious and non-religious subjects alike. The fundamental reason that Barth and Bultmann have for excluding this particular kind of historical judgement from a role in resurrection belief, is the contention that *all* such historical judgements are defective, for they do not lead to fixed and secure results, and therefore have no place in the absolute commitment of faith. But is this reason valid?

The Error of the Basic Historical Presuppositions of Barth and Bultmann

The continuing influence of Barth and Bultmann in contemporary theology can still be felt at this fundamental point. Despite the revival of interest in the historical Jesus, and the wealth of critical historical research that has been carried out on the New Testament texts over the last generation, there is a residual inclination to assume that the decision of faith is utterly independent of such enquiries, which are assumed to have a purely historical rather than a genuinely dogmatic significance.

The strength and tenacity of the methodological principle that the 'certainty of faith' must be 'independent of the unavoidable incertitudes of historical research',[86] may be measured by observing its importance even in the thinking of those who, in more recent years, have revived an interest in the value of the words and deeds of the historical Jesus for Christology. New quests of the historical Jesus notwithstanding, historical conclusions continue to be admitted always to be tentative and insecure. As a consequence faith is still said to be necessarily independent of such results. Gerhard Ebeling, for example, asserts the impossibility of achieving certain, factual knowledge of the past and agrees that there is a deep connection between the critical-historical method and the Reformers' doctrine of justification. For Ebeling, faith is necessarily exposed to the 'vulnerability and ambiguity of the historical' for the uncertainty of historical knowledge and our lack of guarantees is merely the 'reverse side of the certainty of salvation *sola fide*'.[87] Similarly, Ernst Fuchs,

[86] See Paul Tillich's Foreword to Carl E. Braaten's translation of M. Kähler, *The So-Called Historical Jesus and the Historic, Biblical Christ*, p. xii.

[87] Gerhard Ebeling, *Word and Faith*, pp. 56–7. The whole of the chapter entitled 'The Significance of the Critical Historical Method for Church and Theology in Protestantism' is of relevance to the present issue.

following Bultmann, emphasises that historical enquiry 'should not contribute anything to faith, because faith in Jesus Christ dispenses with every security or support; and it cannot contribute anything, because the certainty peculiar to faith cannot be mixed up with the uncertainty and relativity of historical research'.[88] Günther Bornkamm agrees: 'Certainly faith cannot and should not be dependent on the change and uncertainty of historical research'.[89]

Faith has been left mistress in her own household by these thinkers, no less than in the seminal theologies of Barth and Bultmann, because, as Ebeling puts it, the current understanding of the insecurity of historical knowledge has resulted in the 'critical destruction of all supposed assurances'. In effect this is to say that the historian and the philosopher of history, no less than Kant, have abolished reason in order to make room for self-authenticating and free-standing faith. This means that few contemporary theologians, if any, have been motivated to resolve the remaining tensions between Barth and Bultmann by questioning their basic presuppositions.

I have argued elsewhere[90] that this fundamental presupposition of the Barthian–Bultmannian approach to faith, concerning the permanent insecurity not only of general assessments of the life of the historical Jesus, but of *all* historiographical judgements, even relating to a particular and specific fact, is logically erroneous. Even though Paul Tillich estimated that this widespread insight 'is the greatest contribution of historical research to systematic theology'[91] it can now be set aside as a fundamental mistake. For even whilst Ernst Troeltsch seemed to provide a watertight philosophical demonstration of the permanent insecurity of all historical judgements,

---

[88] E. Fuchs, *Studies of the Historical Jesus*, p. 213. See also Heinrich Ott, 'The Historical Jesus and the Ontology of History' in *The Historical Jesus and the Kerygmatic Christ*, especially pp. 154–5 on the problematic nature of all historical judgements.

[89] Günther Bornkamm, *Jesus of Nazareth*, p. 9.

[90] See 'The Poverty of Historical Scepticism' in *Christ Faith and History*, pp. 165–89.

[91] P. Tillich, *Systematic Theology*, Vol. II, p. 125. Tillich himself argued that historical judgements are always made in the face of a theoretical risk because they are open to 'permanent scientific correction'. Ibid., p. 134. The consequence of this is that historical judgements can only be asserted with a 'certain degree of probability' for nothing can be verified with certainty; ibid., p. 135. 'The certitude of faith', therefore, 'does not imply certainty about questions of historical research'. Ibid., p. 125.

his argument in fact rests upon a logical illusion. Troeltsch assumed that, because it is logically possible, or thinkable without self-contradiction, that there might be undiscovered historical evidence that could count against a particular historical judgement, it is entailed that there actually is such evidence and that one cannot ever be certain about any particular historical matter. In other words, he assumed that a purely logical possibility of error entailed an actual possibility of error. However, one claims to be certain precisely when one possesses sufficient evidence to be able to discount the possibility that a future discovery of new and damaging evidence will ever eventuate. Thus the fact that I am certain that there was a devastating war in Europe between 1914 and 1918 means that I am prepared to discount any thought that a document might be found which could show that the evidence upon which my judgement is based is incorrect.

On the other hand, the fact of differences of view amongst historians does not entail that they are all wrong or that any one of them is wrong, unless they not only hold different views but views that are in logical competition with one another. It is possible that some judgements about the past will be different from others and yet complementary. The fact that in different times we see different aspects of a given reality does not mean that we have always been wrong and that therefore knowledge is never attained about the past. Different interpretations of the causes of World War I do not lead to the conclusion that we must doubt whether or not it occurred.

This means that the entire development of this broad strand of twentieth-century theology, in so far as it has accepted sceptical views concerning the results of historical enquiry and subsequently excluded the conclusions of historians from any part in the make-up of faith, has proceeded on the basis of an error. I am gratified that Eric Mascall and John Robinson have accepted my argument in this regard, and that Edward Schillebeeckx agrees that the entire Christological edifice that has been built upon the dogma of the permanent insecurity of all historiographical conclusions is fundamentally mistaken.[92] This means that it is at least in principle possible to go

---

[92] E. Schillebeeckx, *Jesus: An Experiment in Christology*, pp. 587–91; also E. L. Mascall's very full discussion of the matter in *Theology and the Gospel of Christ*, pp. 65–9 and pp. 97–101; and J. A. T. Robinson, *The Human Face of God*, pp. 126–7.

to the traditions concerning the resurrection of Jesus with the tools of critical-historical research, to determine something of the nature of the historical experience which the first disciples concluded was of revelatory and soteriological significance. Indeed over the last decade many New Testament scholars have in fact attempted this and have come to a remarkable consensus concerning the historical development of the Easter traditions, despite the strictures of Barth and Bultmann that the results of such a procedure cannot be dogmatically significant. We shall look more closely at the more secure results of the historical examination of the Easter tradition in Chapter VI.

For the moment, it is necessary to note that, even if the philosophical grounds upon which historiographical judgements have been excluded from the structure of belief are invalid, there might nevertheless be theological and dogmatic reasons, perhaps ultimately enshrined in scripture as basic principles of theological method, which dictate that any attempt to engage in descriptive discourse, including the historian's descriptive discourse about what happened in the past, must be excluded from the structure of belief. Certainly, this has often been argued. In so far as the historian describes events, and also seeks by appeal to evidence to prove that his description is accurate, his work may be said to be alien to the judgement of faith, for 'faith is independent of proofs'. Moreover, historical judgements appeal to reason and this raises the question of whether the historical enterprise is in fact a work of the kind, for example, that is excluded by the Pauline theological principle that justification is by faith alone. Is the gathering of evidential support of a historical nature essentially a rational, human 'work' that is in principle inimical to faith?

There is something circular and just a little spurious about excluding historiographical enquiry from contributing to the makeup of belief under the stimulus of the principle that its results are never fixed and secure enough to qualify as the basis for the absolute commitment of faith and then to expound faith as an utter risk, or venture, a commitment of the will precipitated by the call of the kerygma but without the need of rational supports. On the other hand, it is not at all clear to me, given that the resurrection is a revelatory event with soteriological implications which happened on Divine initiative, why it should not be God's intention that men should utilize their God-given reason precisely for the purpose of perceiving and appropriating what he has accomplished for their salvation. Even if we concede that, as a result of the Fall, human reason is defective, it may nevertheless be God's intention that with his gracious help, reason should be rehabilitated at least to the point where it may be brought into play, precisely in handling and appropriating the divine revelation. So long as it is possible to think, with Aquinas, that grace perfects rather than obliterates nature, it is not incumbent upon us to follow Barth in his argument that grace is antithetical to nature, and that faith must therefore be entirely free of the support of conclusions of natural reason. Nor is it incumbent upon us to follow Barth in his contention that every mode of the exercise of human reason in quest of the knowledge of God is an inherently sinful attempt to reach God by human effort.

The view that the response of faith is utterly inimical and antithetical to the exercise of the historical reason makes no distinction between the exercise of (*a*) reason by man in his sinful and self-assertive attempt to live out his life in independence of God, whereby he tragically forgets God as he immerses himself in creation, and (*b*) reason directed towards the quite different pursuit of earnestly and sincerely seeking fellowship with God himself. It becomes somewhat arbitrary and problematic to classify the exercise of reason as an essentially sinful human work which is antithetical and inimical to the principle of justification *sola fide*. For, why should it be any more of a work to hear the evidence of witnesses and put two and two together than to put oneself in the position of hearing the Word of God by turning the ear and attending to the kerygma? Even Barth and Bultmann are, after all, obliged to concede that, having applied a gag to historical enquiry, an alternative human agency is nevertheless required to trigger faith and devotion. Faith is humanly caused in so far as it is the result of the mediating role of the Church whose work of proclamation becomes, from this theological standpoint, its primary function in the world. While the Pauline declaration that 'faith comes from what is heard' (Rom 10: 17) is utterly determinative for the kerygma theologies of Barth and Bultmann, is is doubtful if even this can be understood in such a way as to eliminate any reliance on the work of a human agent. Hence Paul's rhetorical questions: 'How are they to believe in him of whom they have never heard? And how are they to hear without a preacher? And how can men preach unless they are sent? (Rom 10: 14 f). Human effort is required in the work of proclaiming the gospel so that the Word of God is heard, just as much as it is involved in historical research on the texts. This is to say nothing of the deliberate effort implicit in the human activity of attending to hear or of the exercise of human reason in the hearing. Faith is not acquired as passively as Barth, particularly, suggests. Indeed, one cannot read Barth's account of the meaning of the Easter stories without reflecting that 'this is what Barth makes of the stories' after a good deal of hard work!

Moreover, Barth and Bultmann have to face the embarrassing phenomena of primitive Christian apologetic, which seems to have been an integral part of the early kerygma, and which can hardly be said not to make an appeal to reason: when the early kerygma was proclaimed, arguments were rehearsed which cited evidence and appealed to reason no less than the application of historical techniques to the evidence eventually makes its appeal to reason.

That Barth and Bultmann have difficulty in effectively neutralizing this apologetic aspect of the New Testament presentation of the evidence, which is particularly prominent in the Easter traditions, is amply illustrated by the difficulty they have with the key text of 1 Cor. 15: 3–11. Barth's concerted attempt to argue that the summary of the primitive kerygma in 1 Cor. 15 has nothing to do with an apologetically motivated provision of historical evidence for the resurrection, is heavily conditioned by the assumption that the concept of the kerygma must be interpreted in terms of pure proclamation or announcement of God's deed, an apologetic-free bearing of witness to what God has done, rather than in terms of the more juridical understanding of the notion of the bearing of witness or the giving of evidence, which is more clearly at home in an apologetic context. In so far as he argues that a correct (i.e. Barthian) understanding of 1 Cor. 15 is 'vitally important' for 'understanding the New Testament generally' [93] he comes to the conclusion that the New Testament generally is proclamation and declaration in a technical and religious sense that can be distinguished from the juridical concept of the bearing of witness. This technically religious sense of bearing witness through proclamation is contrasted with the proffer of evidence as the basis of a considered judgement, or the giving of evidence in support of a proposition, which can in turn be cited as the rational justification for its acceptance. Bultmann has

---

[93] *The Resurrection of the Dead*, p. 11.

taken this technically religious understanding of the nature of the kerygma a step further. Under the impact of the attempt to dissociate faith from any suggestion that it involves the critical assessment of evidence, it has become fashionable, particularly amongst theologians influenced by Bultmann, to favour the concept of the kerygma over that of the bearing of witness and even to regard these two concepts as semantic opposites. The kerygma is 'call' and 'address' rather than the bearing witness to the occurrence of an objective event, even of an eschatological rather than purely historical kind. The effect of this has been to rule out the possibility of cross-fertilization so far as the interpretation of the meaning of 'kerygma' and 'witness' is concerned. The proclamation of the kerygma is not to be assimilated to the giving of evidence as in a law court for that would be to suggest that it reports and describes what happened in objectifying language of the kind that Bultmann wishes to exclude. It opens the way for an understanding of faith precisely as a response based on the assessment of evidence. As a result it is now fashionable, particularly amongst some continental followers of Bultmann, almost automatically to assume that the proclamation of the kerygma and the reporting of objective facts bear no relation to one another. F. Gogarten, for example, excludes any suggestion that the proclamation of the kerygma includes the reportage of fact by adopting the slogan 'a herald is not a reporter'.[94] This may be true enough in logical terms, since a reporter of matters of fact by the rehearsing of evidence is not necessarily the herald of what that evidence signifies. But it is nevertheless not false to say that a herald may at the same time be a reporter, since his announcement of 'good news' may report or bear witness to objective occurrences. Even if the kerygma is not just a sterile report of facts from which conclusions as to its religious significance might or might not be drawn, it may nevertheless purport to include reports of an objective state of affairs. This is Barth's position, though in his case it must be understood that the facts reported are divinely caused, transcendent facts of the eschatological order. What is declared or witnessed to is a divinely caused event, belonging to an order which cannot be scrutinized by critical-historical techniques, and which for this very reason must be baldly announced by the Church. It is not offered as evidence, from which a rational conclusion might be deduced, for

[94] F. Gogarten, *Demythologizing and History*, p. 69.

such a conclusion would not only be descriptive or fact-asserting in nature, but the kind of conclusion that is normally made by critical historians. This is precisely what is to be avoided.

Thus, whilst the proclamation of the kerygma is understood to be a key concept, as the means of communicating what God has done for man's salvation (Barth) or as God's own Word of address calling men to salvation (Bultmann), the notion of the giving of witness is shunned. This is because the transmission of factual information as the basis of a considered judgement must be excluded from the understanding of faith if it is not to appeal to reason or rely upon it. In other words, the idea of 'bearing witness' in the solemn context of litigation, like the scientific assessment of evidence by historical-critical techniques, is more clearly a procedure of this world. As such it is to be held at bay in favour of a *sui generis* notion of the operation of the kerygma.

Whilst Barth believes that such an understanding of what Paul announces in 1 Cor. 15 is the clue to a right understanding of the New Testament as a whole, an examination of the New Testament proves that this estimate of its nature is quite invalid. Unfortunately a concentration of attention on the notion of the kerygma in this narrowly technical way actually does violence to the understanding of the New Testament as a whole, where the idea of the bearing of witness is in fact appealed to more often than the notion of proclamation in a simple declaratory sense. In his very important study, *The New Testament Concept of Witness*, Allison Trites has pointed out that the concept of the kerygma is not the only term or even the most used term to denote the function of the Christian missionary, and that the idea of bearing witness, if anything, is more securely established in the New Testament traditions. Moreover, he has shown that the notion of 'bearing witness' does not just have the connotation of a simple announcement, but carries echoes of its original, non-religious meaning in the context of litigation where the bearing of witness is associated with the giving of evidence as the basis of a considered judgement. Thus, once the unwarranted flight from historiographical judgement and from the role of reason in the judgement of faith is seen to be based on false or arbitrary presup-positions, the way is open for a re-assessment of the meaning of the concept of the kerygma in the New Testament. Instead of its being inimical to the idea of the bearing of witness and the considered assessment of the evidence of witnesses, these very concepts may give the clue to a more accurate interpretation of the term kerygma itself.

Moreover, even if Paul was very self-conscious about challenges to his authority and leadership, and whilst he certainly claimed to be an apostle on the grounds that he, like Peter and James, had seen the raised Christ (1 Cor. 9: 1), it is unlikely that his initial preaching in Corinth would have been obsessively concerned with his status and not so much with the content of his message. After all, his message involved the startling claim that Jesus had been seen alive three days after his death and burial. It is a message which prima facie purports to describe a state of affairs. Even in the context of 1 Cor. 15 it is not *only* that he, Paul, should be heard, but that the substance of his message should be heard. And even if Paul did cite what was originally legitimating formulae, he puts it in the context of an appeal to the Corinthians not to abandon the resurrection faith. To this end the evidence of the appearances seems to be cited in order to bolster their flagging commitment and not just to secure Paul's authentic place in the succession of apostolic leaders.

It would be quite abitrary to exclude the element of apologetic from the announcement of the kerygma, where the kerygma is understood in some religiously pristine sense as 'pure announcement' or proclamation. Indeed, such a thing may never have existed. The evidence suggests that the early Christians may always have proclaimed arguments. They appealed to evidence, bore witness to what they had experienced, and offered it for considered, rational assessment. This means that the kerygma is not just a declaration of what God has accomplished which is received and accepted or rejected in a free and open decision of the will. Nor is it a call to obedience devoid of any report of alleged fact. Rather, it is the proffer of evidence that is to be assessed and then accepted or rejected on its merits.

That the notion of giving evidence or bearing witness is to be brought to bear upon the understanding of the nature of the kerygma is suggested in 1 Cor. 15: 15 where, after rehearsing the primitive testimony, Paul declares that if it is not true that Christ is raised, then his preaching and that of his fellow apostles is pointless and meaningless, and 'they are detected as false witnesses' (ψευδομάρτυρες). Here the meaning seems to be not that Paul and his fellow apostles are falsely claiming the authority of leadership and the right to proclaim the kerygma to others without due authorization, but that they are bearing witness to what is false (cf. Matt 26: 60).⁹⁵

It is very pertinent to observe at this point that Paul may have omitted mention of women in his list of primitive witnesses to the resurrection in 1 Cor. 15, precisely because he understood the concept of kerygma in the sense of a bearing witness to what happened that is of a kind with that belonging in a law court, where women were denied the ability to give evidence. The exclusion of women from the list of witnesses would mean that Paul did, after all, understand the primitive kerygma as testimony. It is the proffer of evidence to be considered and assessed, and the proclamation (cf. 1 Cor. 15: 11 and κηρύσσεται in v. 12) of the resurrection is proclamation in the sense of bearing witness to an event whose occurrence is to be inferred from the evidence of testimony.

The same conclusion seems to be implied in 1 Cor. 15: 15, where Paul is not so concerned about whether he is falsely claiming to be authorized to proclaim the kerygma but about whether his testimony is false.⁹⁶ Allison Trites also calls attention to 2 Cor. 11: 13 where ψευδαπόστολοι are castigated, and Romans 9: 1; 2 Cor. 2: 17; 11: 10 and 31; 12: 19 where it is not credentials but sincerity and truth that are insisted upon.

Certainly, by the time we get to Luke the kerygma is understood in terms of the transmission of evidence and faith's reliance on such testimony is clearly accepted: Christians in Jerusalem (Acts 2: 32; 3: 15; 4: 33) and Caesarea (Acts 10: 41) clearly relied on the statements of witnesses. Moreover, in Acts 13: 31 Paul himself does not even appeal to the appearance which he had experienced; rather Luke has him rely on the evidence of testimony of the primitive witnesses.⁹⁷

---

⁹⁵ See A. A. Trites, *The New Testament Concept of Witness*, p. 75; also C. Hodge, *An Exposition of the First Epistle to the Corinthians* p. 320; and H. Strathmann, 'Μάρτυς', *TDNT*, IV, pp. 474–514 (especially p. 514). On 1 Cor. 15: 5 ff as a 'list of witnesses' see E. Bammel, 'Herkunft und Funktion der Traditionselemente in 1 Kor. 15: 1–11', *TZ*, 11 (1955), pp. 401–19; also H.-W. Bartsch, 'Die Argumentation des Paulus in 1 Kor. 15: 3–11', *ZNW*, 55 (1964), pp. 261–74.

⁹⁶ See W. D. Chamberlain, *An Exegetical Grammar of the Greek New Testament*, p. 214.

⁹⁷ See *The New Testament Concept of Witness*, p. 203. Gerhard Delling, in 'The Significance of the Resurrection of Jesus for Faith in Jesus Christ', *The Significance of the Message of the Resurrection for Faith in Jesus Christ*, p. 103, stresses faith's reliance on testimony. This testimony 'was handed down through the links in a chain of tradition' (p. 104).

It is hard to see that the question of the truth of what is reported in the kerygma was not fundamental to Paul's understanding of it; this means that it is rightly understood as a proffer of evidence upon which a rational assessment might be based, and that it is not pure announcement or pure call to obedience, but in some measure report as well. If report, its primitive content may be quite vital to our understanding of faith, not least to our understanding of what kind of reality was originally experienced. As we have already seen, this question of meaning is logically prior to the question of the truth of the claim to have actually experienced an appearance of the raised Christ; it is the first issue to be tackled.

It seems clear enough that the attempt of Barth to hold that 1 Cor. 15 is not intended to be taken as evidence upon which the judgement of faith may be based is largely the product of his *a priori* methodological presupposition that faith must be utterly independent of the historical or rational assessment of evidence. However, it is impossible to hold faith and the critical assessment of evidence apart in the way Barth seeks to do. On the other hand, few will be convinced by Bultmann's contention that Paul's approach here is methodologically mistaken and that the pure proclamation of the kerygma, purged of the temptation to engage in apologetic argument or the inclination to offer evidence for rational assessment, is to be found elsewhere. The fact is that apologetic, in the form of the attempt to argue a case and thus to appeal to reason in order to defend the credibility of resurrection belief, is a perfectly legitimate form for the kerygma to take. Certainly it is an expression of the kerygma in which even the earliest Christians seem to have indulged, without feeling guilty or needing to agonize over whether they were doing something illegitimate.

It is difficult therefore to conclude that we are fundamentally mistaken in regarding the primitive kerygmatic material of 1 Cor. 15, or the other Easter traditions of the New Testament, as evidence. In the case of 1 Cor. 15, the evidence was rehearsed by Paul precisely to support the flagging faith of the Corinthians. It is quite arbitrary to insist that faith must be free of evidential supports and thus entirely free of the arguments of scientific historiography. It therefore seems unlikely that it is in principle illegitimate to argue that the testimony of appearances in 1 Cor. 15 was offered as evidence from which it was inferred that Jesus was raised by God inside the tomb and that as a result he went to live with God in an exalted, heavenly place as Lord of his disciples. Likewise it seems arbitrary to insist on the illegitimacy of employing critical-historical research on the traditions with a view to ascertaining something of the perceived nature of the Easter Jesus. To opt for a purely literary reading of the traditions in the belief that the Holy Spirit will tell us what to make of them (Barth) or to refuse point blank to take any interest in the nature of the object of Easter faith as the first Christians expressed and described their experience (Bultmann) seems quite unjustified.

Both Historical and Eschatological

We saw in the last chapter that the application of critical-historical methods to the resurrection traditions in the New Testament leads directly to an awareness that the first Christians spoke of the resurrection in more than purely historical terms. They spoke of the raised Jesus as a transcendent and glorified being who appeared 'from heaven' as it were. The eschatological nature of that event meant that the apprehension of the presence of the raised Christ was accompanied by an awareness of the drawing near of God to act decisively for human salvation. This eschatological aspect of the event is precisely what caused Westcott and Pannenberg considerable difficulty in their endeavour to handle it purely as a historical event. Despite their concerted attempts to contain the raised Christ within a net cast around him by critical-historical techniques, the raised Christ eluded them; the elusively transcendent qualities defiantly surpass our human attempts to contain him in the conceptual net we prepare in order to ensnare him. Bultmann and Barth, by beginning with an unequivocal affirmation of the eschatological nature of the raised Christ, quite simply abandoned any attempt even to try to do what Westcott and Pannenberg set out to achieve. Bultmann categorically refuses to talk about the nature of the raised Christ at all; Barth allows an uncritical literary reading of the Easter stories to make their own impact in their own way. Unfortunately, this allows the possibility of a very superficial hearing of the stories which leads back in the direction of a mundane restoration. At this point a critical-historical sifting of the evidence seems essential in order to recover and clarify something of the original transcendent and heavenly qualities of the event that are so important to Barth.

This means that, provided the limitations of the historical approach are properly recognized, the application of historical-critical procedures to the assessment of the Easter traditions is essential. The approach to the resurrection as a historical event on one hand and as an eschatological event on the other should be seen not as mutually exclusive but rather as complementary. These two different approaches to the resurrection may both be accorded the status of conceptual models, each of which takes us some way towards understanding the nature of the Easter Event, but neither is satisfactory when isolated from the other. Barth and Bultmann need the help of the methods of Westcott and Pannenberg.

On the other hand, Westcott and Pannenberg are as clearly in need of the eschatological insights of Barth and Bultmann. For all their insistence on their ability to handle the resurrection by the methods of critical-historical research, in the final analysis the raised Christ not only breaks through their attempts to contain him, but they themselves find that they have to appeal to the transcendent and eschatological quality of the resurrection in order to commend assent to it. For when the evidence is assessed in purely historical terms, as we saw in the previous chapter, it fails to warrant the conclusion that Jesus certainly was raised from the dead. This affirmation is only really commended as an article of faith and commitment by both Westcott and Pannenberg by their placing of it in an eschatological context. In other words, they tend to end where Bultmann and Barth begin. In order to defend the validity of the Easter claims, both Westcott and Pannenberg tend to fall back on dogmatic considerations by speaking of it as an eschatological act of God. This means that, instead of being the ground of faith and dogma, faith is in fact presupposed, for appeal is made to the perspective of faith in order to commend the truth of the Easter claims. This does not mean, however, that historical enquiry therefore has no place whatsoever in the structure of resurrection belief. Even if the evidence, as we have seen, is insufficient of itself to prove the occurrence of the resurrection, the historical assessment of it may nevertheless raise the possibility of the 'resurrection of Jesus' in some sense of the term 'resurrection'. Moreover, a historical analysis of the relevant New Testament texts may help us to understand the nature of what it was that the early Christians claimed to have experienced. Such conclusions, even if they fall short of absolute certainty, may not be irrelevant to our faith. Pannenberg is thus right in insisting that, even if the formulas found in 1 Cor. 15: 3–8 had an original use to legitimate the special authority of primitive leaders of the community, Paul certainly 'collected such formulas in order to prove their presupposition, the resurrection of Jesus'.[98] The fact that the evidence may not be capable of warranting a conclusion with certainty, as Pannenberg had hoped, does not alter the fact that at least a historical assessment of the evidence does not lead to the alternative conclusion that the early faith was a complete fabrication. Rather, it at least raises the possibility that Jesus may have been raised from the dead. Moreover, an application of critical-historical techniques to the evidence may yet allow us to arrive at some inkling of the nature of the primitive Easter experience. It may be capable of leading us to some understanding of what it is that the first disciples were talking about, whilst the theologies of Barth and Bultmann leave us high and dry, pending the illumination of the Holy Spirit, who, alas, does not seem to have had much success in leading Barth and Bultmann from contention and confusion to clarity and agreement.

Thus, those who, like Westcott, insist that the resurrection of Jesus is to be handled as though it were a historical event of the past, use methods of critical-historical research which if exclusively relied upon tend to naturalize the resurrection so that it tends to approximate more and more to little else than a mundane restoration of a corpse. Those who follow Barth and Bultmann are plunged into the opposite situation where the resurrected and exalted Jesus becomes so elusive that what his appearance was like, in terms of human experience, almost disappears from view. The net effect of their theology is that we are positively discouraged from employing the techniques of critical-historical research, not only to attempt to *prove* that Jesus did rise from the dead, but even to understand what the primitive Christians seem to have meant when they claimed to experience the presence of Jesus. Instead, the soteriological implications of the resurrection of Jesus are so emphasized that we are left wondering what the resurrection of Jesus involved (as in the case of Bultmann) or else a surface, uncritical reading of the scriptural narratives leaves it to the reader to resolve what happened (as in the case of Barth). The avoidance of a historical-critical approach to Easter faith, initially on the ground that no one can prove that God was the *cause* of the resurrection or that it was for our salvation, leads to the avoidance of any attempt, using historical-critical methods, even to outline what the resurrection experience originally

[98] W. Pannenberg, *Jesus—God and Man*, p. 91.

was. The only alternative to complete bewilderment is to adopt a non-critical reading of the texts in the manner of Barth, which leaves the impression of a set of literal, material, tangible appearances, not substantially different from what Westcott ends with by seeking to handle the matter purely as a historical event!

We can sympathize with Barth and Bultmann in their concern to see the resurrection as a revelatory and salvific event, and not just an occurrence of the mundane order. But because of their inclination to see the exercise of reason, pre-eminently the historical reason, as a human work which in their view is antithetical to salvation by faith alone, they attempt to construct a pathway to the truth via the word of proclamation, which leads them into an unacceptable cul-de-sac. Bultmann works with a self-denying ordinance which forbids him to say what the disciples were trying to talk about; Barth sacrifices critical procedures in favour of a general but ill-defined realism which does not specify the nature of the object of resurrection faith in any detail for fear of falling back into the lap of scientific historiography.

We must therefore conclude that the approach to an understanding of the resurrection as an eschatological event, discontinuous with the ordinary events of the historical order, runs into difficulties no less substantial than those met by Westcott and Pannenberg in their attempt to handle it precisely by assimilating it to other events of mundane order. Whilst the approach of Barth and Bultmann at least does justice to the radical uniqueness of the resurrection, we are left somewhat puzzled as to what the outlines of the original Easter experiences were. On the other hand, we have already seen Westcott and Pannenberg grappling with the inevitable consequence of dealing with the resurrection from the point of view of what it has in common with the events of ordinary history: clarity of understanding is reached at the expense of its dogmatic significance. The raised Jesus is naturalized to the point where his unique revelatory and soteriological significance is lost.

I think this means that we must see these two alternative approaches to an understanding of the resurrection of Jesus and of the structure of the Easter faith, not as antithetical and opposed methods, so much as complementary models, each of which goes some way towards illuminating the nature of the Easter mystery but which by themselves fail to achieve their aim. We must hold them together in order to come to terms with the transcendent mystery and to salvage some understanding of the resurrection, without according either the status of absolute truth. In a subsequent chapter we shall take up the task of probing further into the nature of the original Easter experience in the hope of discerning its outlines a little more clearly and of articulating an understanding of faith that will be appropriate to it.

First, we must pause to consider yet another possibility. This is the suggestion that, far from being a response to an event which can be understood to be in essential respects similar to any other event of world history *or* an eschatological event which is essentially dissimilar from ordinary, humanly caused, events, the Easter faith can be understood without recourse to the idea that it is a response to any kind of objective happening. In this case the contention is that faith can be understood as a self-contained experience of the believing subject, without a dependence upon *any* kind of objective post-mortem event following upon Jesus' crucifixion and death whatsoever.

IV

The Resurrection as a Non-Event

Resurrection and Theological Reductionism

To this point we have examined views of the structure of belief in which the resurrection of Jesus is understood as an identifiable event which is said to have occurred subsequently to his crucifixion on the cross. The basic theological differences that we have noted have had to do with the understanding of the precise nature of the Easter event and the determination of an appropriate means of appropriating it in human consciousness.

Broadly speaking, theologians have been seen to divide over the question of whether the Easter event is to be understood as a historical event, assimilable to other events of the human past, or whether it is an eschatological event which, because of it unique qualities, is discontinuous with natural events. In relation to the human apprehension of the occurrence of this event, these two alternatives resolve into the question of whether it is properly handled with the methods of scientific historiography, or whether it is an event whose revelatory and soteriological character disqualifies it from treatment by such methods, leaving it to be apprehended by faith alone.

We come now to canvass a third possibility. This is the view that the primitive Easter faith is not to be understood as a response to a post-mortem event in any sense at all. Rather, in this case, it is proposed that faith is based upon the completed life of the historical Jesus, a datum that may be said to have begun with his birth and to have ended with his death on the cross. The story of the resurrection is then held to be a way of expressing this faith; it is the product of faith rather than the ground of it, myth rather than record of fact.

In this chapter we shall be chiefly concerned with two comparatively recent statements of this position—the views of Willi Marxsen, a German New Testament scholar and then those of Don Cupitt, a contemporary British philosophical theologian. Both these scholars reach similar conclusions concerning the basic structure of Christian faith, whilst approaching it by quite different routes.

However, the contention that Christian faith may be based upon the datum of the historical life and death of Jesus, without any reliance on a post mortem event in the days immediately after the crucifixion, is by no means new. It is as old as the rise of historical criticism itself and its application to the texts of the New Testament.

The application of critical historical techniques to the assessment of the historical evidence for the resurrection of Jesus, led Hermann Samuel Reimarus to this conclusion in his Wolfenbüttel *Fragments*, which were published by Lessing between 1774 and 1778. Reimarus noted that the Easter stories in the gospels present an impenetrable web of contradictions which cannot be knit together into a single harmonious and unified account. In view of the contradictions, Reimarus concluded that the narratives are little more than pure fiction, the invention of the primitive believers.

The contention that the Easter narratives are fabrications is rather implausible in view of the fact that the primitive Christians were prepared to die for what they claimed to have witnessed: one does not normally give up one's own life in defence of one's own fraud. Nevertheless, the discrepancies and contradictions in the Easter narratives that Reimarus's initial exercises of critical-historical method brought into focus bequeathed a theological problem to nineteenth-century theologians. These discrepancies raised a serious difficulty with which they sought to come to terms in a variety of different ways. Some argued in the manner of Westcott that a few discrepancies of detail were to be expected in any testimony from more than one witness, whilst others of more radical temperament came to the conclusion that the discrepancies so weakened the claim of the Easter stories to be reports of objective fact, that the historicity of the event was seriously called in question. Whilst they saw the difficulties involved in arguing that the primitive faith was a deliberate fabrication, they came to the belief that it was explicable as a delusion produced by purely natural causes. In general terms this was the standpoint of the Tübingen school of biblical criticism associated particularly with the names of F. C. Baur and his more famous pupil D. F. Strauss. Baur himself worked on the basic assumption that scientific historiography must explain events of nature by appeal to other antecedent natural events, and that talk of miraculous interventions were inimical to the very idea of a discipline of scientific historiography. Historians could only operate, he believed, on the presupposition of the uniformity and rational intelligibility of nature. He therefore avoided the difficult problem of the resurrection by arguing that it lay outside the limits of historical investigation.[1] Strauss shared Baur's contention that in so far as events or phenomena purported to be 'produced immediately by God himself' (as in the case of divine apparitions, voices from heaven and the like) or by human beings 'possessed of supernatural powers' (as in the case of alleged miracles and prophecies) they were 'to be considered as not historical'.[2] Nevertheless, he saw the need to explain the origin of primitive Christian faith historically. As he put it in his *A New Life of Jesus*, the need was to explain 'the origin of belief in the resurrection of Jesus without any corresponding miraculous fact'.[3]

Apart from a consensus amongst the Tübingen scholars to the effect that scientific historiography could not deal with miraculous interventions because of its own basic presupposition of the uniformity of nature and the universality of laws which govern the course of events, they were also agreed that discrepancies and internal inconsistencies in historical evidence were sure signs of fabrication. It was quite simply assumed that inconsistency indicated that the account of a purported event was mythical and legendary rather than historical, even if it was piously motivated. This meant that the attempt to penetrate behind the discrepancies to a kernel of truth or underlying harmony of objective fact was shelved in favour of the more stark conclusion that where there was inconsistency there could not be historical knowledge.[4]

These basic methodological principles led Strauss to attempt to explain the resurrection faith of the first disciples other than in terms of a response to an objective occurrence, and thus to propound his now well-known 'subjective vision' hypothesis.

---

[1] F. C. Baur, *The Church History of the Three First Centuries* (Tübingen 1853), p. 39. See D. F. Strauss's comment on F. C. Baur's avoidance of the burning question, *A New Life of Jesus*, Vol. I, p. 398.

[2] *The Life of Jesus Critically Examined*, p. 88.

[3] Op. cit., p. 397.

[4] F. H. Bradley, in his *The Presuppositions of Critical History*, whilst drawing heavily on the pioneering work of Baur and Strauss, went beyond the Tübingen position by seeking to supply a set of criteria for evaluating conflicting testimony. See *The Presuppositions of Critical History*, pp. 31–5.

Strauss ruled out the possibility of the resurrection as a 'miraculous objective occurrence' on the ground that the gospel evidence does not come from eye witnesses and that the accounts themselves do not agree, for in the gospels the raised Jesus is described in self-contradictory ways.[5] Whilst a theologian like Westcott, committed to a mediating or apologetic stance, might argue that it is precisely because the accounts are not from eye witnesses that we must not expect them to be absolutely harmonious, clear and distinct, the conclusion of the more radically-minded Strauss was that 'the whole thing gives the impression, not of a life objectively restored, connected in itself, but of a subjective conception in the minds of those who think they see him'. The original faith in the resurrection is therefore said to be explicable as an internal affair, a matter of 'solely internal states of mind'.[6] Faith in the resurrection arose from the 'recollection of the personality of Jesus himself' and the 'vivid conviction that he was the Messiah'.[7] In other words, Strauss contended that the datum for primitive Christian faith was the life of Jesus from his birth to his death on the cross, and the belief that he was still alive arose amongst his disciples as an imaginative projection from (*a*) their memory of Jesus and (*b*) their interpreting of this remembered Jesus *as* the Messiah.

Consequently, for Strauss, belief in the resurrection of Jesus could be explained as an after-effect of the completed life of Jesus. It was the outcome of 'a renewed search into the scriptures which served to revive the faith of his disciples' plus the confirmatory experiences of visions which could be accounted for in subjective or natural terms.[8] It is important to note that the basis of faith is not just the subjective vision, as is often said, but a recalling of the historical figure in the light of a reassessment of the meaning of scripture, that triggers off the response of faith. It was 'the excitement of the disciples after the sudden death of Jesus, their power of imagination incessantly busy with the recalling of his figure',[9] particularly in the breaking of bread, which continued perhaps as a daily occurrence, and 'the exalted tone of mind which prevailed at this meal, which in particular cases elevated the memory of the Departed into

---

[5] D. F. Strauss, *A New Life of Jesus*, Vol. I, pp. 399–408.
[6] Ibid., pp. 411, 421.
[7] Ibid.
[8] Ibid., p. 423
[9] Ibid., p. 426.

an imaginary appearance'.[10] Thus, faith in Jesus as the Messiah, which by his violent death had received an apparently fatal shock, was subjectively restored, by the instrumentality of the mind, the power of imagination, and nervous excitement.

Similar views were propounded in France by Ernest Renan in his world shattering *Life of Jesus* in 1863, the year before Strauss published his *A New Life of Jesus* in Germany. Renan's book, like Strauss's more popular review of his own earlier work, was directed beyond the narrow confines of professional theology towards the wider reading public.

Like the Tübingen scholars, Renan was disinclined to treat the resurrection at any length at all for, as a historian, he understood that 'the life of Jesus finishes with his last sigh'.[11] Nevertheless he raised the possibility that the first witnesses may have been subject to a delusion—the body could have been removed from the tomb or the resurrection narratives could have been the creation of credulous enthusiasm. In the absence of secure evidence he was content to allow that the matter could never be resolved. However, at the end of the day, it is clear enough that Renan himself believed that the 'strong imagination of Mary Magdalene played an important part in this circumstance.' As he understood the traditions, Mary Magdalene was the only original witness to the resurrection and his suggestion is that the resurrection narratives are the outcome of Mary Magdalene's imaginative projections. Others, whilst following Strauss, attributed the first vision to other apostolic personalities. H. Holtzmann, for example, attributed the initial vision to Peter who, full of remorse because of his having denied Jesus, is said to have had a psychologically induced vision of Jesus risen. His experience is in turn said to have prompted others to have similar hallucinatory experiences.[12]

The appearance of the work of Strauss and Renan in English translation stimulated the proliferation of explanations of the Easter experiences in terms of purely natural causes during the 1870s amongst English theologians as well as amongst the critics of Christianity. Amongst theologians the subjective vision hypothesis was put sensationally by W. R. Cassels in his anonymously published

---

[10] Ibid., p. 429.
[11] *Life of Jesus*, p. 296
[12] H. Holtzmann, *Lehrbuch der neutestamentlichen Theologie*, Vol. 1, p. 431.

Supernatural Religion (1874–7), which went through a series of editions,[13] and by R. W. Macan in his more moderate and carefully argued *The Resurrection of Jesus Christ* in 1877.[14] Meanwhile, John Stuart Mill commented in his *Three Essays on Religion* (1874) that 'of all the miracles of the New Testament' the conversion of Paul in response to an alleged Easter appearance 'is the one which admits of the easiest explanation from natural causes'.[15]

Now, given that these scholars sought to account for the Easter experiences as subjective or psychogenic visions, faith in Jesus, if it was to be defended at all, could no longer be explained as a response to an Easter event, either of a purely historical or of an eschatological kind. Rather the visions were clearly the product of faith rather than the basis of it and the structure of the faith experience itself had necessarily to be explained in other terms.

Most of those who discounted the reality and objectivity of the Easter experiences nevertheless declared their belief in the moral value of the historical life, teaching, and death of Jesus. The datum of Christian faith in this view becomes not just the visions, but the historical life and death of Jesus. What is said to be central to the act of faith is the recalling or remembering of his 'words, acts and doctrines', as Strauss put it. As a consequence of these views, it becomes perfectly clear that the name 'Jesus' therefore has reference to a person of the past, a historical person, who from the present point of view can only be remembered by Christians, though in the

---

[13] W. R. Cassels, *Supernatural Religion, An Enquiry into the Reality of Divine Revelation*, especially Vol. III, part 3, 'The Resurrection and Ascension', pp. 398–586. For the vision hypothesis see pp. 426 ff. See also his reply to Westcott, 'The Christian "Conditions" ' in *Fortnightly Review*, (Feb. 1878), pp. 228–46 and 'The New Revelation' in *Fortnightly Review*, (March 1878), pp. 365–83. A popular edition of *Supernatural Religion* appeared in 1902.

[14] R. W. Macan puts the subjective vision theory in a very clear and cogent statement in *The Resurrection of Jesus Christ*, pp. 28–113.

[15] J. S. Mill, *Essays on Ethics, Religion and Society*, ed. J. M. Robson, p. 480. See also W. B. Carpenter 'The Fallacies of Testimony in Relation to the Supernatural', *Contemporary Review*, (Jan. 1876), pp. 279–95. For a modern statement of the 'subjective vision theory' see H. M. Teeple, 'The Historical Beginnings of the Resurrection Faith' in *Studies in New Testament and Early Christian Literature, Essays in Honour of A. P. Wikgren, Novum Testamentum*, Supp. Vol. 33. (1972), ed., D. E. Aune pp. 107–20.

For an English response to Renan's thesis see the review of 'Les Apôtres' by R. W. Church, first published in *Saturday Review* (14 July, 1866), republished in *Occasional Papers*, Vol. II pp. 205–19. Dean Church's review of Renan's *Vie de Jésus*, originally published in the *Guardian* (9 September 1863), is also interesting—the same volume, pp. 190–204.

judgement of faith he is remembered *as* the Messiah of Old Testament prophecy. Because the reference of the name 'Jesus' is no longer to be thought of as a present, living reality, but as a past and dead one, the traditional theology of the resurrection has to that extent been reduced. There is no suggestion of the need to believe in the objective but heavenly existence of the raised Jesus, and no suggestion that Easter faith involved an encounter with him after his death and burial. Faith may have involved the remembering of the Jesus of the past; it did not involve a knowing of the Christ of the present.

Now, having established this pattern of the 'reductionist' account of the structure of resurrection belief, let us turn to the more recent interpretations of resurrection faith which broadly follow this same reductionist model.

Willi Marxsen

In 1964, Willi Marxsen published an essay entitled 'The Resurrection of Jesus as a Historical and Theological Problem',[16] in which he made the point that no individual of the primitive Christian community ever claimed to have seen or experienced 'Jesus' resurrection as an event, a fact, a happening'.[17] The New Testament evidence represents the actual resurrection as something that occurred in the privacy and silence of the tomb. When the first Christians sought to explain how they had come to believe and how it was that they were carrying on the functions of proclamation and missionary activity, they referred back, not to the actual resurrection of Jesus in the tomb but to his alleged appearances after the crucifixion outside of the tomb: 'this fact alone', says Marxsen, 'is brought into prominence'.[18] Other than this, Marxsen draws attention to what we have already discussed—the enormous variety of the New Testament resurrection traditions and the impossibility of harmonizing them into one basic narrative or story, the diversity that led Strauss and other nineteenth-century Tübingen scholars to doubt the historicity of the event. The one thing which he is prepared to admit is that the emphasis on the basic importance of the *appearances* of Jesus as the beginning point for faith, does come through the variety. At this

[16] Published in English in *The Significance of the Message of the Resurrection for Faith in Jesus Christ*, ed. C. F. D. Moule, pp. 15–50.
[17] Ibid., p. 24.
[18] Ibid., p. 34.

point, Marxsen is less inclined than Strauss to stress the importance of the historical life of Jesus understood in the light of interpretative concepts drawn from scripture. Rather, it is emphasized that it is the appearance of Jesus which is the foundation for faith and the initiating impulse for mission. Marxsen is unconvinced by attempts, notably by von Campenhausen, to prove the historicity of the empty tomb[19] and, in any event, he notes that the traditions of 1 Cor. 15: 5–7, which are without explicit mention of the empty tomb, belong to the earliest extant traditions and 'are probably to be regarded as the earliest altogether'.[20] It is the appearances of Jesus which are stressed in this tradition. From this central datum an inference is drawn, with the help of pre-existing apocalyptic beliefs about the ultimate restoration of the dead, back to what must have occurred in the privacy of the tomb—the resurrection of Jesus from the dead. From the same fundamental datum of the appearances the Church's continuing function of proclamation could be explained. Marxsen therefore points out that the appearance of Jesus alive after the crucifixion ' "came to be spoken of" in opposite directions':[21] back to what occurred in the tomb and forward to what was occurring in the Church—the continuing proclamation. Consequently, we might schematize the pattern of resurrection faith as shown in

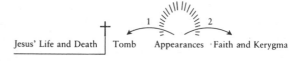

Jesus' Life and Death | Tomb   Appearances ·Faith and Kerygma

Figure 1.

This thesis provoked a good deal of controversy in Germany because Marxsen gave prominence to the second inference, the inference forwards from the appearances, to explain the origin of the kerygma, rather than the first inference back to the actual resurrection of Jesus in the tomb. Indeed, Marxsen gave the impression that this latter inference, which would only be made by interpreting the experience of the appearances in the light of a pre-existing

[19] Ibid., p. 24.
[20] Ibid., p. 26.
[21] Ibid., p. 37.

apocalyptic belief, was relative to the first century which seriously entertained such beliefs, but could now be off-loaded, leaving the second inference to come into its own as the true and continuing significance of Easter.[22]

In 1968 Marxsen published a sequel to this original essay under the title *The Resurrection of Jesus of Nazareth*. This work is in fact presented as a more extended treatment of his earlier position which became necessary because of the bitter controversy that his first essay had produced. However, in the course of this extended treatment, his original thesis is significantly modified. Instead of the appearances of the raised Christ being given centrality as the point from which the community of faith with its characteristic mode of operation is said to have originated, and as the point from which an inference is drawn back to what must have occurred in the tomb, it is now the 'coming to faith' of the disciples after Good Friday that is brought into prominence. Marxsen argues that the affirmation 'Jesus is risen!' is but one way of *expressing* the fact of this 'coming to faith'. Other alternatives are provided in the New Testament talk of exaltation, such as 'Jesus is Lord!' or 'Jesus sits at the right hand of the Father!' Also, it is now the 'having found faith' which is said to have led to mission. When we look more closely at what this 'having found faith' involved we find that it is no longer a faith that is based on a 'seeing' or an 'appearance' of Jesus; on the contrary, the appearances of Jesus are now explicitly said to be an 'externalization of the having-found-faith after Good Friday'.[23] It is here that the parallel with the reductionist views of Strauss begins to appear more clearly for the appearances are now said to be the *product* rather than the *basis* of faith. Indeed faith, to Marxsen's mind, is the kind of faith that is not based on anything. As for Barth, and particularly for Bultmann, so for Marxsen, faith must be a risk, a venture. Jesus requires, he says, 'a trusting faith', a 'daring faith'; he challenges us to have to do with God and faith is a 'trusting commitment to Jesus' challenge'.[24]

In a manner very reminiscent of Bultmann, Marxsen insists that the preacher does not prove that what he preaches is the Word of

[22] See the comments of Hans-Georg Geyer in 'The Resurrection of Jesus Christ: A Survey of the Debate in Present Day Theology' in *The Significance of the Message of the Resurrection for Faith in Jesus Christ*, ed. C. F. D. Moule, pp. 121–6.
[23] *The Resurrection of Jesus of Nazareth*, p. 159. See also p. 156 f.
[24] Ibid., p. 151.

God and that it is pointless to seek for rational legitimation of his message. Thus, faith is not a judgement and a commitment in trust based on evidence or even going beyond the available evidence, but a trusting commitment without *any* reliance on evidence, a free-standing response to the call which is heard in the church's proclamation. Marxsen also follows Barth and Bultmann by attaching dogmatic significance to Paul's statement in Romans 10: 17: 'Faith comes from what is heard'. But what is heard is not testimony of the kind that could ground a rational conclusion.[25] In fact, Marxsen even goes so far as to affirm that we must take the risk of faith, we must dare to have to do with God, 'contrary to all human reason'.[26]

Consequently, Marxsen affirms that what happened after Good Friday was that the first Christians continued to hear Jesus' offer or challenge to have to do with God in this world and to accept the consequences of having to do with God, one of which is the necessity of calling others to the self-same faith. Thus, what happened after Good Friday was that men and women continued to hear the call to faith, which was the same call to faith that they had heard when Jesus walked this earth. The expression 'Jesus is Risen!' is thus one way of expressing the fact that Jesus' cause goes on, for people continue to be plunged into faith.[27] Mission continues, proclamation continues, but it is not necessarily the case that Jesus himself continues.

From time to time Marxsen speaks of 'Jesus going on', or of 'Jesus at work and present in the continuing proclamation'.[28] He also talks of *Jesus' presence* 'in the kerygma of his witnesses'. Marxsen's position is thus reminiscent of Bultmann's contention that Jesus is 'raised into the kerygma'.[29] I say 'reminiscent' here because there are some significant differences between Bultmann and Marxsen. Whereas Marxsen holds that the cause of *Jesus* goes on, that is to say the historical Jesus' call to have to do with God, Bultmann holds that the kerygma, the Church's proclamation of the saving significance of the Cross, goes on as the medium of the revelation of the *raised Christ*. One way of codifying the difference between Marxsen and Bultmann is to say that Marxsen's exposition of the

---

[25] Ibid., p. 142.
[26] Ibid., pp. 183–4.
[27] Ibid.
[28] Ibid., p. 142.
[29] See above, p. 120.

meaning of Easter takes the form of a Jesuology rather than a Christology, whereas Bultmann notoriously propounds a Christology with no (or at least a minimal) Jesuology, in so far as he shows little dogmatic interest in the historical Jesus by substituting talk of encounter with the raised Christ in the proclamation. Marxsen certainly does not equivocate in the manner of Bultmann at this point. It is perfectly clear that for Marxsen talk of Christ being 'present in the kerygma' is metaphorical talk and that its more prosaic and literal meaning is that it is Jesus' *cause* rather than Jesus *himself* which is understood as continuing.

In his critique of Bultmann's theology, Barth raised the possibility that Bultmann should be seen as 'A new David Friedrich Strauss' in so far as he dispenses with the objectivity of the raised Jesus.[30] If Bultmann's actual words are too enigmatic to allow us to be confident that this is a fair representation of his true position, the same cannot be said of Marxsen who, like Strauss, contends that 'the question of the resurrection of Jesus is not that of an event which occurred after Good Friday, but that of the earthly Jesus . . .'.[31]

Thus, if we were to schematize Marxsen's final understanding of the pattern of faith in the resurrection, it could be presented as in

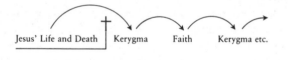

Jesus' Life and Death | Kerygma   Faith   Kerygma etc.

Figure 2.

In this understanding of things faith is not a response to a post-mortem Event, not even an appearance of the raised Christ of a visionary kind. Rather, it is clear enough that Marxsen has here moved much closer to the view of Strauss. The difference between them lies in the fact that, whilst for Strauss faith is precipitated as the disciples remember the historical Jesus by the power of imagination, for Marxsen it is the continuing proclamation of the kerygma

---

[30] 'Rudolf Bultmann—An Attempt to Understand Him', *Kerygma and Myth*, Vol. II, p. 117.
[31] 'The Resurrection of Jesus as a Historical and Theological Problem', p. 50.

of the historical Jesus which precipitates faith. They are both agreed, however, that there is no post-mortem historical event or appearance of Jesus which is the basis of faith.

Now, we must ask: why did Marxsen find it necessary to shift the emphasis from the appearances of Jesus in his first essay to the 'finding of faith', independent of the evidence of appearances, in his more extended work?

There can be no doubt that Marxsen's particular dogmatic understanding of the structure of faith is crucial. For Marxsen, faith is a miracle; a miracle, in turn, is explicitly said to be the result of a divine intervention. Faith is therefore the miraculous gift of the Spirit, not something that is achieved as the result of the believer's own mental effort or ability to draw inferences; it is a grace, not a work. Indeed, Marxsen alleges that it is precisely because faith is a miracle that it became appropriate to use the phrase 'Jesus is Risen!', for what this really means is that faith is *caused* by Jesus or by God rather than a conclusion at which the believer arrives at the end of a process of rational argument. However, while Marxsen insists that reason cannot lead to faith, he is prepared to say that it is nevertheless useful in so far as the exercise of reason, in the course of critical research on the New Testament narratives, helps to sweep away false supports to faith.[32] Reason sweeps away all supports to faith by showing exactly how inconsistent, how disparate and impossible to harmonize the resurrection narratives are. Reason itself shows, in other words, that reason cannot support faith and that faith therefore must be a venture, a risk.

In all this Marxsen shows himself to be a representative of traditional post-Kantian Lutheranism, in which faith and reason are held strictly apart. As we saw in Chapter III with reference to Barth and Bultmann, in that tradition it is assumed that if one relied on the evidence of reason one would destroy the nature of faith as a venture; faith would become a human 'work', not a miraculous gift of God. Faith in the resurrection of Jesus, therefore, cannot be a conclusion that is based on the evidence of seeing Jesus, the empty tomb, or anything else and putting two and two together. And this means that the appearances of Jesus which Marxsen had pointed to as being central to the New Testament tradition in his first essay, have to be elbowed off centre in his subsequent dogmatic treatment.

[32] *The Resurrection of Jesus of Nazareth*, pp. 152–3.

Faith, by definition, is not based on evidence. Evidence must not, therefore, intrude into the understanding of the structure of faith in the resurrection.

This means that the appearances tradition in the New Testament still remains as a very awkward commodity for Marxsen to handle. He cannot avoid the fact that there *is* a tradition of visual or visionary appearances in the New Testament documents, but he argues that the point of the appearance tradition is not to report an occurrence or offer it as evidence on which faith might be based. Rather, he insists that 'the point of these accounts was not to report *the fact that Jesus appeared*', but to explain the 'reason for making disciples of all nations, baptizing them and teaching them to keep what Jesus had commanded (Matthew); the reason for proclaiming repentance to all nations in the name of Jesus (Luke); the reason for knowing oneself to be sent by Jesus, just as Jesus had been sent by the Father (John).[33] One might paraphrase the statement, 'Jesus is Risen!', he says, 'by saying: "it is not our own cause which we are pursuing; it is the cause of Jesus which we are *continuing* to pursue; and we are doing this because he appeared to us after his crucifixion and because that has plunged us into faith and mission" '.[34] But the use of the word 'because' here is very strange. For it seems to imply that Marxsen means to admit that the appearances of Jesus were cited as evidence, as the reason why the first believers had come to faith and as the reason for continuing the proclamation of Jesus' message, but they were not the reasons in fact, because faith and mission originated as an inexplicable miraculous occurrence, independent of reason and reasoning! Marxsen seems to be saying: The first disciples gave reasons for faith which were not their reasons. Or alternatively: Reasons were cited but there were really no reasons, because faith, by definition, has to be independent of reason. Thus Marxsen has got himself into a hopeless logical knot. It is like saying 'E2 occurred because E1 occurred, but I do not wish to suggest that E1 occurred'.

On the other hand, Marxsen looks rather desperately in the New Testament for evidence that the apostolic faith and mission are independent of reason and that faith originated miraculously only as the result of the continuance of the proclamation. He endeavours to

---

[33] Ibid., pp. 83–4.
[34] Ibid., p. 84.

argue, in other words, that in the New Testament the hearing of the call is the occurrence which initiated faith and mission. He cites, by way of example, those in Jerusalem who were found believing in the resurrection and affirming, 'Jesus is risen indeed and has appeared to Simon' (Luke 24: 34). These had apparently come to faith without having 'seen' Jesus themselves, but after having heard the proclamation of Peter. The proclamation precipitated them into faith, not the appearances. But Peter's own case is still a difficulty, for those who were believing in Jerusalem were in fact affirming not only that Jesus was risen, but that he had appeared to Simon. Marxsen in turn seeks to shift attention from this by saying that it is really Peter's 'coming to faith' that is basic and that the appearance to Peter is pointed to as the reason for his faith. Once again, we are meant to understand that it was not the reason in fact. Thus, in the incident concerning Peter which is now found in John 21, Peter is said to have seen, perhaps while fishing, that Jesus was sending him forth. It is clear that Marxsen understands this 'seeing' as an intellectual seeing, the coming to the conviction that he was called to continue the work of proclamation, and that this was externalized or pictorially presented in the story of Jesus appearing by the lake which draws on elements from his social intercourse with his fishermen-disciples during his lifetime.

Now, Marxsen seems to be baulking at admitting that Peter's faith can be traced back to a seeing of Jesus after the crucifixion because he is looking at the narratives as a scientific historian rather than as a man of faith. As impartial historians we can only go so far as to say that Peter was the first to come to faith and that it was claimed that he had seen Jesus; we cannot, as historians, say that he had in fact seen the raised Jesus, and that this seeing of Jesus was the basis of his faith. That would itself be a judgement of faith. When he takes off the historian's cap and becomes a man of faith, Marxsen says that we can say that Peter's faith was caused in some inexplicable way by God or Jesus; we cannot say how faith actually came about, because that would be to supply a reason, justifying grounds, and faith, according to Marxsen's own definition, is independent of such grounds.

On the other hand, Marxsen seems to be excluding all evidence of reason to explain Peter's coming to faith on the assumption that we can only understand Peter's coming to faith on analogy with our own coming to faith. We believe, not because we 'see' anything, he says, but because we hear the proclamation as Jesus' call to faith and we accept the challenge and take the risk of having to do with God. If this is our experience of faith, Marxsen seems to be saying, then Peter's must have been the same.

Thus, it seems clear enough that Marxsen reaches his conclusion about the resurrection from his particular understanding of the nature of faith as his starting-point. He assumes (1) that faith and reason must be held utterly apart and (2) that we do not in any sense see Jesus or perceive his presence; rather, we are plunged into faith by the proclamation. This leads him to shift the emphasis away from the centrality of the appearances in the New Testament and on to the 'coming to faith', despite the fact that in his first essay he had insisted that it is the appearances tradition that 'alone is brought into prominence'.

It is of course possible that some primitive Christians came to believe that Jesus had been raised and exalted to the right hand of the Father as a result of hearing the first reports that some others had experienced an appearance of the raised Christ. In this case their faith would have been an assent to the truth of the contention that Jesus had been raised, a propositional attitude. This seems to have been the case with those whom Luke says were, at Jerusalem, averring that 'Jesus was risen indeed, and had appeared to Simon' (Luke 24: 34). That all Easter faith, including the most primitive, must be reduced to an assent to propositions is another matter.

Marxsen's error is that he has assumed that the faith-response of Christians must be resolved into a single pattern constituted by the central idea of the 'hearing of the proclamation', and cannot be an assent based on evidence. This leads to the effective neutralization of the appearances tradition, which remains as a persistent and embarrassing datum in the primitive accounts of faith.

In subsequent chapters we shall be attempting to re-think the nature of faith understood as a response to an objective event, an appearance of the raised Christ, rather than begin with an understanding of faith which has no room for talk of the perception of evidence in any form and then devalues the dogmatic importance of the appearances tradition. Before we do this, however, we must pause to pay a little more attention to the first of Marxsen's basic assumptions: that faith and reason must be held strictly apart. We can best do this by turning now to a consideration of Don Cupitt's understanding of the nature of faith in the resurrection of Jesus.

Don Cupitt

Don Cupitt presents his views in the important but neglected book, *Christ and the Hiddenness of God*,[35] published in 1971. In this book, Cupitt, like Strauss and Marxsen, arrives at what can justifiably be termed a 'reductionist' thesis. As a philosophical theologian, Cupitt places the emphasis of what he has to say on logical issues rather than historical ones. He says, for example, that the title 'Messiah' or 'Christ', like the title 'Prime Minister' has a meaning but needs a reference. But whereas the office of Prime Minister is occupied at the moment, thus giving the term a present reference (i.e., the present incumbent of the office), the reference of the title 'Messiah' or 'Christ', the man Jesus, is for theologians not present but past. Faith in Jesus is based on the life and death of Jesus; it is a coming to see this remembered or historical Jesus as the Messiah. The real Easter event after the crucifixion is the coming to faith in Jesus as the Messiah, rather than a post-mortem event after Jesus' crucifixion to which men responded in faith. Fig. 3 gives a representation of Cupitt's understanding of things.

Jesus' Life and Death   Faith

Figure 3.

Once again there are similarities here to the thought both of Strauss and Marxsen. For Cupitt, as for Strauss, the datum for faith is the life of Jesus; faith is a seeing of this Jesus as the Christ. Strauss goes a little further and says that the New Testament visions are subjective projections, the product of mental excitement. On this point Cupitt is a little ambivalent. At one place he speaks roundly of the idea of the resurrection as a post-mortem event as being 'like the superstition of tying the doctrine of the Incarnation to an antenatal episode in Jesus' career, namely his virginal conception by Mary'.[36] He also speaks of the 'myth of a posthumous apparition'.[37]

[35] D. Cupitt, *Christ and the Hiddenness of God*, Chs. 9 and 10.
[36] Ibid., p. 165.
[37] Ibid., p. 166.

Elsewhere, however, he says he does not necessarily want to deny the visions; he declares that he is agnostic about them and that, if anything, they are bonuses. They are not necessary to faith and certainly do not provide the grounds or justification of faith; rather, they are superfluous,[38] for the ground for belief in the resurrection (as for the belief in the incarnation) is the completed life of Jesus from birth to death and not a post-mortem event or vision.

On the other hand, Cupitt and Marxsen are at one in insisting that the real Easter event is the coming to faith itself, not something else to which people responded in faith. But it is important to note one key difference between the respective roads which Cupitt and Marxsen outline as the means of arriving at faith. Whereas Marxsen understands faith as a miracle, a sudden inexplicable acceptance of Jesus' challenge to have to do with God, which is independent of all human reasoning and which may even fly in the face of human reasoning, Cupitt's position is exactly the opposite. The judgement of faith is said to be arrived at by rational argument 'as the Apostles put the facts of Jesus' life and death as they had experienced them side-by-side with the Old Testament. In a shocking flash of recognition, he says, 'everything fell into place and they saw the meaning of this man'.[39] Thus, whereas Marxsen says that faith is a response to the proclamation or challenge, independent of the assessment of evidence and processes of argument, Cupitt (rightly to my mind) insists that the first Christians proclaimed arguments. The New Testament reveals that in their arguments the notions of promise and fulfilment were clearly important from an early time. This is reflected, for example, in the most primitive tradition of the resurrection which Paul handed on to the Corinthians in which it was argued that Jesus died for our sins *according to the Scriptures* and was raised to life on the third day *according to the Scriptures* (1 Cor. 15: 3b and 4b). Consequently, Cupitt cites as the model pattern of resurrection faith, the incident on the road to Emmaus where the travellers are turning over the incidents of Jesus' life and death in their minds. The prophecies of the Old Testament are brought to bear on all that had happened, and then, by a kind of dramatic necessity (rather than by a miracle or inexplicable intervention of God) they are said to have come to the conclusion that Jesus must

---

[38] Ibid., p. 167.
[39] Ibid., p. 143.

have been the Messiah. Cupitt's conclusion is therefore well expressed in the words of Gerhard Ebeling, who holds a similar view in so far as he says that the 'faith of the days after Easter knows itself to be nothing else but the right understanding of the Jesus of the days before Easter',[40] but Cupitt's distinctive contribution is that human reasoning plays a key role in the achievement of this 'right understanding'.

Cupitt is therefore led to affirm that talk of Jesus' being alive now really means that he lives in the moral sphere. He lives in the sense that he is morally exalted over this world; he still exercises sovereignty over our lives; he is still our Lord, still the key to our relationship to God. But we must be clear that the reference of the name 'Jesus' for the believer is a historical reference, the historical Jesus of Nazareth, not a present reference.[41] This Jesus of the past is the key to our relationship with God in the sense that he is a model of faith; he shows us what it means to proclaim that God is near and to live as though God were near, even though we find in the ultimate analysis that God is far, remote, sublime, and incomprehensible: 'My God, my God, why have you forsaken me?' is something that we shall all have to utter in the end.

When we look at the reasons which Cupitt gives for arriving at this position we find that he discusses the resurrection in terms of two main kinds of view, which may be called the Event Theory of the resurrection and the Theological Theory of the resurrection. The Theological Theory is that which Cupitt holds himself and which I have just outlined, in which it is held that a theological judgement is made on the basis of the historical life and death of Jesus. The Event Theory is the theory that something happened after the crucifixion which was apprehended in experience and to which men responded in faith. This means that a basic difference between the two theories is that the ground of faith is different; for the Theological Theory it is the historical life of Jesus, for the Event Theory it is an experienced event after his death. Cupitt comes to favour his Theological Theory basically because he believes that the Event Theory is hopelessly incoherent and inadequate for explaining either the meaning of the resurrection or for providing rational or historical justification for belief in it. The Theological Theory is a

---

[40] Gerhard Ebeling, *Word and Faith*, p. 302.
[41] *Christ and the Hiddenness of God*, p. 181.

secure retreat in the face of emergent weakenesses and logical fractures in the Event Theory.

When we come to examine his discussion of the Event Theory we
find that Cupitt in fact distinguishes two different sub-categories of
Event Theory, both of which are held to be equally unacceptable.
One is the 'strict' or 'crude' Event Theory in which it is asserted
that Jesus literally got up and walked out of the tomb and was seen
as plainly as the nose on your face by his disciples. Whilst this version of the Event Theory has the commendable advantage of at least
being reasonably clear, Cupitt argues that it is inadequate either to
explain the nature of resurrection belief or to justify it, because it
can only lead to something approximating to the view of Paulus that
Jesus really did not die but revived in the tomb and pushed his way
out and borrowed the gardener's clothes. The more realism given to
the account of the event of the reappearance of Jesus, the more the
reality of the death is called in question. On the 'strict' Event
Theory the disciples, meeting the risen Jesus, might have said: 'Oh!
we thought they had killed you, but you are not dead after all!'[42]
But Christians do not feel obliged to affirm that Jesus was restored
to *this* life; they normally affirm that he was transformed and
entered upon some eternal, transcendent, heavenly life; a strict
Event Theory cannot be the ground of that, and it must be rejected
as theologically useless. We have already noted that even Westcott
and Pannenberg detect this difficulty and veer away from a naïve
realism of the kind that Cupitt terms the 'strict' Event Theory. But
then there is a second species of Event Theory, which Cupitt terms
the 'Psi' or 'vision' Theory, in which it is argued that the alleged
event after the crucifixion on which faith is grounded is a visionary
occurrence, a revelatory appearance of Jesus 'from heaven' as it
were. This is rejected by Cupitt on the grounds that as soon as we
leave the 'strict' Event Theory our talk becomes vague and incoherent and it does not really help to explain what the term 'Resurrection' means and certainly cannot be used historically to justify
resurrection belief, because the historian cannot know what it is that
he is trying to prove. He cannot say whether or not the resurrection
occurred because he is unable even to say what the resurrection was.
Moreover, it is illegitimate to offer a miraculous, post-mortem event
as the historical basis of faith because we are offering something that

by definition is inaccessible to historical investigation. Taking up the methodological principle of Baur and Strauss, Cupitt argues that miracles are beyond the historian's field of competence and therefore cannot be offered as the historical ground of faith, in the sense of 'capable of proof by the methods of modern scientific historiography'. Cupitt points out that the 'attempt to establish the occurrence of a miracle purely historically with a view to subsequently building a system of doctrine upon it must fail'.[43] One has to have faith in order to believe in miracles themselves; therefore miracles cannot be the historical ground of faith and cannot without circularity of argument be said to provide evidence upon which faith can be built. The same point was made by Reimarus when he argued in his Fragment 'Miracles No Proof' that 'those who would build Christianity upon miracles give it nothing firm, deep, or substantial for a foundation'.[44] For, in order to discover whether miracles are true requires 'as much investigation as that which they are supposed to prove.'[45] In view of the circularity in this argument, Cupitt insists that the Event Theory, which postulates some objective happening after the crucifixion as the basis of our understanding of the resurrection and as the ground for faith in Jesus' continued objective, heavenly existence is too incoherent to be helpful on the question of meaning and incapable of being established by historical research as the historical basis or justification of religious faith. This means that we must swing back to the more concrete, 'strict' Event Theory in order to clarify our meaning, but this, as we have seen, is theologically useless because as soon as we 'naturalize' it in order to handle it with the methods of scientific historiography it suggests a mere *resuscitation* and cannot be the ground of what we mean by the *resurrection*. Both versions of the Event Theory are consequently dismissed.

Cupitt therefore insists that we are obliged to retreat to the Theological Theory, which he proposes as the only viable alternative to the Event Theories. We must note in passing that all the while these theories are presented as strict alternatives: 'Theologians must choose', he says on p. 154, 'between either a strict Event theory or a strict Theological theory'. It is an either/or. But before we take up

[43] Ibid., p. 149.
[44] H. S. Reimarus, *Fragments*, p. 234.
[45] Ibid., p. 230. This point was also noted by R. W. Macan, *The Resurrection of Jesus Christ*, p. 18.

that point let us look at the Theological Theory itself, for there are a number of arguments which count against it.

This theory is, we must remember, that there is no post-mortem event which is the basis of faith; faith is a matter of coming to a theological judgement about the Messianic significance of the completed life and death of Jesus. It is an intellectual seeing of him *as* the Christ, in the light of the Old Testament.

The first argument against this theory is historical. The point arises from a historical examination of the New Testament texts in which the Old Testament is used in Christian apologetic. This for Cupitt is not just apologetic as used by believing Christians in answering their adversaries' objections to the primitive kerygma, but the actual way in which they argued *themselves* into belief, as it were. This shows that the idea that faith originated as the Old Testament was brought to bear on the completed life of Jesus and was then externalized in the vision stories, does not seem possible. For one thing, as Professor C. F. D. Moule has pointed out, in some correspondence between Cupitt and himself, originally published in *Theology*, October 1972,[46] the earthly Jesus scarcely fitted into any recognizably Messianic pattern. The Old Testament concept of Messiah does *not* easily apply to Jesus. He is, in the words of Eduard Schweizer, 'the man who fits no formula'. Even if the disciples came to believe that Jesus was the Messiah in his own lifetime, their conviction was shattered by the crucifixion. There is no known prophecy that the *Messiah* would suffer and die, let alone that he would die as a criminal on a cross. As a result, Professor Moule cannot see that there would be sufficient grounds for interpreting Jesus as the promised Messiah of the Old Testament simply on the basis of his life and death alone. This raises the question: does the bringing of the Old Testament to bear on the life and death of Jesus really explain faith? Professor Moule wants to postulate a transcendent event, a post-mortem happening, which triggered off the faith of the disciples and the efflorescence of Christological talk. This is an example of the so-called 'beaten men argument' which seeks to prove the occurrence of the resurrection of Jesus as nothing

---

[46] See *Theology*, lxxv, No. 628 (October, 1972), pp. 507–19: this correspondence has been republished by Don Cupitt in *Explorations in Theology*, 6, pp. 27–41.

more than the sufficient cause of the observed effect constituted by the conversion of the disciples and the foundation of the Church.[47]

Cupitt's critique of the 'beaten men' argument, however, is very compelling.[48] He notes that there is a big jump from the need of something to trigger off faith to the postulation that Jesus' resurrection is the only adequate thing that will fill the bill. Elsewhere Moule makes the point that his argument is that the distinctiveness and tenacity of the disciples' belief in relation to the pious Judaism to which they otherwise belonged can only be explained in terms of a highly distinctive originating event. In other words, it is not just that the effect, the transformation of the disciples, needs a powerful cause 'strong enough' to explain the beginning of the Church, but that the particularity of the effect calls for the particularity of the cause.[49] The effect thus calls for the postulation of a distinctive and sufficiently striking causal event in order to explain it satisfactorily. However, even in this form the argument claims more than can be sustained by the actual evidence. In seeking to establish the occurrence of the resurrection of Jesus by reference to its effect, the transformation and enthusiasm of the disciples, we cannot avoid the possibility that this effect, even with all its distinctiveness, could have resulted as well from an equally distinctive illusion as from a distinctive fact. A specific but nevertheless erroneous belief, passionately held, would allow Christians to distinguish themselves from the environmental Judaism as much as a passionately held truth. For a passionately held illusion may have the same force and power as reality and so have precisely the same consequence as would the occurrence of an objective event. The beaten men argument cannot get beyond this. Even D. F. Strauss conceded that without the *belief* in the resurrection of Jesus a Christian community would hardly

---

[47] A. Richardson also argues along these lines: 'The real evidence for the resurrection of Jesus is the existence of the Christain Church at all, if we have regard to the circumstances in which the earthly life of Jesus had apparently ended in such crushing failure and disappointment.' The existence of the Church is held to be evidence of the occurrence on the basis of the principle that every effect must have a cause sufficient to produce it. See *Science, History, and Faith*, p. 57. See also G. W. H. Lampe, *The Resurrection*, p. 23: 'the nearest . . . that you can get to objective proof of the Resurrection is the birth of the Christian Church.' Also G. O'Collins, *The Easter Jesus*, pp. 64 ff; Clark H. Pinnock, 'On the Third Day', in *Jesus of Nazareth: Saviour and Lord* (ed.) Carl Henry, p. 149: 'it is difficult to understand how this triumphant conviction was conceived in the hearts of men, unless Christ actually rose'.

[48] See *Christ and the Hiddenness of God*, p. 142.

[49] *The Phenomenon of the New Testament*, pp. 11 and 19.

have come together, but given that 'the disciples firmly believed that Jesus had risen'[50] the question of the validity of the belief remained an open question.

We can agree wholeheartedly with Geoffrey Lampe when he says: 'Unless Jesus' disciples were utterly convinced of his Resurrection their transformation from a dispirited and despairing group of people into valiant defenders of the faith is simply inexplicable.' However, the existence of a fervent belief does not necessarily secure the validity of what is believed, for as R. W. Macan clearly put it: 'given a belief of the same intensity, its results remain exactly the same, whether it is an illusion or an accurate reproduction of facts.'[51]

Professor Moule's postulation of the resurrection as the powerful and distinctive cause of so impressive and powerful a turn-about as that constituted by the conversion of the disciples, therefore fails in logical terms. Nevertheless, and this is the really important matter for our purposes, we do not necessarily have to accept his version of the beaten men argument to accept his point about the failure of Cupitt's Theological Theory to explain the origin of the Easter faith of the disciples. The deficiency of Cupitt's theological explanation therefore remains: it is problematic whether the completed life and death of Jesus would lead to the conclusion that he was the Messiah in Old Testament terms. It is therefore sufficient to note that there are difficulties in arguing, as Cupitt does, that faith is simply a matter of reflecting on the completed life and death of Jesus in the light of the Old Testament, for it is not at all certain, and even positively unlikely, that this would lead to the belief that he was the awaited Messiah.

Secondly, an examination of the actual New Testament texts which do apply Old Testament 'prophecies' to interpret the significance of Jesus suggests a pattern of the origin and development of faith other than that which Cupitt proposes. The earliest proclamation and apologetic seems to have been that Jesus had been appointed Lord and Christ by God who had raised him from the dead and that this Messiah would in the future return in power and glory. This, for example, is the pattern of argument in the early sermon which Luke preserves in Acts 3, and which J. A. T. Robinson

[50] *A New Life of Jesus*, Vol. I, p. 399.
[51] *The Resurrection of Jesus Christ*, p. 123.

conjectures, on the basis of its primitive futurist eschatology, may be the 'most primitive Christology of all'[52] In this passage, if it is early, we have an indication that the primitive Christians first understood the raised Jesus as a heavenly figure who would appear as Messiah and Judge in the future. A subsequent Christology, now reflected in the apostolic sermon in Acts 2, spoke of the raised Jesus as already being the Messiah, present in the early community. Only later still was the title Messiah read back and applied to Jesus during his lifetime as Messianic significance was seen in his historical words and deeds. In other words, the application of the title Messiah to the historical Jesus is something that develops, backwards as it were. This pattern of development is strongly argued for by Barnabas Lindars in *New Testament Apologetic*, where he contends that primitive Christian talk of the heavenly *Christus designatus* gradually gave way to talk of the *Christus revelatus*, as Messianic value was seen in the life and death of the historical Jesus and as incidents of his life began to be fitted to Old Testament prophecies in order to prove that Jesus had been the Messiah all along, even if the disciples had not discerned it.[53] The process of bringing Old Testament prophecies to bear on the historical life of Jesus from birth to death is, in relative terms, late.

Moreover, the same pattern is reflected in the use of the concept *mare*, Lord, in the primitive Aramaic-speaking Christian community. For the remnant survivals of *mare* in Aramaic in 1 Cor. 16 and Didache 10 are both in the context where the one to whom the title refers is understood as a figure of the future, who in these texts is called upon to appear as judge after a rehearsal of the divine law. Eduard Schweizer has argued that it is only later, particularly in the Greek stratum of the New Testament evidence, that we find the notion of Jesus the Lord (κύριος) associated with the present rather than with a future appearance. This is indicated by the use of the term Lord, now a translation from the Aramaic *mare* to the Greek κύριος in the context of eucharistic narratives in 1 Cor. 10: 21 and 11: 20. If the early Christians thought of Jesus as Lord, first in terms of the returning Judge of the future, then only subsequently did they come to the conviction that, amongst members of the Easter

[52] See J. A. T. Robinson, 'The Most Primitive Christology of All?' JTS, NS, 7 Part 2 (1956), pp. 177–89.
[53] See Barnabas Lindars, *New Testament Apologetic*, Ch. 2; also E. Schweizer, *Jesus*, pp. 56 ff. and 65 ff.

community, the raised Jesus was already exercising sovereignty and power over them as their exalted Lord and Messiah, particularly in the eucharistic assembly. It was still later that positive value was seen in the historical and earthly life of Jesus from his birth to his death. In the Aramaic stratum the Lord is already thought of as the exalted and heavenly figure of the future *parousia*; in the later New Testament material only is Messianic value seen in the incidents of Jesus' historical life in the light of the Old Testament. In other words, the orientation of faith as disclosed in a historical examination of the early Christian apologetic seems to have been first to the future and upwards towards heaven, towards the Christ who was understood to have been raised to God's right hand, and designated Messiah and who would return, and only later backwards to reflect upon and see Messianic value in the completed life of the historical Jesus in the light of the Old Testament.

If this is historically correct, it means that the original movement or development of faith seems in fact to have been the reverse of that which Cupitt proposes as the paradigm of the structure of primitive resurrection belief, when he says that first the apostles came to faith in Jesus as the Messiah as they reflected on his life and death and that this was later externalized in visionary experiences of the alleged, heavenly exalted Lord.

On top of all this there is the persistent fact that the Easter kerygma unanimously traces the origin of the early faith and mission back to the appearances in the period after the crucifixion: that is to say, to some kind of post-mortem event in the experience of the primitive disciples. The pattern of the primitive 'coming to faith' proposed by Cupitt does not therefore tally with the historical evidence.

In any event, it must be admitted that it is not for historical reasons that Cupitt comes to his conclusion but for logical ones, so let us now look at his logical objections to the Event Theory.

Logical Objections to the Event Theory

One reason why Cupitt favours his Theological Theory of the resurrection and dismisses the Event Theory is that he insists that, in religious experience, concepts are prior to experience; one must have the concepts *before* one can have the experience. Because a religious experience does not come bearing its own label, 'it is structured, made intelligible, given objectivity by the projection into it of concepts which the experient already has'.[54] Here Cupitt is presupposing a fundamentally Kantian-type epistemology of a two-stem variety in which a distinction is drawn between concepts on the one hand and experiences or intuitions on the other. Kant held that without the concepts with which the raw deliverances of sense are interpreted, intuitions are blind. Concepts, on the other hand, without intuitions that correspond to them, on to which they map or to which they apply, are empty.[55] In any cognitive experience in which a claim is made to know a given object, it seems that the having of a relevant concept is a logically prior factor. When Cupitt declares, therefore, that one must possess a set of relevant concepts before one can have a religious experience, he is working with the very acceptable Kantian principle that interpretative concepts structure experience so that it becomes intelligible. However, there is a certain uncharacteristic looseness in Cupitt's talk at this crucial point. It is possible to introduce a little more precision into the discussion by distinguishing between bare experience on the one hand, and knowledge or cognitive experience on the other. One can have an experience of something without knowing it or claiming to know it. Men had the experience of breathing oxygen long before they claimed to know it. When they finally arrived at the concept 'oxygen', they could order their bare experience in such a way as to be able to claim to know that they breathed 'oxygen'. Consequently, we can agree that the having of concepts is prior to experience only if by 'experience' we mean cognitive experience. Concepts are prior in the sense that one must have the concept before one can know or claim to know what one's experience is an experience of. So when Cupitt says that in religious experience 'concepts are prior to experience' we are to understand him to mean by 'religious experience' that it includes some kind of claim to religious knowledge. Concepts are prior to cognitive experience, for we need concepts to order and interpret the bare experience and thus arrive at knowledge. Now, this is perfectly correct; we can agree that one has to have concepts before one can have the experience of knowing.

---

[54] *Explorations in Theology*, 6, p. 39. See R. W. Macan, *The Resurrection of Jesus Christ*, p. 111: 'They interpreted the facts of their experience by the doctrines already in their mind . . .'.

[55] I. Kant, *Critique of Pure Reason*, A15/B29: 'There are two stems of human knowledge, namely, *sensibility* and *understanding* . . . Through the former, objects are given to us; through the latter, they are thought.'

However, Cupitt argues, on the basis of this, that Easter belief is logically prior to Easter experiences and that faith is prior to vision: 'So far from the Easter Event creating the Easter faith as is commonly said, it was rather the Easter faith which made the Easter Event possible', he says.[56] Indeed, he even argues that if there were experiences such as visions they are logically superfluous and faith must be not only prior to but independent of them. In the Moule/Cupitt correspondence on this subject this is reaffirmed: 'the interpretative work precedes the vision'.[57] But on the contrary, while we admit that concepts are needed in order to interpret experience, the having of concepts is quite a different thing from believing, or coming to faith. For example, suppose I am a zoologist. I have the concept of a yeti, the abominable snowman. I do not yet believe in the existence of yetis, or know if there are yetis or not, but I have a rough idea, pieced together from a number of garbled accounts, of what a yeti might be like. In other words I do not believe but I have the bare concept. I have heard that the alleged yeti is more like a monkey than a crocodile, more like a man with big feet than an elephant. I have also heard reports of what might have been a large, empty footprint or two, allegedly left by a yeti in the snow. All this is enough to give me a vague set of criteria for the use of the term 'Yeti'—not a precise dictionary definition admittedly, but sufficient to give me a vague inkling into what a yeti might be. But if I were walking in the foothills of Mount Everest and suddenly saw in front of me a certain kind of object lumbering about, I might say: 'Ah, that is what they were trying to talk about! This must be a yeti'. I might now claim to know that there are yetis after all and dash back to civilization to try and convince everybody with kerygmatic zeal. But I do not have to believe that there are yetis before I am able to recognize one. Certainly, I do not have to believe with all my heart, and all my mind and all my strength, before the experience; all I need is the concept and a vague set of criteria for its use when the appropriate moment comes. But Cupitt moves from the necessity of *having concepts* prior to cognitive experience to the necessity of the occurrence of *belief* prior to experience and argues that therefore Easter faith preceded any Easter experience. Indeed, Cupitt promiscuously slides from 'having faith' to 'having concepts' and vice

[56] *Christ and the Hiddenness of God*, p. 164.
[57] *Explorations in Theology*, 6, p. 34.

versa. Note, for instance, the following passage: 'Now the birth of the Easter *faith* was, whatever else it was, a religious experience. And in religious experience *concepts* are prior to the experience. You can't have the experience until you have the *concepts* through which it is to be apprehended and understood. So I say the Easter *belief* is prior to the Easter experiences, which express it' [my italics].[58]

This confusion of Cupitt's repeats an identical error made by R. W. Macan in 1877. Macan argued against Westcott's belief that faith and dogma were based on historical facts by contending that dogma was presupposed in any assertion of the occurrence of the event. The dogma interpreted the raw deliverances of sense, and must logically be prior. He therefore concluded that resurrection dogma is prior to the assertion of the occurrence of the resurrection as an event. Today the fact of the dependence of the judgement of faith on the prior existence of apocalyptic beliefs in a future resurrection, which incorporated the concept of the resurrection of the dead as a logical possibility, and which were employed by the disciples to interpret primitive Easter experiences is of course readily admitted.[59] But to entertain the possibility of a general bodily resurrection, not yet as a dogma but as a hypothesis, or just to entertain the bare religious concept as a logical possibility, which is subsequently used to interpret experience, and so to affirm the resurrection in the specific case of Jesus is one thing; it is quite another matter to argue that belief in the dogma of *the resurrection of Jesus* is utterly prior to any post-mortem experiences the disciples may have had.

When Cupitt says that faith is prior to experience he also means not just (confusedly) that concepts are needed prior to experiences in order to interpret them so that we may arrive at knowledge, but also that faith is prior to vision. He is inclined to assume here that visions are subjective visions of the kind that faith might itself generate. Thus he points out that it is no coincidence that Roman Catholic Christians have visions of Mary, and Buddhists have visions of the Buddha, and not the other way around. In the case of

---

[58] *Explorations in Theology*, 6, p. 29.
[59] See R. W. Macan, *The Resurrection of Jesus Christ*, pp. 10 ff. We have already observed Pannenberg and Marxsen's acceptance of the need of a pre-existing apocalyptic belief in resurrection in order to interpret the experiences as evidence for the resurrection of Jesus in the tomb, see pp. 92–3 above.

the Immaculate Conception, 'Bernadette's vision in the Grotto at Lourdes crystallised and expressed beliefs she already entertained . . .'[60] It is for this reason that he holds that the visions are to be regarded as 'gratuities or bonuses',[61] a contingent by-product of the believing which is not *necessary* in itself to the structure of faith. From this Cupitt argues that if there were experiences such as visions of the raised Jesus in the days after Easter they are logically superfluous to faith which must be not only prior to but independent of them.

It would be true that Easter faith is prior to visions if the appearances could definitely be said to be subjective visions after the manner of Strauss's explanation. But we cannot assume precisely what needs to be proved. Nor can we assume that the logical principle that 'concepts are prior to faith' means that 'belief is prior to experience' and that therefore it is entailed that the experiences of Easter were visions produced by a prior faith. This confusion is also already found in the work of Macan. He argued that 'in order to be assured that the Resurrection is a fact we must have, it seems, a body of doctrines already held for true in our minds.'[62] In the course of his argument on the way to this conclusion he points out that Joan of Arc's vision of St Michael is a product of her pre-existing beliefs, not vice versa, that the vision grounded her belief in the existence of St Michael.[63]

But it is precisely at this point that it is absolutely vital to distinguish between believing on the one hand and the having of a concept on the other. One might have a concept of St Michael, but still actually doubt, rather than believe in the existence of a heavenly being answering to that name, until such a belief was precipitated by some kind of experience. The concept of St Michael is logically prior to a cognitive experience in which it might be claimed that St Michael was known by acquaintance. But only *after* an actual experience might one come to believe, rightly or wrongly, that there is in truth a reality to which the concept applies. It is quite another thing to contend that the acceptance of the truth of the belief is necessary prior to *any* experience. All that is needed is the formulation of a belief or concept, that remains entirely hypothetical and

---

[60] *Explorations in Theology*, 6, p. 29.
[61] Ibid., p. 35.
[62] *The Resurrection of Jesus Christ*, p. 111.
[63] Ibid., p. 97.

empty, but which might be said to be confirmed or 'filled' precisely as the result of an experience. It is not necessary to presuppose 'a body of doctrines *already held to be true*' but a set of concepts or doctrines whose corresponding referent in reality needs to be demonstrated.

The importance of distinguishing between having faith, in the sense of believing something to be true, and having a concept, becomes clear also when it is observed that, whilst faith may certainly generate visions, as was almost certainly so in the case of Joan of Arc and Bernadette, it is not equally true that concepts generate that to which they refer and which they are designed to interpret.

To have a concept such as 'presence of Christ' or at least just the proper name 'Christ' and some criteria of correct use may be a necessary presupposition of any claim to identify an experienced reality as 'the presence of the Raised Christ' just as the concept 'table' and linguistic rules for its use is a necessary prerequisite of identifying an object as a table. But it is not necessarily the case that the having of the concept or proper name produces or generates an illusory vision of Christ any more than the possession of a concept 'table' necessarily generates visionary tables. This logical point of Cupitt's about concepts being prior to experience, which is perfectly valid, leaves the question of whether believers encountered and identified the appearance of the raised Christ or saw an illusory vision, which was generated by an existing belief, completely open. Either way concepts would have been required to interpret experience.

The Datum of Faith

This leads me to the next point: when Cupitt treats the Event Theories of the resurrection he treats the alleged resurrection event, the appearances of Jesus on which faith is based, as *past*. One of his major objections is that the historian seeks to establish it and that this is impossible because this alleged event is by definition a suprahistorical or transcendent event. It is therefore said to be beyond the competence of the scientific historian to handle it. This I do not necessarily dispute for it seems necessary to have faith in God before one can begin to assert the occurrence of the resurrection as an act of God. But perhaps we can think of the Easter event which grounds faith in another way. Perhaps we should be prepared to think of it, not in terms of an isolated set of appearances of the past to which a historian might seek to gain access, and which he cannot get at precisely because the only tools available to him are inadequate to handle it, and the methodological presuppositions already debar him from judging with respect to it, but as a long, continuing event which is still with us, and which offers itself for belief in the present. After all, if Jesus has been raised in some sense, he is present with us 'to the end of the ages' as Matthew says, or, as Hebrews 13: 8 has it 'Jesus Christ is the same, yesterday, and today, yea and for ever'. This would mean that the Easter event is not the kind of event to which people can have access *only* as professional *historians*. Rather, if the raised Christ fulfils the promise to be with his people 'to the end of the ages' and if his presence is experienced in the present, then the continuing revelatory event is an event of the present to which believers even today have access. In this case, the event to which faith is a response is not an utterly strange, unique event of the past that we cannot begin to handle as a historical event because of a methodological presupposition of the discipline which is inimical to divine interventions and which we cannot even now understand because we have no present experience with which to compare it; rather it is possible that the claim of Easter faith is that we are involved with a revelatory event which continues into the *present* and to which we have access in the first instance not by historical research but by faith understood as a present cognition, a kind of knowing by acquaintance. In other words, I am suggesting that it is at least thinkable that in the judgement of faith what is brought under a concept, or more correctly what is brought under the proper name 'Jesus' or 'Christ', and thus apprehended in religious knowledge and identified as the presence of Jesus, is a *present* object of *present* experience, the *Christus praesens*. This means that it is thinkable that the contemporary faith of Christian believers may be understood to have essentially the same structure as that of primitive Christians. Irrespective of the question of specific temporal location, faith is always primarily for the believer a response to a present reality, rather than a response of propositional assent based upon historical evidence relating to a past time. If visions of the heavenly, exalted Jesus were claimed by people in the past, that may offer itself for historical assessment and it must be admitted that the modern scientific historian, using his canons of scientific research, may find himself at a loss as to what to make of it all. But the testimony of alleged visionary occurrences of the mid-first century may not constitute the sole evidence which lays claim to be regarded as the experiential anchor or datum of resurrection belief.

By the same token historical research is not the sole, or even the primary, means of apprehending the empirical ground of faith. The presence of Christ which offers itself for perception in faith is not the preserve of historians precisely because it is a reality of the present, and as such available for all who have 'eyes to see'. For this reason, as we shall see in the next chapter, it is important to distinguish the primitive claims to see heavenly visions of the raised Christ and contemporary claims to perceive the presence of the raised Christ. This delivers us from the difficulty of having to assess the reports of heavenly visions in the past and come to a fixed conclusion with tools ill-suited to handling them, and which may in fact positively exclude divine interventions such as the resurrection from the outset.

Whether a coherent account of faith as the present perception of the presence of the raised Christ can be formulated remains yet to be seen. But, for the moment, it is sufficient to make the point that if this is essentially what resurrection faith is, the interpreting of a present religious object as the presence of Jesus, and if faith is based on the perception of a reality in the present, then faith would not just be as in Cupitt's Theological Theory a matter of the making of a theological judgement only about the life of Jesus from his birth to death. The historical life of Jesus would not be the sole datum for faith. The datum for faith would be, in relation to the life and death of Jesus, a post-mortem occurrence, making possible a post-crucifixion experience of the present. This means that we are now conceiving of faith and its structure in a way that broadly fits into Cupitt's Event Theory, for faith is a response to an objective happening or event. Whether the judgement is correct or whether we are mistaken or not is another matter. But it also has something in common with his Theological Theory, because it involves interpreting experience with a pre-existing set of interpretative categories. In this case a person is able to learn, through acquaintance with the Christian community, how to use such concepts as 'God' and 'divine presence' and then not only is he able to bring them to bear in faith on the data of the completed life of Jesus, but he may use them in faith to interpret a religious object of his own present experience. Indeed, it is possible to interpret present experience, not only with concepts deriving from the Old Testament such as 'God' and 'divine presence' but with refinements of those concepts deriving from the fact of the historical Jesus as interpreted to us through the insight of the New Testament writers. In other words, it is possible to think that the mechanism by which a person comes to faith is not just a matter of bringing concepts from the Old Testament to bear on the completed life of Jesus, but also a matter of bringing interpretative concepts to bear on an object of our *own* experience. In this case the datum for faith would be, not just the completed life of Jesus, as in Cupitt's Theological Theory, and as in the theology also of Strauss, but a religious object of present experience. The experience of this, in relation to the completed life of Jesus, is a post-mortem occurrence, and therefore falls into Cupitt's broad category of an Event Theory, but like Cupitt's Theological Theory, it involves interpreting an object of experience with the help of theological concepts deriving from Scripture. In other words, though Cupitt urges that theologians must choose between a strict Event Theory and a strict Theological Theory, I wish to suggest that it may be possible to hold a combination of both. In this case, the interpreting of the completed life of Jesus in a theological way is not an absolute alternative to interpreting an object of present religious experience in a theological way in the light of concepts derived from the Old and New Testaments. Cupitt's concentration on *either* a Theological Theory *or* an Event Theory as mutually exclusive is unnecessarily arbitrary and should not be maintained.

It is possible that Cupitt himself has a suspicion that he has overdrawn the distinction between Event Theory and Theological Theory because at one place he says: 'an Event Theory of the Resurrection cannot *by itself* explain the meaning of and justify Christological beliefs'.[64] Can this mean that some kind of experience of an event after Good Friday, plus theological interpretation, might constitute the basic ingredients of resurrection faith?

This is the first small crack in Cupitt's theological edifice that I wish to widen into a breach. The second small crack appears in the Cupitt/Moule correspondence to which I have already referred. There it is possible to detect a movement in Cupitt's thought, perhaps under the pressure of Professor Moule's insistence that interpreting the completed life of Jesus in the light of the Old Testament would not be enough to precipitate the faith that he was the Messiah

---

[64] *Christ and the Hiddenness of God*, p. 164. My italics.

of God. There Cupitt says, significantly, that faith is arrived at "by theological *and existential* reflection' upon the completed life of Jesus. Or again, Cupitt says that we look at 'the whole picture of the nature of God which the Bible gives us, *and the testimony of our hearts and our own life-situation*'.[65] Faith, it seems, is no longer just a matter of interpreting the completed life of Jesus with the aid of concepts from the Old Testament; our own existential situation in life is also relevant.

Now this comes perilously close to admitting the significance of a post-mortem experience, in the sense of an experience of the present, into the epistemological pattern of faith. For it is at least possible to think that in one's life-situation, perhaps as I shall suggest in future chapters, in the Christian community, one might apprehend what seems to be appropriately described, not only with the help of Old Testament notions of God, as 'the presence of God', but, on the other hand, also an objective reality of the present which seems appropriately described as the 'presence of Jesus' and come to the conviction that the remembered Jesus is present still. Faith would then be not just a matter of making a theological judgement about the completed life of Jesus, but also about a religious object of present experience known in the continuing life of the Christian community. On the basis of such an experience a person might go on to use theological language to affirm that Jesus has been exalted to the right hand of God, and that he is not dormant there, but makes himself known to his people. In this event, what is apprehended and understood in faith in the present then allows us to understand the faith of the first Christians for we can understand their experience on analogy with our own. We can understand that their belief that Jesus had gone to be with God in heaven was also based on a perception of his presence with them after the crucifixion, a post-mortem event.

But now, of course, I have outlined an approach to faith which bristles with problems and which Cupitt would argue falls under the judgement that he has made against Vision theories, that they are too vague to be helpful. For considerable numbers of questions now call for answers: How is it possible for us to recognize a presence as the presence of God? How is it also possible for us to recognize this presence as the presence of *Jesus*? What are the criteria for

---

[65] *Explorations in Theology*. 6, p. 29–30. My italics.

making this identity judgement? And so on. But these are issues which will occupy our attention in the next and subsequent chapters. What I have tried to do in this chapter is to clear the way for an understanding of faith in which something more is involved than an intellectual seeing of a past, historical Jesus as the Messiah. I have sought to clear the way for an understanding of faith which is based on something more than the datum of the completed life and death of Jesus, interpreted with the aid of concepts from the Old Testament. Furthermore, I have endeavoured to outline the possibility of a model approach to faith in which some kind of Easter experience *after the death of Jesus* and continuing into the present also plays a foundational role. The New Testament itself speaks of this in terms of the perception of the continuing presence of Christ. We must therefore devote attention to the more detailed study of this element in the Easter traditions, the appearances of Jesus, and tokens of his continuing presence, and the means of its appropriation in human consciousness.

V

The Raised Christ: Glorified but Disappearing

The Elusiveness of the Easter Reality

IF, as I suggested in the last chapter, Easter faith is understood not just as a judgement about an event which may be said to have occurred in the past, but as a judgement about a reality of present experience, then we must now begin to concentrate on the more detailed configuration of that present experience.

Here we immediately come face to face with the difficulty that, in resurrection faith, the object of the present experience of the believer is understood to be a heavenly, glorified, or exalted and therefore other-worldly Christ. By definition, therefore, that with which we have to do is to be understood as a transcendent and somewhat elusive reality, which will defy our feeble human attempts to express it in words: we cannot expect to be able to describe the Easter mystery satisfactorily in the purely prosaic language of this world. Talk of the perception of the presence of the exalted and heavenly reality of the raised Christ, in other words, generates a particular set of epistemological problems. If the raised and glorified Christ appears 'from heaven', as it were, then we are faced with the problem of expressing something of the distinctive nature of what is revealed. In addition, we must attempt to express something of the structure of the human knowing that is appropriate to it. Apart from seeking to describe something of the unique character of what is experienced we must attend to the epistemological question of how it may justifiably be known and identified as the new presence or appearance in our midst of Jesus of Nazareth.

A discussion of this matter has become particularly important in view of the fact that there has been a tendency in twentieth-century theology to appeal to a present-day experience of the presence of the raised and glorified Christ in order to make up the deficit of a purely historical approach of the kind we examined in Chapter II.

In other words, the sneaking awareness that there is not sufficient evidence to prove the occurrence of the resurrection as an event of the past has led a number of theologians, from Westcott onwards, to affirm that real conviction about the resurrection of Jesus comes from a present encouter with his glorified presence. For example, in the course of his Bampton Lectures, *God as Spirit*, in 1976 Geoffrey Lampe pointed out that 'preachers at Easter often tell their congregations that the real evidence for our belief that Jesus did truly rise from the dead is their present experience of his living presence'.[1] However, without an epistemology of faith, it is hard to see how such claims are to be justified. If a present experience convinces believers that 'Jesus is alive today', then what precisely is the nature of this experience and how is what is known identified as the 'presence of Jesus' alive today? In Easter faith a cognition is regularly claimed but rarely explained.

If this is so, the need for faith to give an account of itself by articulating an epistemology of the present experience of knowing the raised Christ is very urgent. Unfortunately, contemporary theologians have shown themselves to be ill-equipped to perform this task. Most attempts to appeal to the believer's present experience of the raised Christ, in order to clarify and validate the historical account of the first appearances, have run into the difficulty that the raised Christ tends to become so elusive as to recede from view and all but disappear.

Resurrection theology in the twentieth century is not distinguished by its capacity to express what it means by a present experience of the glorified Christ, nor has it explained the structure of the apprehension of his presence. One reason for this is that the over-arching impact of Barth and Bultmann on twentieth-century theology has acted as a discouragement to theologians even to try to articulate the outlines of faith in the raised Christ. Their lack of interest in reason had led to a fideism which does not feel obliged to give an account of itself in the public arena. British philosophical theology of the post-war period, on the other hand, has concentrated its attention on the claim of religious language to refer to and describe God and on the question of the knowledge of God; but the question of the presence of the raised Christ and how the Easter reality may be perceived and identified has by and large been ignored.

---

[1] G. W. H. Lampe, *God as Spirit*, p. 150.

However, if the Easter event is understood, from the perspective of those who came to an awareness of it in time, as a long, continuing event, which began three days after Jesus' death and which is still available to us today, and if we claim a knowledge of the raised Christ in time, we should be able to give some account of the faith that is in us. It should at least be possible to go some way towards expressing what we mean when we speak of the experience of the raised Christ, even if we admit that our finite and limited human understanding must fall short of an exact description. On the other hand, if the object of our present experience is the same exalted and glorified Christ whose eternal presence was also apprehended in faith by the first generation of Christians, then our first approach to this matter may be through an examination of the meaning and appropriateness of the language to which the first Christians themselves resorted in their attempts to express at least something of their experience. This will take us back to a historical study of the nature of the primitive Easter experience.

This is not to say we shall be concerned, in the manner of Westcott and Pannenberg, to try to prove the occurrence of the resurrection as an event of the past. We shall in the first instance need to attend to the meaning of what was said and to the coherence of it, and only then broach the question of truth. We shall also need to be aware of the pitfalls which confront those who seek to approach the understanding of the resurrection through the use of the historical model. In Chapter II we noted that the attempt to handle the resurrection as though it were a historical event, whose occurrence may be rationally demonstrated from the available evidence so that faith in Jesus as the Christ of God might then be built upon it, fails for want of adequate evidence. But, even worse, not only have the considerable efforts of theologians failed to prove the occurrence of the resurrection historically; the very methodological commitment to scientific historiography tends to lead in the direction of a fundamental misunderstanding of the very nature of the Easter event. Such methods tend inevitably to reduce the resurrection to the proportions of a mundane restoration or bodily resuscitation of Jesus to life in this world by suggesting that it enjoys a generic similarity with any other occurrence of human history. Such approaches tend to make for a misunderstanding of the resurrection that renders it theologically useless by naturalizing it. We have also already noted that, in addition to the theological shortfall of this naturalistic outcome, such approaches to the understanding of the resurrection of Christ are vulnerable to historical criticism in so far as they rely too heavily on what appear to be later strata of the New Testament evidence, particularly in the gospels of Luke and John, whose distinctive characteristics can now be explained as developments of the earlier traditions under the pressure of apologetic concerns. At the same time, they tend to ignore the identification of the resurrection and exaltation of Jesus that is found in what seems to be the earlier strata of the New Testament evidence. This underlines the necessity of taking the transformation and glorification of Jesus more seriously as an original element in any reconstruction of what occurred.

In addition, we have already observed that it was precisely a sensitivity to the eschatological dimensions of the resurrection of Christ that led Barth and Bultmann to the view that the historical method has to be abandoned entirely. In their inclination to see things in terms of black and white, they faced the question of whether the historical method should or should not have a place in the structure of Easter faith. It was a matter of either/or. In their violent reaction to what they saw as the futility and positively harmful consequences of approaching the resurrection historically, Barth and Bultmann therefore attempted to articulate understandings of faith which were entirely independent of critical-historical research. The difficulty that we found here was that, though they sought to do justice to the biblical emphasis on the eschatological nature of the resurrection of Christ as a revelatory deed of God with a soteriological purpose, their methodological commitment left the understanding of the nature of the object of faith quite unclear. The essential outlines or qualities of the object with which primitive faith claimed to have to do is left undefined—deliberately by Bultmann, tacitly by Barth. Admittedly, this was in the interests of doing justice to the utterly unique and transcendent nature of the Easter event. However, Barth and Bultmann come to diametrically opposed views of what they themselves understand faith to be all about, so that one of them argues that it is illegitimate to engage in language that asserts that faith is about anything, whilst the other insists that it is about something, even if we know not what it is in detail, and cannot clarify its nature historiographically. We can only rely on the Holy Spirit to make it as clear as it need be in order to provide the ground of faith in our own resurrection.

In view of the elusiveness of the Easter experience at this point, we must now raise the question of whether a more sympathetic disposition towards historical research might not lead at least to some understanding of what it was that the first Christians claimed to have experienced or encountered after the crucifixion of Jesus, and which was said to have led them to affirm that Jesus had been raised. It is agreed that we cannot just assume that what is to be proved historically is the resurrection, pictured more or less as Luke and John portray it, in very concrete and material or naturalistic terms. Likewise it cannot just be assumed that the resurrection was a historical event that could have been observed by anybody who chanced to be there. It is also agreed that the attempt to prove the occurrence of the resurrection by historical methods fails. But, on the other hand, the classical alternative which attempts to handle the resurrection as a transcendent, revelatory event disclosed to specific individuals by God, leaves the nature of the experience elusive and unclear. Given that the early Christians sought to bear witness to a phenomenon of their own experience, it should be possible, however, to come to some historical understanding of what it was that they understood their experience to be an experience of. Even if we cannot prove the occurrence of the resurrection historically, and given that it may be illegitimate to work with a picture of the event primarily conditioned and indeed governed by the graphic imagery of Luke and John, a historical study of the traditions may nevertheless lead us to a clearer picture of the primitive Easter experience. This is the case even if the reality with which the early Christians believed they had to do is understood to have been heavenly and exalted.

Most historical approaches to the resurrection tend to assume that what the resurrection was alleged to be is perfectly clear; the main historical task is to demonstrate whether it occurred or not. Thus, Geoffrey Lampe acknowledges that the historian can investigate the historical evidence for the resurrection as an occurrence of the past and 'pronounce upon the probability or otherwise' that it did in fact occur.[2] Alan Richardson, on the other hand, is quite as definite as Pannenberg in arguing that the resurrection is a historical question, and one which involves the assessment of historical evidence, in order to determine 'whether in fact, Christ rose from the dead'.[3] Both these statements assume that what the resurrection *was*

---

[2] G. W. H. Lampe, *The Resurrection*, p. 33.
[3] A. Richardson, *History Sacred and Profane*, p. 195.

is already known and that the historian's chief task is to determine the question of truth. But this is to tackle the question of truth far too prematurely. Before that issue is broached there is the prior question of meaning to be resolved. When the primitive Christians claimed to have encountered the raised Christ, what exactly did they *mean*? This can only be discovered by a historical-critical analysis of the primitive testimony. What is called for, at least in the first instance, is a phenomenological approach to Easter faith for the purpose of clarifying our understanding, rather than one obsessed by the apologetic concern to verify what was claimed. Even if we agree with Barth and Bultmann that the occurrence of the resurrection cannot be proved by historical-critical methods, in so far as the evidence of the empty tomb and the alleged appearances is inconclusive, we must nevertheless do what both Barth and Bultmann in different ways refuse to do: by employing the historical method we must seek to discern the outlines of the primitive Easter experience including some understanding of the nature of the reality with which faith claimed an acquaintance. Even if we take note of theological questions and acknowledge that a descriptive account of the experience of the raised Christ as a heavenly, exalted reality has to contend with the unavoidable indeterminacy of all religious discourse about the transcendent, we may nevertheless discern something of the broad contours of the claimed object of the primitive Easter experience.

Those who are confident in their affirmation that the resurrected Christ is certainly *not* just a Christ revived and restored to the conditions of the mundane and who could be seen by just anyone, rarely, if ever, balance these negative affirmations by making an attempt to say what they understand the apprehension of the presence of the raised and glorified Christ in faith to be and to have been like. Indeed, in twentieth-century theology this has become a particularly persistent weakness. Don Cupitt is right when he says that as soon as a very prosaic and mundane description of a restored Jesus is abandoned in favour of what he calls a Psi or vision theory of the resurrection, the nature of the object of faith becomes so elusive that historical criticism cannot even begin to demonstrate that it occurred because it is not remotely clear what it is that is being claimed. For whilst the later gospel narratives of the Easter appearances are now regularly set aside as somewhat untrustworthy developments of the tradition, designed to serve a theological and apologetic purpose, very little positive attempt is made to affirm the actual contours of the original Easter experience or to articulate an epistemology of faith designed to explain how the object of the Easter experience was humanly received and appropriated.

It is certainly not enough just to follow the *via negativa* by denying the literalness of the concrete images found in the narratives of Luke and John. The negation of images goes some way towards communicating what is meant specifically by the resurrection of Christ as distinct from the mere resuscitation of a corpse or the restoration of Jesus to life in this world. But it does not really help us to visualize the outlines of the heavenly and transcendent Christ whose presence is said to have been revealed and in faith perceived. Without some understanding of what the earliest witnesses to the resurrection seem to have meant by their talk of encounter with the raised Christ, we are plunged into a thick and unrelenting fog in which the nature of the raised Christ all but entirely disappears from view.

We thus inherit a situation in which we can point to some clearly urgent questions concerning the faith in the 'presence of Christ'. Leslie Houlden has noted, for example, that in resurrection theology talk of Christ's living presence functions chiefly to bridge the gap between the origins of Christianity and the continuing story of Christian life. But he very pertinently raises the epistemologically crucial question: 'how can a person of later times identify his experience as experience of Christ?'[4] It is precisely because of the obscurity of Christian theology at this very point that Houlden raises the question of whether resurrection theology is capable of clarifying contemporary christological difficulties.[5] An examination of some representative twentieth-century theologians who have appealed to the experience of the glorified Christ, will alert us to the difficulties they have encountered and bring us an appreciation of what is theologically wanting.

---

[4] See Leslie Houlden's remarks in 'A Wider Framework' in *Incarnation and Myth*, p. 107.
[5] Alan Bill typifies the current confusion of modern theology in this regard when he says that he does not think he has ever had an experience, spiritual or otherwise, which could be described as a sense of Jesus present and alive. Indeed, he confesses that he finds it hard to envisage what kind of experience is meant and pleads for elucidation of his perplexity: *Theology*, Vol. lxxx (1977), p. 206. One wonders how many other contemporary Christians find themselves in the same difficulty.

Édouard Le Roy

In the first decade of this century, this problem was felt very acutely with respect to the understanding of the resurrection articulated by the French Roman Catholic modernist, Édouard Le Roy. In his work *Dogme et critique* in 1907, Le Roy rejected the straightforwardly materialistic presentation of the Easter event that is derived from an uncritical reading of the gospel narratives, but his failure to fill the empty place left once he dispensed with concrete images quickly led him into ecclesiastical difficulties, as a result of which his book was almost immediately placed on the Index. This does not, of course, diminish the pertinence of the questions that Le Roy raised, nor indeed shake his own ultimate grasp of the truth. Le Roy did not intend to cast doubts on the basic Christian affirmation that after death Jesus 'came back to life',[6] but he was critical of forms of representation of the raised Christ which suggested a reanimation of the dead body in the manner of a second Lazarus.[7] He doubted that a transcendent fact could be subject to conditions that belong exclusively to this world,[8] and saw clearly that the tendency to picture the raised Christ in this way was not just an error of popular religion but the inevitable consequence of the more technical theological quest to treat the resurrection simply as a historical event. The earnest desire to portray the resurrection as a physically observable fact was a product, he believed, of anxiety, lest the resurrection should dissolve into what we would call today myth. Le Roy perceived that the quest for positive historical findings was an understandable but vain attempt to provide an irrefutable basis for apologetics,[9] but the irony was that these very apologetical interests led to a complete falsification and misunderstanding of the concept of the resurrection of Christ. The raised and exalted Christ, he believed, could not be observed in the manner that is normal and appropriate to realities of the physical order alone. If that was so, then how can the historian move in to attempt to prove the occurrence of the resurrection as though it were an event that, like any other historical event, was observed by witnesses?

Le Roy was here putting his finger on a very important point, for which he believed he could claim the support of St Thomas Aquinas

[6] *Dogme et critique*, p. 18.
[7] Ibid., p. 161.
[8] Ibid., p. 171.
[9] Ibid., p. 173.

himself, no less than the biblical testimony.[10] Unhappily, Le Roy nevertheless fell foul of the Roman Catholic magisterium in so far as his own alternative theology seemed, in a manner that anticipated aspects of the more recent work of Bultmann, to dispense with the objectivity and reality of the raised Christ. Having consigned the concrete visual images of the appearances of the raised Christ to oblivion it seemed not only to leave a conceptual vacuum but also that Le Roy had dispensed with the raised Christ altogether.

In fact Le Roy was motivated by a desire to do justice to the transcendent and mysterious dimension of the reality of the raised Christ. The purpose of his book was to establish that dogma cannot be a simple proclamation of truth which ties the intelligence to a determined content of faith—*the* faith specified in a set of fixed formulas. Rather, in a manner congenial to Anglicans acquainted with Mansel's theory of the regulative but non-informative character of theological statements and of the limits of religious knowledge, Le Roy argued that the Christian religion was basically a way of life, a code of behaviour, expressed in terms of a mystery which goes beyond and even contradicts all the theories built upon it. Thus, anybody who seeks to put the resurrection experience into words engages in a very risky business, for regardless of how apt a particular dogmatic statement may seem and however useful to religious living and behaviour it may be, it will nevertheless remain 'pure theory'. Though religiously necessary and practically useful it must be understood to be interpretative of a content that remains strictly inexpressible.[11]

While Le Roy did not intend to cast doubt on the transcendent fact that Jesus had passed through death to a form of heavenly life, he was doubtful, given the mysteriousness of the new state into which Jesus was said to have entered, that any form of representation could be adequate to it. Some popular forms of thought, particularly those which suggested an understanding in terms of a re-animation of a dead body, appeared to him to be particularly inadequate, if not entirely inappropriate and misleading: 'Why should the Resurrection, which is a transcendent fact, be subject to conditions that belong to the physical order?'[12] The occurrence of the resurrection cannot be known in the way that 'the existence of

[10] See *Summa Theologiae*, 3a, Q. 55, art. 5.
[11] *Dogme et critique*, pp. 225–57.
[12] Ibid., p. 171.

Alexander or Caesar can be known', because it is a transcendent affair that cannot be apprehended outside of faith.[13] But precisely what is apprehended *in faith* is not too clear, for Le Roy tended to steer away not only from talk of a physical revival, but of all talk of faith based upon 'appearances'. This unfortunately left Le Roy open to charges of the kind that have since been levelled at Bultmann, that the 'objective' import of Christian speech is annihilated, thus reducing the Easter event to nothing but the fact of the disciples' faith.

It is understandable from the following quotation how it was possible for his critics to construe his meaning in this sense:

There are plenty of reasons for holding that no particular observed event occurred on the morning of the third day . . . What that Easter day was from the phenomenal point of view is something which is today undefinable historically and moreover, as we have seen, physically unimaginable also. We are obliged, therefore, to fall back on a pragmatic interpretation. The Easter date relates less to truth in itself than to the practical reflection of that truth in man. It is a date that relates to the history of mankind's religious attitudes and approaches.[14]

Whilst this kind of statement led both his critics at the time and his more recent interpreters to the conclusion that Le Roy had reduced Easter to a coming to faith on the part of the disciples,[15] and that 'Easter is therefore a date which primarily concerns the Church and its faith and not primarily Christ in his being',[16] it almost certainly misunderstands Le Roy's intention. Even though he denied that the resurrection could be approached by the historian's 'purely rational arguments' or encapsulated in 'purely positive findings' he was anxious also to affirm that 'we must not conclude from the fact that faith recognizes its object, that it creates it'.[17] Indeed, he defined the point of the dogma of the resurrection as a way of affirming that 'the present state of Jesus Christ is such that if the attitude and conduct called for from us are to correspond to its inexpressible reality they must be such as would be appropriate in the case of a contemporary of our own'.[18]

---

[13] Ibid., pp. 178–9, 199.
[14] Ibid., p. 252.
[15] See Lucien Laberthonnière, *Annales de philosophie chrétienne*, Vols. 154 and 155, (1907–8), *Dogme et théologie*, especially Vol. 154, p. 580. Also letters to Le Roy by Maurice Blondel, *Lettres philosophiques de Maurice Blondel*, pp. 251–66.
[16] Gustave Martelet, *The Risen Christ and the Eucharistic World*, p. 71.
[17] *Dogme et critique*, p. 225.
[18] Ibid.

Thus, whilst denying that the resurrection may be established by historical research as 'a reason for believing' he affirmed that the raised Christ is the object of faith, the greatest indeed of all objects.[19] However, it is something 'revealed rather than observed' and the gospel is 'rather a witness of faith than an historical writing to be taken as a purely documentary summary of evidence'.[20] As St Thomas Aquinas put it, the fact of the resurrection is 'not so much a proof as a sign' of God's saving activity.[21]

If the resurrection was not a response to the observed, material or even quasi-physical body of Christ outside of the tomb on the third day, but rather a response of faith to some more mysterious and intangible reality which could nevertheless be interpreted as a sign that Christ was alive, so that people could thenceforth live their lives as though Christ were their contemporary, the ability to express some inkling of what it was that was perceived seems to be implied. Some attempted description of it, even if inadequate, and some notion of how it was perceived and recognized as the raised Christ rather than as some other transcendent reality, such as quite simply 'the presence of God', seems to be called for. But Le Roy really does not succeed in making the transition from a denial of a straightforward visual seeing of a material or physically revived Jesus to an epistemology of faith in which he explains even roughly what it was that was experienced and how it was known. This hiatus means that he, like Bultmann after him, was perpetually in jeopardy of being uncomfortably pushed into a reductionist position. As we shall see, the same difficulty has emerged in the more recent work of Edward Schillebeeckx, who, like Le Roy, has had his work scrutinized by the Roman Catholic magisterium and who has also had to face the charge of reductionism.

Westcott and Kirsopp Lake

This particular problem is not peculiar, however, to modern Roman Catholicism, but is a persistent factor in twentieth-century Anglican theology as well. The absence of a clear epistemology of Easter faith also began to appear in British theology of the resurrection at the

---

[19] Ibid., p. 183.
[20] Ibid., p. 190.
[21] Le Roy, ibid., p. 180, quotes Aquinas, *Summa Theologiae*, 3a, Q. 55, art. 5, ad. 2 um.

turn of the century. In England the inconclusiveness of a historical quest to establish the factuality of the early reports of the resurrection began to dawn upon the theological world during the last quarter of the nineteenth century. We have already noted that, despite Westcott's insistence in *The Gospel of the Resurrection* (1866) that, in dealing with the resurrection of Christ, he was dealing with a historical event which could be verified by appeal to the testimony concerning the empty tomb and particularly the appearances, by 1877 he had begun to treat that particular theme a little more cautiously. At the same time he began to stress the uniqueness of the resurrection of Jesus as a 'new relevation' which needed to be differentiated from, rather than assimilated to, the day to day events with which historical research is ordinarily concerned. On the other hand, he began to admit that all that the historian could really hope to achieve was a demonstration of the fact that the disciples had come to faith. 'Historical evidence alone', he said, 'can go no further than this. It cannot do more than establish the reality of the belief in a particular fact.'[22] But as to the character of the particular fact, and the manner of its perception, Westcott had become somewhat reticent. Indeed, he was more clear and positive about what it certainly was not than what it was. As he began to talk of the radical dissimilarity of the resurrection of Christ from 'popular conceptions of a carnal Resurrection' he found himself speaking of the 'mysterious awfulness' which surrounded the perception of the 'new and glorious conditions of life' that the now transcendent Christ enjoyed.[23] Moreover, at the same time Westcott began to talk of the disciples' original perception of the presence of the raised Christ somewhat vaguely; he spoke in terms of Christ's allowing them 'to feel that He was moving locally among them'. This 'feeling' was confirmed by the 'sensible signs' of the appearances which are rather uncritically understood to have taken the form in which they are reported in the gospels. Westcott came to recognize that it is impossible to prove the occurrence of these signs historically but, more importantly, he recognized that properly speaking they do not in any case really form the basis of our conviction of the reality of the living presence of the raised Christ. This, he believed, was established in the contemporary experience of individual Christians, who on the basis of

---

[22] 'The Resurrection of Christ—a New Revelation', p. 1074.
[23] Ibid., p. 1075.

their own present awareness of the raised Christ were then able to accept the reports of the original appearances rather than vice versa. However, the precise meaning of his talk of 'the testimony of the present experience' is rather difficult to pin down and it is here that his lack of an epistemology of faith in the raised Christ becomes particularly obvious. He insists that 'our endeavour must be not to recall the past work of Christ with the most vivid power, but to realize His present union with His Church'.[24] But just how this is to be done remains vague and ill-defined. He speaks of the 'heart stirred by religious affection' so that it 'knows its own wants and directly recognizes Him who can satisfy them'[25] but how this direct recognition of the raised Christ in faith is possible is not explained. Exactly what kind of reality it is understood to be, given that what is 'seen' today is neither a tangible, material body nor even like the original 'sensible signs' of the alleged first objective appearances, is left in the air. Once again the details of the method of apprehension of the presence of Christ now 'throned in glory on the right hand of God' and 'near alike to all His people' is not explained.

Westcott had virtually no epistemology of resurrection faith to which he could resort. Rather, he was obliged to fuse the findings of the historical method with his own sincere conviction and piety which imagined the raised Christ to be somehow present. But pious imagining is no substitute for a systematic theology or epistemology of faith.

Westcott provides us with a classic example of the difficulties experienced by a multitude of subsequent Anglican theologians who, having been trained in the methods of New Testament studies, have then moved into what we would call today 'systematic theology' but with the limited equipment of the historical, linguistic, and analytical methods that are appropriate enough for New Testament studies but inadequate for the construction of a systematic theology of Easter faith. As Westcott began to move ground, from a belief in the historically provable nature of the resurrection as an observable event of the past to the historical investigation of the nature of the primitive faith, he began to see the importance of a present apprehension of the presence of the raised Christ in faith if the ambiguities and fractures in the historical records were to be compensated.

[24] *The Revelation of the Risen Lord*, p. 40.
[25] Ibid., p. 43.

However, he seems to have been at a loss to articulate the outline structure of that faith. He was equally perplexed about the nature of whatever reality it is in the present, upon which faith is based. He found himself confronted by the problem of the elusiveness of the object of Easter faith, but with only the historical method at hand to deal with it. The fact that he had come to speak of a *present* awareness of the raised Christ rendered the historical method inappropriate as a means of coming to a knowledge of it, yet he had no epistemology to explain how it was that the presence of the raised Christ could be perceived and identified.

By the turn of the century the same tensions that developed during the course of Westcott's lifetime may be seen operating in the work of Kirsopp Lake within a single book. In *The Historical Evidence for the Resurrection of Jesus Christ*, Kirsopp Lake emphasized at the start that the Christian religion could be based upon present-day experience of the raised Christ.[26] However, he wished to make it clear that he intended to investigate the facts in order to establish a knowledge of the resurrection as 'an event of past history'.[27] Quoting some enigmatic words of Dean Inge, he pointed out that 'the inner light can only testify to spiritual truths. It always speaks in the present tense; it cannot guarantee any historical event, past or future'. For this reason the correct method for approaching the resurrection of Jesus is said to be 'the method of historical research'.[28] This in turn is understood as being analogous to the methods of the courtroom: the historian is to 'collect pieces of evidence, discuss its trustworthiness and the meaning of each separate piece', and then the final task is 'to reconstruct the events to which the evidence relates'.[29]

All this seems to be clear enough. However, the results of Kirsopp Lake's ensuing critical-historical analysis turn out to be surprisingly negative, so that by the end of the book Kirsopp Lake appeals unequivocally to the testimony of present experience: 'The argument which alone is convincing is the witness of the Spirit given to men as the proof that on one side of their nature they are the "Sons of God" . . . But the Church will not long survive if the day

[26] Pp. 1–2, The same difficulties are addressed also by W. J. Sparrow Simpson, *The Resurrection and Modern Thought*, pp. 429–35; 443–6; 447–57.

[27] Ibid., p. 5–6.

[28] Ibid., p. 15.

[29] Ibid., p. 6.

ever came when she rests her case on either the theological formulation or the witness of other days, and not on testimony which may
be heard in the present.'[30] This conclusion is forced upon him, precisely because he discerns that, even if the bare historicity of the discovery of the empty tomb is established, it is evidence which
'proves nothing'. On the other hand, it is admitted that the appearing of the raised Christ, and the method of its appropriation in
human consciousness amongst the early believers, is not only
utterly hidden from view but unimportant: 'It is impossible to discover, and it is not very important to ask, precisely what kind of
evidence it was which convinced them of this point'. A mysterious
something led the first Christians to affirm that Jesus was alive but it
is not at all clear what that something was. The manner of its perception is equally unclear, though a stab is made at an explanation:
even though Kirsopp Lake is convinced that the New Testament
evidence points to the apprehension of 'a spiritual being' rather than
something 'physical and material', it is said nevertheless, after the
manner of Westcott's account, to be apprehended by the deliverances of sensory experience.[31] Kirsopp Lake then seeks to explain
why a spiritual being should be apprehended through the senses, by
appealing to the idea of the limitations of finite human understanding: 'if we speak of or think of a spiritual, non-material being, the
nearest approach our minds can make to forming an image of what
is meant is really only a very highly attenuated form of physical
existence . . . '.[32] Though a spiritual being, the raised Christ has to
appear to us as though he were physical because the equipment we
have with which to perceive him is our sensory organs; the form in
which the spiritual being of the raised Christ presented itself was
therefore due 'not to its own nature but to that of the disciples'. It
seems that the raised Christ somehow accommodated himself to the
limited capacities of finite mind and sensory perception so that the
disciples were able to apprehend this sign of his presence. This is
said to be 'a very different thing from saying that the being had itself
no objective existence'[33] but the essential character of the alleged
objective being of Christ and the manner of the continuing perception of His presence remains vague.

[30] Ibid., p. 278.
[31] Ibid., p. 265.
[32] Ibid., p. 270.
[33] Ibid.

Clearly, these attempts to do justice to the transcendent nature of the present object of Easter faith leave the matter very imprecise and ill-defined. It is clearly appreciated that at best the historical method can establish that the first disciples did come to faith, but it is equally clear that it cannot get beyond that to prove that what was believed to have occurred did in fact occur. Indeed, precisely what it was that was believed to have occurred is what first needs to be brought into clearer focus.

On the other hand, when this point of the faith of the first disciples is established and then an attempt is made to understand it, justice must be done to the newness of the Easter experience and its unexpected, unique, and transcendent qualities. This means that the theologian must necessarily follow the *via negativa* more confidently than the *via positiva*. Inevitably he becomes more clear about what is to be denied than what is to be affirmed. We are thus led into a dilemma not unlike that which remains in the theology of Karl Barth. We do not seem to be able to say what it is that is known in faith or how it is recognized as the presence of the raised and exalted Jesus Christ. However, whilst Barth insists on the usefulness of all the biblical evidence, including the tradition of the empty tomb and the Johannine and Lucan appearance stories, modern descendants of Westcott and Kirsopp Lake are often prepared to set aside the evidence of the empty tomb and straightforward accounts of the appearances in terms of visual and literally describable phenomena. But without imagery of this kind, what is left? We may agree that it was not just a resuscitated body that was seen, but what was it? If it is asserted that whatever it was, the first Christians believed it was Jesus, we may well ask how? What religious epistemology lies behind this claim and how is such a claim to be justified? Certainly, surprisingly little attention has been paid to the epistemological question of how a transcendent reality might have been known and identified as the presence of Jesus. Without an epistemology of Easter faith, the raised Christ tends to disappear from view.

This problem is still very much with us. Whilst the Anglican Communion, in particular, has been well served by New Testament scholars, systematicians have been few and far between. Thus, as a consequence of the popularity of critical-historical research on the traditions of the New Testament a situation has arisen in which the historical reliability of the very concrete, materializing presentations of the appearances of the raised Jesus, is called into question. This is then set aside as relatively unimportant in view of the fact that faith is said to be grounded in a *present* revelatory experience of the raised Christ. However, few details of what is involved in such an experience are ever given; just how what is apprehended might justifiably be identified as the raised *Jesus* is left undefined. Thus, Geoffrey Lampe, for example, is convinced that when St Paul speaks of Jesus' appearing and of his having been seen 'he doesn't mean "seen" as you see me now with your two eyes. He means that a revelation came to him in the way that one might see God'.[34] We might be forgiven for wondering what this involves more precisely. Lampe simply assures us that 'there are moments in life when one *does* see God'.[35] The lack of definition at this point is typical of a great deal of contemporary theology, whose almost exclusive attachment to New Testament studies at the expense of systematic theology has left the Church in a residual state of semi-agnosticism and unclarity. The lesson for contemporary theology to learn from this is that an epistemology of Easter faith in the resurrection is absolutely vital. If the more concrete presentation of the resurrection as a physical restoration is set aside as a later development of the Easter tradition, then some attempt must be made to articulate the nature of the Easter reality and how it was apprehended, in so far as the most primitive stratum of the tradition will allow us. Simply to negate the very positive images communicated by Luke and John will not do. We need to identify the nature of the reality experienced by the primitive Christians, of which the gospel narratives are later developments. If the raised and exalted Christ is understood to have appeared 'from heaven' as it were, we nevertheless need to be able to describe something of the object experienced. On the other hand, we need to be able to articulate an understanding of the structure of Easter faith that will be appropriate to it.

Edward Schillebeeckx

The most impressive modern attempt to expound the nature of Easter faith in a way that does justice to the heavenly and exalted status of the raised Christ is that of the Roman Catholic theologian

[34] *The Resurrection*, p. 8.
[35] Ibid. See also p. 36 where ὤφθη in 1 Cor. 15 is interpreted in the sense of a 'vision of God or of God's angel' rather than an optical seeing of the ordinary kind.

Edward Schillebeeckx. Once again, however, as we shall see, an epistemological deficit plagues his theology. This is similar to that which rendered the work of Le Roy, Westcott, and Kirsopp Lake vague and ultimately unsatisfactory. Even so, Schillebeeckx does at least make a concerted attempt to fill in some of the gaps in so far as he tries to describe the outlines of what he believes is the nature of the primitive Easter experience of the exalted, heavenly Lord. The fact that he works one hundred years on from Westcott and is sensitive to the achievements of New Testament scholarship over this period, means that he cannot just accept a pre-critical or surface reading of the Easter texts as an account of what originally occurred. He is therefore reluctant to speak of 'sensible signs' or anything that would suggest the re-appearance of a resuscitated corpse. Yet he is just as assuredly convinced that something occurred, an event to which faith responded. His task is to outline its fundamenal configuration.

Schillebeeckx sees perfectly clearly that the crucial point for Christology and for an understanding of the Easter faith which gives rise to Christology, is 'whether the entire Christian interpretation of Jesus rests solely on experiences with the earthly Jesus or whether it is not partly undergirded by new experiences after his death'.[36] As far as he is concerned, the Easter faith certainly involves a post-mortem experience of encounter with the raised Christ. He, therefore, very self-consciously, distances himself from Marxsen, in so far as he declares his own personal conviction that there is a need to proceed from the 'Easter experience'. But, like Le Roy, he is equally convinced that the evidence of the empty tomb and the alleged appearances, so far as they are spoken of in concrete and materializing terms, are now more of a hindrance than a help in our understanding of the nature and character of the original experiences. These original experiences, as Schillebeeckx understands them, have to do with a transcendent Christ who is revealed rather than observed, and thus with an object that was perceived by faith rather than by sight. As a result, Schillebeeckx says he does not even understand Pannenberg's lengthy attempt to prove the occurrence of the resurrection as an outward, historical event. Indeed, he labels this as a 'pseudo-empiricism' which raises all sorts of false problems concerning whether the Christological mode of seeing was a sen-

---

[36] *Jesus: An Experiment in Christology*, p. 394.

sory seeing of Jesus, whether it was an 'objective' or 'subjective' seeing, a manifestation or a vision, and so on. Even if the bodily emergence of the raised Jesus from the tomb could be demonstrated, he asks 'what would a straight appearance of Jesus in the flesh prove?'[37] Clearly we are meant to conclude that it would prove that a mere resuscitation occurred rather than a resurrection and that this would be theologically useless. But this means that the more precise nature of the experiences upon which resurrection faith was originally based cries out for further elucidation.

Before we attempt to understand his conception of the nature of this foundational Easter experience, we should observe that there are a number of respects in which Schillebeeckx's theology is reminiscent of that of Barth and Bultmann, particularly in so far as he also wishes to do justice to the revelatory and soteriological aspect of the Easter faith. However, he is not, like them, committed to the methodological principle that the Easter event is by definition inimical to treatment by the methods of critical-historical research or that historiographical judgements must necessarily be excluded from the structure of belief. Nor is he beguiled by the principle that any objectifying language must be ruled out of court as fundamentally mistaken or even alien to theology. He is therefore not under the pressure of a prior methodological commitment to avoid saying anything about the nature of the early Easter experience or about the alleged character of the object experienced on the ground that this would admit historical judgements into the make-up of faith. As it turns out, however, Schillebeeckx's actual *historical* treatment of the New Testament resurrection traditions leads to an exposition of faith in the raised Jesus which is in fact remarkably free from the need of evidential supports of a historical kind, for he feels no need to appeal to the narratives of the empty tomb or to the cycle of stories of alleged visual appearances of the raised Jesus to the first disciples. In Schillebeeckx's view the crux of faith is not an

---

[37] *Jesus*, p. 710, n. 119. Schillebeeckx has in mind Pannenberg's lengthy exposition in *Grundzüge*, pp. 93–103. (*Jesus—God and Man*, pp. 95–106). He says that 'faith is emasculated if we insist on grounding it in pseudo-empiricism, thereby raising all sorts of false problems: whether, for instance, this "Christological mode of seeing" was a sensory seeing of Jesus, whether it was "objective" or "subjective" seeing, a "manifestation" or a "vision", and things of that sort. To the New Testament all such questions are alien'. He is equally disenchanted by the work of Br. O. McDermott, *The Personal Unity of Jesus and God according to W. Pannenberg* (St Ottilien), pp. 262–9, though this work has not been available to me.

acknowledgement of the truth of certain statements which assert that the original disciples of Jesus had experiences of an outward, visual, and quasi-empirical kind, but rather that their faith was essentially an inner and more clearly religious conviction of knowing themselves to be forgiven by Jesus who, on the basis of this experience, was declared to be risen. This religious experience of understanding oneself to be forgiven and to be a member of the community of the forgiven-by-Jesus, is then said to be the essence of the Easter experience, not only of the first believers but of Christian believers through the ages. In this way, Schillebeeckx concentrates attention, not upon the visual appearance of the raised Jesus or upon the discovery of the empty tomb, so much as upon an experience of his forgiving presence, the 'conversion process' undergone by the disciples and their 'encounter with grace' after Jesus' death.[38] For him, the Raised One is an essentially divine and heavenly entity apprehended from within the context of faith and repentance: He is the Raised Christ the Forgiver.

The net result is that the stories of outward appearances tend to recede into the background. Indeed, the bare kerygma of Easter appearances preserved by Paul in 1 Cor. 15: 3–8 also becomes secondary. Instead, we may substitute a kind of *metanoia*, a change of heart, for which the living Jesus is said to be responsible. The scattering of the early community at the crucifixion is therefore said to have been reversed as the community gathered once again to be reconstituted as the community of the forgiven. This is the crux of his understanding of the Easter experience of the exalted Lord. Schillebeeckx thus argues that 'the resurrection *kerygma* was already present even before the traditions about the tomb and appearances had arisen. The Easter faith emerged independently of these two traditions'.[39]

It should be pointed out that in his more recent apologia *Interim Report*, Schillebeeckx is anxious to say that a misunderstanding of his earliest work *Jesus* has tended to suggest that he wishes to dethrone the appearances of Jesus from a key place in the structure of resurrection belief when in fact he is really concerned only to set aside the later *stories* of the appearances.[40] These alone are said to be later developments of the tradition and we are meant to understand

[38] *Jesus*, p. 394.
[39] Ibid., pp. 333–4.
[40] E. Schillebeeckx, *Interim Report on the Books* Jesus *and* Christ, p. 74.

that Schillebeeckx is not so anxious to dispatch the actual appearances themselves. Even so, this disclaimer is not sufficient to correct a tendency in the original book *Jesus* to set aside not just the narratives of the appearances as a secondary and somewhat insignificant element in the make-up of primitive Easter faith but the very fact of the appearances themselves, for it is not only that the narratives of the appearances are down-graded by Schillebeeckx. Apart from the more detailed and graphic stories of the appearances found in the gospels, the net result of Schillebeeckx's work is that all New Testament passages which suggest that a visual seeing of the raised Jesus stood at the beginning of the history of Easter faith recede into comparative unimportance, including the early credal formula in 1 Cor. 15. Here, once again, Schillebeeckx's thought bears comparison with that of Barth and Bultmann. For whilst Barth interprets the list of original appearances in 1 Cor. 15 otherwise than as evidence upon which a considered historical judgement might be based, and whilst Bultmann concedes that Paul's attempt to do just that in this same passage of 1 Cor. was mistaken, Schillebeeckx regards any attempt to base faith on the evidence of appearances, including the list of appearances in 1 Cor. 15, as a secondary form of the kerygma rather than its original kernel.

Like both Barth and Bultmann, Schillebeeckx gives a certain primacy to the proclamation of the kerygma, but he has his own distinctive understanding of what constituted the substance of it. It is his view that historical-critical research on the New Testament Easter traditions is able to demonstrate the priority of the preaching of a kerygma and an experience of faith that gave rise to it that is independent of the alleged appearances of Jesus. If this is correct, then faith, in Schillebeeckx's view, is not only a judgement that is independent of the story of the empty tomb or the gospel *narratives* of the alleged appearing of the raised Jesus, but independent also of the proclamation of a kerygma in which it was simply declared that Jesus had appeared.

It is not that Schillebeeckx argues that the appearances of Jesus cannot be the subject of critical-historical assessment because of their revelatory or eschatological nature, so much as the fact that he believes that historical enquiry demonstrates that the appearances were really not essential to faith. Instead, Schillebeeckx believes that faith was based upon the perception of the operation of eschatological grace. The appearances were thus not vitally important in the rise of primitive faith, nor therefore did they feature in the earliest kerygma, even if they do qualify for mention in 1 Cor. 15. In other words, Schillebeeckx does what Barth and Bultmann refuse to do. He submits the Easter traditions to historical scrutiny in order to determine the outlines of the historical ground of the primitive faith and the exact nature of the heavenly reality upon which faith was based. But he finds that the original ground of faith is not constituted by external quasi-empirical appearances of the raised Jesus from heaven any more than the empty tomb. Nor is it based upon the *proclamation* of appearances and the empty tomb. Rather, he believes that historical enquiry demonstrates that the ground of faith lies elsewhere. It lies in the experience of eschatological grace, conversion and forgiveness rather than in 'appearances' or the proclamation of appearances.

Now, we have already seen from the discussion of the evidence relating to the empty tomb that its inconclusiveness from a historical point of view arises because it may well be a tradition of relatively late origin. The story of the empty tomb may well represent a development of the original Easter proclamation. It may have emerged as an early attempt to counter Docetic tendencies, or else it may have been a natural consequence of a prior Easter faith, given a pre-existing understanding of resurrection as something which necessarily involved the raising up 'without remainder' of the mundane body of flesh and bones. In so far as Schillebeeckx says that Easter faith and the early Easter proclamation may be historically prior to the emergence of the empty tomb tradition, he may well be quite correct, even though, as we saw in Chapter II, the historical evidence is not clear enough to lead to an unequivocal determination of this matter. There is insufficient evidence to allow an absolute confidence in pronouncing the empty tomb tradition later than the original emergence of faith, based upon some other grounds, though Schillebeeckx may well be right in thinking that this is where the balance of probabilities lies.

Some of the appearance narratives, it is true, may, in the form we have received them, also be judged to be late. It has already been admitted that the developed traditions in the gospels of Luke and John for example, with their references to the bodily appearance of Jesus in a very material or concrete form, may certainly be later than the original Easter proclamation in 1 Cor. 15 which is devoid of such details. However, it is far more difficult to maintain that the unadorned appearances tradition is necessarily later than both the emergence of Easter faith and the commencement of the first Easter proclamation. The contention that the earliest proclamation was without any reference whatsoever to the appearance of the raised Jesus or that faith was earlier than and independent of any tradition of appearances, is open to question. This is particularly problematic when we note that the tradition concerning the resurrection of Jesus which Paul preserved in 1 Cor. 15 and which has a good claim to be considered 'early', possibly even having an original Aramaic form, declares that Jesus appeared, and this not once but four times over.

Schillebeeckx is clearly somewhat embarrassed by this Pauline kerygma, containing, as it does, references to a list of appearances, but he does not follow Bultmann in his attempt to pass it off as Pauline error nor does he seek to focus attention away from the character of its content as historical evidence by following Barth in speaking of the Pauline intention in using it as legitimation formulae only. Rather, he seeks to deflect its claim to be taken as of quite fundamental importance in discussions of the origin and nature of the early Easter faith by relegating it to a secondary position.[41] Indeed, he clearly finds the contemporary, post-Barthian concentration of interest in 1 Cor. 15: 3–8 and the contention that this is the correct point of insertion into the New Testament for an understanding of the primitive Easter proclamation and faith rather tiresome.[42] Thus, whilst Barth discounts the use of 1 Cor. 15: 3–8 as historical evidence and Bultmann accepts it but sets it aside as a mistake, Schillebeeckx downgrades its dogmatic significance by pointing out that there is an even earlier Pauline Easter tradition than that quoted in 1 Cor. 15 which does not so much as mention the alleged appearances. This, he says, is found in 1 Thessalonians 1: 10 and 4: 14. Schillebeeckx contends that in this tradition faith seems to have focused on the future return of the raised Christ at the *parousia* without any reliance on the evidence of appearances of the raised Jesus between the time of the cross and his future return. Here, he says, there is no mention of appearances; 'everything centres on the imminent parousia of Jesus'.

It is true, that the tradition in 1 Thess. 1: 10 and again in 4: 14 does seem to be primitive. The appearance of the Greek ὅτι in

[41] *Jesus*, p. 350.
[42] Ibid.

4: 14 functions as quotation marks and this shows that, like the substance of 1 Cor. 15: 3–8, Paul is quoting a tradition which he had received. Whether this silence with respect to appearances should be held to be evidence that there was in fact no reliance on appearances of the raised Jesus in the primitive coming to faith is another matter, for we have here an argument which, precisely because it is an argument from silence, may not be conclusive. Given that there is an explicit mention of the future parousia of Jesus and no explicit references to the appearances of the raised Jesus, it may still be the case that it came to be believed that Jesus would return and manifest his glory in the future as Messiah, precisely because he had appeared in the manner indicated in 1 Cor. 15: 3–8. After all, the prior conviction that Jesus was alive and in heaven is a logical precondition of the affirmation that he would return. The appearance of Jesus is also reiterated in what looks like another early credal statement preserved by Luke in Luke 24: 34: 'He is risen indeed and has appeared to Peter'. The later and more detailed appearance narratives of the gospels are thus anticipated by unambiguously clear affirmations of the Easter message that Jesus had in fact appeared. Even if we agree with Schillebeeckx that the most primitive faith cannot have relied upon the appearance narratives as we now know them in the developed tradition of the gospels, that does not dispense with the proclamation of the fact of the appearances which stubbornly persists in the early stratum of the New Testament. Whilst Schillebeeckx lifts the tradition of 1 Thess. 1: 10 and 4: 14 above 1 Cor. 15: 3–8 in terms of dogmatic importance, on the grounds that 1 Thessalonians is an earlier epistle than 1 Corinthians, this does not necessarily mean, of course, that the tradition contained in 1 Corinthians is necessarily later than that in the letter to the Thessalonians. Indeed, it is sometimes the case that literary texts that are usually held to be late in fact preserve the earliest form of a tradition. This may be the case, for example, with the tradition of Mary Magdalene's discovery of the empty tomb which seems to come to us in its most original and unadorned form through the text of St John's Gospel rather than the synoptics.

Schillebeeckx's tendency to weaken the dogmatic impact of the tradition of the appearances is also evident in his explanation of the meaning of 1 Cor. 15: 3–8. On each of the four occasions in 1 Cor. 15: 3–8 when Paul affirms that Jesus appeared, the Greek word which we translate 'he appeared' is ὤφθη and on a purely linguistic level this may be translated 'he appeared' or 'he allowed himself to be seen' rather than 'he was seen'. This immediately suggests that the revelatory initiative lay with the raised Christ himself rather than with the experient subjects who allegedly became aware of his presence. However, that Christ was understood to have taken the revelatory initiative tells us nothing concerning the way in which that revelation, once initiated, was received and appropriated by the human subjects; nor do we know sufficient concerning the nature of the object that allowed itself to be perceived to infer the nature of the appropriate means of apprehending it. If we ask for more information concerning the precise nature of the object said to have been revealed or seen, it is, of course, possible to think of a fairly straightforward visual seeing of an object. In this case the human apprehension through the deliverances of sense seems an unavoidable corollary. However, once again, Schillebeeckx is clearly anxious to reduce the significance of the appearances tradition as an element in the earliest proclamation. He first argues that the word ὤφθη which we normally translate 'he appeared' and which thus suggests an objective appearance is only insecurely rooted in Pauline theology for it is not used in any other place. Secondly, when he comes to discuss the meaning of ὤφθη he argues that it is a mistake to think in terms of a visual seeing of the raised Jesus. Rather, it is be understood as a 'making epiphanous' of the raised Jesus. Here Schillebeeckx draws on the support of André Pelletier, who observes that in the Septuagint ὤφθη is frequently used in Genesis for revelations, 'even when no visual element at all is present'.[43] He therefore concludes that ὤφθη is a technical term which in its use by Paul in 1 Cor. 15: 3–8, avoids the idea of the re-animation of a corpse such as might be implied in ocular seeing. This leaves us with the task of discerning what the 'making epiphanous' of the raised Christ might be and exactly how it is to be understood to differ from a visual seeing. Some of Schillebeeckx's remarks certainly suggest a moment of inner illumination in which the believer 'sees', not visually, but in a metaphorical or intellectual sense, 'that Jesus was the Messiah'. This way of putting it suggests not so much an encounter or an awareness of the presence of Christ, as a coming to a clear conviction as to

---

[43] *Jesus*, p. 706. See André Pelletier, 'Les Apparitions du Ressuscité en termes de la Septante', *Biblica*, 51, (1970), pp. 76–9 where ὤφθη is translated largely on the basis of Genesis 12: 7 as 'God made him epiphanous'.

the historical Jesus' true identity and to some insight into the significance of his role in the restoration of a right relation between men and God.[44] In this case Schillebeeckx's position would be barely distinguishable from that of Don Cupitt and it is understandable that his theology has also been classified as reductionist.

Whilst Schillebeeckx relies heavily on the work of André Pelletier, a very substantial weight of theological scholarship, predominantly Protestant, also suggests this same general emphasis. In his article ὁράω in *The Theological Dictionary of the New Testament* (Vol. V, pp. 315–82) W. Michaelis is at pains also to insist that ὀφθῆναι and ὤφθη are technical theological terms of Septuagintal origin denoting 'the presence of revelation as such without reference to the nature of its perception or to the presence of the God who reveals Himself in His Word'.[45] Michaelis also insists that it is possible to think of the meaning of ὤφθη in such a way as to assimilate it to an intellectual kind of seeing. The visual element, he says, is never stressed. When ὤφθη is used as a term to denote the resurrection appearances, as in 1 Cor. 15, 'there is no primary emphasis on seeing as sensual or mental perception. The dominant thought is that the appearances are revelations, encounters with the risen Lord who herein reveals Himself, or is revealed'.[46] This once again begs all the epistemological questions as to the nature of the object revealed and the manner in which a 'revealed' content is appropriated in human consciousness and identified as the raised Christ. But the epistemological question of how such identity claims are justified is not even raised. Michaelis simply insists that 'the appearances are to be described as manifestations in the sense of revelation rather than making visible'.[47]

Having dispensed with any idea of concrete appearances, Michaelis then abandons the category of 'vision' as the method of apprehension and speaks more technically of 'revelation'. This is entirely empty and mysterious, however, until Michaelis astonishingly contends that revelation is to be understood as a kind of hearing, so that the resurrection appearances are 'auralised' and reduced to inner whisperings: 'seeing becomes hearing. Paul bases faith only on hear-

---

[44] See also *Jesus*, pp. 347–8 and p. 387 where Jesus' becoming epiphanous is an experience in which we are said to 'grasp who he is'.

[45] *TDNT*, V, p. 358.

[46] Ibid.

[47] Ibid., p. 359.

ing apostolic preaching'.[48] Clearly, Michaelis is pulling the interpretation of Paul's talk of appearances in 1 Cor. 15 into line with
Romans 10:16 ff where the coming to faith is said to be precipitated
by hearing. In this case, the appearing of Jesus would tend to
become an inner conviction; ὤφθη would be understood in the
sense of insight rather than of sight, an intellectual seeing rather
than sensory perception.

Willi Marxsen argues the same point by bringing Galatians
1: 15 f., where Paul speaks of a 'revelation' or *apokalypsis*, and also
1 Cor. 9: 1 to bear upon the meaning of ὤφθη in 1 Cor. 15. He says
that it was not a vision of the Risen One which was claimed so much
as 'a vision of Jesus the Lord, the Son'. By this he seems to mean
that what was seen was the truth of the proposition that Jesus was
'The Messiah', 'The Lord' or 'The Son of God' and that he was
sending the disciples forth on a mission.[49] U. Wilckens comes to
very similar conclusions. Whilst rejecting Harnack's thesis that 1
Cor. 15: 5 and 7 constitute evidence for an early rivalry between
Peter and James, Wilckens nevertheless accepts that we are dealing
here with formulae which were used in the early community to
legitimate the authority of the early leaders. Even so, he then allows
his discussion to drift away from the idea of a visual seeing to a seeing of a more intellectualized kind. He is, like Marxsen, inclined to
interpret ὤφθη from the point of view of Gal. 1: 15 where Paul
speaks of an *apokalypsis*. Here God reveals 'his son' to Paul for him
to proclaim him to the heathen. Because υἱὸν refers to the exalted
Jesus it implies the heavenly status of him who is revealed. Thus,
what is *seen* in resurrection faith is the truth of the new status of
Jesus: 'God shows Jesus as his Son' or he reveals the truth that Jesus
is his exalted, vindicated Son.[50] This seeing seems to be related not
so much to sight, for as Wilckens himself puts it, it was a 'sudden
miraculous *insight*'. This suggests that Paul did not see Jesus so
much as 'see clearly' that Jesus was 'in heaven with God'.[51]

[48] Ibid., p. 349.

[49] *The Resurrection of Jesus of Nazareth*, p. 101–5.

[50] U. Wilckens, 'The Tradition–History of the Resurrection of Jesus' in *The Significance of the Message of the Resurrection for Faith in Jesus Christ*, p. 68.

[51] For Wilckens' argument that the formulas of 1 Cor. 15 are legitimizing formulae rather than reports which are intended to be understood in terms of visual seeing,
see U. Wilckens, 'Der Ursprung der Uberlieferung der Erscheinungen des Auferstandenen, Zur traditionsgeschtlichen Analyse von 1 Kor. 15: 1–11' in W. Joest and
W. Pannenberg, eds., *Dogma und Denkstrukturen*, pp. 59–95.

R. Pesch, following Wilckens, seeks more clearly to dispense with an 'occurrence of seeing Jesus' in the time after his death by pointing to the foundation of faith in Jesus' eschatological message, which is said to have been clearly 'seen' for what it was. This means that faith is the result of reflection and does not require any acquaintance with a Jesus who is seen in a visual sense in order to touch off the new beginning.[52] The effect of this is to move the meaning of ὤφθη away from 'seeing' towards 'hearing', and even here it is not outward audition that is intended, so much as an 'inner' hearing of the truth about the historical Jesus and his message.

This definition of the meaning of ὤφθη as a technical theological term to denote the means of receiving the revelation of God, owes a good deal to Michaelis, who as we have seen, contends that it is meant to denote the presence of revelation as such, without meaning to communicate anything with regard to the nature of the perception.[53] He argues that the way the appearance is appropriated is subordinated to the theme of theological evaluation, so that it is actually neutral as to the structure of the perception. Having thus neutralized it as a term denoting 'revelation', Michaelis then fills it with his own highly specific understanding of revelation through the medium of Word. Given the importance that the early community placed on its kerygma, and having in mind John's words about those who do not see being blessed (John 20: 29) and Paul's words about faith being based on the apostolic preaching, 'seeing thus becomes hearing'. Ὤφθη is then assimilated to the hearing of the kerygma, in so far as Michaelis says that when ὤφθη is used 'there is no primary emphasis on seeing as a sensual or mental perception' and that 'the appearances are to be described as manifestations in the sense of revelation rather than making visible'. The double-talk here does not circumvent the same urgent epistemological question: How is what is heard to be identified justifiably as the presence of the raised Christ? There is no advance here over the 'arbitrary assertions' of Barth and Bultmann. This leads W. Kasper, quite justifiably, to conclude that Michaelis intends ὤφθη to mean

[52] R. Pesch, 'Zur Entstehung des Glaubens an die Auferstehung Jesu. Ein Vorschlag zur Diskussion', TQ, 153 (1973), pp. 201–28.
[53] ὁράω in *TDNT*, V, pp. 358 f. R. Rendtorff, 'The Concept of Revelation in Ancient Israel', *Revelation as History*, pp. 23–53.

that instead of sensory perception the disciples were overwhelmed by an 'anonymous numinous transcendence'.[54]

Certainly, the revelation of the raised Christ tends to be internalized so that external seeing is denied in favour of an inner conviction. The end result is that the 'appearance' of the raised Christ evaporates almost entirely as an outward or external phenomenon with which the believer has to do. Whilst Schillebeeckx does not draw directly upon this Reformed understanding of what is meant by the appearances of the raised Christ as proclaimed by Paul, his own exposition is remarkably similar. He so stresses the idea of the inner experience of concrete forgiveness that the place of the objective appearances in the structure of the primitive faith tends to recede into the background. Indeed, one could be forgiven for wondering whether some special pleading is not going on which turns 'he appeared' into some kind of inner conviction on the part of believers. One can appreciate why it is that Schillebeeckx has suffered a similar fate ecclesiastically to that endured by Le Roy, and he certainly does not correct the tendency of the book *Jesus* to down grade the kerygma of the appearances when he says in his *Interim Report* that is only the gospel *narratives* of the appearances which are to be understood as secondary.

It must be observed, however, that in the *Interim Report* there is a tendency for Schillebeeckx to restore the place of the fact of the appearances in the kerygma by emphasizing simply the diversity of the early preaching so that the tradition of Easter appearances of 1 Cor. 15: 3–8 becomes one among many forms of the proclamation of Easter faith. In this case some primitive Christians are said to have begun with a resurrection kerygma based in an experience of perceiving the presence of the raised Jesus, whilst others had no experience but simply looked forward to the manifestation of a Jesus of the future and thus proclaimed a kerygma containing a parousia Christology. However, even in his *Interim Report* he continues from time to time to go beyond the mere assertion of kerygmatic diversity to insist upon the historical priority and importance of the parousia Christology over one containing reference to appearances or present experiences of the raised Jesus. He thus continues to insist that '*parousia christology is the mother of all*

---

[54] W. Kasper, *Jesus the Christ*, p. 138.

Christianity: Jesus is "the one who is to come" '.[55] This suggests that parousia Christology is to be accorded a temporal and logical priority over a proclamation of the kerygma which asserts that Jesus had appeared. Clearly, Schillebeeckx has not shaken himself free from a residual inclination to favour a parousia Christology over one asserting the fundamental importance of resurrection appearances.

This inclination of Schillebeeckx to favour the future parousia over present appearances, conditions his assessment of the remainder of the New Testament evidence. For example, Schillebeeckx is impressed by the fact that the hypothetical document Q includes a well-formed and specific parousia Christology but no explicit resurrection Christology.[56] He goes on to argue that the Q tradition is evidence of the existence of an early Christian community, the so-called 'Q-community', which, in its understanding of faith, placed no importance on the appearances or on an awareness of the presence of the raised and glorified Christ, but instead espoused the more fundamental parousia Christology. This entails the postulation of a 'Q-community' which was to some extent separate from other Christian groups and with a self-contained intellectual life of its own. This community is said to have looked forward to the return of the raised and exalted Christ at the parousia but not back to any appearances in the form of visions.

We may take the point that there was a plurality of traditions amongst the first generation of Christians and that the 'Q-tradition' may have been one of them. However, the contention that the Q-community was isolated to the point where access to any underlying acquaintance with the tradition of appearances which are so central to Paul's kerygma relies too heavily on the silence of the Q material. After all, the Q-tradition, as a collection of sayings, does not contain any explicit proclamation of the passion either, but this does not lead us to the view that in the so-called 'Q-community' there was no acquaintance with the fact of the passion and crucifixion of Jesus. Likewise, the consequential fact of the resurrection appearances may not have been foreign to the Q-community, even despite the Q-tradition's concentration of attention on the parousia.

More seriously, despite Schillebeeckx's explicit denial that he has

[55] *Interim Report*, p. 71.
[56] Ibid., p. 42.

a proclivity for Q, in practice he goes beyond the assertion of the diversity of the traditions to elevate the Q tradition with its parousia Christology above other alternative possibilities. This is done in such a way as to devalue their dogmatic importance. Indeed, Schillebeeckx is inclined to interpret other traditions in such a way as to bring them into congruence with the parousia Christology which he favours. Not only is Paul's kerygma displaced from its usual centrality; Mark is also brought into line with the alleged Christological approach of the supposed Q-community.[57] Schillebeeckx somewhat surprisingly maintains that the empty tomb tradition of the Marcan gospel should also be accorded a paradigmatic place in the understanding of the primitive Easter experience. This is understandable enough, given the thesis that Schillebeeckx is seeking to substantiate, for Mark has no tradition of appearances. Schillebeeckx is not prepared to give much credence to the view that there was an original Easter story in which an appearance of Jesus was narrated at the end of Mark's gospel and which is now lost, though many Marcan scholars are still prepared to accept this possibility.[58] Rather, Schillebeeckx argues, in a manner reminiscent of Lohmeyer and Lightfoot, and more recently of Marxsen, that the Marcan story of the empty tomb with the direction that it puts on the lips of the angel, to 'Go into Galilee, there you will see him', is not meant to refer to an anticipated appearance of the raised Jesus in Galilee, of the kind that was later narrated, for example, in Matthew 28 and John 21, so much as the imminent *parousia* of Jesus in Galilee. In this way Schillebeeckx is able to say that Mark's gospel truly reflects the early resurrection kerygma as found in 1 Thess. 1: 10 and 4: 14 and also Q and this in turn means that the early Easter faith and the proclamation which expressed it was independent of a tradition of visual appearances. Moreover, the early proclamation of a future *parousia* is said to have brought the scattered community together in Galilee, where together they became conscious of the operation of Christ's forgiveness and grace amongst them.

Schillebeeckx does not discuss the views of Lohmeyer, Lightfoot, and Marxsen in this regard. Indeed, he does not make any reference

---

[57] The use of the Q material by Schillebeeckx has been critically assessed by P. Schoonenberg, 'Schillebeeckx en de exegese', *Tijdschrift voor Theologie*, 15 (1975), pp. 255–68 and A. L. Descamps, 'Compte Rendu', *Revue Théologique de Louvain*, 6 (1975), pp. 212–23.

[58] See for example, E. Schweizer, *The Good News According to Mark*, pp. 365 ff.

to any of them at this point, though either Lohmeyer or Marxsen may well be the source of his ideas in view of the fact that he refers to the relevant works elsewhere.[59] Whatever the truth of this matter, he uncritically accepts the same point of view. It should be noted, however, that many scholars do not agree with the Lohmeyer–Lightfoot thesis with regard to the interpretation of the meaning of the angel's direction at the tomb, and the standard criticisms apply equally well to Schillebeeckx's statement of the position.

Lohmeyer and Lightfoot contended[60] that the ending of St Mark's gospel itself suggested that what was to be witnessed in Galilee was not an appearance of the raised Christ, but the end of the world, the *parousia* or return of Christ as Judge to inaugurate the Kingdom of God. This, they argued, would be the proper climax of a gospel. In addition, it dispenses with the need to argue for an original ending, now lost, in which an appearance of the raised Jesus was narrated. The gospel could be said simply to end at Mark 16: 8 with the direction to 'go into Galilee' to await the eschatological return of Christ there. It is because this cataclysmic event did not occur that we have no description of it at the end of the gospel. Marxsen has revived this thesis[61] with the added suggestion that if, as is often said, the gospel was written around AD 65, the advance of the Roman legion on Jerusalem in AD 66 could be interpreted as an intimation of the events of the end in which God would show himself and his power once and for all and Jesus would be revealed as his Messiah. Marxsen contends that it is for this reason that Mark is able to have Jesus say in Mark 13: 14 f.: 'When you see the desolating sacrilege set up where it ought not be . . . then let those who are in Judaea flee to the mountains . . . shortly after the Son of Man will appear in the clouds of heaven with great power and glory'. In other words, the terror of the times evoked the expectation of the parousia in the imminent future, as has since often been the case in times of wars and rumours of wars and natural disaster. This provides the context for the understanding of the angel's command to go into Galilee, there to await, and ultimately to see, the returning Jesus. Willi Marxsen, following Lohmeyer, makes the suggestion there-

---

[59] E. Schillebeeckx, *Jesus*, p. 43.
[60] In *Galiläa und Jerusalem*, FRLANT, 35 (1936), pp. 1088 ff. and *Locality and Doctrine in the Gospels*.
[61] In *Mark the Evangelist* pp. 83 ff.

fore that the 'seeing' foreshadowed by the angel (ὄψεσθε) really refers to the parousia, the revelation of Jesus as Messiah at the end-time, rather than to what we have come to call Easter appearances. The angel's command then becomes a command to the women to tell the others to gather in Galilee for the glorious denouement of the return of the Lord.[62]

If the ending of Mark's gospel is to be interpreted in this sense, then Schillebeeckx is on firm historical ground in contending that the earliest gospel reflects an Easter kerygma in which it was declared that Jesus had been raised from the dead and that he would return in the imminent future, but without any reference to the claim of early witnesses to have 'seen' the raised Jesus.

Unfortunately there are good reasons for not following either Schillebeeckx, or Marxsen, Lightfoot, and Lohmeyer, at this point. For one thing the words put into the mouth of the angel at the tomb are not the only indication we have of Mark's understanding of this matter. Apart from the words of the angel concerning what was to happen in Galilee, Mark has a parallel saying in Mark 14: 27–8 which is attributed to Jesus himself as a kind of prophecy: 'You will all fall away, for it is written, I will strike the shepherd and the sheep will be scattered. But after I am raised up I will go before you into Galilee'. In view of Schillebeeckx's heavy reliance on the theme of the scattering of the early community at the time of the crucifixion and the re-gathering in Easter faith, this is a very relevant passage. R. H. Lightfoot argued that though the alleged statement of Jesus in Mark 14: 28 sounds like the promise of a future resurrection appearance, it should be read in the light of Mark 16: 7 which, as we have seen, in his view refers to the parousia. However, the word 'go before' (προάξω) here in Mark 14: 28 and again in the statement of the angel in Mark 16: 7 (προάγει) does not suggest a parousia, a *coming* in the clouds, so much as a leading, analogous to the way in which Jesus 'went before' on the way to Jerusalem *from* Galilee (cf. Mark 10: 32). Furthermore, Christopher Evans has pointed out[63] that the image of the shepherd in Mark 14: 27 suggests that in Gali-lee the Risen Lord will appear as shepherd of his people to gather

---

[62] See W. Marxsen, 'The Resurrection of Jesus as a Historical and Theological Problem' in *The Significance of the Message of the Resurrection for Faith in Jesus Christ*, pp. 15–50. See also N. Perrin, *The Resurrection Narratives*, pp. 29–30, 36–38 and Ulrich Wilckens, *Resurrection*.

[63] *Resurrection and the New Testament*, pp. 80–1.

those who had been scattered by the event of Calvary around himself precisely as the Raised One.[64]

This means that the idea that Mark knew nothing of an early kerygma which included the declaration that the raised Jesus had appeared to his disciples and gathered them around himself, but simply affirmed instead that Jesus had been raised and would be revealed in the parousia of the end-time, cannot be substantiated by the evidence. From a consideration of Mark's gospel, it is not at all clear that there was an early Easter faith which was independent of the tradition of the appearances and which simply focused attention on the hope of the parousia of the crucified and raised Jesus. On the other hand, from a purely logical point of view, without a revelatory experience of some kind, it is difficult to see what could have grounded the hope of the future imminent parousia of Jesus. It may still be very cogently argued that Mark knew of a tradition of resurrection appearances and that the original version of his gospel concluded with an account of at least one occasion when Jesus was alleged to have appeared. This means that it is extremely precarious to erect a systematic understanding of resurrection faith which dispenses with any talk of the appearances of Jesus, on the basis of this particular piece of New Testament evidence from Mark. Apart from the methodological questionability of preferring Mark's gospel to the tradition of 1 Cor. 15: 3–8, as giving an indication of the nature and content of the earliest proclamation of the resurrection, it is clear that Schillebeeckx's interpretation of Mark is itself open to question.

The resulting mis-exegesis of Mark may be more damaging to Schillebeeckx's resultant theology than he is prepared to admit. In his *Interim Report*, he tends to pass off criticism of his book *Jesus* on exegetical grounds. Exegetical difficulties are said to be incidental to his fundamental theological position. It may be, however, that a revision of the exegetical grounds of Schillebeeckx's account of the fundamental Easter experience does severely challenge Schillebeeckx's basic lack of interest in Easter appearances in favour of a concentration of attention on the parousia. Moreover, the priority given by Schillebeeckx to the parousia has the effect of displacing

[64] See also C. F. Evans, 'I Will Go Before You Into Galilee', *JTS*, N. S., 5 (1954), pp. 3–18 where the meaning of προάγω, 'to lead', is fully discussed. Also W. Michaelis, *TDNT*, V, pp. 356, 360 and W. Kümmel, *Introduction to the New Testament*, pp. 78–9 and E. Schweizer, *The Good News According to Mark*, pp. 364–73.

the appearances of the raised Christ so that the cognitive element in faith becomes vague. In the understanding of the Easter event which appeals most to Schillebeeckx, the experience of forgiveness is said to ground the conviction that the Forgiver is alive and will return. How the Forgiver is actually known *in* the experience of forgiveness is left very unclear. Indeed, it is precisely the vacuum which Schillebeeckx tends to leave at this point which opens the way for others to charge him with a form of theological reductionism. His talk of a conversion experience and of 'concrete forgiveness' is capable of a psychologizing interpretation which does not really include a reference to the raised Christ as an object of knowledge.

Under the pressure of criticism evoked by his book *Jesus*, Schillebeeckx is therefore anxious to avoid being pushed into a reductionist position in which the Easter experience becomes a self-contained exercise in self-understanding. At this point the work of Schillebeeckx is once again reminiscent of that of Bultmann, with whom he shares the common concern to ensure that justice is done to the soteriological element in the Easter experience. Indeed, his understanding of faith as an experience of forgiveness is not dissimilar to Bultmann's existential experience of self-understanding. In so far as talk of a visual seeing of the raised Jesus recedes into the background proportionately as the emphasis on the subjective experience of forgiveness is stressed, there is an added resonance with Bultmann. In Schillebeeckx's case, the believer knows himself to have been forgiven in the moment when Christ becomes 'epiphanous', but the objectivity of the raised Christ becomes somewhat problematic. In Bultmann's understanding of the moment of encounter, it is a moment of illumination in which the man of faith grasps hold of himself in relation to the salvation of the cross and responds in obedience. It is true that, whilst Bultmann resorts to the use of existentialist categories to speak in terms of a transition to authenticity at the hands of God, Schillebeeckx retains the traditional language of forgiveness, which has the virtue of being more recognizably biblical. One further difference between them is that Schillebeeckx's account of salvation is less individualistic than Bultmann's. Whereas in Bultmann's account of the coming to faith, it is very much the individual who sees himself in relation to the cross and its saving significance; for Schillebeeckx the Easter experience of being forgiven is essentially a communal experience. Thus, he says that Jesus is presented as the risen one 'within a collective-ecclesial experience'.[65] What he means by this ecclesial experience of forgiveness in which Christ became 'epiphanous' can be gleaned from his own actual description of what he believes occurred at the first Easter, three days after the crucifixion. This experience, which initiated the early Christian mission to the Jews and then to the Gentiles, is essentially what Schillebeeckx calls a 'conversion experience',[66] but it also precipitates at the same time the birth of the primitive community. Schillebeeckx places great weight on the motif of 'scattering' and 'gathering' in giving content to the idea of an ecclesial experience of *conversion*. He argues that at Calvary the disciples scattered to Galilee and that the Easter experience was essentially an experience of re-grouping.[67] I suspect also that by 'concrete' forgiveness Schillebeeckx has in mind that it is an experience of forgiveness and conversion which has a quite real and tangible side to it. Just as the sin of the apostles is concretely expressed in flight and dispersion as they deserted Jesus, so their feeling of forgiveness coincided with their concrete and visible coming together, as they re-gathered around him. In other words, what Schillebeeckx has in mind is a conversion experience not just of a private, inner kind, but an experience with a public face to it. Moreover, Schillebeeckx would resist any charge that he dissolves the Easter experience into the non-objective, inner or psychological experience of the religious subject. The experience of being forgiven is an experience not just of inner peace and calm or a kind of subsidence of former guilt. He claims that it is a concrete experience of being forgiven *by Jesus*. It is here that the fundamental epistemological weakness of his position begins to appear, for whilst he asserts all this, he does not really explain the identifying characteristics of this experience in such a way as to connect it *necessarily* with Jesus. In other words, the logical connection between the experience of forgiveness and even re-grouping, and the declaration that *Jesus* is alive and doing the forgiving or causing the re-grouping is extremely weak. Schillebeeckx simply says that 'a dead man cannot forgive' and therefore that Jesus may be said to be alive, forgiving. But he has not explained why the forgiveness must be understood as the

---

[65] E. Schillebeeckx, *Jesus*, p. 352.

[66] Ibid., p. 385.

[67] Against this we must note Von Campenhausen's contention that the 'flight' to Galilee is no more than a 'legend of the critics', 'The Events of Easter and the Empty Tomb', p. 79. See Pannenberg, *Jesus—God and Man*, pp. 104–5.

specific forgiveness of this particular human/divine agent: If the Christians' Easter experience is one in which they see themselves as forgiven, why can it not be interpreted as an experience of *God's* forgiveness? Why should it be spoken of as *Jesus'* forgiveness? In other words, what precisely is it in this experience that leads the Christian to feel constrained to speak of Jesus as risen?

In his defence and explanation of his position Schillebeeckx categorically denies that he has reduced the Easter experience down to a matter of self-understanding; on the contrary, the experience of *metanoia*, which is so vital a part of the resurrection event, is said to contain within it a cognitive element. Indeed, in the *Interim Report* Schillebeeckx goes to considerable lengths to underline the fact that he understands the Easter experience as 'a process of conversion in which the cognitive element is fundamental'.[68] The importance of a cognitive element within the experience of conversion and new life is now heavily emphasized.[69] However, exactly what this cognitive element is remains far from clear. Even in his *Interim Report*, where he is under pressure to avoid a reductionist interpretation of the resurrection, some of Schillebeeckx's statements continue to suggest that the cognitive element in faith is an intellectual seeing in which the believer comes to 'recognize Jesus as the Christ'.[70] In this case the object about which the judgement of faith revolves is the historical Jesus prior to the crucifixion. He also speaks of the object of faith as 'the historically tangible earthly appearance of Jesus of Nazareth'.[71] This is congruent with his contention that ὤφθη is not to be understood as an ocular seeing but as a technically religious seeing akin to insight. However, under the pressure of the criticism of those who believe Schillebeeckx has tended to reduce the objective reality of the raised Christ to a matter of self-understanding coupled with a new vision of the meaning of the historical Jesus, Schillebeeckx tends in his *Interim Report* to deny that his book *Jesus* reduces the cognitive element in faith to a judgement about the identity of the historical Jesus. Instead he insists that in faith the early Christians were able to recognize Jesus as the Christ and experience his 'renewed presence among them'.[72] This is now said

---

[68] *Interim Report*, p. 75.
[69] Ibid., p. 82.
[70] Ibid., p. 23.
[71] Ibid., p. 32.
[72] Ibid., p. 79.

to be the 'new presence of the now glorified Jesus'[73] and not just the historical Jesus: 'When I call the Easter experience a process of conversion', he says, 'its all-embracing cognitive aspect should not be forgotten, i.e. the experience of the new (spiritual) presence of the risen Jesus in the gathered community'.[74] It is clear that even though the earliest Christians are said in the book *Jesus* to have proclaimed a parousia kerygma of the returning Christ of the future, the fundamental emphasis of *Interim Report* is to ensure that the perception of the present Christ is not omitted from view. Certainly our own faith is said to be more than merely a matter of new self-understanding.[75] We must take account of 'the experience in faith of the living presence of the risen Jesus in the community, as a cognitive nucleus' of what Schillebeeckx calls 'the Easter experience as a process of conversion'.[76] Schillebeeckx thus speaks of the 'uniqueness of the structure of the Easter experience'[77] and is most concerned to insist that 'the experience of the glorified presence of Jesus in the community has a structure of its own which is not identical with the structure of the interpretation of the life-work of Jesus in faith'.[78] However, despite these protestations, his original tendency to place an emphasis on a parousia Christology and to steer away from the empiricist interest in the manner of the original appearances, leaves the alleged 'cognitive nucleus' of faith and repentance undefined. An emphasis on the cognitive element in the response of faith and repentance should lead Schillebeeckx back in the direction of the need for a religious empiricism, in so far as it raises a set of questions about the exact nature of the object cognized and how it was recognized and identified. If such questions are raised about the 'cognitive nucleus' of the present-day experience of faith, then it is legitimate to ask what the cognitive nucleus of the experience of salvation was understood to be by the *first* Christians. Given that the primitive Easter experience was an experience of concrete forgiveness in which the presence of the new life of Jesus was recognized, we will want to know how that presence was experienced and what conditions made it possible to claim to recognize it as *Jesus'* pres-

[73] Ibid., p. 81.
[74] Ibid., p. 80.
[75] Ibid., p. 81.
[76] Ibid., p. 93.
[77] Ibid., p. 93–4.
[78] Ibid., p. 93.

ence. Indeed, an appreciation of the importance of the cognitive nucleus to present-day Christian experience should lead Schillebeeckx back to a greater interest in and appreciation of the appearances tradition in the New Testament and in the resurrection kerygma of the manifestation of Christ as present, as against his preoccupation with the parousia Christology to which he gives such prominence. Unfortunately, such an enquiry is exactly what he condemns in Pannenberg as 'pseudo-empiricism'.

Schillebeeckx rightly emphasizes the importance of our own present experience to the understanding of faith. Faith is primarily not a matter of the reception and appropriation of biblical and doctrinal truths, so much as a matter of the interpretative use of biblical concepts and doctrines to illuminate the present experience of salvation. However, if the experience of salvation within the milieu of the Church is interpreted, in the light of the Easter kerygma, as an experience of forgiveness and of encounter with the presence of the exalted Christ as the one who mediates the divine forgiveness, it is encumbent upon theologians to give an account of the structure of this faith. They must make some attempt to explain the nature of the experienced reality which is identified as the presence of Christ and how such an identification may be made. Schillebeeckx speaks of a current 'fatal gulf between exegesis and dogmatics'[79] and rightly chides contemporary theologians for their 'inability to make anything of the critical results of present-day exegesis'.[80] This gulf certainly exists. However, whilst Schillebeeckx has made his own valiant attempt to bridge it, his concluding talk of a cognitive element within the salvific experience of concrete forgiveness still leaves the fundamental work to be done: what is this cognitive nucleus of faith?

Our task in subsequent chapters will be to probe the shape and structure of the original Easter experience with a view to clarifying the nature of the renewed presence of the glorified Jesus amongst the disciples. Given that we appreciate Schillebeeckx's insistent demand that this cognitive nucleus be situated within a broader experience of conversion and new self-understanding, we shall want to come to some clearer understanding of how it was that the early Christians came to identify the continuing presence of which they

---

[79] Ibid., p. 34.
[80] Ibid., p. 2.

became aware as the presence of *Jesus*. Indeed, we shall want to know how it is that we ourselves are able to justify the claim that we identify the presence of the glorified Jesus within our own experience of conversion and faith.

This chapter began with the observation that twentieth-century theology has tended to compensate for the failure of a historical approach to the resurrection of Jesus, whether as a purely historical or as an eschatological event of the past, by affirming the importance of the *present* believer's experience of faith. The shortfall in the historical evidence which leads to its inevitable failure to prove the occurrence of the resurrection is balanced by the confident affirmation of faith as an acquaintance with the raised Christ here and now. However, the contemporary discussions of what is involved in this experience have, without exception, failed to grapple with the epistemological questions raised by such a contention. Not only is the nature of the raised Christ who is said to be encountered left unclear and undefined to the point where he tends to disappear from view, but the epistemological structure of resurrection belief which explains how his presence is identified awaits its articulation. To this double-sided task we must now address ourselves, by first tackling the question of the nature of the object of the Easter experience, the appearance and presence of the raised Christ.

VI

The Raised Christ:
Appearance and Presence

He Appeared: ὤφθη

WE have seen that Edward Schillebeeckx's attempt to argue on exegetical grounds that the tradition of the Easter appearances may be displaced by an exclusively parousia Christology will not stand up to scrutiny. A systematic theology of the resurrection must therefore come to terms with the central place of the appearances tradition in the early preaching. Indeed, the appearances seem to have a clear prima facie claim for inclusion in what Schillebeeckx himself calls the 'cognitive nucleus' of faith and repentance.

In speaking of a 'cognitive nucleus' of faith we are in fact referring to what traditional theology has called *fides* as distinct from *fiducia* or trust. *Fides* is faith understood as knowledge and it may be cogently argued that whilst the response of faith may include both elements simultaneously, *fides* or knowledge is in fact logically prior to *fiducia*. This is for the perfectly straightforward reason that it would be unwise to trust the untrustworthy; one must first know something of the person in whom one trusts. Thus, faith in God in the sense of knowledge is logically prior to faith as trust. Faith is not a blind leap in the dark but a rationally justified commitment of trust in one whom one knows as trustworthy.

The cognitive nucleus of faith is therefore constituted by the knowing of God, or in the case of Easter faith, the knowing of the raised Christ. Just how the raised Christ makes his presence felt and known and how human beings are able to claim a knowledge of him is our problem.

Given that the appearances of the raised Jesus have an immediate prima facie claim to be taken seriously as that to which faith first responded, we must pursue the possibility that Easter faith was, in the first instance, precipitated by an acquaintance with the Christ who may be said to have 'appeared'. Certainly, a more sympathetic treatment of the appearances tradition may yet yield some helpful results concerning the fundamental structure of resurrection belief. We are therefore driven back to the primitive proclamation in 1 Cor. 15.

Despite the attempted embargo of Barth and Bultmann on treating the statements contained in verses 3–11 as evidence from which historical inferences might be drawn in order to provide a cognitive basis for faith, a great deal of historiographical attention has in fact been paid to the question of the precise meaning of these primitive traditions in recent years.[1] Not all of what has been written is relevant to our present discussion. However, it is unanimously agreed that the central claim of these traditions is the claim that Jesus *appeared*: he appeared to Peter and the twelve, to more than five hundred on one occasion, to James and the apostles, and finally he appeared to Paul. Even allowing the arguments of Barth, Marxsen, and others that Paul is not citing the appearances as rational evidence upon which faith is to be inferentially based, it nevertheless remains that the early kerygma asserts four times over that Jesus appeared. Regardless of the particular intention that was originally in mind when this information was first used, there can be little doubt that in Paul's mind importance certainly attached to the actual occurrence of the appearances. Moreover, the gospel narratives hardly differ from the affirmations of the Pauline kerygma at this central point. Despite the many discrepancies amongst the gospel narratives and the discontinuity of the gospel records with these Pauline assertions of the bare fact of the appearances, at least there is agreement over the basic contention *that Jesus had appeared*. Prima facie it seems that the appearances and the accompanying experiences of 'seeing' the raised Christ provided an empirical anchor in the period immediately after the crucifixion for the affirmation of resurrection belief. Primitive Christian resurrection belief was therefore naturally expressed in claims to have encountered or perceived an object of religious awareness, which could be identified

---

[1] See J. Jeremias, *The Eucharistic Words of Jesus*, pp. 101–5; Hans Conzelmann 'On the Analysis of the Confessional Formula in I Corinthians 15: 3–5,' *Interpretation*, 20 (1966), pp. 15–25, and J. Jeremias, 'Artikelloses Χριστός', *ZNW*, 57, 1966, pp. 211–15 and 60, 1969, pp. 214–19; C. F. Evans, *Resurrection and the New Testament*; Reginald H. Fuller, *The Formation of the Resurrection Narratives* and essays by Willi Marxsen, Ulrich Wilckens, Gerhard Delling, and Hans-Georg Geyer in *The Significance of the Message of the Resurrection for Faith in Jesus Christ*.

with a deal of confidence as *Jesus*, alive and known by acquaintance in the historically datable consciousness of primitive Christian believers. The alleged appearances therefore seem to have provided the experiential ground for the inference that Jesus had been raised in the tomb and also for theological speculation concerning the heavenly place where Jesus had gone and whence he had appeared. The experience then invited speculation about why he had gone there and about the theological significance of his going. The same experience led to assertions as to what could be expected to happen in the future as a consequence of it, in statements of an eschatological kind concerning the imminent return or parousia of Christ. In other words, a resurrection Christology and a parousia Christology are not just alternative forms of expression of Christian faith. It is not just that the early kerygma could take either form, for there is a logical connection between them: in the Pauline literature there is evidence to suggest that the declaration that Jesus would return presupposed and logically depended upon the belief that he had been raised 'to the right hand of the Father' and had appeared to his disciples. In other words, faith is to the Easter appearances as hope is to the parousia: faith dimly perceives the flickering presence of Christ; hope anticipates his clearer manifestation when he shall come in his kingdom. But hope is saved from being mere wishful thinking precisely because it is grounded in and justified by what is perceived and known, at least in a partial way, in the response of faith.

The purported experience of 'seeing' the raised Christ seems therefore to have provided a basis for the generation of resurrection beliefs and doctrines and of eschatological hopes, and the appearances rooted the resurrection itself and the anticipated consequences of it into human history.[2] And even if historical-critical techniques are not competent to judge whether or not God was the heavenly author of this alleged event, or whether or not it was 'for us and our salvation', these same techniques may nevertheless be used as we take an interest in discovering what it was in human experience that led the first Christians to affirm that Jesus had been raised from the dead in the first place. A historical examination of the details of the reports of these alleged foundational experiences is vital, not so

---

[2] The process of early Christian dogmatic construction and doctrinal development on the basis of this experience, employing Old Testament texts to justify it, is clearly expounded by Barnabas Lindars in *New Testament Apologetic*.

much in order to discover where and when they were purported to
have occurred, to whom, and in what order, for that is precisely the
kind of detail that historical-critical study has demonstrated to be
irreconcilably diverse (and not only is it an area where few positive
results are possible, but, in any case, the answers to such questions
are inconsequential with respect to the question of the more fundamental nature of the primitive Easter experiences). Rather, our real
interest is in the nature of the basic structure of the experiences as
far as they were understood by the first witnesses. In other words,
we need to uncover the epistemological pre-suppositions and implications of the primitive Christian claims.

It was noted in the previous chapter that, despite Schillebeeckx's
reassurance that a 'cognitive nucleus' is important to Easter faith,
his theological writing does not outline with any clarity the detailed
components of this 'cognitive nucleus'. Moreover, we also noted
that the fundamental exegetical emphases of the book *Jesus* build
into a tendency to evacuate the experience of faith of any clear content. The raised Jesus and the manner of his self-disclosure tend to
disappear behind talk of the experience of 'concrete forgiveness'.
Indeed, as the experience of forgiveness becomes more concrete the
raised Christ becomes more ethereal. We have noted, for example,
that Schillebeeckx, following André Pelletier and, less directly, W.
Michaelis and a succession of contemporary Protestant theologians,
argues that the 'seeing' which is implied by the use of ὤφθη in 1
Cor. 15: 3–8, is a religiously technical 'seeing' different from rather
than similar to natural perception of an ocular kind. The word is
said to denote the perception of the revelation of God rather than
the seeing of a natural object or anything like the seeing of a natural
object.

It must now be observed that this particular understanding of the
meaning of ὤφθη does not stand unchallenged in contemporary
theology. A less technical interpretation of the meaning of the term
ὤφθη has its contemporary proponents both in Reformed as well as
modern Roman Catholic theology. For example, K. H. Rengstorf
argues, in response to Michaelis, that in 1 Cor. 15 perception
through sight is meant. The same position is followed by G. Delling
who, whilst admitting that ὀφθῆναι can signify the coming of God
to someone without becoming visible, nevertheless claims that this
is not so with respect to the perception of the presence of the raised
Jesus. In this case, he says, it means to make 'visibly present' for

Jesus appears in bodily form.³ Others, just as confidently, speak of ocular vision as though there could be no debate about the matter. Karl Rahner, for example, contrasts any religious perception that Christians may come to by way of insights in the present, with the clarity of sight of the foundational apostles.⁴

It is unfortunate that something of an alignment has tended to develop between those who seek to interpret ὤφθη in an ordinary ocular sense and those who see it in a more technical sense as a term for the reception of revelation. The result is that an antithesis has been drawn between the visual or ocular seeing of the raised Christ and the intellectual seeing of a truth about the meaning of the historical Jesus, a coming to an inner conviction concerning his messianic identity. This is unfortunate, for the truth probably lies somewhere between these two alternatives and this truth can only be grasped by appreciating what is common between the religious and the purely secular use of the word.⁵

Though a discussion of the meaning of a single word must avoid the false standardization which comes by failing to attend to nuances that arise from its use in particular contexts, it does seem that, generally speaking, when ὤφθη is used religiously to refer to the apprehension of revelation it is intended to mean something more than the mere intellectual grasp of a propositional truth, for it speaks of encounter and engagement with the Divine. And yet it means something less than the clarity of sight that is experienced in seeing a material object through the natural mechanism of the eye and optic nerve. Whether we can clarify the nature of 'seeing' that is peculiar to religious faith remains to be seen. But those who opt for 'insight' rather than 'sight' and indeed draw some kind of antithesis between the two, do not take into account that the word ὤφθη does have a natural as well as a technical or supernatural application, even

---

³ K. H. Rengstorf, *Die Auferstehung Jesu. Form, Art und Sinn der urchristlichen Osterbotschaft*, pp. 93–100; G. Delling, 'The Significance of the Resurrection of Jesus for Faith in Jesus Christ' in *The Significance of the Message of the Resurrection for Faith in Jesus Christ*, p. 84.

⁴ Karl Rahner, *Sacramentum Mundi*, Vol. V, p. 330. See also W. Kasper, *Jesus the Christ*, p. 138.

⁵ For example see K. Lehmann 'Die Erscheinungen des Herrn', in *Auferweckt am dritten Tag nach der Schrift. Früheste Christologie, Bekenntnisbildung und Schriftauslegung im Lichte von 1 Kor. 15, 3–5*, Quaestiones Disputatae, Vol. 38, pp. 370 ff. In respect to the opposed views of Michaelis and Rengstorf, he argues that the question cannot be resolved on the level of these two alternatives.

in the Septuagint. Michaelis and Pelletier, for example, omit to note that the religious or technical meaning of the term is drawn from and dependent upon its ordinary use, and that apart from its specifically religious use with respect to the perception of the presence of the Divine (as in Genesis 12: 7) the same word is also used in the Septuagint to connote the seeing or appearance of natural objects. For example, the word is used in cases where natural objects which were formerly hidden or concealed from view come into vision: after the Flood in Genesis 8: 5 the mountain tops are said to have been 'seen' as the water receded, for example. On the other hand, people are commanded to 'appear before' Yahweh,[6] as one might today appear before a magistrate in a law court. The suggestion of this ordinary use of the word with respect to persons or things in this world is that an object is seen or a person is seen or appears and shows himself, perhaps as a missing person might come forward and present himself alive. It is this ordinary or literal use of the term that is then given an extended meaning in the Septuagint, where it is used in specifically religious contexts to refer to the epiphanous appearance of a religious object such as we find in Genesis 12: 7 and Exodus 3: 2 f. The same word is used, not only of the appearance of the worshippers before Yahweh but of the disclosure of Yahweh himself, his glory or his angel, from his radical hiddenness, as worshippers became aware of his presence. This religious use of the term flows on into the New Testament.

The suggestion of the sudden 'coming into view' of a previously hidden reality is contained in Mark 9: 4 where ὤφθη is used of Elijah's appearance with Moses in the context of the story of the Transfiguration of Jesus. The tongues of fire are similarly said by Luke 'to appear' in a dramatic and sudden way at Pentecost (Acts 2: 3) and, in the resurrection tradition, it is the presence of Jesus himself which is disclosed, when he is said to have appeared to those mentioned in the chronological list passed on by Paul in 1 Cor. 15.

The use of the same word in both a natural and a religious or technical context suggests at the outset that, given a clear difference between natural objects and the object of religious faith, the structure of the seeing and recognizing which belongs to Christian faith may be understood as being similar to the structure of the seeing and recognizing of natural objects in this world generally. In other

---

[6] Exodus 23: 15.

words, we are justified in assuming a 'family resemblance' in the meaning of the word when used in the two different contexts, the one relating to the natural world, the other to religion. In this case, it could be argued that the seeing of natural objects in this world and the apprehension of a religiously significant reality is essentially the same kind of thing in terms of its structure and exhibits the same basic epistemological pattern, even though the objects may be of a radically different kind.

It is true that in religious contexts the word ὤφθη, when God himself is the object, may be being used in a metaphorical or extended sense, rather than in the literal sense of its use with regard to the direct, visual seeing of mountain tops and tables and chairs, people and other straightforward natural objects. But, even if this is the case, it is still entailed that there must be some features of the seeing of an object in the natural world which are similar to features of the less direct perception of the presence of a religious object. Whilst the metaphorical use of a word does not explicitly assert a similarity, as does a simile, it is based on some similarity that holds between the standard and the metaphorical application of the term. Indeed, the standard use of the term is presupposed by the metaphorical use, and we would not understand the metaphor without it.[7] As William Alston has pointed out, we would have trouble assigning meaning to the words, 'Sleep that knits up the ravell'd sleeve of care',[8] unless, at the very least, we had some idea of what the words 'knitting up a ravelled sleeve' mean when used literally. Similarly, the meaning of the word ὤφθη when used with respect to the appearance of the raised Jesus may be difficult to pin down and specify in exact terms, but it cannot mean anything at all without a reliance on what the same word means when used of ordinary or natural objects such as the mountain tops after the Flood or the appearance of ordinary people from a former obscurity. This at least disarms attempts to understand the theological use of ὤφθη by divorcing it from its ordinary use and to turn it into a purely esoteric and technical term denoting an 'inner conviction or hearing'.

When we ask the vital question, what features of ordinary perception are being presupposed when ὤφθη is used in relation to the perception of the presence of the unique religious object which in

[7] See W. Alston, *Philosophy of Language*, pp. 98–103.
[8] *Macbeth*, Act II, Scene ii.

faith is identified as the raised Jesus, the answer seems to be some kind of awareness of acquaintance with an objective reality, akin to the seeing of a material object in the natural world but in some as yet unspecified way, different. The difference flows from the peculiar qualities that attach to the religious object, its uniqueness, elusiveness and transcendence, but the epistemological pattern may nevertheless be the same as the seeing of material objects.

In Chapter IV it was observed (pp. 172–3) that the knowing by acquaintance of an ordinary object of the material world involves two elements: the deliverances of sense and the interpretative apparatus of the concepts of a linguistic system. One identifies a particular object when one encounters it in sensory experience and brings it under an appropriate identifying concept. If the knowing which is appropriate to faith is to be understood on analogy with natural perception of objects in the world, rather than some utterly *sui generis* knowing, the religious perception would necessarily display the same twofold epistemological structure. Easter faith would necessarily involve (*a*) the perception or apprehension through the deliverances of sensory experience of an objective presence and (*b*) the interpreting of that object of religious experience *as* the appearance or presence of Jesus Christ.

In this case a religious object, of whose presence one becomes aware through the deliverances of sense, would be interpreted and identified with a set of appropriate concepts or proper names. These concepts and names, and the grammatical rules for their correct use, may be understood to have been evolved in the course of religious history of the Church which, like any linguistic community, passes them on from generation to generation. With this linguistic equipment the Christian is able to order his experience by the application of an appropriate concept such as 'presence or appearance of Christ' in just the same way as he may note an object of the natural world and indentify it by using the concept 'tree' or 'mountain top' or whatever. The pattern of the knowing between religious and natural perception is the same, even if the object of religious awareness is unique.

The Heavenly Vision

Some further understanding of the uniqueness of the kind of seeing implied in Christian claims to have 'seen' the raised Christ may be gleaned from a consideration of the nature of the object seen.

Indeed, a better understanding of the nature of the reality of the raised Christ will help us define the manner of the human perception that is appropriate to it. In other words, when we leave a consideration of the term ὤφθη in order to consider what Paul had to say elsewhere about the nature of the resurrection body, the manner of perception implied by it may come into clearer focus. Here, once again, we are in the position of having to grope for understanding from meagre fragments of evidence but the general drift of things seems clear enough.

At the outset it must be admitted that Paul's notion of the nature of the resurrection body must be understood in the light of prevailing opinions in contemporary Judaism to which he was heir and that these were various. There was by no means a clear and uniform tradition which can be used to clarify Paul's views. Paul inherited a wide spectrum of beliefs which had evolved in Hellenistic Judaism, ranging from the belief in a mundane restoration of the actual physical remains of the dead to a more refined, spiritualized understanding in terms of a transformed, heavenly or 'spiritual body'.

The resurrection had come to be envisaged in a very 'materialistic' way, especially in apocalyptic Jewish circles, as a return to life on earth with the same body, even with the same blemishes and, so the rabbis said, with the same clothing.[9] On the other hand, there is the tradition of the Apocalypse of Baruch, Chapters 49–51, in which the body of the resurrection is spiritualized. Kirsopp Lake speaks of this as a 'transubstantiation' of the body of flesh and blood into a 'spiritual body', where 'spiritual' clearly is meant in the sense of 'immaterial'.[10]

Just where we should place Paul's understanding of things in this spectrum is not entirely clear, but the general tenor of his thought is away from crude conceptions of a mundane restoration. Apart from the fact that Paul nowhere mentions the empty tomb, which suggests that the body of the raised Christ need not necessarily be understood to have been of such a kind as to have left the tomb

---

[9] See H. L. Strack and P. Billerbeck, *Kommentar zum Neuen Testament aus Talmud und Midrasch*, III, p. 475; also IV, p. 1175–6.

[10] Kirsopp Lake, op. cit., pp. 22 ff; for the non-material nature of the 'spiritual body' see p. 35. For evidence of 'mundane restoration' see 2 Macc. 7: 11 and 2 Macc. 14: 46; behind belief in physical restoration stands Ezekiel 37. On the other hand, in Matt. 22: 30 and Luke 20: 35 f the raised are said to be like angels, neither marrying nor being given in marriage. See also Qumran *Benedictions* I Q Sb, IV, 24, 25.

'without remainder', Paul explicitly says that 'flesh and blood cannot inherit the Kingdom of God' (1 Cor. 15: 50).[11] It is true that Paul is here speaking of resurrection in general terms rather than the resurrection of Jesus in particular. However, it is clear enough that in 1 Cor. 15 Paul understands the resurrection of Jesus to which he refers in verses 3–8 as a truly representative sample of the resurrection of all believers to which he makes reference in verses 42–50. Indeed, the resurrection of Jesus was itself understood by interpreting the experience of the appearances with pre-existing apocalyptic concepts and beliefs of a general kind: Jesus is the first fruits of *all* the dead (1 Cor. 15: 20). Paul's discussion of the nature of the resurrection body of all believers is therefore pertinent to the question of the way in which he thought of Jesus' own raised and exalted body. There is a parallel between the resurrection of Christ and the resurrection of Christians at the eschaton,[12] and given that Paul speaks of resurrection in general in terms of the 'spiritual body', Jesus' resurrection must be a prime exemplification of it. This suggests that Paul did not entertain a simplistic notion of a mundane restoration with respect to the particular case of the resurrection of Jesus, a factor which is congruent with his failure to speak of an 'empty tomb'. Moreover, in Philippians 1: 22–24 Paul contrasts 'departing this life to be with Christ' with 'staying in the flesh'.[13] Even more revealing in his argument in 2 Cor. 5: 1 ff. Here he speaks of the body as an 'earthly tent' which if destroyed will be replaced by 'a house not made with hands, eternal in the heavens'.

C. F. D. Moule detects a change in one significant detail of Paul's

[11] See J. Weiss, *Der erste Korintherbrief*, KEK, (1910), pp. 345, 377, (1 Cor. 15: 50a may apply to those still living at the parousia); J. Jeremias, ' "Flesh and Blood Cannot Inherit the Kingdom of God" (I Cor. 15: 50)', *NTS*, 2, 1955–6, pp. 151–9; C. K. Barrett, *I Corinthians*, p. 379; though see also, E. Schweizer, *TDNT*, VII pp. 128 f.

[12] As Kirsopp Lake put it, 'If Christ's Resurrection is described as the first-fruits of the dead, this idea must be implied'; op. cit., p. 243. See also p. 20 where concerning Chapter 15 of 1 Corinthians Kirsopp Lake says that Paul 'is basing his teaching as to what will happen to Christians at their resurrection on what has already happened to Christ; it is therefore a perfectly sound method of argument to reverse this process and to reconstruct his views as to the Resurrection of Christ, to which he only alludes, from the full statement which he gives of his hopes for the resurrection of Christians'.

[13] See also Phil. 3: 20–1: 'For our citizenship is in heaven; from whence also we wait for a saviour, the Lord Jesus Christ, who shall fashion anew the body of our humiliation, that it may be conformed to the body of his glory, according to the working whereby he is able even to subject all things unto himself.'

thought between writing 1 Cor. 15 and 2 Cor. 5.[14] He argues that whereas 1 Cor. 15 speaks of the new spiritual body as though it were to be added to the old physical body ('the perishable putting on the imperishable'), in 2 Cor. 5 the implication is that the new spiritual body is received in exchange for the old body of flesh and bones. This, however, may be to push a chance remark too far, for in 1 Cor. 15: 50 Paul already appreciates the transformative impact that death has on the human body when he declares that 'flesh and blood cannot inherit the Kingdom of God'. Certainly this parallel between the resurrection of Christ and the resurrection of Christians means that Paul is more likely to have thought of the raised Christ in terms of a glorified 'spiritual body' than the 'yet to be glorified' mundane, visible, and tangible body envisaged by Luke and John.

More importantly, in his attempts to explain the nature of the body of the resurrection, it is significant that Paul does not call on his experience of the appearance of the raised Jesus to explain the resurrection of Christian believers; rather he calls on his vaguely formed ideas concerning the resurrection of Christian believers to illuminate the understanding of the nature of Christ's raised body, and whilst Paul certainly contrasted the spiritual body with the physical body, he seems to have been at a loss when it came to explain exactly how the 'spiritual body' should be understood. He does not resort to his own experience of actually seeing the body of the raised Jesus but gropes for understanding by using the analogy of the seed planted in the ground (1 Cor. 15: 35–44). It is clear that Paul is struggling imaginatively to explain the nature of the resurrection body. This suggests that, whatever his Damascus road experience was, it was sufficiently ambiguous and unclear as not to be of real help in explaining the detailed nature of the body of the resurrection. The evidence thus leads us back to the view that his initial experiential encounter with the raised Christ was in the nature of some kind of 'heavenly vision'. The fact that the nature of the body of the resurrection seems to have been open to speculation indicates that this was indeed a speculative matter that was brought up rather than settled by the encounter with the raised Jesus on the Damascus road.

[14] C. F. D. Moule, 'St. Paul and Dualism: The Pauline Conception of Resurrection', *NTS*, 12, 1965–6, pp. 106–23.

This view of the nature of the appearance as a 'heavenly vision' seems congruent with an understanding of the meaning of ὤφθη which suggests that it is in some way similar to the perception of a physical object yet at the same time in some way different. It is similar to ordinary seeing in so far as it implies acquaintance with an object, yet the object itself seems not to conform to the limitations of physical existence, but is rather to be understood as 'spiritual' or 'heavenly'. There is, however, little to suggest that an interpretation of the meaning of ὤφθη can dispense with some reference to an involvement with an object of acquaintance by being understood purely as a self-contained intellectual insight or a new descriptive understanding of the significance of the historical Jesus. Rather than being a matter of experiencing a psychological feeling of forgiveness or diminishment of guilt, it is a matter of knowing the presence of one who is accepting and forgiving.

The Gospel Narratives of Appearances

Though Paul spoke of the body of the resurrection as a 'spiritual body' appropriate to the eschatological order to which Jesus was understood to have gone, and though the appearance of the raised Christ 'from heaven' must therefore be understood in some sense as a 'heavenly vision', the gospel writers, somewhat notoriously, did not hesitate to narrate the Easter story in such a way as to suggest that the appearances were of such a kind that the perception of them was purely a matter of ocular sight. This has led J. Lindblom to make an important and useful distinction between those accounts of the appearance of Jesus which suggest that he was seen walking again on this earth, which Lindblom calls *Christepiphanies*, and those which, taking account of the glorified status of the raised Christ, suggest that he appeared 'from heaven', which Lindbolm calls *Christophanies*.[15] In terms of the epistemological implication of this distinction, a Christepiphany would be more like a straightforward ocular seeing and a Christophany from heaven would be something more technically religious and revelatory, different from visual seeing in some way but nevertheless akin to it.

John E. Alsup, in a history-of-tradition analysis of the appearance stories,[16] makes a similar distinction between what he calls the

[15] J. Lindblom, *Geschichte und Offenbarungen*, pp. 104 f., 108 f., and 111 f.

[16] John E. Alsup, *The Post-Resurrection Appearance Stories of the Gospel Tradition: A History-of-Tradition Analysis with Text Synopsis*, Chapter 2.

more 'anthropomorphic' type of appearance (in Matthew 28, Luke 24, and John 20 and 21) and the 'heavenly radiance' type as found in the appearance to Stephen in Acts 7 and to Paul in Acts 9, 22, and 26. These distinctions between two kinds of appearances suggest something of the diversity of resurrection belief, from mundane restoration to a more spiritualized understanding of things, which was a feature of Hellenistic Judaism and which is reflected in the gospel narratives as different writers sought to visualize the first appearances. We have already noted that the implication of the gospel tradition of Jesus' appearances in Luke and John, particularly, and at one isolated place in Matthew as well (Matt. 28: 9), is that the seeing or perception which belongs to the original resurrection faith was almost completely identical in epistemological pattern with the ordinary perception of persons and things in the natural world. Luke and John, particularly, tend to emphasize the very concrete, physical nature of the body of the Jesus who allegedly appeared or was seen: in Luke and John the raised Christ, who is said to have been not only seen but handled, seems hardly different from the historical Jesus of the days before the crucifixion.

If these were the only gospel accounts of the appearances of the raised Jesus we had at our disposal, we might happily bring them into association with the kerygmatic formulae of 1 Cor. 15 and conclude that the appearance of the raised Jesus upon which primitive resurrection belief was based is to be understood as being precisely the same as the seeing of an ordinary object in this world. Even here there are, of course, peculiarities and problems posed by the fact that Jesus is said in the same gospel sources to move about in an ethereal manner (Luke 24: 31,36) and to pass through walls (John 20: 19,26). Additional queries might be raised by the fact that the disciples on occasion are said not to recognize the raised Jesus. This gives the hint that there is something unfamiliar and strange, or 'not quite up to expectations' about the object of their experience. The initial failure to recognize the Lord tends to suggest an ambiguity in the appearance which renders recognition neither immediate nor inevitable. However, as a general rule, Luke and John nevertheless leave us with the overall impression that Jesus appeared in a clear, physical, and unmistakable way, even if his identity was at first problematic. This allows us to assume that the manner in which his presence was first appropriated in human awareness was of a piece with the seeing of ordinary objects in the natural world.

However, other parts, even of the gospel evidence, will not allow us to rest in this relatively simple and straightforward view. Indeed, there is good reason to believe that an earlier resurrection tradition which is also embedded in the gospels, thought of the appearance of the raised Jesus in a much less concrete or material manner. In this case the 'seeing' of the raised Jesus may not have been as alike to the seeing of ordinary objects of the natural world as might first appear from a surface reading of the narratives.

The missing ending of St Mark's Gospel leaves us bereft of information on this matter and this means that we do not possess an original gospel paradigm from which alleged developments at the hand of Matthew, Luke, and John can be clearly demonstrated. The belief that Mark intended his gospel to end at Chapter 16: 8, without any narrative of an appearance of the raised Christ, has by no means been utterly abandoned by scholars, but if the alternative theory, that the ending was lost and that Mark originally included an account of an Easter appearance, is true, then it is just possible that Matthew followed the Marcan original when he wrote his account of the appearance of the raised Christ to the assembled disciples in Galilee. In other words, Matthew 28: 16–20 may have been based on Mark's now lost ending. In view of Matthew's dependence on Mark elsewhere it is therefore possible that in Matthew we are encountering the outline of the more primitive tradition which in turn lies behind the expanded stories narrated by Luke and John. We must therefore look carefully at what Matthew implies concerning the nature of the Easter appearances. J. D. G. Dunn claims that Matthew's appearance story is one narrative which cannot be assigned firmly to the category of a Christophany from heaven or a more earthly Christepiphany and concludes that the original experience was 'sufficiently ambiguous that it could be understood either as a Christophany or as a Christepiphany'.[17] I do not think it is quite as open as this. For one thing, Matthew in this episode certainly suggests a less concrete and more heavenly and elusive appearance than those more earthly manifestations narrated by Luke and John. Matthew places words on the raised Jesus' lips which suggest that it is the already exalted Christ who is speaking 'from heaven' when Jesus is made to say: 'All authority in heaven and on earth has been given to me . . . '. There is no suggestion

---

[17] J. D. G. Dunn, *Jesus and the Spirit*, p. 124.

that Jesus had yet to be exalted. He is exalted to a place of heavenly authority already. The only indication in this pericope that Jesus was understood to have appeared as a material or physical body walking on this earth (as in a Christepiphany), rather than more elusively 'from heaven' (as in a Christophany), are the words 'Jesus came near and said' in verse 18. But this phrase is a typical Matthean one which is found some thirty times in Matthew's gospel but nowhere else in the New Testament. It is clearly an editorial comment which Matthew elsewhere adds to his source material and it seems likely he has added it here also, to an original resurrection tradition which, without it, unequivocally implied that Jesus appeared 'from heaven'.

Moreover, the Matthean tradition suggests that the appearance of the raised Jesus 'from heaven' was unclear and ambiguous enough to leave room for some of those present to doubt that the raised Jesus had appeared at all, for Matthew records that 'some doubted' (Matt. 28: 17) whilst others saw Jesus and worshipped him. This immediately introduces some important epistemological complications, but it does seem to exclude rather than allow for a Christepiphany, which is more congenial to scrutiny in both a visual and tactile way by anybody present. The appearance now becomes somewhat elusive. Instead of a clear and unequivocal appearance of Jesus in a way that would allow his raised body to be assimilated to other objects of this world, what is said to have been seen now becomes the appearance of a heavenly being, in some sense at least, discontinuous with natural objects of the mundane sphere. It is also important to be aware that this tradition in Matthew of the appearance of the raised Jesus 'from heaven' does not stand alone in the gospel traditions. Even Luke preserves a remnant of the same kind of tradition concerning the heavenly appearance of Jesus when he speaks of Paul's Damascus road experience in terms of the seeing of a light and the hearing of a voice from heaven and where he has Paul refer to his own Damascus road experience as a 'heavenly vision' in Acts 26: 19. The visionary or heavenly nature of this Pauline experience, as narrated by Luke in Acts, approximates to Paul's own understanding of the nature of the resurrection body which he speaks of as a 'spiritual body' and which is to be contrasted with the 'physical body' of flesh and bones. We may now raise the possibility that the appearance to Paul and that said by Matthew to have occurred to the assembled disciples on the Mount in Galilee are both to be understood to be of the same 'heavenly' kind. This possibility is strengthened by Matthew's placing of the words, 'Lo, I am with you always' on the lips of the raised Christ, for this suggests continuing experiences of a similar heavenly nature, even to the present day. It is also pertinent to note that the perception of the raised Christ is understood by Matthew to occur 'wherever two or three are gathered together in his name'. (Matt. 18: 20). On the other hand, Paul himself, in 1 Cor. 15: 3–8, lists the appearances which he witnessed along with those of the other disciples as though it was one of a series of experiences of similar quality. From this it could be inferred that he understood the first experiences of Peter and the twelve, of more than five hundred brethren, and James and the Apostles, also to have been experiences of the raised Christ 'from heaven', and that they were not understood to be different in kind from his own experience. The same implication attaches to Paul's claim to enjoy an apostolic authority of similar status to the original apostolic band, on the ground that he, like them, had seen the raised Christ (1 Cor. 9: 1).[18]

Does this mean that all the foundational appearances of the raised Jesus were in the nature of 'heavenly visions' and that the tendency to make Jesus more material and concrete is a later embroidering of the tradition? Unfortunately, we are prevented from coming to an easy conclusion in this regard because the matter is further complicated by Luke. It is an identifiable feature of Luke's theology that he not only makes the appearances to the original apostles more concrete than other New Testament resurrection traditions imply, but that he distinguishes the status and authority of the original apostles from that of Paul. At the same time, he differentiates the quality of the first disciples' experiences from that of the raised Christ to Paul on the Damascus road. For Luke, apostolic status involves the qualification of having been a witness of all that the historical Jesus said and did, from the time of John the Baptist (see Acts 1: 21–22). On this ground Paul failed to qualify. Consequently, on the few occasions when Luke speaks of Paul (and Barnabas) as 'apostles' it seems to have been by accident rather than by design; indeed, we may here be hearing the voice of a more primi-

---

[18] A point underlined by U. Wilckens in his argument that the statements of 1 Cor. 15: 3–8 are primarily legitimation formulae to secure the authority of early leaders. See U. Wilckens, 'The Tradition-history of the Resurrection of Jesus' in *The Significance of the Message of the Resurrection for Faith in Jesus Christ*, p. 69.

tive state of Pauline affairs lingering on. Luke's own more deliberate tendency seems to be to refuse Paul the status which he accords to the foundation apostles. This in turn may be the reason why he portrays Paul's vision of the raised Jesus as a heavenly one, less concrete and material and therefore less clear and authoritative, than the first cycle of appearances as he understands them. Christopher Evans comments that the operation of Luke's theological persepective may mean that Paul would not have recognized Luke's account of his own Damascus road experience and that Luke in this case has, for theological reasons, made an original tradition of concrete appearances rather more elusive and heavenly in nature.[19] If this is correct, then we must say that the first appearances were of the concrete and material kind that could have been visually seen and that a similar kind of encounter of Jesus with Paul on the Damascus road became more ethereal and heavenly or 'visionary' at Luke's hand. But it is more likely that Luke's theological perspectives worked the other way round. In view of the Matthean intimation that the original experience in Galilee was of the raised, exalted Christ 'from heaven', it is more likely that Luke made the first foundational appearances more concrete and material in order to distinguish them from the appearance to Paul, but that in fact there was originally no such differentiation of quality. This means that the Pauline experience of a heavenly vision as narrated by Luke in Acts, in terms of a light and a voice, may have reflected the true nature of all the original experiences at least in so far as even the appearances to the first believers were 'visionary' rather than 'visual', or appearances 'from heaven' rather than being more like the observation of an object of the natural world.

This contention is supported by the fact that Luke elsewhere shows a tendency to make heavenly realities visible and concrete. His tendency to materialize spiritual realities may be seen in the narrative of the Baptism of Jesus (Luke 3: 22) where he adds the word σωματικῷ ('in bodily form') in relation to the appearance of the dove: the dove cannot be understood in a symbolic way; it is a concrete, material dove. Likewise he is anxious to deny the possibility that the transfiguration experience of Luke 9: 32 was a dream by insisting that Peter and those who were with him were awake. On the other hand, it is pertinent to note that he speaks of the appearance of the Holy Spirit in 'tongues like fire' rather than 'like tongues of fire' in Acts 2: 3. Also, Luke's angels are not just dream-messengers as in Matthew, but concrete historical agents who become actively involved in human affairs (Acts 12: 7–10; 1: 10–11). Even in his account of Paul's Damascus road experience, the same tendency may not be absent. Although Paul himself nowhere speaks in his own epistles of having heard words during his Damascus road experience, Luke furnishes the scene with 'a voice from heaven' which in one account at least is said to have been heard by Paul's fellow travellers (Acts 9: 7). This part of the tradition may have originated simply as an inner conviction on the part of Paul. The materializing tendency in Luke's resurrection narratives may therefore be said to be of a piece with the inclinations revealed in other parts of Luke's work.

In view of Matthew's intimation that at Easter an already exalted Jesus appeared somewhat ambiguously to the first disciples 'from heaven' and that Paul himself seems to have thought of the appearance of Jesus to the disciples and to himself in similar terms, and in addition speaks of Jesus' raised body as though it were of a piece with his understanding of the 'spiritual bodies' of Christians at the eschaton, we must conclude that the Lucan tradition that Jesus appeared on this earth for forty days in a very clear, concrete, physical form before his exaltation to heaven must be regarded as a development of the tradition at Luke's hand: from a temporal distance and without exact information he imagined what originally took place. But even so, Luke means that the appearances were spread over forty days rather than that Jesus was uninterruptedly with his disciples for forty days and certainly does not suggest that between appearances Jesus was somewhere else on earth, though not with the disciples. This means that his own account of Paul's heavenly experience in Acts could be closer to the facts of the case with respect to the nature of all the primitive experiences, than his account of the earlier, concrete appearances to the inner circle of disciples, and that we should regard the first unembroidered accounts of the appearance of the raised Jesus as also 'heavenly visions'.

Whilst the diversity represented by the distinction between the more earth-bound Christepiphanies and the more heavenly Christophanies certainly cannot be added together to make one complete and clear picture of the early appearances, it is thus possible to penetrate behind the evidence to the earlier of the two patterns. It seems clear enough that the more heavenly and revelatory Christophany is to be given priority. The more material and anthropomorphic Christepiphanies may be seen as alternative developments of the tradition. I do not think it is satisfactory either historically or dogmatically to accept the suggestion that qualitatively quite different experiences were given to different people, so that some might be said to have seen Jesus in a concrete, material form and others in a more ethereal, visionary or spiritual form. To speak of an array of Christophanies and Christepiphanies simply introduces a superficial harmony into the diversity of the tradition which is better explained in terms of a variety of attempts to visualize and articulate what was essentially 'heavenly' and ambiguous and thus open to a range of speculative interpretations and developments.[20]

This is not to say that the narratives of the appearances are simply paradigm illustrations of the primitive kerygma, which arose in a missionary context, more or less as we would today use visual aids in teaching. This has been argued by Dibelius and has by and large gone unchallenged, but there is no suggestion in the actual gospel narratives that they are dependent upon the kerygmatic formulae of 1 Cor. 15: 3–8 or that they are an amplification of it in dramatic and picturesque detail. The gospel narratives seem to have been developed independently. On the other hand there is no suggestion that the gospel narratives are a development of the 'heavenly radiance' type of experience involving light, of the kind said by Luke to have been experienced by Paul on the Damascus road, to which German scholars refer as the *Lichtglanz* type. The motif of light which figures in the appearance stories in Acts is not present in the more anthropomorphic imagery of the other gospel appearance narratives, though there may be some connection in the story of the Transfiguration. Whilst they are in competition with the more materialistic or anthropomorphic appearance stories, it is very unlikely that they were the precursors of those stories. This stratum of the tradition must be understood to be independent and to have served another purpose.

[20] John E. Alsup, *The Post-Resurrection Appearance Stories of the Gospel Tradition*, p. 265; J. D. G. Dunn, *Jesus and the Spirit*, p. 124. The similarity of some of the appearance narratives with Old Testament theophanies was noted by C. H. Dodd in 'The Appearances of the Risen Christ: An Essay in Form-Criticism of the Gospels' in *Studies in the Gospels*, p. 34.

In his study of the literary style or *Gattung* underlying the appearance stories, John Alsup has pointed out that what he classified as the 'anthropomorphic appearances' reach back to an Old Testament tradition of anthropomorphic theophanies. These Old Testament stories are found in Genesis 18, Exodus 3, Judges 6 and 13, and 1 Samuel 3. To this list we may add the story of Elijah's experience of an anthropomorphic theophany at Mt Horeb in 1 Kings 19: 1–15 and the extra-canonical stories of Tobit 5 and 12, and Testament of Abraham. These seven 'anthropomorphic theophanies' exhibit similarities with the Easter narratives in terminology, motifs, structural elements, and conceptual scope and Alsup concludes that the appearance narratives exhibit a distinct literary type, which suggests that the stories are the product of primitive Christian preachers who sought to 'approximate' to what took place by drawing on the Old Testament models rather than eyewitness information. We are therefore led to conclude that the first appearances took the form of 'heavenly visions' or Christophanies of the raised and glorified Christ and that when, in the ensuing weeks and years, attempts were made to express the 'heavenly vision' or 'appearance' in verbal form, a variety of different images was used. Behind the 'verbal ikonastasis' lies the original experience, which is transcendent and thus elusive. It is not that the various images are later illustrations of the Pauline kerygma, or that one kind of verbal picture of what happened is a development of another, for there is an absence of literary interdependence. Rather, all are verbal attempts to express the inexpressible, for behind them all is not a more simple verbal expression of which they are amplifications so much as original Easter experiences of the raised Christ as one who appeared 'from heaven'.

Now, what are the epistemological implications of the contention that the first Easter experiences were in the nature of 'heavenly visions'? Given that the entire thrust of the evidence is towards the view that whatever was 'seen' appeared 'from heaven', as it were, any attempt to interpret ὤφθη as being identical with the visual perception or inspection of ordinary objects of the natural world is extremely precarious. On the other hand, nothing we have been able to glean from the gospel records suggests that the original Easter experience was a matter of clever or revelatory 'insight' as distinct from or even antithetical to sight. Rather, the suggestion is that the first Christians believed they perceived the presence of an objective reality rather than that they came to a positive inner conviction about the messianic identity and status of the historical Jesus. The apparent objectivity of the experienced reality meant that the manner of perception could be denoted by a word whose ordinary use applied to the sight of natural objects. One thing therefore remains constant: whilst the raised Christ as a supernatural rather than a natural object might not necessarily be open to visual observation, there is nevertheless no initial requirement for Christians to think of religious perception as a *sui generis* affair or to separate natural perception from the perception of a divine reality by a sharp divide: the appearance of an object of religious devotion from the radical hiddenness or invisibility of heaven, may be understood on analogy with the appearance of the worshipper himself at a place of worship so that the ensuing encounter may be conceived as a kind of meeting. This means that the 'seeing' appropriate to Easter faith is to be understood as a 'knowing by acquaintance' rather than just an intellectual seeing of the truth of a proposition about the historical Jesus' true identity.

Nevertheless, we may wish to avoid talk of a seeing that is absolutely identical with the ordinary vision appropriate to the perception of a material object. The reality of the religious object, the raised Christ, may not be doubted, but it is not understood as a reality that can be said to have been seen in a perfectly straightforward sense. As we have already noted, Geoffrey Lampe provides us with a typical example of one struggling to articulate this position. He confidently excludes the element of visual seeing: Paul, he says, 'does not mean "seen" as you see me now with your two eyes. He means that a revelation came to him in the way that one might see God. And there are moments in life when one *does* see God.'[21] Though the manner of this 'seeing of God' seems obvious enough to Lampe, it is precisely what we must try to understand. A little later he says that at Easter 'eyes were opened to know Jesus as their Lord'.[22] This is not to be interpreted as the merely intellectual seeing of the truth that the historical Jesus was their Lord, for Jesus is said now to be 'not just a remembered figure of the past, but their living Lord'.[23] This suggests that the presence of the raised Christ is

[21] *The Resurrection*, p. 8.
[22] Ibid., p. 11.
[23] Ibid., p. 10.

known by acquaintance in an experience which, in this respect, is like ordinary seeing, but at the same time, in an unspecified but significant respect unlike it. Lampe does not go on to say how this can be so, but seeks refuge in the concept of 'mystery'.[24]

Whatever the similarities between the seeing of the raised Christ and the seeing of ordinary objects of the natural world, there certainly were differences enough in the object seen to make it insufficiently clear to compel the assent of everybody and therefore difficult to talk about and describe, even from the point of view of those who did claim an acquaintance with it. However, it might be argued that if the apprehension of the raised Jesus, upon which primitive faith was allegedly based, is to be understood as some kind of 'heavenly vision' or Christophany, and if the apprehension of it seems to be spoken of as a perception that is in some way analogous to the vision of ordinary objects, yet in some unspecified way different, the explanation of a 'subjective vision' such as D. F. Strauss postulated on the basis of the diverse and contradictory nature of the traditions seems as good an explanation as any. Certainly, it has been followed by a great number of recent theologians, including, as we have already seen, a succession of representatives from Strauss and Renan through to Bultmann, Marxsen, and Cupitt. Even a relatively conservative scholar such as James Dunn admits that the subjective vision hypothesis is a possibility given the evidence we have.[25] Moreover, we have already noted that if there were 'visions' we need an answer to Pannenberg's question about the lack of criteria for distinguishing between subjective visions and objective visions: we need to explain how it was that the Easter visions could be understood as signs of the objective but heavenly existence of Jesus rather than as mere dreams and psychogenic delusions. Pannenberg confesses that the criteria elude us and that all we know is that a distinction was made between subjective visions and the objective visions which were foundational for faith. Indeed, Pannenberg's account of Easter faith as a historical inference fails pre-

---

[24] Ibid., p. 10: 'How this can be is mystery.'
[25] J. D. G. Dunn, op. cit., p. 133. See also Robert C. Ware, 'The Resurrection of Jesus II', in *Heythrop Journal*, 16 (1975), p. 190: 'There is no warrant to conclude from the representations documented in the New Testament directly to the specific concrete reality of the resurrection of Jesus'. Also, X. Léon-Dufour, *Resurrection and the Message of Easter*, pp. 263 f.

cisely at the point where he seeks to demonstrate the objectivity of the visions as against the subjective vision hypothesis. This means that the 'subjective vision' hypothesis is still on our agenda as an item of business yet to be resolved.

In addition, we have already observed that those who wish to follow Grass, in his contention that it is possible to distinguish 'objective' from 'subjective' visions, need criteria for making such a distinction meaningful (pp. 69–71 above). The attempt to argue that there were criteria for distinguishing between ecstatic visions and revelations from Jesus, such as Paul mentions in 2 Cor. 12, and the more fundamental encounters on which faith is alleged to be based, will not get far unless we can indicate what those criteria were. Thus, if we follow the chain of historical reason back behind us to what appears to be the first, experiential anchor of resurrection belief, we find that we get some insight into what the original Easter experience was like, as a kind of perception or sight of a religious object, but we cannot get beyond the original tradition of 'heavenly visions' or appearances of the exalted Christ 'from heaven'. And we simply do not have the evidence to judge whether these initial Easter experiences were objective disclosures of the raised Christ of a visionary kind or something more akin to 'subjective visions' having a psychological cause.

It may be noted in passing that, if we were inclined to resort to the so-called 'subjective vision hypothesis' and to interpret the visions as psychological phenomena, this would not in itself necessarily dispossess us of belief in the reality and objectivity of the Easter event. It is pertinent to note, for example, that if Carl Jung is right, even dreams and visions are not to be written off as so much irrelevant psychological phenomena, entirely without meaning and significance. For Jung a dream or vision is a means of communication whereby we become aware of something we should know but do not. Even if we had sufficient evidence to demonstrate the early disciples' proclivity for 'subjective' dreams and hallucinations, which we do not, we should beware lest we undervalue the unconscious as a means of communication of information which in our conscious lives we suppress. To explain a vision as a product of the 'subconscious' or 'personal unconscious' does not mean that it does not serve some purpose. Only an entirely rationalistic 'psychologism' could so devalue the purposive nature of psychic functions. Jung himself once complained that: 'If, in physics, one seeks to explain the nature of light, nobody expects as a result there will be no light. But in the case of psychology everybody believes that what it explains is explained away.'[26] This comment may help us see that, even if the appearances are explained as 'subjective visions', that does not mean that we are free to ignore the role they played in the transformative Easter experience of Jesus' followers. The importance of the experience of the visions cannot be gainsaid by talk of 'mere vision'. Unless we are speaking of pathological phenomena of mental illness, the deliverances of psychological experience carry a certain meaning and veracity. They cannot be dismissed as non-entities or as insignificant. They are signs and tokens of something real. Only those who devalue the events of their own psychological life or are asleep to this dimension of experience could so misunderstand the importance to the first disciples of the visions, even if they are judged to be 'subjective' visions. Strauss lived before the rise of modern psychology; he may be excused for failure to see the importance of what he tended to set aside as mere 'subjective visions'; today we are in a different circumstance. Even if the visions are today explained as psychological phenomena they are not explained away. They may be understood as tokens and signs of something real, whose meaning needs to be interpreted.[27]

Meanwhile, there is no doubt that the first disciples interpreted the Easter visions or appearances as signs of the heavenly presence of Christ. Why they should be minded to do this with the degree of conviction that is so clearly reflected in the early testimony is what we must seek to explain.

Apologetically minded scholars are inclined to urge us to accept

---

[26] See C. G. Jung, 'Answer to Job', (1952) in *Psychology and Religion: West and East*, CW 11, p. 463 n. Jung also says: 'I do not underestimate the psyche in any respect whatsoever, nor do I imagine for a moment that psychic happenings vanish into thin air by being explained.'

[27] Robert C. Ware has attempted to explain the resurrection experience on psychological lines: 'the origin of the concrete symbol "the resurrection of Jesus"—with all its symbolic variants—can be understood psychologically from the fantasies, images, representations brought about by effects aroused through the experience of the crucifixion . . . and by the experiences of encounter, reconciliation and conversion . . . '. See 'The Resurrection of Jesus', I and II, *Heythrop Journal*, 16 (1975), pp. 22–35; 174–94, especially pp. 185 ff. This is an interesting field of investigation which is deserving of further attention. I am more interested in this book, however, to probe the epistemological structure of the 'experiences of encounter, reconciliation and conversion' rather than the psychological aspects.

the objectivity of the visions on the ground that if Jesus has been raised from the dead, then he must have had the sovereign freedom to appear to selected disciples had he chosen to do so. However, this argument, if it is to escape circularity, presupposes an existing faith in the resurrection on other grounds, which is then receptive to the acceptance of the appearances as being objective phenomena. The appearances cannot be the ground of the Easter faith; they can only be accommodated to it and justified by it.

Given faith in the reality of the raised Christ on other independent grounds, who is to deny him the ability to bring people to an awareness of his presence through the medium of what might be called 'objective visions'? Thus, G. E. Ladd argues that 'If Jesus actually entered a new realm of existence at his resurrection, there remains no reason to deny the possibility that he could appear to his disciples in completely human form, as the Gospel witness said he did'.[28] If we overlook the implication of the concluding words of this sentence to the effect that the appearances may be uncritically accepted in precisely the manner they are said to have occurred in a surface reading of the developed gospel texts, Ladd's point is that *on the presupposition of the occurrence of the resurrection* it is logically possible, or thinkable without self-contradiction, that Jesus appeared to the apostles and that the visions were 'objective' ones. Of course, it is logically possible: with God anything is possible or thinkable. The remaining question then becomes, is there evidence to lead us to think that it is actually the case? On the other hand, Ladd's presupposition is that an Easter appearance is logically possible, given a prior belief in the resurrection. This means that we should need other grounds on which to base our Easter faith, which in turn would incline us to accept rather than reject the possibility that the visions to which the apostles were subject were real and actual rather than purely subjective. J. D. G. Dunn concedes that the experiences of the appearances are too vague and imprecise to warrant a clear historical judgement about their historicity or otherwise,[29] and that the additional evidence of the empty tomb is needed to confirm the objectivity of the appearances, but we have already noted that the empty tomb tradition is equally ambiguous

---

[28] G. E. Ladd, *I Believe in the Resurrection of Jesus*, p. 126.
[29] *Jesus and the Spirit*, p. 120.

and problematic from the point of view of historical enquiry. We cannot rely on it alone to clarify the tradition of appearances by providing the initial ground for faith, for it also stands in need of more corroborating evidence.

We thus seem to be caught in an impasse. After considering the gospel evidence Norman Perrin ventures to suggest that the first witnesses were 'in some way' granted a 'vision of Jesus which convinced them that God had vindicated Jesus . . . and that therefore the death of Jesus was by no means the end of the impact of Jesus upon their lives and upon the world in which they lived'.[30] Why we should reach the same conclusion or why they were convinced remains unanswered. The question is: if we have no criteria for deciding the historical question of whether the visions were 'objective' or 'subjective', why do many Christians nevertheless think of them as more than visions of a purely subjective or psychogenic kind? Why do Christians take the visions to be tokens and signs of the objective reality of the Heavenly Jesus? In the remainder of this chapter I wish to argue that, in fact, the tradition of the 'heavenly visions' of the raised Christ did not stand alone in the experience of the first Christians and that they had access to a second empirical anchor of their resurrection beliefs and eschatological hopes. This additional datum in the 'cognitive nucleus' of faith explains why the visions are usually not taken as purely psychological and subjective particulars but as pointers to the objective, if heavenly, existence of the raised Jesus. Moreover, this additional datum is one to which we have direct access in the present so that it grounds our continuing Easter faith no less than theirs. This, as I have already suggested at the end of Chapter IV, is the continuing presence of a reality in the life of the Christian community which is identified as the 'presence of Christ'. In other words, if we, like G. E. Ladd, incline to the view that the visions were indicators of the objectivity and reality of the Christ who was said to have appeared, even if we cannot prove this objectivity, it seems that we must be relying on other evidence to persuade us. Otherwise we are in the uncomfortable position of turning the judgement of faith into an unjustified because unevidenced propositional attitude. The requisite and necessary additional empirical evidence of the fact that Jesus was raised is the experience of his continuing presence as Spirit.[31] If the perception of this continuing reality has the capacity to secure our Easter faith, then we shall be in a position to argue, as Ladd has done, that the appearances are at least possible and believable, even if we do not have the actual evidence to prove their occurrence.

The Spirit of Christ

Our inability to decide whether the appearances of the raised Christ, as they are reported by Paul and described in graphic visual detail in the stories of the later gospels, were originally based on reports of objective visions or merely subjective ones, may therefore not be ultimately detrimental to faith. Even from the start, the appearances or visions do not seem to have provided the only empirical anchor for verbal expressions of resurrection belief and eschatological hope or for the more formal articulation of doctrines. The mistake of a great many current theologies of the resurrection is that they assume that the evidence of the 'heavenly visions' is the only evidence, apart from the clearly inconclusive story of the empty tomb, by which Easter faith might be rooted into experience and history. It is therefore particularly noteworthy that the belief that Jesus was alive and that he had been raised to God's right hand, whence he would at the Last Day return as Messiah and Judge, as this belief is articulated in the Pauline literature, is not exclusively traced back to a visionary experience of the past that we might today seek to pronounce either subjective and illusory or objective and real. Rather, Paul's own exposition of the nature of faith and hope is regularly traced back, not to an experience or vision of the bodily Jesus of some kind, but to the continuing presence of the

---

[31] This is contrary to Geoffrey Lampe, whose lack of interest in the continuing significance of the resurrection, as distinct from the experience of the Spirit, becomes clear when he says, not only that 'present faith is not constituted by, and dependent upon, historical evidence for a resurrection event' but 'neither can present faith in any way corroborate that evidence and substantiate the event.' *God as Spirit*, p. 151. Contrary to Geoffrey Lampe, our present experience of the Spirit of Christ convinces us that the stories of the empty tomb and appearances are '*substantially true*': i.e. they convince us that Jesus was raised from the dead. The occurrence of this past event is the ground of our current experience. Without the substantial truth of the occurrence of the resurrection event, our present affirmation of Jesus' presence would be meaningless. On the other hand, if faith is based upon the present perception of the Spirit of Christ, then it may be that the visions were subjective or psychological phenomena which functioned nevertheless as signs of the substantial truth that Jesus had been raised.

Spirit of Christ. This provided Paul with an additional empirically based indication of the fact that Jesus was alive as one who had been raised as a 'spiritual body' and exalted to the heaven whence he would return. In this case the alleged knowing of the raised Christ which logically grounds the continuing claim that he was alive and exalted, could be spoken of not in terms of inner conviction or insight only, or of a seeing of a 'heavenly vision' of his 'spiritual body', so much as the continuing perception of the presence of his Spirit in the lives of the first Christians and particularly in the life of the fellowship which they corporately constituted. Certainly, this continuing reality of the Spirit was said in an early stratum of New Testament evidence to have been identified as the presence of the raised Jesus himself.

The New Testament evidence makes it clear that the identification of the experienced reality of the Spirit as the 'Spirit of Jesus' constituted an important ingredient in the make-up of primitive Christian understanding. Despite this, it is often passed over in modern systematic treatments of the structure of resurrection belief. Indeed, the importance of New Testament claims to perceive and know the 'Spirit of Christ' to a dogmatic understanding of the structure of resurrection faith has been regularly ignored in Western dogmatic theology, which tends to look back exclusively to the traditions of the empty tomb and the original appearances. Karl Rahner, for example, declares that 'we have no experience of the same kind as the Easter experience of the first disciples, at least if we leave out of account the experience of the Spirit (Gal. 3: 1 ff.).'[32] But why should we 'leave out of account' the experience of the Spirit?

There are reasons to explain why, almost as a matter of theological and historical accident, the Spirit has been ignored in Western dogmatics of the resurrection. Not least, this has been because Easter and Pentecost, the raised Christ and the Spirit, have, under the influence of a pre-critical reading of the Lucan dogmatic schema, been seen as quite separate sets of terms denoting quite distinguishable realities. This schema, which separates Easter from Pentecost by fifty days, plus those elements of the New Testament which highlight the distinction between raised Christ and Spirit, particularly the trinitarian formula of 2 Cor. 13: 14 and Matt. 28: 19, pro-

---

[32] K. Rahner, *Sacramentum Mundi*, Vol. V, p. 330.

vided the biblical foothold for the eventual articulation of the doctrine of the Trinity. Since the late fourth century the distinction
between Father, Son, and Spirit has been foremost in Western theology, even to the point of fostering at times a popular tri-theism.
Once the distinction of three persons was accepted there was an
inevitable disinclination to refocus importance on those biblical passages which implied the close identification of raised Christ and
Spirit. As a result, the experience of the Spirit has rarely been considered in expositions of resurrection belief, which are almost automatically understood to concern only the second person of the
Trinity. The doctrine of the Trinity, as it has been popularly understood and despite its own emphasis on the essential unity of persons, thus encourages us to think of Christ and Spirit as two distinct
persons and hence of the human experience of them in the economy
of salvation as two distinguishable experiences. Indeed, even in
recent treatments of the resurrection tradition in the New Testament, such as those of Christopher Evans, Reginald H. Fuller, Willi
Marxsen, and others, the early Christian claim to have experienced
and known the 'Spirit of Christ' is not included as even relevant.

   Despite the systematic theologians' neglect of the relevance of the
Spirit to Easter faith, New Testament scholars have nevertheless
pointed from time to time to the early identification of the raised
Christ and the Spirit. For Paul, the metaphysical distinctions of later
Trinitarian theology were not even felt to be a question at all. If we
are to hold Paul to a Trinitarian belief we must say that it is the
unity of the three persons rather than their distinction that is implicit in his thought. For example, in pointing to Paul's identification
of the raised Christ and the Spirit, exegetes have in the past shown
considerable interest in Paul's words in 2 Cor. 3: 17a: 'The Lord is
the Spirit'. It seems from this reference that what the Church called
the Spirit was also understood to be none other than the living presence of the raised Christ himself. However, it has to be admitted
that the exegesis of these words of 2 Cor. 3: 17 is disputed, for the
reference to 'the Lord' in this context could refer to God the Father,
just as 'Yahweh' is 'the Lord'. This means that it would be unwise to
put too great a reliance on this single text or to draw dogmatic
significance from it. Even so, it is possible to argue that Paul con-
sistently reserves the title 'Lord' for Jesus and can elsewhere call
the Spirit 'the Spirit of Christ' (Rom. 8: 9), the 'Spirit of Jesus
Christ' (Phil. 1: 19), and the 'Spirit of the Son' of God (Gal. 4: 6).

Consequently it would not have been foreign to Paul's thought if he were understood to say with reference to the raised Jesus, 'The Lord is the Spirit' or 'The Spirit is the Lord'. Indeed, in 1 Cor. 15: 45, Paul, speaking of Christ, says 'The last Adam became a life-giving Spirit'. Thus, while the identification of Christ and 'The Lord' who 'is the Spirit' of 2 Cor. 3: 17a may be problematic, the identification is elsewhere quite positively made by Paul.[33]

---

[33] E. Schweizer, πνεῦμα, *TDNT*, VI, p. 433. Paul is hardly touched by the metaphysical question how God, Christ and the Spirit are related to each other.

On the exegesis of 2 Cor.3: 17 see D. R. Griffiths, 'The Lord is the Spirit' in *Expository Times*, iv (1943), pp. 81–3, where the literature up to that date is discussed and a verdict given in favour of the identification of the Spirit and the Resurrected Lord. See also W. D. Davies, *Paul and Rabbinic Judaism*, Chapter 8: 'The Lord the Spirit'. C. H. Dodd, *The Apostolic Preaching and its Developments*, p. 147 favours the view that in 2 Cor. 3: 17 the Spirit and Christ are identified; R. H. Strachan, *The Second Epistle of Paul to the Corinthians*, reaches the same conclusion (p. 88); C. A. A. Scott, *Christianity According to St. Paul*, pp. 258–61 thinks of 'equivalence' rather than 'identity' but the distinction is unclear; Neill Q. Hamilton, 'The Holy Spirit and Eschatology in Paul', *Scottish Journal of Theology, Occasional Papers, No. 6* (1957), p. 4, says that Paul 'in some sense equates the Spirit and the resurrected exalted Lord'. E. Schweizer, *TDNT*, VI, p. 418 favours some kind of identity. Against an absolute identification, see E. F. Scott, *The Spirit in the New Testament*, pp. 177 ff., especially pp. 180–1; however, Scott admits some kind of identity between the Spirit and the risen Christ on the basis of other statements of Paul if not on the basis of 2 Cor. 3: 17 (see pp. 185–6). Similarly, A. E. J. Rawlinson, *The New Testament Doctrine of Christ*, p. 155 n, argues that the identification of Spirit and resurrected Christ is not justified on the basis of 2 Cor. 3: 17 but goes on to admit that if Paul 'is not invariably careful to discriminate precisely between the idea of the Spirit and the idea of the indwelling Christ, it is . . . much truer to maintain that he regards the one as being the medium of the other than that he identifies the two. The risen Christ indwells his Church through the Spirit—that is St. Paul's real thought' (p. 159). Similarly, G. W. H. Lampe, 'Holy Spirit' in *The Interpreter's Dictionary of the Bible*, Vol. II, p. 636, is prepared to say that the 'Spirit is the mode of apprehension of the risen Christ', and admits that Paul makes some kind of identification of Spirit and resurrected Christ. He adds however, 'Yet Paul's identification of the Spirit of God with the operation of the risen Christ in and among his people does not lead him to make a substantial identification of the Spirit as a divine "person" with Christ as a divine "person". His statement: "Now the Lord is the Spirit" (II Cor. 3: 17) is not to be read in this sense.' More recently, James Dunn in 'II Corinthians 3: 17— "The Lord is the Spirit" ', *JTS*, NS 21 (1970), pp. 309–20 follows E. F. Scott and A. E. J. Rawlinson in affirming that an identification of the Spirit and the raised Jesus is unjustified on the basis of 2 Cor. 3: 17 but is prepared to affirm the identification on the basis of other Pauline passages; see 'I Corinthians 15: 45—Last Adam, Life-giving Spirit', in *Christ and Spirit in the New Testament: Studies in Honour of C. F. D. Moule*, ed. B. Lindars and S. S. Smalley, pp. 127–41 and *Jesus and the Spirit*, Ch. X. On the other hand, other recent opinion, perhaps less anxious to preserve a rigid Trinitarianism, is prepared to make the identification with little qualification even with respect to the contested passage 2 Cor. 3: 17. See E. Käsemann, 'The Pauline Doctrine of the Lord's Supper' in *Essays on New Testament*

Apart from these explicit Pauline identifications of the Spirit and the raised Jesus, the idea of a kind of identity between Christ and the Spirit pervades Paul's thought. In the eighth chapter of Romans, for example, πνεῦμα and κύριος are apparently used interchangeably when he speaks first of the Spirit 'dwelling in you' (Rom. 8: 9) and then of 'Christ in you' (Rom. 8: 10). Meanwhile, at the beginning of the same epistle (Rom. 1: 3–4), the raised Christ is closely associated with the Spirit, for though the historical Jesus is said to have been descended from David 'according to the flesh' his designation as 'Son of God in power' is said to have been accomplished 'according to the Spirit of holiness' by his resurrection from the dead.[34] Elsewhere in the New Testament, a very similar association of raised Christ and Spirit appears in 1 Peter 3: 18 where Christ is said to have been 'put to death in the flesh' but 'made alive in the Spirit' and in 1 Tim. 3: 16, where Jesus is said to have been 'manifested in the flesh, vindicated in the Spirit'.

W. D. Davies has also noted parallels between references to the work of the raised Christ in the believer and the work of the Spirit. To die and rise with Christ, for example, involved a dying to sin and a living to righteousness, and to be possessed by the Spirit is to bear good fruit—love, joy, peace, long-suffering. Also, just as to be in Christ is to belong to the Body of Christ, so there is a unity of the Spirit; indeed, in giving himself to us as πνεῦμα, the Christ incorporates us into his Body.[35]

Wolfhart Pannenberg has noted that a close connection existed

Themes, p. 113—'Christ himself . . . is identified with πνεῦμα in II Cor. 3: 17;' and, p. 114 ' . . . the Lord is the *Pneuma*.' W. Pannenberg, *Jesus—God and Man*, p. 171, stresses the identity of *kyrios* and *pneuma*, and Ingo Hermann, *Kyrios und Pneuma: Studien zur Christologie der paulinischen Hauptbriefe*, concludes 'that Paul answers the question of the relation between Kyrios and Pneuma in the sense of identity' (p. 140). Also, see E. E. Ellis, 'Christ and Spirit in I Corinthians' in B. Lindars and S. S. Smalley (eds.), *Christ and Spirit in the New Testament, Studies in Honour of C. F. D. Moule*, pp. 269–77. W. D. Davies in *Paul and Rabbinic Judaism*, Chapter 8, 'The Lord the Spirit', discusses the symbolism of light in the Lucan accounts of Paul's Damascus road experience with reference to Rabbinic parallels as a symbol of the Spirit. See p. 185, n. 1.

[34] See on this J. D. G. Dunn, 'Flesh and Spirit: An Exposition of *Romans* 1: 3–4', *JTS*, NS 24 (1973), pp. 40–68.

[35] See E. Käsemann, 'The Pauline Doctrine of the Lord's Supper' in *Essays on New Testament Themes*, p. 113. J. Knox, *Life in Christ Jesus: Reflections on Romans 5–8*, p. 46 and 'The Church *is* Christ's Body', *Religion in Life*, 27, (1957/8), pp. 54–62; C. F. D. Moule, *The Phenomenon of the New Testament*, and *The Origin of Christology*, Ch. 2.

for Paul between πνεῦμα and the reality of the resurrection and that
κύριος and πνεῦμα belong together. Indeed, quoting Ingo Hermann, he says that 'all "genuine", theologically pregnant statements
about the Spirit in the principal Pauline letters are Christologically
stamped'.[36] Whilst this is a very sweeping statement it must be
taken with the utmost seriousness.

It should be noted also that whilst the identity of the raised Christ
and the Spirit has often been ignored in the theology of the resurrection, it has not been overlooked in recent studies of the Holy Spirit.
H. Berkhof has concluded that 'the Spirit is always and everywhere
the Spirit of Jesus Christ' and George S. Hendry has likewise noted
that 'the Spirit continues the presence of Christ beyond the brief
span of his historical appearance and completes it by effecting its
inward apprehension among men . . . There is no reference in the
New Testament to any work of the Spirit apart from Christ. The
Spirit is in an exclusive sense, the Spirit of Christ'.[37] More recently,
G. W. H. Lampe has made the identification of the raised Christ
and Spirit the central theme of his Bampton Lectures, *God as
Spirit*.[38] Lampe points out that, apart from the identification of
raised Christ and Spirit in the early Pauline stratum of the New Testament, evidence of the identification may be detected elsewhere in
the New Testament documents. John, for example, is as insistent as
Paul that the Spirit, whose ultimate source is the Father, has been
sent by Christ and is the medium through which Christ himself
continues to be present with his people.[39] Despite the literary constraints of the gospel narratives of the Easter appearances which
tend inevitably towards the use of more graphic imagery, it is
important to note that the same very close identification of raised
Christ and Spirit is expressed in the story of the Easter appearance
which is now found in John 20. Here the raised Jesus is portrayed as
one who breathes on his disciples, and they, in this gesture, are said

---

[36] W. Pannenberg, *Jesus—God and Man*, p. 171, quoting Ingo Hermann, *Kyrios
und Pneuma*, p. 144.

[37] H. Berkhof, *The Doctrine of the Holy Spirit*, p. 24; George S. Hendry, *The
Holy Spirit in Christian Theology*, p. 26.

[38] G. W. H. Lampe, *God As Spirit* especially Chs. 1–3.

[39] Cf. G. W. H. Lampe, *God As Spirit*, p. 91: 'John is as insistent as Paul that
the Spirit, whose source is God the Father, is sent by Christ. It is the Spirit
"which he has given us", and the presence of the Spirit is the sign and assurance
that Christ himself dwells in us and that we dwell in him.' See John 3: 24, 4: 13;
15: 26–7; 16: 7; 20: 22.

to have received the Spirit: John does not know of a clear and absolute distinction between a separate object of the Easter experience and the Spirit. The same identification is also made prior to Good Friday when John has Jesus follow up his promise to send 'another comforter' after his death to be with his followers 'for ever' with the words, *'I will not leave you desolate, I will come to you'* (John 14: 16 f). This would suggest that to know the Spirit is in some sense to know the raised Christ himself and is in line with the Pauline identification of raised Christ and Spirit.

It must be observed, however, that despite the clear identification of raised Christ and Spirit, particularly in Pauline thought, some distinction between the raised Christ *himself* and *his Spirit* may be made.

Eduard Schweizer agrees that the Spirit of early Christian experience is 'not anonymous or unknown' because it is 'identical with the exalted Lord', but he adds the significant qualifying words, 'once this Lord is considered, not in Himself, but in His work towards the community'.[40] He also wants to say that, when Christ is seen in terms of his role for the Church and of his works of power within the Church, he can be identified with the Spirit; but in so far as Christ is also Lord over his own power, he can be distinguished from that power, 'just as the I can be distinguished from the power which goes out from it'.[41] In similar vein, Ingo Hermann comments that '*Pneuma* is a functionary concept (*Funktionsbegriff*): It is the divine power by which the exalted Lord as the possessor of the *Pneuma* is present and active in his Church . . . This *Pneuma* is the Kyrios Christ himself, *in as far as he gives himself to man and can be*

[40] E. Schweizer, 'πνεῦμα' in *TDNT*, VI, p. 433.
[41] Ibid., p. 419. See also W. Grundmann, 'δύναμις' in *TDNT*, II (1964/5), p. 312. Grundmann draws attention to the fact that, as an eschatological reality present in the Christian community, 'the concept of power is linked indissolubly with that of Spirit.' Also, R. Bultmann, *Theology of the New Testament*, Vol. I p. 156–7; and Alan Richardson points out that the 'πνεῦμα of a man is his δύναμις, his person in action', *Introduction to the Theology of the New Testament*, p. 104. It is relevant to note Paul's words in 1 Cor. 2: 4: 'My kerygma was not in persuasive words of (human) wisdom but in demonstration of Spirit and power that your faith might not rest on the wisdom of man but in the power of God'. See also 1 Thess. 1: 5 and Gal. 3: 5. On the relation of Spirit and power see also E. E. Ellis, 'Christ and Spirit in I Corinthians' in *Christ and Spirit in the New Testament, Studies in Honour of C. F. D. Moule*, pp. 269–77.

experienced by man'.[42] Likewise, Neill Hamilton qualifies his assertion of the identity of Christ and Spirit by saying that it is clear from statements of Paul in 2 Cor. 13: 14 and 1 Cor. 6: 11 and 12: 4–6 that 'it is not a simple statement of absolute identity'.[43] He then goes on to affirm: 'The identity here posited is not ontological, an identity of being, but dynamic, an identity which occurs in redemptive action'.[44]

It seems clear enough that the Spirit is the reality of the raised Christ *in so far as the raised Christ is experienced*. Or, to put it another way, the exalted Christ is the hidden source of the Spirit which is experienced and apprehended in faith. The raised Christ himself in his 'spiritual body' is in heaven, hidden from earthly scrutiny. He is known in human experience not in an immediate and direct encounter but indirectly, through the influence of the Spirit.[45] And, precisely because the Spirit was understood as the Spirit or power of Jesus, it could be regarded as an indicator of the fact that Jesus, in some kind of body suitable to his new eschatological heavenly life, was 'at God's right hand'. This was originally argued by primitive Christians on the basis of Psalm 110: 1 and Psalm 16.[46] This means that the presence of the Spirit itself was the object of faith in so far as faith was based in human experience.

The New Testament can therefore speak of the Spirit as 'given' by the ascended Lord himself and the Spirit itself may be seen as the gift to which faith responds. This entails that we should say that the Spirit itself is the gift which is perceived in faith, rather than that

---

[42] Ingo Hermann, *Kyrios und Pneuma*, p. 57 (my italics). See R. H. Strachan, *The Second Epistle of Paul to the Corinthians*, pp. 88–9 where he says that 2 Cor. 3: 17 'identifies Jesus and the Spirit, at least in the experience of men'. Strachan may be wrong in identifying the Lord of 2 Cor. 3: 17 as Christ but the notion of the identification of the Spirit with the Christ of human experience remains. On p. 89 he says: 'In the experience of men, the power of God, as the exalted Christ, and the Spirit are identical'. See also Alan Richardson, *An Introduction to the Theology of the New Testament*, pp. 109 and 122.

[43] Neill Q. Hamilton, 'The Holy Spirit and Eschatology in Paul', *Scottish Journal of Theology, Occasional Papers, No. 6* (1957), p. 4.

[44] Ibid., p. 6. Cf. R. H. Strachan, *The Second Epistle of Paul to the Corinthians*, p. 88: '*The Lord means the Spirit* identifies Jesus and the Spirit, at least in the experience of men.'

[45] As Barnabas Lindars puts it: 'The Messiah is unseen, but known in the experience of the outpouring of the Spirit', *New Testament Apologetic*, p. 55.

[46] Ibid., Chapter 2.

faith is the gift of the Spirit.[47] Moreover, fragments of tradition in Acts 2: 33, 5: 31–2 and Ephesians 4: 8 indicate that from an early time, the justification for this belief was apparently drawn from Psalm 68: 18, which was interpreted with the help of the Aramaic Targum to mean that the Messiah functioned in terms of his gifts.[48] However, the gift is not something separate from Jesus, but the active extension of the raised Christ himself. As Barnabas Lindars puts it: 'It is because Jesus is where he is that the signs of the Spirit are now seen in the life of the Church'.[49] In John's gospel the same idea is preserved, even if the language is a little different. In his talk of the living water in Chapter 4: 10–15 and in Chapter 7: 37–9, John speaks of the Spirit as a personal gift of the glorified Jesus himself.[50]

Thus, what is perceived in faith is the Spirit of Jesus, the Holy Spirit, which the exalted Christ mediates to his people, and which, in the light of the early Christian commentary on Psalm 68: 18, came to be seen as the gift of the Messiah; the Messiah himself was therefore known in his gift of himself as Spirit.

Given the rich diversity of view found in the New Testament and the high degree of development of the theological ideas discernible within it, it is remarkable that on the particular issue of the experience of the Spirit there are such clear signs of an original uniformity of understanding. There are, of course, obvious differences of a conceptual kind which arise from the different *Sitz im Leben* of the various writers. Paul, for example, believed that with Christ's death and resurrection 'the bell for the final lap of this world's history had sounded'[51] and that the imminent End had begun decisively to influence the course of human history. He therefore understood the experience of the Spirit, which people had earlier thought must be reserved for the age to come, as an anticipation of the End.[52] For Paul the Spirit of Christ is thus the eschatological Spirit, the sign in

---

[47] See 2 Cor. 1: 22; 5: 5; Romans 5: 5; 8: 23; 1 Thess. 4: 8. Also Luke 11: 12–13; Acts 2: 38; 5: 32; 8: 18–20; 10: 45; 11: 17; 15: 8. See also, Rudolf Bultmann, *Theology of the New Testament*, Vol. I, p. 330 and W. Pannenberg, *Revelation as History*, p. 136.

[48] See Acts 2: 33; Eph. 4: 8; Acts 5: 31.

[49] Barnabas Lindars, *New Testament Apologetic*, p. 55.

[50] See also John 14: 16; 15: 26; 16: 7; 1 John 4: 13.

[51] J. D. G. Dunn, *Jesus and the Spirit*, p. 308.

[52] See 2 Cor. 5: 17: 'When anyone is united to Christ there is a new creation; the old is finished and gone, everything has become fresh and new'.

present experience of the coming full disclosure of the Messiah at the Day of the Lord. However, whilst for Paul the Spirit of Christ was the anticipation in the present of the imminent return of Christ, by the time Luke wrote, perhaps early in the second century, the Spirit had come to be understood as a *substitute* for the non-return of Christ. For Luke, therefore, the Spirit stands in place of the presence of Jesus himself rather than simply being the Spirit of Jesus himself and this emphasis has naturally strengthened as the belief in imminence of the return of the Lord himself has waned in Christian consciousness to the point where the ultimate connection betwen raised Christ and Spirit is overlooked. Even so, Luke's dogmatic standpoint is not quite thoroughgoing enough to eliminate every trace of a persisting identification of the raised Christ and Spirit. For example, whereas in Luke 12: 11–12, the Holy Spirit is said to be the author of a Christian's inspired defence in circumstances of trial and persecution (cf. Mark 13: 11), in Luke 21: 15 where an almost identical situation is described, it is the raised Christ who is understood to be the author of similar utterances. In Acts 16: 7 the identification which is implicit in these references is made explicit when Luke (perhaps inadvertently) allows the identification to slip through the grid of his dogmatic inclinations by speaking of 'the Spirit of Jesus'.

Given that the assessment of the significance of the Spirit was open to various nuances of interpretation, it is an impressive fact that there was apparently such a fundamental agreement about the original experience of the Spirit as the medium of the presence of the raised Christ with his people.[53] Certainly, it would be perilous to attempt a systematic theology of Easter faith without taking the Spirit into account, even though it has in the past barely been regarded as even relevant to an understanding of the structure of resurrection belief. Furthermore, once the evidence relating to the identification of the raised Christ and Spirit is taken into account it allows us not to over-work the question of 'what really happened?' in connection with the visions and appearances, for which we have very little evidence, in order to focus instead on what can in principle even now be experienced and known: the continuing presence

---

[53] C. F. D. Moule, 'The Individualism of the Fourth Gospel', *Novum Testamentum*, 5 (1962), p. 179 observes that the experience of the Spirit is 'conceived basically in the same way in Luke, Paul and John'.

of Christ as Spirit as a datum of faith in the life of the contemporary Church.

Epistemological Implications

It is clear enough that though the first Christians resorted to a variety of different terms including Spirit, Holy Spirit, God's Spirit, and Spirit of Christ in their talk about their Easter experience, these terms referred to the same experienced reality. Even if they connoted slightly different things, they seem to have been used somewhat indiscriminately to denote the same experienced reality. It was not just that the first Christians came to believe that there was such an entity exercising sovereignty over them and thus governing their lives; rather, they seem to have intended to say that they experienced a given, empirical reality in their lives, and that its active presence was something they could thus claim to perceive and know not just by description but by acquaintance. To read the passages of Paul's letters where he makes reference to the experience of the Spirit, is to be aware that he conceived of the Spirit as a concrete, objective phenomenon with which he had to do.

In those places where the New Testament tradition speaks of the presence of the Spirit of Jesus as something that is 'seen' and as a reality 'given' and 'received' it prima facie suggests that we are to understand the Spirit as a reality that is perceived in a kind of partial 'knowing', in which the knower is acquainted with some kind of religious object, outside of himself (*extra me*). The tradition suggests, in other words, that faith involves a knowing by acquaintance. If we prefer to speak in terms of a 'seeing' rather than a 'knowing', then it seems that we are to understand this as a perceiving of some kind of religious object, or of some kind of presence, rather than as a contrasting intellectual kind of perception, like that implied in the claim to 'see' the point of a joke or to 'see' what a particular proposition means. On the other hand, if the Spirit is 'seen' or 'known' by acquaintance, there is no suggestion that we are required to understand the perception of the presence of the Spirit as any kind of esoteric or *sui generis* experience, that is utterly discontinuous with ordinary seeing and knowing. On the contrary, faith may be understood as being in some way continuous with or of a kind with, ordinary perception. The 'seeing' of the presence of the Spirit may be understood to be akin to natural perception, in exactly the same way that ὤφθη was seen to connote a religious seeing that is continuous with the ordinary seeing of objects in the natural world, even if the object of religious awareness is unique.

Though the Spirit may be given by divine initiative, there is no necessity to assume that the abilities for receiving or 'seeing' the Spirit's activity lie other than with the human capacities of the Christian believer. If we are to employ Don Cupitt's distinction between an Event Theory of the resurrection and a Theological Theory we must say that here we have a combination of both. The experience of the Spirit is a post-mortem event; but at the same time it involves bringing an object of experience under a set of interpretative concepts. The experienced reality of the Spirit was identified and referred to as 'the Spirit of Christ' or 'the Spirit of God', 'the Holy Spirit', terms which were constructed out of commonplace elements in the Jewish mentality. Thus, the perception of the Spirit of Christ was a post-mortem occurrence in which, after the crucifixion, early Christians brought a given reality of their religious experience under interpretative concepts which they had received as part of their tradition. In addition they interpreted the reality with which they were acquainted by applying the proper name 'Jesus' to it, for they experienced it also as *his* presence.

Now, if the Spirit of Christ was an experienced reality which could lead men and women to the conviction that Jesus himself had been raised from the dead and exalted to God's right hand in heaven, then we are able to explain why it was that Paul and others were free to speculate about the nature of Jesus' raised and heavenly body. Indeed, they were obliged to do this precisely because the bodily Jesus was not actually available to scrutiny but was understood to be hidden—in heaven! What was actually perceived or seen was the activity of the Spirit which they traced to Jesus as the heavenly source or origin of it. This means that, in enquiring into structure of resurrection belief and its empirical basis we must not just focus on the term ὤφθη and on the discussion of whether Jesus appeared in a visual and material sense or whether his appearances were visionary appearances 'from heaven' as it were, and ask what kind of seeing would have been appropriate to the apprehension of such an object. We must also ask how it was that the experienced reality of the Spirit could be apprehended and known and, indeed, how such a reality could justifiably be identified as 'the Spirit of *Jesus*' and thus how it could logically lead back to the belief that Jesus was the living, heavenly source of it. Certainly, once we place the appearances or visions in the broader context of the perception and identification of the continuing Spirit as the Spirit of Jesus, then we have an answer to the otherwise unexplained question of how it was that the early Christians could with such confidence conclude that the visions were signs of his objective reality and presence rather than merely subjective illusions. The conclusion that the visions could be interpreted as signs and tokens of the heavenly existence of Christ was reinforced by the perception of the presence of the Spirit as a second element in the 'cognitive nucleus' of faith.

Moreover, on the basis of this experience they inferred not only that Jesus was himself alive and exalted in heaven but that this was where he would come from at the time of his eschatological return. Indeed, it is clear from the New Testament evidence that the early hope for a fuller outpouring of God's Spirit on all flesh and the return of Christ in sovereign power at the eschaton was sustained not by 'heavenly visions' but precisely by the experience of the Spirit, interpreted as a promissory guarantee of what was to come.

It is in relation to this element of early Christian understanding that it is possible to point to another sense in which Paul does, in some way, distinguish between the Spirit of Christ and Christ himself, despite his inclination to identify the Spirit and the raised Christ of which we have already taken note. If Paul makes no clear distinction between the raised Christ and the Spirit, in the sense that the Spirit is understood to be the experienced reality of which Christ himself is the source, a further distinction may be made in so far as he speaks of the Spirit as a reality of the present; whereas Jesus himself is understood as the returning one of the future eschaton (see 1 Thess. 4: 16). In 2 Cor. 1: 22 and 5: 5 where the Spirit is spoken of as the 'guarantee' or 'first instalment' of an expected fulfilment and in Romans 8: 23, where he speaks of the Spirit as the 'first fruits' of a greater yield to come, the tension between the reality of present experience and the future object of hope is already operative. However, as Wolfhart Pannenberg has pointed out, the expressions 'earnest' and 'first fruits' also imply that the difference between the present and the future with regard to the Spirit is only quantitative, so to speak, and Pannenberg goes on to say that 'Paul does not make any basic qualitative distinction between the present reality of the Spirit and that of the resurrected Lord'.[54] The Spirit is

<hr />

[54] W. Pannenberg, *Jesus—God and Man*, p. 178.

thus the first instalment of the future revelation of the returning Christ himself, the genuine anticipation of what is yet to come.[55] The fact that Paul makes a temporal and quantitative distinction between the (present) knowledge of the Spirit of Christ and the (future) revelation of the returning Christ, but not a qualitative one, points to the importance of refraining from separating talk of the apprehension of the raised Christ from eschatology. On the other hand, the real connection between Christ and Spirit is reflected in the logical connection between faith claims and expressions of hope. In faith the Spirit is experienced and identified as 'the Spirit of Christ'; in hope the person of faith is orientated towards the full vision of the returning Christ, of which his experience of the Spirit is down payment or guarantee. Thus, faith and hope are intimately connected in so far as what is known in faith is precisely the ground of hope. The Spirit which is apprehended in faith is itself the anticipation in the present of the object of hope, the clear manifestation of the returning Christ in the world.

Another epistemological implication of the understanding of the Spirit which flows out of a consideration of its eschatological dimension is therefore that the present knowledge of it in faith is in some sense partial or ambiguous. The object of hope is the full or clear manifestation of the presence of the Lord on the day of revelation. What we perceive now in Easter faith, the Spirit, is ambiguous, fleeting, unclear, and in some sense provisional (pro-visional). It is an inkling only, which, precisely because of this, can be interpreted as a promise of clearer vision to come. Thus in 2 Cor. 5: 6–10 Paul says that the Spirit which we perceive in faith whilst we are away from the Lord in this world, in the body, is a guarantee of the clear sight of the Lord when he appears before us as the returning judge of the world. Until that day we walk by faith not by clarity of sight. This ambiguity in the present perception of the presence of the Spirit is of a piece with the appearances tradition of the resurrection in which the visionary appearances are understood to be unclear enough to allow for an element of doubt (cf. Matt. 28: 17). The witnesses to the resurrection seem to have been understood to have been free to see or not see, for the appearance of the raised Lord did

[55] Roland de Vaux in *Ancient Israel*, p. 490 f reflects that the 'first fruits' may be interpreted as the first sheaf of the harvest of the end-time; the experience of the Spirit denotes the beginning of the eschatological harvest of redemption.

not bring full or immediate conviction to all beholders. Likewise, the perception of the Spirit of Christ, is not clear and distinct, for final clarity lies in the future, at the eschaton: 'Now I know in part, *then* I shall understand fully' (1 Cor. 13: 12). The epistemological implication of this is that whilst the empirical anchor of faith and hope must be of such a kind as logically to ground faith and hope, it cannot be expected to be so clear and unambiguous that it in fact eliminates the nature of faith as a free, uncompelled response or so clear that it eliminates the need for hope in an unmistakable clarity of present awareness. As St Paul says: 'Nobody hopes for what he already sees' (Rom. 8: 24). Thus, the clearer vision of the returning Christ himself, is distinguishable from the partial apprehension of his presence as Spirit in this world. Even so Paul speaks of this 'partial knowing' as a 'seeing' or 'perceiving'. He says, for example, in Romans 8: 23, that we 'have' the first fruits of the Spirit as experienced realities. The uniqueness of the Spirit and its divinely transcendent qualities entails, however, that it is an ambiguous and elusive reality, for some people claim to perceive and to identify what they see as 'the Spirit', and indeed do so with vehemence, whilst others apparently do not perceive anything religiously significant at all. This means that we are not required to conclude that God has determined, for some reason only known to himself, to give believers a knowledge of the presence of Christ and to withhold it from others depending on the whim of the moment.[56] Rather, the Spirit is a reality of such a kind that men and women are either free to perceive and claim to know its impact in their lives or are able not to be aware of it at all, primarily because of its own very elusive and transcendent nature and their own inclination either to see and attend or not to see by immersing themselves in the natural and material world.

As a consequence the presence of the Spirit of Christ which is to be experienced and apprehended in faith must be a reality of such a kind that men and women are free either to perceive its presence or to ignore it and allow it to pass unnoticed. In other words, it must be an ambiguous reality which does not compel assent and it is precisely the element of freedom to look and not to notice which distinguishes the religious perception appropriate to faith from the ordinary perception of everyday objects of the natural world. This is why it is appropriate for Paul to speak in 1 Cor. 13: 12 of the response of faith in terms of a partial knowing which awaits further clarity of sight.

Believing in the resurrection does not just involve a one-sided historical quest to define the *fons et origo* of Christian belief in the Lordship of Jesus and the source of the existence of the Church.[57] Indeed, such a retrospective pursuit, whether it be to pin the resurrection faith to the empty tomb (H. von Campenhausen) or the appearances (H. Grass) or both (Pannenberg) or the beginning of preaching (Marxsen) or even the history of the transmission of the tradition (U. Wilckens) have all been found wanting. But believing in the resurrection of Jesus is not just a retrospective or past-centred matter. Because it is said to have been an event which occurred at a specific time and place an approach to it through the avenue of the model of 'historical event' is not irrelevant. However, believing in the resurrection means accepting the resurrection on the basis of a decision which combines knowledge of past facts with an interpretation of present experience. There is a kind of existential correlate in the present of what the first witnesses reacted to and described in the past. The present access to the Spirit entails that the possibility of an empirical understanding of Easter faith is therefore not exhausted when the findings of historical-critical research on the tradition of original appearances are found to be inconclusive.[58] What has become clear is that the ground of resurrection belief is not found only in *appearances* but in the *presence* of Jesus as well.

The crucial question for the epistemology of faith is how such a reality could, with any justification at all, be identified as the Spirit of Jesus. If the knowing of the raised Christ as Spirit is in principle open to anybody who has eyes to see and ears to hear, and is not a gnostic secret knowledge granted to a few privileged individuals, then we must be able to explain how it is even possible for people to identify the Spirit as Jesus. In other words, we are faced with the problem of explaining how the Spirit, as a present object of religious

[57] C. F. Evans, op. cit., pp. 148–9: The resurrection is 'the *fons et origo* of Christian faith—the lordship of Jesus . . . the source of the existence of the Church'.
[58] 'God's revelation received and expressed in the community of faith is the horizon within which the meaning and significance of the resurrection can be discerned.' R. C. Ware, op. cit., p. 33. Also p. 184.

experience, can be identified by employing the name of a person who lived some two thousand years ago. By what criteria do we use the name Jesus and how do these criteria allow us to identify his continuing presence as Spirit?

VII

The Raised Christ as the Remembered Jesus

The Remembered Jesus

WE have arrived at the point where we must grasp a particularly prickly nettle. I have argued that resurrection faith may be understood as a kind of knowing by acquaintance of the presence of the raised Christ as Spirit. Whatever status is accorded by the heavenly visions or appearances of the raised Christ which were claimed by the first witnesses, whether they are regarded as objective visions or psychological phenomena of a more subjective kind, we are able to interpret them as tokens and signs of the real and objective existence of Christ 'at the right hand of the Father' because we have access to the presence of his Spirit as an additional datum within the 'cognitive nucleus' of faith.

Moreover, I have suggested that the perception of the presence of Christ through the medium of the Spirit may be understood to be similar in terms of its epistemological structure to the knowing by acquaintance of ordinary objects of this world, even if the Spirit of Christ is unique. If this is so, then we must recognize that this kind of perception involves an identity judgement in which the Spirit of the Christian fellowship is identified as the gracious presence of Jesus. The Raised One whom the first witnesses claimed to recognize from Easter Day onwards was not a new and anonymous presence but the very presence of their remembered master and teacher who had been crucified on the cross. This means that the identity judgement of faith in which an ostensively given reality is recognized as 'the Spirit of Jesus' involves a double reference. It is a matter of recognizing the presence of the Spirit of Christ, and this act of recognition involves or implies the memory of Jesus as he was. What is recognized in the present is identified by reference to the Jesus of the past. As Jürgen Moltmann puts it:

Christian theology speaks of 'revelation', when on the ground of the Easter appearances of the risen Lord it perceives and proclaims the identity of the risen one with the crucified one. Jesus is recognized in the Easter appearances as what he really *was*. That is the ground of faith's 'historical' remembrance of the life and work, claims and sufferings of Jesus of Nazareth.[1]

This entails that if faith is not just a perception of the presence of the Spirit of the Christian community but an identifying of that Spirit as the Spirit of Jesus, then the 'cognitive nucleus' of Easter faith must necessarily include a memory of Jesus as he was when he walked this earth. It is by virtue of this memory of the historical Jesus that the judgement of faith is made possible.

Whilst this may have been a relatively straightforward matter for those primitive Christians who had lived in Jesus' own time and who had enjoyed his company and witnessed his death, it is clearly questionable whether a present-day Christian can justifiably make any such claim. How can a person living in the twentieth century possibly claim to 'remember Jesus'? The use of the word 'remember' normally implies that the individual who is said to remember, actually witnessed the event said to be remembered by him at the time of its occurrence or once knew by acquaintance a person now said to be remembered by him. How can one ever claim to remember what one has not oneself previously experienced? It makes sense for me to claim to remember my grandfather, who, though he did not visit our family house often, was nevertheless a regular enough childhood visitor to allow me to recognize him again, should he knock on my door today. But what sense is there if I, as a twentieth-century person, were to say 'I remember Napoleon' or 'I remember Henry II'? One does not normally claim to remember persons who lived prior to one's own birth, for remembering presupposes some former original experience that supplies the content of the remembrance. How valid is it, therefore, for Christians to claim to recognize and identify the presence of the Spirit of Jesus, on the ground that the object of their present experience is numerically identical with the person who is 'remembered' to have lived in the first century and to have died upon the cross?

Whilst there seems to be a prima facie problem here concerning the nature of the Christian's memory of Jesus upon which his

[1] Jürgen Moltmann, *Theology of Hope*, pp. 84–5.

identification of the presence or Spirit of Jesus so crucially depends, talk of the 'memory of Jesus' or the 'Church's corporate memory' of him has in fact constituted an important theme in some twentieth-century theology.

The most sustained treatment of the theme of the 'Church's memory of Jesus' has been provided by the Anglican New Testament scholar John Knox, whose work was very widely read on both sides of the Atlantic during the 1960s. Systematic theology should have been able to get more mileage out of Knox's insights than in fact it has done, for there is a sense in which interest in Knox's writing petered out prematurely. Apart from the vicissitudes of theological fashion, this was almost certainly because of the imprecision with which Knox articulated his ideas. Before we shall be able to put his notion of 'the Church and her memory' to constructive use in the service of clarifying the structure of resurrection belief, it will be necessary to submit it to considerable scrutiny and revision.[2]

The first thing that must be said about Knox's talk of the 'Church and her memory of Jesus' is that it is rather promiscuous,[3] for he moves with bewildering rapidity from talking of the first Christians and their 'memory of Jesus' to talking of contemporary Christians

---

[2] Knox's writing on this theme dates from 1938. See 'Our Knowledge of Jesus', *Christendom*, 3 (1938), p. 644. Also 'A Few Memories and a Great Debt', *Criterion*, 5 (1966), pp. 24–6; *Chapters in a Life of Paul*; *Christ and the Hope of Glory*; 'Christianity and the Christian', Chapter 5 of *The Christian Answer*, pp. 160–90; *Christ the Lord*; *Criticism and Faith*; *Jesus: Lord and Christ*, a trilogy comprising 'The Man Christ Jesus' (1941), 'Christ the Lord' (1945), and 'On the Meaning of Christ' (1947); *Life in Christ Jesus: Reflections on Romans 5–8*; *On the Meaning of Christ*; *The Church and the Reality of Christ*; 'The Church *Is* Christ's Body', *Religion in Life*, 27 (1957/8), pp. 54–62; *The Death of Christ*; *The Early Church and the Coming Great Church*; 'The Epistle to the Romans: Introduction and Exegesis' in *The Interpreter's Bible*, ed. C. A. Buttrick *et al.*, Vol. IX, pp. 353–668; *The Ethic of Jesus in the Teaching of the Church*; 'The Hope of Glory: Ingersoll Lecture 1960', *Harvard Divinity Bulletin*, 24 (1960), pp. 9–19; *The Humanity and Divinity of Christ*; *The Integrity of Preaching*; 'The "Prophet" in New Testament Christology' in *Lux in Lumine: Essays to Honor W. Norman Pittenger*, ed. R. A. Norris, Jr., pp. 23–34. (There is a full bibliography of Professor Knox's writings in W. R. Farmer, C. F. D. Moule, and R. R. Niebuhr (eds.), *Christian History and Interpretation: Studies Presented to John Knox* (Cambridge, 1967). Those cited here are those having a particular reference to the theme of corporate memory.)

[3] See E. L. Mascall's criticisms of Knox's views in *The Secularisation of Christianity* and in *Theology and the Future*, where Mascall notes that the use of the notion of the Church's memory, as Knox employs it, is so enigmatic and baffling that he calls it 'somewhat "Pickwickian" ' (p. 106).

and their 'memory of Jesus' as though there were no differences between the two.

One reason for this is that there is a basic ecclesiological emphasis in Knox's theological writing which is marked by a strong feeling for the continuity of the Church through the ages. Thus, Knox says, for example, that the Church reflected in the New Testament documents 'is not the *primitive* Church only, but is the Church I know. As I read the passages in which its distinctive life is most clearly expressed, my primary experience is not that of *learning* something about the past, but of *recognizing* something in the present. In a word, the Church is one, not only in space, but in time'.[4] It is because Knox so strongly holds to the conviction of the continuity of the Church through time that he is able to argue, first, that one of the distinctive characteristics of the early Church as expressed in the New Testament is that it possessed a 'corporate memory of Jesus' and then, that this 'corporate memory' is also a distinctive characteristic of the Church in the present. Consequently he declares that 'This memory of Jesus himself was a central element of the life of primitive Christianity and still belongs to the very being of the Church.'[5] In other words, Knox exemplifies the kind of problem which I have just identified, by passing with remarkable, even alarming, ease from speaking of an experience of the first Christians to that of contemporary Christians, and by claiming that the Church in the present has a 'memory of Jesus', or to use the cognate verb, that the Church in the present 'remembers Jesus': Jesus is 'the human being, human hands once handled and human hearts remembered and remember still'.[6] The ease with which it is possible to slip from speaking of the 'corporate memory' of the first Christians to speaking of the Church in the present as a community that 'remembers Jesus' is an invitation to philosophical enquiry for it raises in a direct and acute form the question of the very propriety of claiming that twentieth-century people can 'remember' a person who lived two thousand years ago.

On the other hand, if there is continuity of logical pattern

---

[4] *The Church and the Reality of Christ* (hereafter *CRC*), p. 30. See also *CRC*, p. 44 and *The Early Church and the Coming Great Church* (hereafter *ECCGC*), p. 137.
[5] *ECCGC*, p. 54.
[6] *The Humanity and Divinity of Christ* (hereafter *HDC*), pp. 110–11; see also p. 2; of Jesus and the Church he says, 'he is *remembered* there'.

between the faith of primitive Christianity and that of Christians today, it is important that the relation of the early Christian memory of Jesus and any similar memory that Christians might claim today should be carefully examined. The problem here is one of multivocality. The first Christians remembered Jesus in a quite straightforward, literal sense of the word. But today, it might be said, we 'remember Jesus' in some less than literal sense, perhaps metaphorical. This seems to have been understood by Knox himself for he often draws on examples of individual memory to illustrate what he means when he speaks of the 'Church's memory'. He asks his readers, at one place, for instance, to consider the case in which they remember a friend, and then to consider the role that an independent biographer would play in relation to this memory. He then goes on to say that the Church's memory of Jesus and the role of an independent historian in relation to this memory is 'not too different'.[7] This very statement implies, however, that despite alleged similarities there is *some* difference and elsewhere Knox says, 'I hope no one will suppose that I am arguing that I can remember Jesus in the way Peter or John or Mary did', thereby indicating that his use of the term is not to be understood in a literal way.[8] In *The Humanity and Divinity of Christ*, moreover, he sometimes uses the word 'memory' in inverted commas to warn his readers that it is predicated in some unusual sense.[9] Even so, at other points in his writing he uses the term as though there were in fact no differences at all between the logic of its literal predication of individuals and its logic when predicated of the Church metaphorically. For example, at one place he speaks of his memory of his father and then goes on to say, 'So Jesus was remembered'.[10] Consequently, Knox tends to move not only from speaking of the early Church to speaking of the present Church with a rapidity that is deceptive, but from a literal or standard use of the words 'memory' and 'remember' to what appears to be a metaphorical one with somewhat bewildering facility, and we shall not be happy with talk of the 'Church and her

---

[7] *Criticism and Faith* (hereafter *CF*), p. 39. See also *CRC*, pp. 38–40.
[8] *CRC*, p. 39.
[9] *HDC*, p. 77.
[10] *Christ the Lord* (hereafter *CL*), p. 56. Speaking of an alleged certitude that attaches to the Church's memory of the Christ-Event, he says, 'it is of the very nature of the community to remember the event and the person around whom it occurred; and *one* simply cannot doubt the existence of what *one* remembers'. See *ECCGC*, p. 78.

memory of Jesus' until we can come to some better and more precise specification both of the differences and the similarities that hold between the literal and the metaphorical application of the concept. In addition, and very importantly, we shall want to know whether any differences that hold between the early Christian, literal 'memory of Jesus', and the contemporary Christian's 'memory' of Jesus, whatever it may involve, are sufficiently far-reaching to upset an understanding of faith in which the presence of the Spirit of Jesus is recognized and identified for what it is, precisely on the basis of the alleged 'memory' of Jesus, which alone makes such an identity claim possible.

John Knox's View of the Church and her Memory

At this point we must look at Knox's ideas of 'the Church and her memory of Jesus' in more detail. At the outset it is important to note that Knox makes an initial distinction between 'authentic primitive memories' or 'earliest shared memories'[11] about Jesus, on the one hand, and on the other 'the memory of Jesus himself' or the Church's 'common' or 'corporate memory' of Jesus.[12] The 'authentic primitive memories' about Jesus are the memories of the first Christians which the New Testament historian tries to separate from the mass of theological interpretation with which they were from the start clothed, and in which they are still embedded in the narratives of the New Testament. However, when Knox speaks of 'the memory of Jesus' he has in mind, not a memory possessed by the first Christians only (though he does not deny that it was entertained by them), but a memory of Jesus that has been transmitted in the life of the Church, through the ages. It is not the scientific historian's task to *discover* the content of this memory because it is a memory of Jesus that is already possessed by contemporary believers. It is, indeed, *the memory* of Jesus, shared in the continuing life of the Church, which constitutes a central factor in establishing the essential and continuing identity of the Christian community. Having made the distinction, the validity of which we shall assess in a moment, we may say that if the historian is able to discover some of the 'authentic primitive memories' of the first Christians with a greater or less degree of probability, he can aid

---

[11] *DC*, p. 29; *CRC*, p. 53.
[12] *ECCGC*, p. 54; *CRC*, p. 38 ff.

and enrich the life of faith. But, if he cannot reach any certain and fixed results, or even highly probable results, it is of little consequence to faith because the judgement of faith is actually made on the basis of 'the memory of Jesus'. Because this is transmitted in the life of the Church it may be said to be independent of historical research.[13] *The memory* of Jesus, indeed, was passed down in the life and worship of the Church long before the relatively modern science of historiography began. Consequently, the difficulties the historian experiences in trying to achieve fixed and assured conclusions concerning the particular 'primitive memories' about Jesus should not alarm the believer, for while he cannot feel absolute confidence in the original authenticity of many separate words or acts of Jesus[14] and must often be content with probabilities and the most tentative of conclusions, *the memory* of Jesus *himself* may be said to be secure and may be held with confidence and assurance.

In a way that highlights Knox's tendency to slide from talk of individual memory to that of the corporate memory of the Church with rather bewildering facility, he says that 'It is of the very nature of the community to remember the event and the person around whom it occurred; and *one* simply cannot doubt the existence of what *one* remembers'.[15] The point is that the Church cannot without ceasing to be the Church, doubt its fundamental memory of Jesus any more than an individual can doubt his own memories of the past. This statement seems to mean that an individual cannot intelligently claim to remember some past event and at the same time doubt that it occurred. In logical terms this is a correct presupposition because one cannot assert, 'I remember that p' and at the same time doubt 'that p', since the assertion 'I remember that p' entails 'that p' and to deny 'that p' would be to fall into self-contradiction.[16]

---

[13] *CF*, p. 9. Also see pp. 21 and 41. Here we see Knox striving for an incontrovertible base for faith in the face of the alleged permanent insecurity of historiographical judgements similar to that which so troubled Barth, Bultmann, and Tillich and others before them.

[14] *On the Meaning of Christ* (hereafter *OMC*), p. 38.

[15] *ECCGC*, p. 78. The italics are mine.

[16] The logic of the word 'remember' thus runs parallel to that of the word 'know'; one cannot claim to know something and at the same time doubt it. Indeed, if I claim to remember something it is entailed that I must also claim to know it. See G. E. Moore, *Philosophical Papers*, especially 'Four Forms of Scepticism', p. 214; also see Sydney Shoemaker, 'Memory', in *The Encyclopaedia of Philosophy*, Vol. V, 5, p. 266.

For the moment, it is sufficient to note that Knox does distinguish the memory of Jesus, which he says is a secure and vital ingredient of faith, and 'authentic primitive memories' *about* Jesus, which are additional to faith and which are established with varying degrees of probability by scientific historical research on the New Testament records. Given this distinction we must ask, what is the precise content of this memory of Jesus as distinct from the specific 'primitive memories'? If the scientific historian cannot be absolutely certain about individual words and deeds of Jesus, and if he experiences difficulty in separating the 'earliest memories' from the theological interpretation with which they were clothed, what is the content of the memory of Jesus of which the Christian is said to be reasonably certain?

Knox argued that while we cannot regard every item in the gospels as belonging to this 'authentic and abiding memory'[17] of Jesus there is a certain small but essential minimum of historical truth of which the Christian believer is sure. The memory of the Church assures the believer of the historicity of Jesus[18] and then, not just the bare fact that there was a Jesus, but something of the distinctive quality of his character. However, when we speak of what is remembered we are referring not so much to specific facts *about* Jesus, but to the person himself as *he* is remembered in the Church.[19] In other words, the irreducible minimum of historical truth that is passed down from generation to generation as the Church's memory, is not constituted by a plethora of facts *about* Jesus. Facts about Jesus are the 'authentic primitive memories' of the first Christians and are the object of historical research. What is transmitted in the life of the Church, and what is vital to the judgement of faith, is a memory of Jesus *himself*.

This same distinction lies behind a statement in his early work *Christ the Lord* where Knox says that, 'However much of what (Jesus) did and said was forgotten, or half-forgotten, *he* was remembered'.[20] In endeavouring to communicate his meaning at this point Knox says that the first Christians remembered Jesus, and 'remembered him in just the concrete, quite indescribable way we always

---

[17] *OMC*, p. 38.
[18] *CF*, p. 36.
[19] *CF*, p. 37.
[20] *CL*, p. 55. See also *HDC*, p. 77.

remember persons we have known and loved'.²¹ For the purpose of further clarification he then appeals to an analogy from his own experience. The distinction between remembering facts *about* persons and remembering persons *themselves* is illustrated in his memory of his own father. While he has a memory of his father, he cannot actually recall with any precision fully or accurately one incident in which his father took a significant part, and though he listened to him privately and publicly on many occasions he does not believe that he can quote a single phrase from his lips or put into definite form a single idea that he remembers from him.

And yet (he goes on) I remember him . . . So Jesus was remembered . . . they remembered *him* more vividly and more truly than any fact about *him* or anything he said. And it was that memory of Jesus himself upon which the Christian community, with all its life and faith, was in the first instance based.²²

In other words, in giving content to the notion of the Church's memory of Jesus, Knox clearly distinguishes between facts about Jesus which are said not to be part of the Church's memory and the memory of Jesus himself.²³ Clearly, if any mileage is to be got out of his notion for the purpose of explaining how it is that Christians are able to identify the Spirit as the presence of Jesus, the memory of Jesus himself, rather than a memory of particular incidents in which he was involved, is what appears to be of crucial interest.²⁴ Those who remember him will clearly be in a position to identify his living

---

²¹ *CL*, p. 55.
²² *CL*, p. 56.
²³ *ECCGC*, p. 54. Knox affirms that the 'memory we are considering was a memory of Jesus himself, not of any fact about him or any word he spoke'.
²⁴ *CRC*, pp. 51-2: 'When I say . . . that the Church remembers Jesus, I do not mean that it remembers *facts about him*. Indeed, it is doubtful that we can ever properly be said to *remember* a fact about anything. Facts about things are abstractions; only the things themselves can in the strict sense be remembered'. See also *CF*, pp. 49 and *CRC*, pp. 35 and 54, especially footnote 3. It is because the memory of the Church does not contain facts about Jesus, over and above those found in the New Testament, nor doctrinal formulations, that Knox says he prefers his term 'memory' to 'tradition'. For accounts of what has been conceived as a 'tradition' in the history of the Church see G. Tavard, *Holy Writ or Holy Church* and Y. Congar, *Tradition and Traditions*, especially Chapter 2. Even so, Knox says that what he calls 'memory' is obviously related to what the Church has called 'tradition'. For the use of this concept in recent theology see Hans von Campenhausen, *Tradition and Life in the Church*, especially Chapter 1, 'Tradition and Spirit in Early Christianity' and Gerhard Ebeling, *The Word of God and Tradition*.

presence. But first we must test the coherence of talk of the Church's remembering of him. Certainly, the relation of the Church's continuing memory to historical research will depend largely on the validity of this distinction, for, implicit in the distinction between two kinds of content, facts *about* Jesus on one hand, and Jesus *himself* on the other, is a distinction between two ways of acquiring knowledge, historical research and a continuing process of transmission within the life of the Church. If the distinction between facts about Jesus and Jesus himself cannot be maintained, it may also follow that it may not be possible to maintain a rigid dichotomy between historical research and the processes of transmission in the life of the Church either.

Malcolm on Memory

Before we seek to test the validity of distinguishing between authentic primitive memories of a specific kind and the continuing memory of Jesus himself in the life of the Church, it will be necessary to raise the prior question of the validity of claiming that it is possible for the contemporary Church to 'remember Jesus', given that it has had no direct experience of him. Knox says that he believes that it is doubtful if we can ever properly be said to remember a fact but that 'only things themselves can in the strict sense be remembered'. At this point Knox is certainly mistaken. The verb 'remember' enters into a variety of grammatical constructions and it is wrong to think that it is properly used in only one of them. Professor Norman Malcolm, for instance, has distinguished three different forms of memory each of which is expressed by employing the verb 'remember' in a different, but perfectly correct or 'strict' sense.[25] There may well be more than the three forms of memory that Malcolm has defined, but a consideration of Malcolm's distinctions will help us to analyse the nature of the contemporary Christian's 'memory of Jesus' generally.

Malcolm calls the three forms of memory *perceptual* memory, *factual* memory and *personal* memory respectively. The meaning of perceptual memory as Malcolm defines it, is roughly, though not exactly, equivalent to an original definition given the term by C. D. Broad. Broad said that 'perceptual memory' is 'the memory of

[25] 'Three Forms of Memory', in Norman Malcolm, *Knowledge and Certainty*, p. 205.

particular events, places, persons, or things'.[26] Perceptual memory is memory *of* some past object rather than memory *about* a past object; it is the memory of a past event *itself* or of a past person *himself*. For example, perceptual memory is expressed in such assertions as 'I remember its raining last week' or 'I remember the launching of the *Queen Elizabeth II*' or 'I remember him, though I do not remember his age'. Perceptual memory is roughly what Gilbert Ryle calls a man's occurrent recollecting of something, his 'recalling, reviewing, or dwelling on some episode of his own past'[27] in distinction from habit memories or memories of *how* to perform certain tasks, such as remembering the way to the bank or remembering how to tie one's shoelace.

Malcolm's definition of perceptual memory differs from Broad's in that he requires that the memory *of* past persons, places, events, or things always involves mental imagery: 'It belongs to the concept of perceptual memory, that it requires mental imagery', he says, and notes that Bertrand Russell seems to be conceiving of the same kind of memory when he says that the 'process of remembering will consist of calling up images . . . '.[28] Perceptual memory, as Malcolm defines it, involves seeing a past person, place, event or thing 'before the mind's eye'.

Malcolm's second form of memory, factual memory, is quite different. It is not memory *of* a person, place, event or thing, but it is memory of facts *about* persons, places, events or things. To Malcolm's mind it is distinguishable from perceptual memory because it does not involve mental imagery. Rather, factual memory denotes a use of 'remember' 'in which this verb is followed by a clause of the form "that *p*" where for "*p*" there may be substituted any sentence expressing a proposition'.[29] The parallel kind of memory is referred to by Broad as 'propositional memory', but Malcolm calls this form of memory 'factual memory' because, when the subordinate 'that-clause' expresses a true proposition, it expresses a fact. Moreover, whereas perceptual memory is memory of concrete persons, places, events or things of the past, factual memory may be quite abstract.

[26] C. D. Broad, *The Mind and Its Place in Nature*, p. 222.
[27] G. Ryle, *The Concept of Mind*, p. 258.
[28] N. Malcolm, op. cit., p. 208. Bertrand Russell, *The Analysis of Mind*, p. 175, quoted by Malcolm p. 210.
[29] N. Malcolm, op. cit., pp. 203–4. For further definition of factual memory see pp. 222–40, 'A Definition of Factual Memory'.

For example, the statements, 'I remember that $2 + 2 = 4$' or 'I remember that Jones is 31 years of age', are examples of factual memory.[30]

On the other hand, the facts expressed in statements falling under the heading of factual memory may relate to or be about past events, such as, 'I remember that the *Queen Elizabeth II* was launched in 1968' or 'I remember that Jones won the chess championship'. The difference between factual memory and perceptual memory becomes clear if somebody claims to remember 'that the *Queen Elizabeth II* was launched in 1968' but adds, 'however, I do not remember the actual launching *itself*', or if somebody claims to remember 'that Jones won the chess championship' but adds, 'however, I do not actually recall the occasion *itself*'.

Malcolm goes on to say that the distinction he is making between factual memory and perceptual memory could be stated as the distinction between 'memory by description' and 'memory by acquaintance'.[31] Perhaps a better way of putting this distinction would be to say that factual memory is 'memory by description' and perceptual memory is 'acquaintance by memory'.[32]

Another important distinction between these two forms of memory is that, while in examples of perceptual memory the referent is always past, a factual memory may be about the past, present, or future. Thus, all the following examples are examples of factual memory: 'I remember that Napoleon lost the Battle of Waterloo'; 'I remember that the mayor is opening the flower show'; and 'I remember that there will be a May Ball next week'.[33] But perceptual memory must always be *of* a person, place, event or thing in the past. One cannot intelligently claim to have a memory *of* the mayor opening the flower show at the present moment, nor to remember, recall or have a memory of next week's May Ball.

Something must now be said about the third of Malcolm's three forms of memory, personal memory. Malcolm defines personal memory as memory of persons, places, events, or things, that one has previously perceived or experienced *in one's own lifetime*. It is

---

[30] Cf. C. D. Broad, op. cit., p. 272: 'The propositions which I remember . . . *may* be about past events, but they need not be'.

[31] Op. cit., p. 208.

[32] For the phrase 'acquaintance by memory' see Bertrand Russell, *The Problems of Philosophy*, p. 76.

[33] Cf. G. Ryle, op. cit., pp. 257–8.

represented in statements of the kind, 'I *personally* remember *p*'. The examples that have already been cited to illustrate perceptual memory can also be expressed as examples of personal memory. For example, one could say, 'I personally remember its raining last week'; 'I personally remember the launching of the *Queen Elizabeth II*', or 'I personally remember *him*, though I do not remember his age'. Indeed, all perceptual memory is personal memory since one cannot claim to remember a previous acquaintance with persons, places, events, or things that lie beyond one's own personal experience. That is to say, one cannot have perceptual memory of objects and events that lie temporally or geographically outside the bounds of one's past experience. One cannot have perceptual memory of events which occurred before one was born, or of persons who died before one was born, or of places and things that lie geographically outside the field of one's past experiences. There would be an absurdity in saying that I, a twentieth-century person, 'personally remember Napoleon losing the Battle of Waterloo', or, if I have never been to the South Pole, that 'I personally remember the South Pole'. As Gilbert Ryle put it, 'these are not the sorts of things that can be recalled, in the sense of the verb in which what I recall must be things that I have myself witnessed, done or experienced'.[34]

However, while perceptual memory is always personal memory, personal memory is not always perceptual memory, for personal memory does not always involve seeing images 'before the mind's eye'. Personal memory *may* be expressed as factual memory. One may say, 'I personally remember *p*' or 'I personally remember that *p*'. On the other hand, whilst all perceptual memory is personal memory, and while personal memory may be either perceptual or factual, not all factual memory is personal memory, for what is said to be remembered in factual memory need not necessarily be about a person, place, event or thing previously witnessed or experienced in one's own lifetime.

Many philosophers have thought that all memory must be of the personal/perceptual or personal/factual type. That is to say, many have thought that the only permissible form of memory is memory of persons, places, events, or things that one previously witnessed or experienced oneself. W. von Leyden, for example, says: 'Everyone would agree that what we can remember is not just any past event or fact, but a certain kind of past events or facts, namely those that form part of one's own previous experience.'[35]

This contention cannot claim our assent, however, for a number of reasons. First of all, we are inclined to claim to remember events which were not actually previously witnessed or experienced, but which we otherwise came to know about at the time of their occurrence. For example, though one has not actually experienced the Second World War, one is inclined to claim to remember it if one was alive at the time it was going on, and if one knew that it was going on at that time. Similarly, one is inclined to say, 'I personally remember the assassination of President Kennedy' though one did not actually witness it, but came to know about it at the time of its occurrence through various media of communication. However, even if these claims are allowed as legitimate memory-claims, this still limits memory to events or facts that have occurred within one's own lifetime. Malcolm correctly insists that even this limitation is invalid. Factual memory need not be of facts falling within the rememberer's previous experience, or occurring within one's own lifetime. It is perfectly correct to say, 'I remember that Napoleon lost the Battle of Waterloo'. That is to say, not all factual memory is personal memory.

G. E. Moore said at one place that we do not *personally* remember William the Conqueror winning the Battle of Hastings in 1066.[36] It is true that we cannot intelligently claim to have personal or perceptual memory of William the Conqueror winning the Battle of Hastings; we can hardly claim to see an image of William winning the Battle 'before our mind's eye'. If we do we are imagining not remembering. However, it is perfectly correct for a twentieth-century person to claim to remember 'that William the Conqueror won the Battle of Hastings'. Broad also affirms this: 'I certainly do remember that Caesar crossed the Rubicon', he says, 'and I certainly do not remember the event which is described as "Caesar crossing the Rubicon" '.[37]

Moreover, it would be incorrect to object that what is really meant when one claims to remember 'that William the Conqueror won the Battle of Hastings' or 'that Napoleon lost the Battle of Waterloo', or 'that Caesar crossed the Rubicon' is that one remem-

[35] W. von Leyden, *Remembering*, p. 60.
[36] G. E. Moore, *Philosophical Papers*, p. 215.
[37] Op. cit., p. 272.

bers past occasions in one's lifetime when these facts were learned. I myself do actually remember all these facts, and many more besides, but I do not remember the occasions when I first learned them, nor do I actually remember *how* I first acquired the knowledge of them. Claims to possess factual memory do *imply* previous occasions in one's past experience when such facts were learned or acquired. If I claim to remember 'that William the Conqueror won the Battle of Hastings' what is meant is that I previously learned or knew that William the Conqueror won the Battle of Hastings and I still know it.[38] That is say, factual memory *implies* knowledge and previous occasions in one's personal experience when the facts in question were learned or acquired. They may have been previously known on the basis of observation, or the testimony of others, or inference from evidence. I may have acquired the facts that William the Conqueror won the Battle of Hastings and that Napoleon lost the Battle of Waterloo by reading a reliable history textbook, or by being told by a teacher whose accuracy in such matters had usually been unquestioned. However, though experiences such as these are *implied* by factual memory, these things are not what I *remember* when I say, 'I remember that William the Conqueror won the Battle of Hastings' or 'that Napoleon lost the Battle of Waterloo'.[39]

In summary, the basic relations between the three forms of memory as Malcolm defines them may be expressed as follows:

(*a*)   All perceptual memory is also personal memory;
(*b*)   Not all personal memory is perceptual memory since personal memory may be factual or perceptual;
(*c*)   Not all factual memory is personal memory, since remembered facts may be very remote ones, lying outside one's own personal experience.

Now, these distinctions may be employed to clarify statements concerning the Church's 'corporate memory' of Jesus.

First of all, when Knox makes the distinction between remember-

---

[38] See Norman Malcolm, 'A Definition of Factual Memory', in *Knowledge and Certainty*, pp. 222–40, especially p. 223. Malcolm defines factual memory as follows: 'A person, B, remembers that *p* if and only if B knows that *p* because he knew that *p*'.

[39] For comments relevant to this point see Norman Malcolm, op. cit., p. 217; also Sydney Shoemaker, 'Memory', in *Encyclopaedia of Philosophy*, ed. Paul Edwards, Vol. V, pp. 256–6.

ing his own father, and remembering particular facts about him, he is saying something of importance. Knox is making a distinction similar to Malcolm's distinction between perceptual memory and factual memory. Knox does not explicitly say that his memory of his father involves seeing a mental image of his father, but as much is implied. He remembers his father *himself*, and this is to be contrasted with remembering facts *about* him. However, when Knox says that 'in the strict sense' we can only be said to remember 'things themselves', he apparently means that *only* what Malcolm calls 'perceptual memory' can strictly be called memory. In other words, he claims that only memory *of* an actual person or event in the past and not abstract facts *about* them can be strictly called memory. This view is understandable. Bertrand Russell and Henri Bergson both held similar views. Both held that what Malcolm calls 'perceptual memory', as distinct from habit memory or factual memory, is the true or real kind of memory.[40]

It does not follow, however, that we can never properly be said to remember facts about things, and when Knox says, 'One does not "remember" ideas or concepts or generalisations or formal definitions, however true they may be; one *remembers* only persons and things and happenings'[41] he is clearly mistaken. It is perfectly correct to say that we remember 'that $2 + 2 = 4$', 'that Napoleon lost the Battle of Waterloo' or even, providing these propositions are true, 'that there was a Jesus' or 'that he displayed a particular quality of character'. Factual memory, indeed, is the only form of memory which allows references to persons, places, events, or things which lie outside one's own experience. It would be as absurd to say, 'I remember Jesus dying on the cross' or 'I personally remember Jesus' or 'I personally remember Jesus himself' as it would be to say, 'I personally remember William the Conqueror winning the Battle of Hastings', or 'I personally remember Napoleon losing the Battle of Waterloo'. However, one can claim to remember that there was a Jesus, as properly as one can claim to remember that there was a Napoleon.

But factual memory seems exactly the kind of memory that Knox will not allow. He claims that he remembers his father, but that he

---

[40] See Bertrand Russell, *The Analysis of Mind*, pp. 167 and 175–6; Henri Bergson, *Matter and Memory*, pp. 86 ff. See also Norman Malcolm, op. cit., p. 210.

[41] *CRC*, p. 46.

does not remember facts about his father. Similarly, he insists that the Church's memory is not comprised of factual memories *about* Jesus but that we remember *him*; we remember Jesus *himself*. This seems to suggest that the Church has a perceptual memory *of* Jesus. But this is exactly what the Church cannot have because perceptual memory is always also personal memory; it is a recalling of persons, places, events, or things previously experienced in one's own life-time. No doubt Knox would claim that while we cannot *literally* claim to have a perceptual memory of Jesus himself, in just the way the apostles, Peter or John, or Mary, his Mother, did,[42] the Church's memory of Jesus himself is *like* perceptual memory, and that it is perceptual memory that provides the basis from which the metaphorical predication of the concept 'memory' of the Church derives. This, at least, seems to be the implication of his contention that the Church's memory of Jesus is similar to his own memory of his father. In this event, perhaps we are to conclude that when Knox speaks of the 'Church's corporate memory of Jesus' he means to refer to a reality in the life of the Church that is in some way similar to perceptual memory, but distinct from it in the sense that while perceptual memory is always of persons, places, events or things that one has oneself previously experienced, the Church's memory of Jesus is a memory of a person who lived two thousand years ago, and thus of a person whose existence stands outside the experience of contemporary Christians. The Church's memory of Jesus would thus be similar to perceptual memory, but unlike it in the sense that it is not also personal memory.

But in exactly what way is the Church's memory of Jesus similar to perceptual memory? Knox states the similarity only negatively. Given the fact that the Church's memory is not literally an instance of perceptual memory, he says it is analogous to perceptual memory in so far as it is independent of factual memory. It is independent of factual memories about Jesus, just as his own memory of his father is independent of the memory of facts about him. In other words, the similarity between the Church's memory of Jesus and Knox's memory of his father is conveyed by saying that as he remembers his father but not facts about him, so Christians remember Jesus himself, but not facts about him.

This leaves the concept of 'the memory of Jesus himself' far from

---

[42] *CRC*, p. 39.

clear. But even these contentions are untenable. The argument implicit in Knox's statements is that it is possible to have perceptual memory of one's father and a memory of Jesus that is in some way analogous to a memory of one's father, without having factual memories about one's father, and without having any factual memories about Jesus. Now let us, for the moment, set aside what he says about the Church's memory of Jesus and concentrate on what Knox says concerning his memory of his father. He claims to remember his father, but not facts about him. Is this a defensible contention? I do not think it is.

While a person may claim to have factual memories without also claiming to have perceptual memory, since one can claim to remember a fact without conjuring up an image 'before the mind's eye', it is doubtful if it makes sense to claim to have perceptual memory and at the same time to deny all factual memory about the object of perceptual memory. If a person claims to have a perceptual memory of a past person, or to remember the person himself, which, if we accept Norman Malcolm's definition of perceptual memory involves summoning up an image of the person concerned or seeing him 'before the mind's eye', it follows that the rememberer must be able to state some facts about him. If he cannot state at least some facts about him, we will hardly be convinced that he really has a perceptual memory of the person;[43] we may doubt that he is really seeing an image of the person 'before his mind's eye'. In other words, perceptual memory is logically dependent on factual memory, for the capacity to state some factual memories is implied by claims to have perceptual memory. Factual memory, on the other hand, is not logically dependent on perceptual memory. One can remember facts about persons, places, events, or things without conjuring up images in the mind's eye; indeed, we have argued that one can have factual memories about persons, places, events, and things that lie outside one's past experience and of which, therefore, one cannot have perceptual memory.

Moreover, what are prima facie examples of perceptual memory are often reducible to cases of factual memory. When I say, 'I remember what I had for breakfast', I may be understood to be asserting that I have an image of my breakfast before my mind. On

[43] See Norman Malcolm, op. cit., p. 220. Also p. 222: 'Both personal and perceptual memory imply factual memory' (footnote 2).

the other hand, I may simply be understood to be asserting something like, 'I remember that I had eggs, bacon, and toast for breakfast'; I may not necessarily mean that I am seeing my breakfast 'before my mind's eye'. However, if I claim to be able to see my breakfast 'before my mind's eye' I must be able to state some facts about it, such as, 'that I had, eggs, bacon, and toast', before I will convince another person that I am really seeing my breakfast 'before my mind's eye'. If I claim to have a memory of what I had for breakfast and cannot state some facts about it there is something decidedly wrong. Indeed, a hearer will probably conclude that I do not know how to use the word 'remember'.

Perceptual memory thus depends on factual memory; factual memory does not depend on perceptual memory. Consequently, we may conclude that factual memory is logically the more primitive kind, for whilst it does not itself imply other kinds of memory, it seems always to be implied by other kinds of memory.

Now, if I claim to remember Winston Churchill himself, that is to say, if I claim to have a perceptual memory of Churchill, and claim to have an image of him presented 'before my mind's eye', I must be able to state some facts about Churchill. I must be able to say that he had a roundish face, stern features, and a cigar in his mouth. If I cannot state at least some facts about him I shall hardly convince others that I am remembering him. In the light of this we may conclude that if Professor Knox is not able to recall 'with any precision fully and accurately' one incident in which his father took a significant part, and does not believe that he can quote a single phrase from his father's lips, unless he can state *some* facts about his father we shall have grave misgivings as to whether he really has a memory of his father at all.

Similarly, we may concede that the kind of memory that Knox has in mind when he speaks of 'the Church's memory of Jesus', whilst not being personal/perceptual memory may be called 'memory' in some extended or metaphorical sense; however, unless *some* factual memories about Jesus can be stated we shall be inclined to doubt that the Church has a 'memory of Jesus' in any sense of the word. Indeed, we seem close to the conclusion that a 'memory of Jesus' that cannot be expressed in terms of at least *some* facts about him is an entirely vacuous notion.

Professor Malcolm says that he has been unable to find an example of memory that is not logically dependent on factual memory. We are prevented from stating categorically that the 'Church's memory of Jesus' is logically dependent on factual memory because we have not yet been able to come to a precise and clear conception of what the 'Church's memory of Jesus' actually *is*. This may yet be an exception to the rule; it may yet be that what the Church means by the 'Church's memory of Jesus himself' is independent of factual memories about him. However, we have been able to say that there is good reason to think that unless some factual memories about Jesus can be stated the idea of the 'Church's memory of Jesus' is empty. This at least points to the logical primitiveness of factual memories in this case.

Curiously, however, the logical primitiveness of factual memories about Jesus in relation to the 'Church's memory of Jesus himself' is actually demonstrated in Knox's own writing, for the notion of 'the Church's memory' is thoroughly shadowy and vague and Knox's references to it are quite bewildering until Knox begins to give it precise content by resorting to certain facts. Even in *The Man Christ Jesus* (1941) Knox argued that the Church remembers Jesus as a person 'supremely great and good'. What is this but a memory of the fact that Jesus was supremely great and good? On the other hand, in his more recent work *The Humanity and Divinity of Christ* (1967) Knox emphasized that the Church remembers Jesus as an actual human being; what the Church ' "remembers" is a man— a man "full of grace and truth", but nevertheless a *man* . . . '.[44] An 'essential constituent' of the memory of Jesus is that it is 'the remembrance of a truly human person'.[45] In other words, the memory of Jesus himself is at least the memory that Jesus was a truly human person.[46]

However, even at the outset we noted that Knox claimed that the Church's memory of Jesus contains more than the bare fact that there was a Jesus. It also contains something of the distinctive quality of his character. Certainly, if the memory of Jesus is to give the Church the ability to recognize his spiritual presence we should expect it to contain much more than the bare fact that there was a Jesus and that he was a man. Knox is true to his word. He claims

---

[44] *HDC*, p. 78. See also p. 55: 'the one we know in memory is fully human'. And *DC*, p. 112: Jesus is said to be 'a vividly remembered individual'.
[45] *HDC*, pp. 76 and 78–9.
[46] *HDC*, p. 79. Jesus is the '*humanly* human Companion we remember him to have been'.

that in remembering this man we remember his particular and uniquely individual character, which can be described in a number of statements of fact. In *The Death of Christ* Knox argued that 'the moral personality of Jesus and the character of his life'[47] is remembered, for the memory is constituted not only by 'the fact of the historical life but also the quality of it as a life in which . . . agape . . . began to be revealed'.[48] Indeed, Knox says:

It belongs to the very nature of the Church to know not only that Jesus lived but that *Jesus* lived. I mean that it is of the nature of the Church to remember a man who in word and act expressed that agape which later became the breath, the spirit, of the Church's life and which even then began to evoke a characteristic response.[49]

Again, in *The Church and The Reality of Christ* Knox affirms that *agape* is 'remembered as the essential and distinctive quality of Jesus' own life'.[50] His character is remembered as the character of the 'full integrity and utter abundance of love'.[51]

In other words, in giving content to the concept of the 'memory of Jesus *himself*' we are obliged to resort to certain statements of putative fact, namely, that Jesus existed, that he was a man, that he was supremely great and good, that he possessed a distinctive moral character, that the quality of this distinctive character can be expressed as '*agape*'.

On the other hand, we must continually stress the importance of the fact of Jesus' death in the Church's memory of him. To remember Jesus is to remember his cross.[52] Jesus was 'the man and Master whose death was remembered';[53] he was 'poignantly remembered to have suffered a terrible death'.[54]

Indeed, for the early Christians the remembrance of Jesus himself would have been associated in their minds with the remembrance of his death. Because the cross was for the first Christians the centre of their memory of Jesus, and since our memory of him is theirs con-

---

47 *DC*, p. 110.
48 *DC*, p. 111.
49 *DC*, p. 11.
50 *CRC*, p. 56. See also *LCJ*, pp. 21–2, 51, and 74.
51 *HDC*, p. 45.
52 *CL*, p. 56. See also *DC*, p. 114: 'thence forth to remember Jesus was to remember first of all his Cross'.
53 *ECCGC*, p. 61.
54 *DC*, p. 36.

veyed to us, it is also the centre of ours.[55] Thus, the cross has a place of special significance in the event to which we find ourselves looking back in memory and faith, for the cross is the focus of the community's memory.

In other words, though Knox avows that the memory of Jesus which is transmitted in the life of the Church contains no facts *about* Jesus, when we come to give content to what would otherwise be a strange and shadowy notion, we are obliged to resort to statements of a factual kind. Not only may the Church be said to remember that Jesus possessed a distinctive quality of character, but it remembers also that he died on the cross. This demonstrates the logical primitiveness of factual memory in this case. Indeed, we are obliged to conclude that when Knox says that the Church remembers 'Jesus *himself*', and not facts *about* him, he is confused. We must in fact treat the construction 'the Church remembers Jesus *himself*' as an ellipsis, in the grammarians' sense, the meaning of which is given in a series of putatively factual statements. It may be that the Church's memory of Jesus is not fully accounted for when it is said to contain the facts that we have so far stated; at least these facts are required, however, in order to give some specific content to the notion of 'the Church's memory of Jesus *himself*'.

It was noted at the outset that when Knox said that we do not remember facts about Jesus but that we remember Jesus himself, he clearly believed that he was making a distinction of importance. If we are prepared to try to appreciate his insight and ignore the infelicities that have been exposed in his attempt to communicate it, it will be useful at this point to make a distinction between dispositional and episodic statements.

Dispositions and Episodes

It is fairly clear that when Knox says that the Church does not remember facts *about* Jesus he really means that the Church does not remember particular incidents of his career of an episodic or occurrent nature. For example, he says 'Jesus is remembered . . . and therefore his existence cannot be doubted by the Christian. But no mere incident or circumstances in Jesus' career belongs to this memory.'[56] Or again, he asserts: 'I am not suggesting that it (the

[55] *DC*, p. 113. See also p. 117; *OMC*, p. 39 and p. 38; *ECCGC*, p. 53. See also *LCJ*, p. 34.

[56] *CF*, pp. 48–9.

memory) contains a single specific datum concerning the circumstances or incidents of Jesus' career or a single sentence from his lips . . . '.[57] In other words, the Church does not remember that Jesus said or did this or that, that he went here or there, that this or that thing happened to him or in his presence.[58] It seems fairly clear, then, that when Knox says that there are no facts in the memory of Jesus, he means that there are no factual statements reporting episodes or incidents in Jesus' career.

This leads me to suggest that when we say that the Church remembers 'Jesus *himself*' we are endeavouring to say that the Church's memory of the bare fact of Jesus' existence can be given content in statements reporting certain dispositions relating to Jesus. Gilbert Ryle has pointed out that dispositional statements do not report 'observed or observable states of affairs . . . They narrate no incidents.'[59] 'When a cow is said to be a ruminant, or a man is said to be a cigarette-smoker, it is not being said that the cow is ruminating now or that the man is smoking a cigarette now. To be a ruminant is to tend to ruminate from time to time, and to be a cigarette-smoker is to be in the habit of smoking cigarettes.'[60] That is to say, a dispositional statement, as distinct from a categorical statement of fact, does not report any particular incident or occurrence; rather, it has a tendency-stating or capacity-stating function. Its logical behaviour has much in common with general laws or open hypotheticals which do not themselves assert particular states of affairs, but, precisely because they are general or 'open' statements, can be 'filled' by particular instances of states of affairs. Dispositional statements, in other words, are capable of expression in universal conditional form; they can be cast in the form 'if *p* then *q*' or 'whenever *p* then *q*' and are universal or 'open' in the sense that they can be filled by particular instances of *p*'s and *q*'s. To say that a glass is brittle means that if it is hit with a hammer then it will shatter and fly into splinters, not that it is now shattering and flying into splinters; to say that a sheep is a grass-eating animal is to say that if a sheep is put into a field, then it will tend to eat grass, not that it is at this instant eating grass. Or to say that sugar is soluble in water is to say that whenever sugar is put in water it will dissolve, not that it it now dissolving.

---

[57] *CRC*, p. 51.
[58] *CRC*, p. 52.
[59] *The Concept of Mind*, p. 120.
[60] Ibid., p. 113.

Now, qualities of character are dispositional statements and, despite the fact that they refer to specific persons, are capable of expression in universal conditional form. To say that Bill is an angry person is not to say that he is even now exhibiting anger, nor that he is always at every moment exhibiting anger, but that if he is crossed he will tend to show anger rather than forbearance. To say that Tom is compassionate is to say that in certain kinds of situations he will tend to exhibit the quality of compassion, not that he is always or at every instant exhibiting compassion. Sometimes he goes to sleep, at other times he reads books and is engrossed in his work. To say that he is compassionate is to say that he is liable to exhibit compassion in specific situations.

Now, we have said that the Jesus who is remembered in the life of the community of faith is a truly human person, and that he exhibited a specific quality of character called '*agape*'. This does not report any particular incident or occurrence. Nor does it mean that in every instant of his career Jesus was exhibiting this quality of character. Rather, it means that it is remembered by Christians that in certain kinds of circumstances he tended to act in such a way as to exhibit what is called '*agape*'. This disposition can be cast in universal conditional form: 'Whenever Jesus was in circumstances of kind *k*, he tended to exhibit the character of kind *L*'.

Consequently, when the Church remembers Jesus *himself*, this involves not just the bare fact of Jesus' past existence but something of the distinctive or specific quality of his character. The content of this memory can be given not in categorical statements reporting particular incidents, but in statements of hypothetical form. Jesus is remembered as a person who exhibited *agape*; that is to say, he allegedly exhibited a liability or regular tendency to act in a certain way. Thus, to 'remember Jesus' is to remember a disposition, not an episode. The Church remembers not specific words or deeds of Jesus so much as Jesus *himself* and the kind of person he was.

Though we may not know with certainty that Jesus said or did any particular thing, we do know with a high degree of confidence that he said and did a certain kind of thing. In other words, Jesus is remembered to have been 'the kind of person he was', and if we cannot be certain that he spoke particular words, we can be sure that he was the kind of person who could have spoken them.[61] Or again,

[61] *OMC*, p. 37.

though we cannot feel absolute confidence in the original authenticity of specific separate words or acts of Jesus merely as such, he is remembered to have been a specific kind of person.[62] It is at this point that the current theological interest in the category of 'story' is of importance. Though particular incidents and episodes in the Jesus story may be open to question on the grounds of dubious historicity, the story itself may be said to be true in so far as it has the ability to communicate with accuracy the kind of person Jesus was, the general disposition of his character.

Such an understanding of the nature of the content of the Church's memory is suggested also, when we talk of the transmission of an 'image' or 'picture' of Jesus. It is the general impression, rather than reports of particular episodes, that is transmitted as the Church's memory of Jesus himself. Thus when we rehearse the Jesus story we may trust the impression of the person the story conveys, even if we have reason to doubt the accuracy of some of the reports of his specific words and acts.

These statements may seem to suggest that the content of the Church's memory of Jesus has been determined largely under the restraining influence of the findings of contemporary critical-historical research on the New Testament. However, it is a mistake to jump to the conclusion that accounts of incidents in Jesus' career have been excluded from the content of the Church's memory simply because we have been obliged to do so by the somewhat tentative results of much historical criticism. Even Paul seems to have been very little interested in specific incidents and episodes of Jesus' career and yet Paul's epistles reveal that he had a clear impression of the kind of person Jesus was, a vivid sense of the personality of Jesus. In other words, when Paul speaks of Jesus, he speaks of a person remembered; the memory unmistakably underlies Paul's knowledge of Christ and is presupposed in every reference he makes to him. The Lord Jesus Christ is no vague mythological personage; the *remembered Jesus* was Lord. Consequently, it was the fact of Jesus' unique humanity that was important to Paul, rather than specific incidents of Jesus' career. One only has to read again the famous kenotic passage in Philippians 2: 5–11 to recognize that Paul is holding before his readers the memory-image of Jesus and the particular quality of his self-giving: He is the one who emptied

---

[62] *OMC*, p. 38. See also pp. 62–3.

himself and, taking the form of a servant, humbled himself and was obedient, even unto death.

However, this is not to say that dispositional statements are not or cannot be putatively factual. Even dispositional statements do state facts. It is a fact that sheep are grass-eating animals, that glass is brittle, that sugar is soluble in water, and it may be a fact that a certain person is a cigarette-smoker. It may also be a fact, if it is true, that Jesus exhibited a certain quality of love. Dispositional statements are no less capable of being shown to be true or false than episodic statements, even though 'they do not state truths or falsehoods of the same type as those asserted by the statements of fact to which they apply'.[63]

However, having said this, one qualification must be made. 'That Jesus displayed a certain moral character' and 'that he exhibited a particular quality of love' are dispositional statements. They are also putatively factual. But we may affirm quite explicitly that the memory of Jesus includes not only these facts but also the fact that Jesus died on the cross: it 'remembers' the human Jesus and his goodness, but also his death. This is clearly not only a dispositional but an episodic statement. It reports an occurrence. On the other hand, it is clear that the memory of Jesus' death on the cross does not simply report a bare incident. In so far as the cross constitutes part of the content of the Church's corporate memory of Jesus, it is clear that it is not a bare incident but a symbol. It is the symbol of the whole concrete impact of Jesus' life. Indeed, it was the moral personality of Jesus and the character of his life, as these were known and remembered, which made the death significant. Consequently, the death of Christ was not only the vivid and poignant focus of the Church's memory of Jesus, as death is always likely to be in our memory of another person, but also the symbol of what was realized to be the crucial meaning of the Christ-event. It is an incident, in other words, which took on supreme significance as a particular instantiation of the kind of love that Jesus exhibited, and because of this, became the symbol of the quality of his life. Therefore, in one sense, to remember the cross is to remember Jesus himself for the remembered character of Jesus is symbolized by the cross. Thus the memory of the death comes very near to being the memory of the man. One cannot remember Jesus without thinking

---

[63] G. Ryle, *The Concept of Mind*, pp. 116–7.

of his cross, or remember the cross without thinking of him who died upon it.

In other words, when we say that the memory of Jesus includes the memory of his death on the cross, this incident is regarded as a symbol of Jesus himself. In particular, it symbolizes the quality of character that was remembered to have been exhibited in Jesus' life. It symbolizes what can otherwise be stated in dispositional terms— that Jesus exhibited the distinctive character of *agape* or self-giving which was lifted up in the awful beauty of his self-sacrifice. A great deal of what has been written about the category of story in contemporary theology suggests that the importance of stories is in the communication of truths of a doctrinal kind that can be expressed in no other way. Thus, as we have already noted, Stephen Sykes speaks of the Church as a community which gathers around the rehearsal of the Jesus story. It must also be appreciated, however, that stories about Jesus communicate truths of a dispositional kind concerning the distinctive quality of Jesus' character. Even if as incidents they may not be true in every detail, as the unit of meaning for the communication of a disposition, the story remains invaluable.

There is still much more to be said about the content of the Church's memory of Jesus, but it will be useful at this point to draw out some conclusions for the structure of resurrection belief from what has been already said.

First of all, we have noted that though Knox insists that there are no facts in the Church's memory of Jesus and that the Church remembers Jesus himself, he in effect treats this as an ellipsis to which meaning is given by employing a number of factual statements about Jesus. We have suggested, on the other hand, that Knox's intention is served if this assertion is amended to read, 'there are no particular *incidents* in the Church's memory of Jesus', but even so, we must add, 'with the exception of the death on the Cross'.

It can therefore be argued that what is meant when contemporary Christians claim to 'remember Jesus' is that they claim to remember the facts that Jesus existed, that he was a man, that he exhibited the moral character of *agape*, that he died on the cross, that his death on the cross symbolized the same quality of character of self-effacing love that he had exhibited in his lifetime. They may claim to remember more facts than these, indeed, but at least these seem essential constituents of the Church's 'memory of Jesus'.

In other words, the notion of the 'memory of Jesus *himself*' can be translated into a set of factual memories. Now, this helps enormously to dispel some of the elusiveness that attaches to the use of the metaphor of the Church's memory. When a contemporary Christian claims to remember Jesus *himself*, it at first seems that he is engaging in a bit of 'deviant discourse', for he seems to be claiming to have a perceptual memory of Jesus, yet Jesus is a person of whom he cannot have had a previous experience. Therefore it is impossible that he can have a personal or perceptual memory of Jesus. Consequently, we are inclined to regard the contemporary Christian's claim that he 'remembers Jesus' as an odd or abnormal use of words, apparently metaphorical. However, our contemporary Christian may admit that he is employing the verb 'remember' in an odd or 'extended' sense; he may agree that he does not literally have a personal or perceptual memory of Jesus. Instead he may make his meaning clear by saying that when he claims to remember Jesus he actually means that he remembers a certain set of facts about Jesus.

Now, we must note that factual memory denotes a use of the word 'remember' which is not metaphorical but perfectly literal. If I claim to 'remember that Napoleon lost the Battle of Waterloo' or if I say, 'I remembered that William the Conqueror won the Battle of Hastings in 1066' I am not employing figurative or metaphorical language. I am employing a perfectly standard sense of the verb 'remember'. It therefore follows that if a Christian claims to remember 'that there was a Jesus' or, if he claims to remember any of the other facts to which regular appeal is made in order to give content to the Church's memory of Jesus, he is not using the verb in a metaphorical sense but in a perfectly standard sense. Consequently, we are able to say that the extended or metaphorical use of the verb 'remember' can be reduced to more precise specification by employing the same verb 'remember' in a literal or standard sense. And in so far as we talk not of Christian individuals 'remembering Jesus' but of the '*Church's* memory of Jesus' we may say that once the metaphorical use of the verb is reduced to a literal or standard use we no longer have a metaphor but a case of metonymy. The claim that the Church remembers certain facts, is simply a way of saying that Christians remember these facts about Jesus, or that individual persons, as Christians, share with their fellow Christians, the remembrance of certain facts about Jesus.

That the metaphorical use of the verb 'remember' can be reduced to more precise specification by employing the same verb in a standard sense is a peculiarity of the logic of the particular verb. Moreover, the fact that the verb can be used both metaphorically and literally and that the metaphorical use can be reduced to the literal use, perhaps explains why we are able to slide from metaphorical language to what seems more nearly literal language with such facility.

There are now two final comments to be made. We noted at the beginning of this chapter that in juxtaposing the Church's continuing memory of Jesus *himself* and the memory of facts about him, Knox was also contrasting information that is acquired by a process of transmission with information that is acquired by critical-historical research. However, if we reduce the metaphor of 'the Church's memory of Jesus *himself*' to a set of factual memories about Jesus, it seems that this distinction begins to collapse. The only distinction that remains is that while the content of the Church's corporate memory of Jesus can be stated in dispositional terms, the 'authentic primitive memories' that the critical historian seeks to establish are memories of particular episodes and incidents. This leads us to ask if Knox's contrast between the process of transmission and critical-historical research can really be maintained. For even though the content of the Church's memory of Jesus is dispositional, is it not something nevertheless that could be established or confirmed by the critical historian? Certainly, if the radical contrast between the processes of transmission in the life of the Church and critical-historical research is based on different kinds of *content* it can hardly be justified.

Finally, if 'the memory of Jesus *himself*' can be reduced to a set of factual memories about him, we are able to say that its content is given in a set of uniquely referring statements about Jesus. Indeed, a set of descriptive statements must be presupposed when the Church uses the proper name 'Jesus' referringly. Possession of at least some uniquely descriptive statements is a precondition of the use of the proper name.

John H. Searle has pointed out that, strictly speaking, proper names denote but do not connote; that is to say, proper names refer but do not have meaning or sense.[64] However, to use a proper name referringly is to presuppose the truth of certain uniquely referring descriptive statements.[65] Though it is not ordinarily to assert these statements or even to indicate which of an unspecified number of possible descriptive statements are presupposed, some must be pre-supposed as a precondition for using the proper name, and proper names, therefore, must have sense 'in a loose sort of way'. We would not be able to use the name 'Napoleon' referringly unless we knew, for example, that he was a French General, the husband of Josephine, and that he lost the Battle of Waterloo. Some of the descriptive state-ments which are presupposed when we use the proper name 'Napo-leon' may turn out to be false, but a sub-set of the possible descriptive statements about Napoleon must nevertheless be true; if all of them were found to be false there would be no criteria for using the proper name at all. Similarly, we would not be able to use the proper name 'Jesus' referringly unless we knew, for example, that Jesus was a person who died on the cross, that he taught such and such a thing, or exhibited a certain kind of character. The use of the proper name referringly presupposes the knowlege of certain descriptive characteristics about him. The same goes for the use of the proper name to identify a given object ostensively as 'the pres-ence of Jesus'. In order to use the proper name in this way it is necessary to remember certain characteristics of Jesus by virtue of which the object of acquaintance can be identified as 'Jesus'.

It therefore seems that the statements that the Church makes con-cerning what is remembered about Jesus qualify as the kind of state-ments that are presupposed whenever the proper name 'Jesus' is used either referringly or identifyingly in the life of the Church. In other words, when the Church uses the name 'Jesus' it seems to refer not to a mountain, nor to a kind of hair spray, nor to a mytho-logical figure, but to a man, a human person, who died on the cross, and who exhibited a distinctive quality of character, and that this quality of character can be expressed in terms of the concept 'agape'.

---

[64] John R. Searle, 'Proper Names' in *Philosophical Logic*, pp. 89–96. This article was originally published in *Mind*, 67 (1958), pp. 166–73. See also Searle's article 'Proper Names and Descriptions' in the *Encyclopedia of Philosophy*. Cf. J. S. Mill, *A System of Logic*, Book I, Chapter 2, especially Sec. 5, and L. Wittgenstein, *Philoso-phical Investigations*, paras. 4–79.

[65] Ibid., p. 94.

Moreover, it was noted at the beginning of this chapter that a 'memory of Jesus' is presupposed when, in Easter faith, the Church makes claims to recognize *his* living presence. Unless the Church first 'remembers Jesus', it can hardly claim to recognize and identify the Spirit of its own corporate life as the 'Spirit' or 'presence' of *Jesus*. This 'memory' which is thus an integral element in the cognitive nucleus of Easter faith, seems best understood as an identifying description, a set of identity criteria which can be expressed in descriptive statements about Jesus, and to which appeal may be made to justify the claim to perceive and recognize his presence. In other words, if 'the corporate memory of Jesus himself' is reduced to a set of factual memories about him, or factual descriptions of Jesus, this goes some way towards supplying what is needed to enable the believer to make the identity judgement of faith.

However, we may ask whether the descriptive statements that have so far been drawn upon are sufficiently specific to qualify as an identifying description. They may go some way towards describing who Jesus was, or who is referred to when the name 'Jesus' is used, but do they convey sufficiently detailed information about Jesus to enable the present-day Christian to recognize his living presence? With this question in mind we must now examine the function of the 'memory of Jesus' within the structure of Easter faith and then we shall consider what more may be said about the content of the Church's memory of Jesus *himself*.

VIII

Easter Faith as Remembering and Knowing

Remembering and Knowing

AT one place in the course of a discussion of the Christology of Johannes Weiss, Rudolf Bultmann entertains the possibility that an image of the personality of Jesus may have been preserved and transmitted by the Christian community.[1] He is disinclined to place much importance on this idea, however, because he believes that, in any event, such an image would be irrelevant to faith. At best, a kind of backward-looking remembrance of Jesus, as a hero of the past, could inspire the present-day Christian to imitate Jesus' faith and love:

Even on the assumption that an image of his personality was preserved in the community, the most that such an image can effect would be to make faith in God and love of neighbour appear to me as beautiful and desirable. It can never give me that faith and love—only pietism and romanticism could so misjudge what is possible.[2]

Indeed, the outcome of the Christology of Weiss, says Bultmann, is that 'the imitative discipleship *of Jesus* is the only legitimate relation to him'.[3]

It is perfectly clear that the Church's 'memory-image' of Jesus is far from being irrelevant to faith as we are here understanding it. Certainly, we should not conceive of the Christian's relation to Jesus in terms of a mere backward-looking 'imitative discipleship'. It is a mistake to think that Jesus 'lives' only in the mind and memory of the Church, for the Church 'remembers Jesus' not in the spirit of a romantic hankering after a past hero, but precisely in

---

[1] 'The Christology of the New Testament' in *Faith and Understanding*, pp. 266–7.
[2] Ibid., p. 267.
[3] Ibid.

order to recognize the *Christus praesens*. As Christians we remember the Jesus of the past but only in order to know his living presence in the here and now. In the cognitive nucleus of faith we must therefore be careful to distinguish two elements: first the object of religious experience which is apprehended in religious sensibility and interpreted with a set of interpretative concepts, including the concept 'Spirit' and the proper name 'Jesus' itself. These conceptual tools are called into service to interpret and identify the object of religious experience as 'the presence or Spirit of Jesus'. Thus, the response of faith involves the apprehension of an objective, spiritual presence, particularly in the life of the Christian fellowship. But I have also pointed out that this particular claim to know the presence of Jesus by acquaintance itself leads to an appreciation of the importance of the second main element in the cognitive nucleus of faith. This is the remembering of the Jesus of the past, which alone renders such an identity judgement possible. Without the memory of the man who lived and died in the first century and to whom the name 'Jesus' originally referred, we have no criteria for its continued use either referringly or identifyingly. For this reason we have sought some basic information about the remembered person to whom the name Jesus refers and in the previous chapter we have tried to understand the nature of this 'memory of Jesus' and its relation to facts of the kind that are established by the scientific historian.

Before we turn to the more detailed discussion of the content of the memory of Jesus that may be said to be an essential constitutive element in the cognitive nucleus of resurrection belief, we must pause to consider more fully the question of the epistemic function of this memory in the response of faith. It is easy to slip into misunderstanding at this point. Whilst we have been speaking of a *knowledge* of the present Christ-Spirit and a *memory* of the Jesus of the past, it is important not to confuse the two. A possible confusion arises because memory is itself a kind of knowledge; to remember Jesus is to know something about him. In other words, the verbs 'know' and 'remember' may be used almost synonymously or interchangeably, since to claim to 'remember' Jesus is also to claim to have some knowledge of him. For this reason it is important to note that in this book the words 'know' and 'remember' are normally used in a contrasting sense. The Jesus who may be said to 'have been remembered' or to be 'remembered' is Jesus as he was in the days of his flesh from birth to death on the cross. The content of the Christian memory of Jesus must therefore be drawn from the period of his earthly life-span in first-century Palestine. If this 'memory of Jesus' is understood as a kind of knowledge, it is for us a knowledge by description, rather than by direct acquaintance. On the other hand, the Jesus who may be said to be 'known' is the raised Jesus, who is known by acquaintance in the present. It is the Spirit of Jesus in the here and now which in faith is identified and thus known. Thus, Jesus as an object of the Church's memory is always past; as the object of knowledge he is always thought of as present. Between the Jesus who is remembered and the Jesus whose Spirit is known stands the cross. This marks the decisive break.

Because the judgement of Easter faith is an identity judgement in which the past, remembered Jesus is allegedly recognized in the Spirit to be living still, the judgement of faith has a reference both to past and present; it is a matter of remembering *and* knowing. For the primitive Christians it was a matter of recognizing one previously known or of recognizing the presence of one who was *also* remembered. For the contemporary Christian it is a matter of knowing one who is also remembered to have lived in the past, or of knowing the presence of one who is also still remembered.

Moreover, these two distinguishable elements of remembering and knowing are not logically independent or discrete in the make-up of faith. Rather, they are logically interrelated, precisely in so far as the one known is recognized as the present Jesus, only because he, Jesus, is still remembered. The knowing or recognizing depends upon the logically prior remembering but is not to be confused with it.

I have taken time to emphasize this distinction between 'remembering' and 'knowing' because I do not wish it to be thought that in the post-Easter period the first witnesses simply remembered Jesus in a particular way or knew him in vivid memory. This, as I understand it, is where the theologies of D. F. Strauss, Don Cupitt, and Willi Marxsen lead.

In the 1960s Paul van Buren said the same thing very explicitly. It was van Buren's view that the resurrection of Jesus is to be understood in a non-objective way as the disciples' act of coming to remember Jesus from a particular point of view. He contended that what happened at Easter was that the early Christians came to see the messianic significance of the remembered Jesus. In van Buren's own words, the resurrection is simply a way of describing the fact that 'against the background of their memory of Jesus' the disciples 'suddenly saw Jesus in a new and unexpected way'. They came to remember him as the 'one who had set them free'.[4] Thus, van Buren also arrived at a reductionist understanding of faith in which it became nothing more than a kind of remembering.

Essentially the same view was espoused by Josiah Royce earlier this century. Whilst Royce declared that he had 'no positive theses to maintain regarding the person of the founder of Christianity' and 'no hypothesis whatsoever to offer as to how the Christian community originated'[5] he ventured nevertheless to say that Jesus 'suffered and died' that the Church 'might have life' and that through 'his death and in his life the community lives'.[6] Indeed, Royce says *'He is now identical with the spirit of this community'*. However, while he says that Jesus is a supernatural being whose Body is the Church, it is clear that Jesus' Spirit is to be 'identified with the will and with the mind' of the community.[7] The Spirit of the community, as Royce understands it, is not a transcendent object that is perceived through the deliverances of sensory experience; it is, rather, a 'compounding of consciousness', for a community, he says, can be possessed of 'one mental life'.[8] One of the things that makes the men and women of a community to be of one mind is the sharing of a memory of the community's past. Consequently, the Spirit is conceived in idealist terms as the Absolute Mind of the community. It is not a transcendent activity or a presence to be recognized by virtue of the possession of a memory of Jesus; rather, the Spirit is generated by the sharing of a memory for the sharing of the memory unites men by 'ideal ties'.[9] Royce concedes that the common memory must be 'enlivened by love', but the fact that the raised Jesus cannot be thought of as himself an object of love and devotion is perfectly clear. Instead, Royce proposes a 'religion of Loyalty' where 'loyalty' means 'the *practically* devoted love of an individual for a community'.[10] Religion thus becomes, not the matter of a relation of trust (fiducia) based on the recognition (fides) of

[4] Paul van Buren, *The Secular Meaning of the Gospel*, p. 136.
[5] Josiah Royce, *The Problem of Christianity*, Vol. I, p. xxvi; p. xxviii.
[6] Ibid., p. 187.
[7] Ibid., p. 202.
[8] Ibid., Vol. II, pp. 30 and 39.
[9] Ibid., p. 95.
[10] Ibid., Vol, I, p. xvii. See also p. xxxvii.

the Spirit as the Spirit of Jesus; rather, it is a matter of 'loyalty to the "Beloved Community" '. Consequently, the individual is exhorted by Royce to 'Love the Community. That is, be loyal'.[11]

The distinction between these notions and the understanding of resurrection faith here advocated must be made unequivocally clear. Whereas for Royce, the sharing of a common memory constitutes the community because it promotes a common mind, I wish to emphasize that the idea of a common memory of Jesus is that by virtue of which the believer is able to make judgements in which a graciously given object of religious intuition is identified as 'the Spirit of Jesus'. Faith is not just a matter of the mere remembering of Jesus or the mere sharing of a corporate memory of him. It is a matter of remembering and knowing. In other words, in the judgement of faith, it is important to recognize that there are two distinguishable stems of religious knowledge.

That is not to say that the sharing of the memory of Jesus does not have a value and an importance in the life of the Church in its own right, in independence of its role in allowing men and women of faith to recognize the Spirit of Jesus in the here and now. It is possible to argue that the members of the Church are united in so far as they share a common mind concerning the significance of Jesus and his role in their assessment of the relation of men and women to God. This shared common memory itself generates a sense of community, just as in any other community the rehearsal of the history of its past gives it a sense of its own unique identity. As Peter Selby points out, 'the assumption of common memories is something that gives reality to membership of a community'.[12] But, whatever value this may have, it would be untrue to the nature of the early response of faith to think of it purely in terms of the remembering of Jesus, as a kind of backward looking adulation of a dead hero. The first Christians certainly remembered Jesus and his death on the cross and may well have been drawn together after the

---

[11] Ibid., p. xxv; p. 375. See also pp. 401 and 410.
[12] Peter Selby, *Look for the Living*, p. 37. John Knox has written very fully on this aspect of the sharing of common memories. See *The Church and the Reality of Christ*, Chapter II, especially p. 42: 'When Lincoln in the final sentence of his First Inaugural Address predicted that "The mystic chords of memory stretching from every battle field and patriot grave to every living heart and hearthstone over this broad land, will yet swell the chorus of Union when again touched, as surely they will be, by better angels of our nature", he was not being either sentimental or fanciful, but was appealing to the deepest element in the actual unity of the nation.'

crucifixion by virtue of their shared memory of him. Indeed, as they
re-grouped in Galilee after the crucifixion and looked back in
memory and recalled that the Jesus whom they had deserted had
been a very loving and forgiving leader, accepting of their human
fragility and failings, their feelings of guilt may well have subsided.
In this experience, to which Schillebeeckx refers as the experience of
'concrete forgiveness', the memory of their crucified master may
have operated therapeutically as they 'worked upon' and 'processed' their trauma. However, resurrection faith is more than this.
Their resurrection faith affirmed precisely that he whom they affec-
tionately remembered by description they also knew by acquaintance as a heavenly and exalted presence among them.

Knowing

It is clearly of great importance not to assimilate the understanding
of faith to the notion of memory alone; faith is a kind of knowledge
that derives from two distinguishable stems. Through the first stem
Jesus is remembered as an object of thought; through the second his
living Spirit is apprehended as an object of religious experience in
the present. To eliminate the second stem from the cognitive nucleus of resurrection belief would be to reduce it to an idealistic affair
of thought alone.

We must now focus upon the second of these two elements—
faith as knowledge. It is a form of religious cognition which
involves the ordering and interpretation of experience using conceptual tools supplied in the religious language of the Christian community. This presupposes that there is in the make-up of faith, as in
the cognition of objects generally, a duality between bare experience
and knowledge. This duality can also be expressed as a duality
between the receptive faculty of religious sensibility and the active
faculty of understanding. This basic pattern ultimately derives from
Kant's epistemological distinction between sensibility and understanding, or what he called 'intuitions' as distinct from 'concepts'.
Kant says: 'There are two stems of human knowledge, namely, *sensibility* and *understanding* . . . through the former, objects are given
to us; through the latter, they are thought'.[13] Moreover, Kant
argued that, without concepts which grow out of human thinking,
sensibility is blind, for it is the use of concepts to order the chaotic

---

[13] I. Kant, *Critique of Pure Reason*, A15/B29.

deliverances of the bare experience of sense perception that leads to knowledge. Thus, if I claim to know that I am experiencing a table, I must have the sense-experience of seeing and touching a concrete object of my awareness plus the concept 'table' and a set of criteria or a rule for its correct use, which alone allows me cognitively to isolate and identify the object to which that concept refers from the kaleidoscopic givenness of the deliverances of sensory perception. The mere concept, on the other hand, without an object of sense perception to which it answers, is purely empty. It is a figment of the mind, an item of abstract thought, without any corresponding empirical reality in the world.

The use of this basic epistemological pattern to understand the structure of Easter faith entails, of course, that the exercise of human reason has a role to play in the active faculty of understanding. By this I do not mean the discursive reason whereby the steps of an argument are followed with a view to proving the existence of God or the occurrence of the Resurrection of Christ in the manner of Westcott and Pannenberg. Rather, reason is brought into play when 'the penny drops' or 'two and two are put together', and in faith the believer recognizes that a reality of his or her present experience is what the first Christians were celebrating when they spoke of the transcendent presence of 'the raised Jesus' in their midst. Reason, in other words, has a role in the choice of the appropriate interpretative concept with which experience is ordered. In addition, the making of such a judgement in the decision of faith commits the believer to cite the justification for his or her decision. This will involve citing the criteria or grammatical rule which may be said to warrant the application of the appropriate concept or name. Despite the role of reason in the active faculty of understanding and interpreting what is given in experience, much twentieth-century theology has not so much as imagined that such a pattern of faith might be a 'live option' for Christianity. This is precisely because in the influential opinion of dialectical theology reason has been assumed to be inimical to faith.

The overpowering success of the dialectical theology of Barth, Bultmann, and Gogarten in the first half of our century has meant that faith has tended to be seen as an esoteric or *sui generis* form of the apprehension of God, rather than a perception that is continuous with ordinary perception employing natural human endowments. Indeed, one of few theologians to see the possibilities of a religious empiricism of this kind earlier this century, Ernst Troeltsch, was not treated kindly by the dialectical theologians and, as a consequence, his attempt to articulate an understanding of faith on the basis of a fundamentally Kantian epistemology was quickly set aside as an entirely mistaken enterprise along with all 'natural theology' and other 'sinful' attempts of human reason to reach God by its own effort.

Now that dialectical theology has to a large extent run its course, we are free to re-examine the Troeltschian alternative which that earlier generation felt justified in passing over on the meagre ground that its fundamental error was assumed to be self-evident.[14]

Troeltsch began to develop his theory of religious knowledge from about 1904 onwards. At this time he had begun to turn his attention in the direction of Kantianism and was already set upon the logical track which led him to his distinctive treatment of the theme of 'the religious a priori', the idea of a universal religious consciousness which is expressed across the broad spectrum of world religions.[15] Indeed, Troeltsch utilized the concept of the religious a priori in an epistemology of religious faith which was worked out on the basis of an essentially Kantian understanding of the structure of human knowing. This theoretical concern, however, was not alien to Troeltsch's overriding empirical and historical interest in

[14] During the last decade the intellectual legacy of Ernst Troeltsch has been subject to some welcome critical reassessment. See John Powell Clayton (ed.) *Ernst Troeltsch and the Future of Theology*. In these essays written for a colloquium on Troeltsch, sponsored by the University of Lancaster in 1976, it is possible to discern the stirrings of a desire to rescue Troeltsch's contribution to twentieth-century theology from the limbo to which it was prematurely consigned by the over-shadowing eminence of dialectical theology.
During the course of the 1920s Troeltsch's theology was very quickly eclipsed in Germany by the dazzling and programmatic work of Barth, Bultmann, and Gogarten, who were fundamentally unsympathetic to his entire theological method. They tended to regard Troeltsch's approach to an understanding of the structure of Christian faith through the history of religions as a remnant survival of nineteenth-century liberal protestantism and thus as just another futile attempt of sinful man to reach God by the exercise of his own rational powers. They therefore tended to dismiss his work as a clear example of all that they were wedded to putting down. See especially Robert Morgan, 'Ernst Troeltsch and the Dialectical Theology', pp. 33–77.
[15] This formula is found in an article which Troeltsch published in 1904 and it is clear already from the very titles of his other publications of the same period that Kant was exercising an important influence upon him at the time. See his article on the philosophy of religion in *Die Philosophie im Beginn des 20. Jahrhunderts*, essays in honour of Kuno Fischer (1904) and 'Psychologie und Erkenntnistheorie in der Religionswissenschaft' (1905) which was published with the sub-title 'An enquiry into Kant's account of religion for the science of religion today'.

the history of religions. On the contrary, his epistemology of religious knowledge was developed as a reflection upon the historical phenomenon of what he believed was a universal aspect of religious devotion and which he termed the 'radical religious individualism of Mysticism'.[16]

Despite the centrality of Troeltsch's well-known distinction between the two ideal types of Christianity, the church type and the sect type, to the main argument of his great work, *The Social Teaching of the Christian Churches*, Troeltsch believed that it was an inadequate distinction to account fully for Christian social thought. To those two types a third type had to be added, which he designated the mystical type. This third type was distinguishable by the fact that, while the church type was characterized by a positive relationship to the world and the sect type by a negative relationship, it was characterized by the absence of any concern with questions relating to involvement or non-involvement with the world. Moreover, as a correlative to this, the mystical type was said to concentrate its attention solely on 'a relationship to God'. Troeltsch had thus isolated the Christian expression of the 'radical religious individualism of Mysticism' as a topic for intensive study. Because he believed that this was shared with other religions his epistemology of religious knowledge was developed as a reflection upon this allegedly universal religious phenomenon.

Troletsch's writings with regard to the way in which the individual's relationship to God was established and the structure of the religious knowledge involved in it, provided the outlines of what was called at the time a 'religious empiricism'.[17] North American theologians were alerted to Troeltsch's views in this regard by an article he wrote in criticism of William James which was published in the *Harvard Theological Review* in 1912.[18] Troeltsch's criticism

---

[16] *Gesammelte Schriften* I, p. 420; *The Social Teaching of the Christian Churches*, Vol. II, p. 377.

[17] A term coined by D. C. Macintosh. For Macintosh's appraisal of Troeltsch's view of religious knowledge see 'Troeltsch's Theory of Religious Knowledge' in *American Journal of Theology*, XXIII (1919), pp. 274–89. For this aspect of Troeltsch's thought see *Gesammelte Schriften*, I, p. 967; *The Social Teaching of the Christian Churches*, II, p. 993. The concise delineation of the distinguishing characteristics of the three types of Christianity is discussed by Benjamin A. Reist in *Toward a Theology of Involvement: The Thought of Ernst Troeltsch*, pp. 116–8.

[18] 'Empiricism and Platonism in the Philosophy of Religion', *Harvard Theological Review*, V (1912), pp. 401–22.

of the theological writing of William James hinged on James's concentration of attention on the subjective psychological states of religious experience as the empirical basis of religion. This concentration of attention on psychological states, argued Troeltsch, is inadequate to account for religious knowledge. He believed that in this respect James could be compared with Schleiermacher, whose theology constituted a kind of 'dogmatic agnosticism' in so far as it renounced exact and adequate knowledge by concentrating attention on the psychological feelings of absolute dependence experienced by religious believers. Troeltsch himself was interested in the transition from the psychology to the epistemology of religion which, as D. C. Macintosh observed, seemed to give promise of liberating theology 'from its former perpetual oscillation between helpless agnosticism and the sheer dogmatism of *exclusive* supernaturalism'.[19]

Troeltsch's approach to theology through the history of religions had convinced him that the common denominator in religion 'wherever human life exists' is faith in the revelation of a religious object. This inevitably raised the question of 'how revelation is to be recognized as such or, in other words, how religious knowledge is possible'.[20] We may today wonder if Troeltsch was not naively over-confident in this claim concerning the universal occurrence of this religious phenomenon, but this does not alter the fact that he nevertheless refused to confine his attention to Christianity and sought to outline a theory of religious knowledge that would be universally valid. Thus, he engaged in what was, in effect, *a critique of religion* by attempting to define the a priori conditions of all religious knowledge. In this enterprise Troeltsch discerned that if we are to reach assured reality in religion, as against mere psychological appearance, the appeal must be back from James to Kant.[21] His theory of religious knowledge was thus worked out on the basis of an

---

[19] See D. C. Macintosh, 'Troeltsch's Theory of Religious Knowledge', pp. 286, 277. Troeltsch's essay entitled 'Psychology and the Theory of Knowledge in the Science of Religion' (1905) which was influential on Macintosh, was in fact delivered by Troeltsch as a lecture in North America at St Louis. See 'Empiricism and Platonism in the Philosophy of Religion', p. 420.

[20] 'Troeltsch's Theory of Religious Knowledge', p. 279.

[21] Ibid.

essentially Kantian epistemology.[22] And while he believed
that William James's approach to theology from empirical foundations was right as far as it had gone, he was convinced that if it was
not to lead to agnosticism it would have to appeal to a critical
rationalism. Moreover, he seems to have implicitly assumed that the
specific knowledge of the divine or heavenly object appropriate to
religion was of a piece, in terms of its basic epistemological structure, with the knowledge appropriate to the perception of ordinary
objects in the natural world and that what Kant had said concerning
the way we perceive and know natural objects could be extended to
cover the knowledge of the unique and transcendent object which
offers itself for religious perception. It is at this point that Kant's
understanding that in ordinary perception there is a basic duality
between bare experience and knowledge comes into play. This distinction can also be expressed as a duality between the receptive
faculty of human sense experience and the active faculty of understanding.

Troeltsch took this basic two-stem theory of natural perception
from Kant and applied it in the religious arena by arguing that
religious knowledge involves the bringing of empirically given or
mystically intuited data under the logically prior concept of 'God'.

In other words, Troeltsch pointed out that the possession of the
bare concept or idea of God did not amount to religious knowledge.
An additional essential ingredient of religious knowledge is that the
believer must have, over and above the possession of the concept or
idea of God, material furnished through religious sensibility, or
intuition.[23] Troeltsch believed that this understanding of the structure of religious belief would avoid the empty dogmatism of high-
flown, speculative rationalism in religion. It would dethrone
abstract supernaturalism of a very cerebral kind and provide the
opportunity of replacing it with a truly scientific or empirical theology, involving the bringing of concretely given or experienced
religious data under an appropriate set of interpretative concepts—
such as 'God', 'Spirit', or 'Divine Presence'. Thus, mysticism, as

---

[22] The Kantian overtones are unmistakable in Macintosh's summing up of
Troeltsch's position: 'Troeltsch would say that without concepts which grow out of
the a priori categories of human thinking, religious sensibility is blind. But he would
be quite as emphatic in arguing, on the other hand, that the a priori alone, even when
it is "the religious a priori", can give no religious knowledge but only empty concepts.' Ibid., p. 279.
[23] Ibid.

Troeltsch understood it, 'is the union of pure or rational religion with impulse, the actualizing of the religious a priori', or 'the union of rational form with empirical content'.[24]

It will already be apparent that I am eager to bring this outline pattern of religious knowledge, involving the interpreting of the ostensively given data of religious experience with a set of concepts, to the service of a systematic presentation of resurrection belief. However, before we move on to that, there is one point where we shall find it necessary to divert from the broad pattern of Troeltsch's thinking. This is the incorporation into his theory of religious knowledge of the notion of the religious a priori with its implication that the concepts of the divine which the religious person is said to use to interpret his religious intuitions are *utterly prior* to experience. In Germany R. Köhler came to quite negative conclusions concerning this aspect of Troeltsch's thought,[25] and few were moved to take it seriously. It is important to note, however, that Troeltsch's critics on this score tended to pay too much attention to the mysterious idea of the religious a priori itself and not sufficient attention to the broader contours of the epistemology which provided the context for it. However, in the United States of America, D. C. Macintosh saw that the broader outline of Troeltsch's theory of religious knowledge might well provide a useful model for Christian faith without necessarily following the details of his developed notion of the religious a priori. Troeltsch seems to have believed that the concept of God which religious men were said universally to employ to order their religious experience was absolutely a priori, but even the sympathetic Macintosh found difficulty with this. He proposed as a substitute for 'dogmatic absolute a priorism' an 'empirical relative a priorism', 'such as would recognize the "religious a priori" as but relatively a priori, and the product, ultimately, of the activity of the human psychical subject in experimental relations with the religious Object'.[26] By this he seems to have meant that the having of a concept of God is logically prior to any claim to know the experience of God, without necessarily saying

[24] Ibid., pp. 280, 281. An essentially similar understanding of the nature of faith as a kind of religious cognition may be found in J. Hick, *Faith and Knowledge*, Chapters 5 and 6.

[25] R. Köhler, *Der Begriff a priori in der modernen Religionsphilosophie: Eine Untersuchung zur religionsphilosophischen Methode*, pp. 3–22.

[26] 'Troeltsch's Theory of Religious Knowledge', p. 289.

that the requisite concept of God has to be plucked in an a priori manner out of the miasma of wholly abstract thought or 'born into' all human individuals as an aboriginal endowment. We must take account of the evolution of religious concepts in the course of religious life and activity and of the role of tradition in delivering religious concepts and the rules for their correct use to the believer. The individual receives the interpretative concepts, with which he is able in faith to order his religious experience, from the Church, understood as a linguistic community.

In the philosophy of the later Wittgenstein it has been very powerfully demonstrated that the meaning of words is established by their use in a linguistic community which settles on conventionally agreed-upon meanings.[27] Moreover, as members of linguistic communities we cannot estrange ourselves from the deeps of history. Conventional use in its temporal aspect becomes tradition. This is never static but always subject to a process of refinement and reform in the light of successively new insights and experiences. Religious language, like all language, evolves, if ever so slowly.

The idea of the generation of concepts within the historical particularity of the Hebrew–Christian tradition immediately moves the Troeltschian theory of religious knowledge some way from Troeltsch's original intention.[28] Troeltsch used the notion of the religious a priori, which he seems to have understood as a universal factor in all human religious experience, in the belief that it would facilitate the articulation of a general epistemology of religious knowledge that would be relevant to any world religion. In reality, however, it could not have had the universal application that Troeltsch seems to have envisaged. For one thing, it could only be applied to theistic religions, but in addition Troeltsch's own recognition of the historical plurality of religious traditions should have alerted him to the possible violence that would be done to them by over-simplifying the conceptual framework of each in order to achieve a common denominator. Certainly, once the universality of

[27] L. Wittgenstein, *Philosophical Investigations*.
[28] Curiously, Troeltsch, for all his concern with the history of religions, tended to promote the superiority of Christianity as the 'pinnacle of religious development', and it seems likely that his theory of religious knowledge is really more suited to this 'pinnacle' than to other 'less advanced' religions. In other words, his theory of religious knowledge may be more congenial to an understanding of Christian faith and less congenial to 'religion' generally conceived. See *The Absoluteness of Christianity and the History of Religions*, p. 131.

the religious a priori is abandoned, the way is opened for an appreciation of the plurality and historical particularity of religious concepts and beliefs. We should therefore be wary of oversimplifying the conceptual apparatus of diverse religious traditions in order to reach a common factor and be more sensitive to the particularity of religious traditions. Certainly, this revision of Troeltsch's theory of religious knowledge is particularly pertinent when we come to consider its usefulness to the specifically Christian understanding of faith as the perception of the presence of the raised Christ. It invites us to think of the Christian community as, in the first instance, an ongoing linguistic community, within which a religious vocabulary is evolved, transmitted, and progressively refined.

The development of a satisfactory linguistic apparatus is a historically conditioned enterprise, for experience plays a part in the process of the refinement and reform of concepts and ideas. In the case of the Christian religion, for example, the object of faith may in the first instance be said to be the 'Spirit of God'. By this the believer means to refer to God as he makes himself known as distinct from God as he is in himself. The Godhead is the hidden source of the Spirit which goes out from him; the 'Spirit of God' is the empirically experienced object of faith. If the first prerequisite for the knowledge of this reality is some kind of contact with the Christian Church, conceived of as a historico-linguistic community which transmits a stock of distinctive religious concepts and interpretative ideas, the first concept with which the prospective believer must become acquainted is the long-evolved Hebrew–Christian idea of God as Spirit or non-embodied person. But a decisive place in this developing tradition is occupied by the historical Jesus as the decisive revelatory prism through whom, in human experience, a new and refined understanding of the character of the Spirit of God comes to definition. This means that, for Christians, the concept of the 'Spirit of God' cannot be understood in independence of the imprint of meaning put upon it by the memory of the life and death of Jesus. Thus, if one is to learn the rules for the distinctively Christian understanding of the concept 'Spirit', reference must be made to the stamp given it in the course of the historical life and teaching of Jesus, not to mention his self-giving on the cross which stands as the episodic symbol of the character and unique disposition of his active life. For this reason it is necessary to have a reasonably secure historical knowledge of the kind of person Jesus was said to have been. In so far as early Christians spoke of the distinctive quality of Jesus' self-giving in terms of *agape* (cf. 1 Cor. 13) they were also defining something of the distinctive quality of the presence of the Spirit of God in his life, for the anointing of the Spirit was understood to have shown itself in Jesus' character of *agape* or self-giving. Likewise something of the nature of the Spirit of God was understood to have been exhibited in his equally distinctive selflessness and the humility of one who self-consciously chose the role of a servant (cf. Phil. 2: 5–11). Thus, if primitive Christians were asked what they meant by the concept of the 'Spirit of God' they could draw upon the traditional images of 'wind' and 'fire' and they could speak of a 'spring of living water' to indicate something of the experience of the Spirit; but they could also speak of the distinctive love revealed in Jesus' words and deeds. This entails that the object of Christian faith is not just 'God' or even the 'Spirit of God', such as might be apprehended with the so-called 'religious a priori'. For Christians the object of faith is not just to be identified as the 'Spirit of God' but, as an implicate of the Easter experience, as the 'Spirit of Jesus'. Entry into the life of the Christian community, amongst other things, therefore involves access to the distinctively Christian religio-linguistic tradition in which these religious terms and conventionally agreed upon criteria for their correct use are learned. The word of proclamation is not just a word of call and address, which precipitates the existential decision of faith, but a word of report in which succeeding generations hear of the faith experiences of former generations and, in the rehearsal of stories, are simultaneously introduced to the set of religious concepts and ideas which have been evolved and refined in order to come to terms, admittedly ever so inadequately, with those experiences. In this way, the revelatory initiative of God may be said always to require a correlative human ideology or system of theological concepts if the believer is to be capable of receiving and interpreting what of God is revealed to him. Likewise in order to recognize the revelatory presence of the Spirit of Jesus it seems necessary to have not just the proper name 'Jesus' but some 'idea' or 'concept' of Jesus and what he was like in the days of his flesh.

Barth seems never to have understood that a set of interpretative concepts is presupposed in claims even to the knowledge of revelation. Bultmann, on the other hand, comes close to seeing the point with admirable clarity at least with respect to the knowing of God through the medium of the Word of proclamation if not through the broader medium of human experience in the community life of the Church:

> . . . *the comprehension of records about events as the action of God* presupposes a prior understanding of what may in my case be termed the action of God—let us say, as distinct from man's action, or from natural events. And if this is countered by saying that neither can man know who God is before his manifestation, nor consequently, what God's action may be, then we have to reply that *man may very well be aware who God is,* namely, *in the enquiry about him.*

Otherwise, 'neither would he know God as God in any manifestation of him'.[29] Barth, in arguing for 'open-mindedness' and 'freedom', apparently thinks it possible to come to a knowledge of the revelation of God with a 'blank mind' as it were, and castigates Bultmann for restricting the interpretation of the experience of the revelatory Word of God to existentialist categories of Heideggerian type. The basic epistemological insight of Bultmann in his contention that a presupposed concept of God is an element in claims to know any manifestation of him, however, has a Kantian origin and is independent of anything Bultmann may have learned from Heidegger, though Bultmann has a very individualistic approach to the matter and little comprehension of the importance of belonging to a linguistic community.

Another implication of the perception of the Spirit of Christ as an objective presence in the life of the post-Easter community is that the deliverances of sense are important in the structure of resurrection belief. Rudolf Bultmann at one place indicates that apprehension 'by the physical senses' in the manner of natural, ocular seeing, indicates necessarily that the resurrection must be understood as the resuscitation of a corpse.[30] This, however, is to delimit the possibilities unnecessarily.

In so far as Paul speaks of the Spirit, as an 'indwelling Spirit' (Romans 8: 11) and as a reality that is 'poured out (Romans 5: 5) amongst those who share in the life of the Christian fellowship, it seems clear that the Spirit is to be perceived in, with, and under the myriad words and deeds, actions and reactions, that make up the texture of the Christian *koinonia*. Charles Williams has spoken of

---

[29] See R. Bultmann, 'The Problem of Hermeneutics' in *Essays Philosophical and Theological*, p. 257.
[30] *Kerygma and Myth*, Vol. I, p. 39.

the 'co-inherence of the divine Spirit and the created order' and John V. Taylor, building on this insight, sums up his understanding of the primitive Christian experience in the following words: 'When the members of this new fellowship talk about the Holy Spirit it is obvious that they are not speaking of moments of sudden possession or exceptional endowment but of a permanent presence; not so much of a power as of a partner who lives in their life; not so much of an individual encounter as of a life in fellowship'.[31] If the Spirit is perceived in and through the texture of community life, it seems to be entailed that its presence is appropriated through the deliverances of sense. To take a secular analogy, when people speak of the lack of 'team spirit' amongst the members of a hockey team, they are referring to the absence of a non-material reality whose presence they would normally become aware of by observation. An acquaintance with the team and some observation of their play might in better days lead to the perception of the presence of 'team spirit'. Team spirit is not a material object, but it is a reality which we can nevertheless perceive and judge to be either present or lacking through sensory perception of the physical activity of the team. Likewise, it is thinkable that, through the texture of the life of the Christian community what the believer apprehends in faith through the deliverances of sense, may be the heavenly or graciously transcendent reality of the Spirit of Christ, and not just a material object. Even the presence of a humanly generated 'team spirit' is, after all, apprehended by the senses and it may be that something less material than a resuscitated corpse might also be apprehended by the deliverances of sense perception in the case of the Easter Jesus.

At this point, it will be useful to distinguish between 'the mere presence' of the Spirit and the 'revelation' or 'revelatory presence' of the Spirit, for it seems possible to think of the Spirit as being present, and yet to think of it as remaining unnoticed, just as many other aspects of what is presented to sense go unnoticed. If the Spirit is mediated to the believer through the warp and woof of life in the natural world, and particularly through his or her contact with the common life of the Christian fellowship, then it seems possible to think of the Spirit as being in some kind of competition with other objects which in that context vie for attention. This means that it is logically possible to conceive of the presence of the Spirit as a

---

[31] John V. Taylor, *The Go-Between God*, pp. 84–5.

somewhat ambiguous reality which does not necessarily compel assent but which leaves men and women the freedom not to notice it, should they choose to focus their attention elsewhere. The mere presence of the Spirit for this reason does not guarantee revelation. In so far as the early Christians claimed to perceive and know the active presence of the reality of the Spirit, it seems to be entailed that what they claimed to perceive was 'carved out' or 'isolated' from the rest of what they perceived in their experience of life in the Christian fellowship, by the use of the concept of 'Spirit of Christ' not only referringly and descriptively but identifyingly.

In our experience of God there is a merging of many experiences, and the precise form or phase which gives us data for the knowledge of God is not clearly distinguished from that which gives us data for our knowledge of earth, and sky, and fellow man, and social group. But just as we have learned to break up the stream of experience into discrete data by selecting more or less well-defined elements from out of it and noting them, so we must acquire the habit of recognizing the presence of the Divine. We need concepts and the rules for their use if we are to be able to recognize, for concepts shape our perception. We come to knowledge only if we order and interpret experience with certain acquired conventional modes of understanding, with a certain store of previously evolved concepts. Following Kant's dictum, we might say that religious knowledge involves the experience of a given religious object to which people would be blind save for the capacity to interpret that object with appropriate concepts, but that these concepts would be quite empty without an empirically disclosed point of reference.[32]

In the specific case of Easter faith the empirically given reality which is the object of faith is identified as 'the Spirit or presence of Jesus'. This judgement is only possible, however, because the proper name 'Jesus' and criteria for its correct use have been learned in the context of the believer's acquaintance with the Church understood as a linguistic community whose processes of proclamation and catechesis equip the believer with the ability to identify the 'presence of Christ' by bringing a concretely given element of

---

[32] For the preliminary explorations of D. C. Macintosh see *The Problem of Religious Knowledge.* Also, Peter A. Bertocci, 'Macintosh's Theory of Natural Knowledge', *Journal of Religion*, xxiii (1943), pp. 164–72 and 'An Analysis of Macintosh's Theory of Religious Knowledge', *Journal of Religion*, xxiv (1944), pp. 42–55.

religious experience under an interpretative name. This in turn presupposes the possession of criteria for the correct application of the appropriate name, hence the importance of the memory of Jesus to the believer if that presence is to be identified as the presence of Jesus Christ. Let us therefore turn to a more detailed examination of what is involved in this element of 'remembering' in the cognitive nucleus of faith.

Remembering

I have argued that the use of the proper name 'Jesus' is backed by a memory of him which supplies the criteria for the correct use of the name. This is the case when the name is used identifyingly, but also simply when it is used referringly. Certainly, when the Church claims the ability to employ the proper name 'Jesus' to identify a certain ostensively given object, a 'memory of Jesus' seems to be implied or logically required. One would not be able to bring a given reality of experience under the proper name 'Jesus' unless one 'remembered' the person to whom this name originally referred.

However, to say that a 'memory of Jesus' is 'presupposed' is not to say exactly what kind of entity it is. It is now pertinent to ask whether we are talking about a psychological particular when we are speaking of the 'Church's memory'.

Given that Easter faith may be understood in realist rather than idealist terms, as the apprehension of the presence of an object of religious awareness in the present, we may well ask is 'the memory of the Church' by virtue of which this reality is recognized, a kind of 'mental image' that is available to introspection?

In other words, we have seen that within the judgement of faith, the Church's 'corporate memory' is something that is presupposed by claims to recognize the presence of Jesus. The 'memory of Jesus' is a presupposition of the exercise of the active faculty of understanding. Even if the presence of the Spirit of Jesus is understood as a reality outside of the mind of the beholder which is perceived through sense experience, the 'memory of Jesus' may be an introspectible particular of the beholder's psyche. In this case talk of 'the memory of Jesus' would be closely associated with a state of consciousness. This suggests that what is presupposed when the Church makes claims to recognize the presence of Jesus, by applying the name 'Jesus' to a given object, is that the Church must be in a certain psychological state of 'remembering Jesus'. Indeed, it might be thought that the Church must not only be in a psychological state of remembering, but that this state consists of consulting a mental image. The Church's memory of Jesus, for example, could be thought of as a 'picture', an 'impression', or an 'image' or 'mental ikon' of Jesus. For example, in discussing St. Paul's ability to recognize the presence of Jesus, even though he apparently had no direct contact with Jesus in the days of his flesh, John Knox argues that Paul had received the 'memory of Jesus', and that this is to be understood as a 'picture of Jesus' that is located 'in the mind': 'Is it not a fact', he says, 'that we often . . . have in our minds an impression of the appearance of any person about whom we have thought or heard much?'[33] This suggests that the 'memory of Jesus' is to be understood as an introspectible particular, a psychological entity that is inwardly accessible.

Clearly, it is possible to speak of an 'idea' or 'image of Jesus' or of the 'memory of Jesus', without giving any indication of exactly how these entities should be conceived. Given the claim that Jesus is in some way remembered by the contemporary Christian and that this remembrance of Jesus gives access to his living presence as the Spirit of the Christian fellowship, we must attempt to say exactly what we mean by the phrase 'the memory of Jesus' for it is thinkable that we could interpret the concept in a psychological sense to denote an introspectible mental object.[34] Are we bound to this understanding of things? Does the believer, for example, have the capacity to recognize the 'Spirit of Jesus' precisely because he or she is able to summon up a 'mental image of Jesus' in memory and compare what is encountered with the remembered image and thus identify the two? In this case it might be thought that we are thinking in terms that are analogous to the classical representative theory of memory in which individuals are said to entertain mental images or copies of past objects and events, which are accessible to introspection. If this

---

[33] *Christ the Lord*, p. 9, footnote 3. See also *The Church and the Reality of Christ*, p. 35 where the memory of Jesus is said to be 'an image in men's minds and hearts' and M. Kähler, *The So-Called Historical Jesus and the Historic, Biblical Christ*, p. 88, where he speaks of a 'picture impressed upon their hearts and minds'. C. C. Morrison in *What is Christianity?*, p. 164 says that the Church 'carries in its communal consciousness the memory of an actual figure of history'.

[34] In *The Humanity and Divinity of Christ*, Knox speaks of the Christian's awareness of Jesus as a human and divine person. He says that the humanity and divinity of Christ are found 'not as abstract ideas but as existential realities, and the Christian needs only to look into his own heart . . . ' Op. cit., p. 55. See also p. 77.

is so we would be obliged to think of it as something introspectible or psychological which leads to the ability or capacity to use the proper name 'Jesus' in assertions about the identity of a certain empirically experienced phenomenon. The procedure for applying the proper name 'Jesus' in the judgement of faith would, in this event, be that, in circumstances where Christians think that they may be having a sensory experience of the impact upon them of the presence of the Spirit of Jesus, they conjure up and consult a memory-image or mental picture of Jesus as he was in the days of his flesh and check it against the object with which they are alleged to be acquainted. Correspondence of some characteristics of the mental image with the object encountered would enable them to call that object 'the Spirit of Jesus' or 'Jesus' presence'.

This understanding of the nature of the 'memory of Jesus' and its role in the judgement of faith is quite untenable. To begin with we tend to speak of the 'corporate memory' of Jesus as something which Christians publicly share. Mental imagery is by definition private rather than public; and how could a mental image be transmitted? Indeed, in speaking of the Church's 'living memory' we are referring not to a memory, however sharp and vivid, in the minds and hearts of individual disciples, but rather a shared remembrance. It would be absurd to suggest that the Church's 'memory of Jesus', as something in the 'mind of the Church' rather than in individual minds, is a kind of corporate or shared mental image of Jesus.

Moreover, Wittgenstein has given the best of reasons for abandoning theories of knowledge in which objects are said to be identified by comparison with a mental image or copy.[35] If a person were to summon up a mental image of a patch of yellow in order to identify a yellow flag as yellow he is first faced with the problem of having to identify the memory-image as 'yellow'. And if it is conceded that it is possible to conjure up a mental picture of a person, this does not actually explain the ability to use the proper name. How would we know that the image we have is an image that can be called an 'image of *Jesus*'? In other words, in summoning up an image of a person we are faced with the problem of identifying or applying the proper name to the image. To insert a mental picture of

[35] See L. Wittgenstein, *The Blue and Brown Books*, pp. 3–5; *Philosophical Investigations*, pp. 2 ff. For a discussion of the application of concepts with respect to Kant's thought see Jonathan Bennett, *Kant's Analytic*, pp. 143–8, 'How to apply concepts'.

Jesus between the proper name 'Jesus' and putative instances of his living presence simply duplicates the problem of identification, for in this situation we would have to cope with two applications of the proper name, one to a mental image, one to a given object with which we are acquainted. The having of 'a mental image of Jesus' would not explain the Christian's ability to use the proper name.

On the other hand, it may well be that when we speak of the 'memory of Jesus' as a 'picture', 'impression' or 'memory-image' we mean to refer, not to a mental picture, impression or image, but to a verbal one. That is to say, when we say that the 'memory of Jesus' is 'entailed' or 'presupposed' in claims to recognize his living presence, we mean that what is presupposed or entailed is not a mental particular but the possession of certain publicly shared concepts relating to the identity of Jesus.

In this case, we are able to avoid a psychologizing interpretation of the nature of the Church's 'memory of Jesus' altogether. Wittgenstein made a clear distinction between 'concepts' and sensory or psychological states in so far as he stressed the importance of the public or corporate nature of concepts. This understanding of things helps explicitly to avoid the notion that the meanings of words are to be explained in terms of the introspection of private mental imagery. Concepts are corporately shared or conventionally agreed upon signs of standardized meanings. Likewise, the Church's 'memory of Jesus' may be understood, not as a psychological particular, but as a corporately shared verbal image of Jesus as he was in the days of his flesh, which gives the Church, understood once again as a linguistic community, the capacity to use and communicate with the name 'Jesus'. In this case, what is presupposed when the Church makes claims to identify the presence of Jesus, is not the having of a particular psychological experience in which a mental image is introspected, but the communal possession of certain identity criteria for using the proper name 'Jesus'. This means that we should think of the Church's 'memory of Jesus' not in terms of a psychological or mental object, but in terms of certain publicly shared criteria of a conceptual nature that back the Church's claims to recognize the presence of Jesus.

Consequently when, in the life of the Church, certain claims are made concerning the presence of Jesus, what is in fact presupposed is the possession of certain identity criteria for using the proper name. In this event, the 'memory of Jesus' which is transmitted and

shared within the life of the Church and which is presupposed in the
judgement of faith may be understood not as an inner, mental image
of psychological kind that can be introspected, but a public set of
identity criteria for the object Jesus. The 'memory of Jesus' may be
understood, in other words, in terms of a set of descriptive factual
statements that were formulated on the basis of empirical observation by the first Christians and transmitted in the early life of the
Church, and then from generation to generation, and that now
provide the descriptive backing for the name 'Jesus' and thus the
criteria for applying this name in demonstrative assertions or judgements of faith.

Thus, 'the memory of Jesus' may be understood not as an introspectible mental particular, but as a set of uniquely referring
descriptive statements about Jesus as he was in the days of his
flesh—a *verbal* picture or ikon of Jesus that is shared by the members of the Christian community. And what is presupposed by the
judgement of faith is not the having of a psychological experience,
involving the introspection of an inner mental particular, but the
possession of a set of statements, which express a sufficient but
unspecified number of descriptive characteristics, by virtue of
which we are able to teach and use the name 'Jesus'.

This seems, at least, a possible explanation of the reality in the life
of the Church to which we refer when we employ the metaphor of
the Church's 'corporate memory' of Jesus in our understanding of
the nature of the judgement of faith. Moreover, having said this, it
must be noted that this discussion of whether the Church's
'memory of Jesus' is to be understood as a 'psychological particular'
has led us back to the conclusion we arrived at at the end of Chapter
VII. Talk of the Church's 'memory of Jesus' can be expressed as a
set of factual memories about him. Though John Knox mistakenly
denied that the memory of Jesus is to be understood as a set of factual memories about him, such a set of factual memories is precisely
what is positively required by the logic of claims to recognize his
living presence. Indeed, a set of putatively factual statements about
Jesus is presupposed in the use of the proper name Jesus both referringly and identifyingly.

Knowing and Remembering

We have seen that despite the fact that 'remembering' and 'knowing'
must be clearly distinguished, they are nevertheless associated

together as two interwoven and thus interrelated elements or strands within the cognitive nucleus of faith. The memory of Jesus is presupposed when his living presence is apprehended and known as a concrete, empirically given reality and there would be no recognizing without it. On the other hand, the memory of Jesus does not stand alone as a backward looking and sentimental following of the human Jesus of liberal protestantism. But is it the case that these two stems are always associated together in serial order, as it were, first 'remembering' and then 'knowing'? In other words, given the distinction between remembering and knowing in the Christian response to Jesus Christ, there is a prima facie relation between these otherwise distinct elements in so far as the one known as the Christ could only be recognized as Jesus on the basis of some logically prior memory of the person referred to by that name. Does this mean that in terms of the cognitive experience of faith 'remembering' always precedes 'recognizing'?

H. H. Price has argued that the recognition of individuals depends on recognition of characteristics and that to recognize an individual person or object one 'must first recognize a characteristic, characterizing a present particular'. However, he goes on: 'But I must do more than this. I also remember an earlier particular— Jones-as-he-was-last-Wednesday—which was an instance of that same characteristic.'[36] This confirms my contention that recognizing or knowing the presence of the risen Christ *presupposes* a memory of Jesus. However, Henri Bergson expressed a view that is apparently contrary to Price's analysis of recognizing, when he pointed out in *Matter and Memory* that 'not every recognition implies the intervention of a memory image' and, indeed, that 'in most cases recollection emerges only *after* the perception is recognized'.[37]

It has already been noted that the memory that is presupposed in recognition may not be conceived in terms of the introspection of a mental-image and that when one claims to recognize a particular individual one may instead rely on a factual memory of certain descriptive characteristics. But in any case, we may nevertheless ask whether Bergson is right in saying that it is possible to recognize without *first* remembering. That is to say, is it possible to recog-

---

[36] H. H. Price, *Thinking and Experience*, p. 39.
[37] Henri Bergson, *Matter and Memory*, pp. 109 and 107. My italics.

nize without first remembering, either in the sense of calling up and introspecting a mental-image or in the sense of recalling certain descriptive characteristics?

At first sight it seems that Bergson may be right. For example, the fact that we first recognize and only then remember seems to be entailed when we focus attention on one person at a crowded party and say 'I recognize you . . . now, where have we met before?' In other words, it does seem that we have experiences in which we recognize persons *before* we actually remember them.[38] In such cases, however, we are undoubtedly recognizing certain characteristics, or perhaps remembering having been previously acquainted with a person having these particular characteristics, without being able to identify the actual person to whom they belong. For it is possible to recognize certain characteristics or features of a person without being able to identify the person by name. However, the kind of recognizing with which we are here concerned is the kind in which we not only claim to recognize certain characteristics or features of a presence, but in which we claim to recognize these features or characteristics as the characteristics of *Jesus*. And the question is, does this act of recognition entail that we must have *first* 'remembered Jesus' or remembered certain descriptive characteristics of Jesus? Or is it possible *first* to recognize his presence and only then actually 'remember'?

Gilbert Ryle has pointed out that we do not normally require that a person must be able to see an image of a past person or event 'before his mind's eye' before we are prepared to concede that he 'remembers' that person or event, but that the criteria by virtue of which we judge that a person 'remembers' are various. We are normally prepared to acknowledge that a person 'remembers' a past person or event if he is able to describe that past person or event *without recourse* to publicly observable evidence or without needing to be prompted by others.[39] Similarly, if a person correctly recognizes another person we should normally be prepared to concede that he remembers that person, or, at least, that he remembers certain descriptive facts about him. A person who has the capacity

---

[38] Cf. J. O. Urmson, 'Recognition', *Proceedings of the Aristotelian Society*, 56 (1955–6), p. 279: 'It is not uncommon', he says, 'to find oneself saying "I recognize him; when and where on earth can I have met him before? I have no recollection".'

[39] Gilbert Ryle, *The Concept of Mind*, p. 260. Cf. L. Wittgenstein, *Zettel*, para 650–9; also, Sydney Shoemaker, *Self-Knowledge and Self-Identity*, Chapter 4.

to recognize another person is one who has not forgotten what the person concerned was like. Thus, we say for example, such things as, 'I was able to recognize him at the airport because I remembered that he had a tattoo of a snake on his arm', or 'Though we had been apart for twenty years and she had changed considerably, I recognized her because I had not forgotten the distinctive way she laughed'. In other words, when we recognize a person and are able to cite, without recourse to criteria of a publicly observable kind and without needing to be prompted, the descriptive characteristics which constitute the identity criteria by virtue of which we are able to recognize, this is normally a sufficient demonstration of the fact that we remember him.

Even so, though we may do this *after* we have recognized a person, it is not necessarily true that we *first* either call up an image, as a kind of souvenir or replica of the person, and check what we see against it, or recall and rehearse a list of all factual memories, and check off what we see against them, one by one. Indeed, we seem to recognize *without* first having an actual experience of remembering, whether it be an experience of perceptual memory in which we see an image 'before our mind's eye', or an experience of factual memory wherein we recall certain facts. When I recognize my wife each morning, I do not first hesitate, introspect a mental memory-image, compare it with what I see and then confidently make the assertion that what I see is my wife. Nor is it an accurate account of the experience of recognizing to say that we call up a number of factual memories against which we check what we see before us, rather in the manner of a housewife checking though the items of the grocery delivery to make sure they are all there. If asked, we are normally able to state sufficient descriptive characteristics to justify our claims to recognize given persons or objects, but we do not normally 'tell them to ourselves' before we recognize.[40]

All this points to the fact that, whilst recognizing presupposes a memory, this presupposed memory is not necessarily an occurrent memory or memory-experience. Just as, when a person is said to remember the A–B–C, it is not being said that he is actually going through the processes of repeating the A–B–C to himself at that instant, but that he has the skill or capacity to do so if an occasion

---

[40] Cf. L. Wittgenstein, *Zettel*, op. cit., para 659. Also, see Urmson's criticism of H. H. Price's views in 'Recognition', pp. 277 ff.

arises in which this would be an appropriate thing to do, so we do not have the actual experience of remembering before, or even at the same time as, we make claims to recognize. For, if we are able to recognize a person correctly, it will normally be acknowledged by others that we also 'remember' or have 'not forgotten' him or her, and if we do claim to recognize a particular person, it is entailed that we should be able to state the characteristics on which our claim to recognize is based, if we are asked to do so. Thus, the memory which is 'presupposed' when we recognize may not necessarily be an occurrent memory; it may be a dispositional memory. It is the kind of memory that could be actualized in occurrent memory-experiences if we are asked or if we find it necessary, for some reason, to do so. This seems to confirm Bergson's observation, if he is understood to mean that we may have an experience of recognizing before we actually have the experience of remembering or even without having any actual experience of remembering.

It seems to follow from this that, when it is said that the Church 'remembers Jesus' and 'knows his living presence', we are not obliged to think in terms of two synchronous or coupled occurrent experiences. When we say that the Church 'remembers Jesus' it is not necessarily being said that the Church, at that instant, is in an actual psychological state or experience of remembering. Indeed, this would be absurd, for half the Christians of the world would almost certainly be asleep at any particular moment when this claim is made. In other words, there is an important difference in meaning between the statements, 'the Church *remembers* Jesus' or 'the Church *remembers* that Jesus died on the cross' and the statements, 'the Church *is remembering* Jesus' or 'the Church *is remembering* that Jesus died on the cross'. When we say that the Church is the community which 'remembers Jesus' we are not obliged either to think in terms of occurrent memory, or to psychologize the memory. We are not engaging in 'ecclesiastical psychology'. Instead of implying that Christians are in a particular psychological state we may simply mean, when we say that the Church 'remembers Jesus', that the Church is in the position to make certain claims. We mean that the Church is in a position, or has the skill or capacity, to make claims to know certain things about Jesus, such as 'that he lived', 'that he died on the cross', and 'that he exhibited a certain quality of character which came to be designated by the word "*agape*" '. Or else, we mean simply that the Church has the skill or capacity to recognize the presence of Jesus, for if a Christian correctly recognizes the presence of Jesus, we would normally concede that he had not 'forgotten Jesus', or, more correctly, that he had not forgotten certain descriptive characteristics of Jesus by virtue of which his living presence is recognized.

However, when we claim that the Church has the skill or capacity to state certain things about Jesus, or the ability to make claims to recognize Jesus' living presence, and that this is what we mean when we say that the Church 'remembers Jesus', we also imply that these things *could* be stated or that the Church *could* give reasons to justify her claim to recognize the living presence of Jesus, at particular moments, in occurrent memory-experiences if she is required to do so. Thus, though the memory that is presupposed in recognition may be dispositional memory, it is entailed that this dispositional memory may be actualized in particular, occurrent memory-experiences.

There is no doubt that sometimes we may speak of the Church as 'remembering and knowing' and have in mind two occurrent experiences. Though the Church's memory of Jesus may be understood in a dispositional sense, there are certainly specific times or occasions when the Church (at least when it is conceived of as a local community) may be said to have an occurrent memory or memory-experience of Jesus, in the sense that it actually gathers in its eucharistic assembly to recall that there was a Jesus and certain additional facts about his character, or perhaps to recall the fact that he died on the cross: The Lord's Supper is an occasion for the conscious recalling of Jesus for it is done 'for the remembrance of him'. But, besides the fact that on particular occasions the Church as a local, gathered community may be said to have a corporate experience or be in the state of remembering or recalling Jesus, or certain facts about him, there are specific occasions when the Church also 'knows Jesus'. Once again the Eucharist is an occasion for knowing Jesus: his living presence is known in the breaking of the bread. The liturgy of the Eucharist indeed is both a remembering of the human Jesus and a receiving of and communing with the divine Lord as Spirit.[41] It is not surprising that Easter narratives were developed in which Jesus 'breaks bread with' his disciples—thus to associate the

---

[41] See E. Käsemann, 'The Pauline Doctrine of the Lord's Supper' in *Essays on New Testament Themes*, pp. 112–13.

resurrection with the eucharistic faith and practice of the early Church. Thus, it is no accident that the actual occasion when Christians have claimed to be most deeply aware of the presence of the raised Christ is in the eucharist when the community gathers to break bread and share the cup *in remembrance of Jesus*. In the proclamation of the cross, Jesus' self-giving is set firmly before the Christian consciousness. But the eucharist is not just a backward-looking memorial. It is the means of encounter with the presence of the Lord as Spirit. Moreover, it is not just an occasion for recalling the Jesus of the past *and also* for enjoying a heightened awareness of the presence of the Lord, but it is the one *because of* the other. In the eucharist we know him as present because we first remember him. In proclaiming the Lord's death 'till he come' we are not only remembering or recalling Jesus' death and self-giving in an occurrent sense of the word 'remember'; we may also claim to know his living presence, in an occurrent sense of the word 'know'.[42] However, not every moment in the Christian's life can be like this, and more often than not the Christian's memory of Jesus is dispositional.

On the other hand, we do not necessarily have an experience of remembering Jesus before recognizing his presence as the raised Christ. 'Remembering' and 'knowing' do not follow each other in regular succession or serial order but are inextricably mingled. We remember him whom we now know; we know him whom we remember. More important, the fact that the experience of knowing may precede the experience of remembering comes to our attention when not only is the Spirit's presence discerned and identified as the undubitable present reality of the risen Christ but also the memory of the man Jesus comes alive with a new vitality and meaning.[43] The idea that after the resurrection the disciples remembered and then, only for the first time really understood, the words of Jesus, is rooted in St Luke's gospel where, indeed, it is emphasized in the

[42] Cf. S. J. Case, 'The Resurrection Faith of the First Disciples', *American Journal of Theology*, 13 (1909), p. 192: 'As he lived on in the spirit world his touch made their hearts burn, and the fires of their spirit were kindled as they reflected upon his teaching and broke bread together in loving remembrance of their former common fellowship.'

[43] See for example, John 12:16: 'His disciples did not understand this at first; but when Jesus was glorified, then they remembered that this had been written of him and had been done to him.' Also, John 14: 26; and 16: 13–4. Cf. G. W. H. Lampe in *The Resurrection*, p. 90 and C. C. Morrison, *What is Christianity?* p. 178.

narration of the Easter story.[44] Thus, though recognition entails a
(dispositional) memory of at least sufficient facts to enable the presence of Jesus to be recognized, the apostles may be understood to have had a full and clear (occurrent) memory of Jesus only after recognizing his living presence.[45]

Moreover, the two kinds of experience are so inextricably mingled that they *are not without effect upon each other*. The memory cannot be explained as a mere projection backwards of the Church's later experience, but our present knowledge of the Spirit of Jesus is decisively affected by our memory of him; and it is probably just as true that our memory of him has to some extent been shaped by our knowledge of his present reality. Thus, there is a sense in which the Spirit is informed by the memory; the memory, by the Spirit.

There is now one important and outstanding question which must be addressed. We have seen that if faith is correctly understood as the apprehension and identification of the presence of the Spirit of the Christian fellowship as the presence of Jesus Christ, then it is logically entailed that those who make the judgement of faith must have recourse to a set of factual memories about Jesus, which makes such an identity judgement possible. The crucial question that now concerns us is whether the set of factual statements about Jesus which constitutes the content of the Church's 'memory of Jesus' is sufficiently precise as to refer uniquely to Jesus. In order to identify the presence of the Spirit of Jesus, as distinct from some other spirit, the believer must rely on a set of *uniquely referring* characteristics which would justify that particular identity judgement to the exclusion of other possibilities. With this question in mind we must now return to a further consideration of the precise content of the Church's memory of Jesus.

44 See Luke 24: 8. Also Luke 2: 50 and 18: 34.
45 John 2: 22.

IX

Easter Faith and the Self-Giving of Jesus

The Particularity of Love

ONE feature of the early Christian proclamation, as it is reflected in
the first sermons of the apostles, which are now found in shorthand
form in the early chapters of Acts, is that there is an emphasis on the
continuity of the Jesus who was remembered and the Christ who
was known in the response of faith. Acts 2: 23–4 insists that it was
Jesus of Nazareth—this Jesus whom lawless men had crucified—
whom God raised up. Similarly, it was 'this same Jesus' whom the
Jews crucified whom God 'made Lord and Christ' (Acts 2: 26). The
content of this primitive preaching as Luke relates it was not just
that *a man* had risen from the dead, or that there was an anonymous
Risen One whom God had raised, but that *Jesus* had been raised
from the dead. The person whom the first Christians claimed to
know in faith was understood to be numerically identical with the
very Jesus whom they remembered.

The same emphasis on the continuity of identity of the one 'who
died for our sins according to the Scriptures' with the one who was
'raised on the third day according to the Scriptures' is also present in
the primitive kerygmatic formula of 1 Cor. 15: 3–4 and is, of course,
a feature of the appearance narratives of the gospels either implicitly
or explicitly.[1]

The question of the identity of the one known as the Christ of
faith with the one remembered as the historical Jesus is as crucial for
present-day Christians as it was for the first witnesses. Given that
the gospel narratives register an initial failure to recognize and even
a residual doubt on the part of at least some witnesses as to whether
it really was *Jesus* whom they encountered, we must ask how it is
that in faith we make the identity judgement that it is in any sense
Jesus with whom we have to do. Even if it is a divinely exalted and

---

[1] It is clear that a chief concern of at least some appearance narratives is to establish the very point. For example John 20: 26–9; Luke 24: 39.

heavenly Jesus with whom we are dealing it is still central to the affirmation of Easter faith that the heavenly one enjoys a personal continuity of identity with the man of Nazareth. This is an issue of fundamental importance for the theology of the resurrection, for, if resurrection faith is not clear in its reference to Jesus of Nazareth, then it is in danger of dissolving into a pious ideology. Indeed, our very talk of 'resurrection' becomes problematic. For this reason, many find Bultmann's exposition of Easter faith, in terms of an awakening to new self-understanding before God, uncomfortable from a Christian point of view, despite its positive attractiveness in terms of the enhancement of human existence. Similarly, Geoffrey Lampe's concentration of attention on the Spirit and its power to bring present-day believers to a consciousness that they are 'Sons of God in Christ Jesus' (Galatians 3: 26), seems at times to be only very loosely attached to an originating event involving *Jesus*. Whilst he speaks of the Spirit as the 'Spirit of Christ', he so concentrates upon the exposition of its implications for the transformation of human lives that he sees little need to 'refer back to an original resurrection event' without which faith would collapse.[2] It is almost as though Christianity could perform a pragmatically useful role by alerting believers to the transformative presence of what is called 'the Spirit of Christ' without any reference to the originating event of the raising of Jesus from the dead. Clearly, if Christians are to continue to identify the Spirit not just as the 'Spirit of Christ' but more specifically as the 'Spirit of the raised *Jesus*' some attention must be paid to the question of the particularity of this identity claim.

Now, if the 'cognitive nucleus' of resurrection faith is a kind of knowledge exhibiting the same fundamental epistemological pattern as ordinary perceptual knowledge, despite the fact that its object, Jesus the raised Lord, is unique, then one way in which the judgement of faith may be said to conform to the pattern of ordinary per-

---

[2] See *God as Spirit*, p. 151. Thus he says: 'it is not really the case that the on-going experience of Christian people, of the kind to which the Easter preacher appeals, is actually constituted by, and dependent upon, the resurrection as an event.' Also, R. C. Ware, *op. cit.*, p. 35: 'Resurrection faith must be concrete, too, in its reference to Jesus of Nazareth. Otherwise Christian faith is in danger dissolving into still another ideological superstructure. Much speculative theological reflection tends to gravitate in this direction, so that one is often left wondering whether the specific conception of resurrection still has any relationship to the profession of God's raising of *Jesus* from the dead.'

ceptual knowledge is that the Spirit of the raised Christ can *only* be known also as the presence of *Jesus* by those who remember something of him. The New Testament witness indicates that Jesus was first recognized only by those who had known him previously or by those who, like Paul, had received information concerning Jesus through contact with the 'living memory' of the primitive Christian community.[3] Thereafter faith 'comes through hearing' (Romans 10: 17) in the sense that the proclamation of the kerygma both alerts and equips the hearer to perceive the presence of the Spirit as the redemptive presence of Christ. It is not possible for people to recognize and believe in one 'of whom they have never heard' (Romans 10: 14) just as those at Ephesus did not receive or perceive the presence of the Spirit because they 'had not so much as heard that there is a Holy Spirit' (Acts 19: 2).

We have already noted that, in cases of natural perception, a person who claims to recognize another as one, let us say, to whom he was introduced during the previous week, must be able, if asked, to give some reason for supposing that person to be the same person as the one to whom he was previously introduced. Ordinarily this will entail citing certain descriptive characteristics of the person concerned. Similarly, the Christian believer must be able to give some reasons for supposing the presence of the 'Spirit of Christ' to be identical with the *Jesus of Nazareth* of whom he or she has heard.

In the previous chapter it was noted that the 'memory of Jesus' which is presupposed when the Church makes claims to recognize Christ's living presence seems best understood not as a mental-

---

[3] Bultmann's idea that Paul was interested only in the mere *Dass* of Jesus' historical existence is, of course, today widely challenged. See Graham Stanton, *Jesus of Nazareth in New Testament Preaching* especially pp. 99 ff., 'Paul and the Character of Jesus'. Also 'The Gospel Traditions and Early Christological Reflection' in *Christ, Faith and History*, pp. 191–204; also of relevance is G. D. Kilpatrick's translation of Galatians 1: 18, concerning Paul's visit to Jerusalem, as 'to get information (about Jesus) from Cephas', in 'Galatians 1: 18 "ΙΣΤΟΡΗΣΑΙ ΚΗΦΑΝ" ', *New Testament Essays* pp. 144 ff. Also, C. H. Dodd, *The Apostolic Preaching and Its Development* p. 26. Concerning Paul's visit to Jerusalem, he writes: 'At the time he stayed with Peter for a fortnight, and we may presume they did not spend all the time talking about the weather'. Günther Bornkamm points out in *Paul*, p. 238 that 'in spite of the almost two thousand years' interval, we today probably know more about the Jesus of history than did Paul. At the time, on the basis of what Paul did know of him, his death on the cross and resurrection, he proclaimed Christ's liberating work and conceived his person as the "Yes and No" confirming God's promises (2 Cor. 1: 17 ff)'.

image but as an identifying description, a set of identity criteria or descriptive statements about Jesus. If the concept of 'the corporate memory of Jesus himself' is reduced to a set of factual memories about him, or factual descriptions of Jesus, this goes some way towards supplying what is needed to justify the identity judgement of faith. However, we may ask whether the descriptive statements that have so far been suggested are sufficiently specific to qualify as an *identifying* description. To say that Jesus was a man who lived in the first century, who was crucified on a cross and who was remembered to have exhibited a distinctive character, may go some way towards describing who Jesus was, or who is being referred to when the name 'Jesus' is used. But do such statements convey sufficiently detailed information about Jesus to enable the present-day Christian to recognize *his* living presence?

In order to justify a claim that an object of present perception is identical in a *numerical sense* with one remembered, it is necessary that the claimant should be able to cite certain *uniquely referring* characteristics. Gottlob Frege held that proper names do have sense as well as reference and that the sense of a proper name contains the 'mode of presentation' which identifies the referent.[4] We have noted that John R. Searle has argued that, though proper names do not strictly speaking have sense, certain descriptive statements are at least presupposed when proper names are used. However, if a proper name is used to identify an object, it is essential that the presupposed sense of the proper name should be specific enough to indicate a 'mode of presentation'. Consequently, we may say, not only that when the name 'Jesus' is used referringly the knowledge of certain descriptive characteristics is presupposed, but that these same descriptive characteristics may also be cited to justify claims to recognize Jesus' living presence. But this will only be possible if the descriptive statements are specific enough to indicate the 'mode of presentation' of *Jesus*. This means that the Christian must possess an identifying description of Jesus—a description of such a kind that one and only one person—Jesus—can fill it. Given, then, that the Church's memory of Jesus may be understood as a set of descriptive statements concerning Jesus, or as a set of factual memories about Jesus, the crucial question is whether the factual memories which

---

[4] G. Frege, 'On Sense and Reference' in *Translations from the Philosophical Writings of Gottlob Frege*, p. 57.

have so far been brought forward to provide the content of the Church's 'memory of Jesus' are specific enough to constitute an identifying description. Is the Church's 'memory of Jesus' specific enough to do the job that faith requires it to do?

Clearly, a single descriptive predicate, such as 'man' does not provide us with a 'mode of presentation', for, though the statement 'Jesus was a man' is true, the predicate 'man' is not specific enough to describe *Jesus*. Nor do the assertions that Jesus was supremely good or that he exhibited a distinctive quality of character help us. It is true that qualities of character could conceivably specify the means whereby a particular individual is to be recognized. For example, one might say 'You will recognize him because he is the most boisterous member of the group', or 'You will know him because he is the most shy and retiring member of the family', or 'He is the British politician who is disposed to make inflammatory speeches on race'. However, in order to identify Jesus' presence we should at least want to know something specific about Jesus' distinctive quality of character. This leads us to ask whether the concept *agape* is specific enough to provide us with a 'mode of presentation'; does the description of Jesus' character in terms of *agape* constitute a sufficiently specific description to permit the Christian to distinguish his presence from other objects?

If the term *agape* is employed, along with *eros* and *philia*, in its pre-biblical sense, as a class name of a general kind of love, it would hardly suffice.[5] However, *agape*, as used by early Christian writers, did not simply denote one of three or four species of the genus 'love'. The variety of love is incalculably greater than such classifications suggest. In fact, it is possible to argue that there are as many kinds of love as there are individual persons. If love is self-giving, then it is the giving of particular human selves and every human self is unique. Loving, in other words, is not just one of a number of attributes a person may be said to possess; a person's loving is the person himself or herself, going out to and giving him or herself to another.

In his devotional studies on Romans Chapters 5 to 8, entitled *Life*

---

[5] See Ethelbert Stauffer, 'The Words for Love in Pre-Biblical Greek' in 'ἀγαπάω, ἀγάπη, ἀγαπητός', by Gottfried Quell and Ethelbert Stauffer in TDNT, I, pp. 35–8. Also, J. Moffatt, *Love in the New Testament*, pp. 35–40, and Cyril C. Richardson, 'Love: Greek and Christian', *JR*, 23, 1943, pp. 173–85.

in Christ Jesus, John Knox provides an excellent statement of the distinctiveness of love:

If love is one's giving of oneself to another, there are as many kinds of love as there are persons loving and beloved. The man and woman in love who feel that what has happened to them has never happened before are quite right—for he is himself and she is herself, and their love for each other is as unique as they are. Even if each of them has been in love before, this is still true. For the way we give ourselves—indeed *what* we give when we give ourselves—is partly determined by the character of the person to whom the gift is made. I can remember my mother answering the complaint of one of her four children that she loved one of us more than the others by saying that she loved each us, not more, or less, but differently. And so she did.[6]

In the light of this highly particularized conception of the nature of love, it is understandable that when the first Christians came to speak of the love that was remembered to have been in Jesus, they thought in terms of the distinctive quality of *Jesus'* self-giving. Indeed, it is precisely the particularity of Jesus' love that is expressed in the New Testament's distinctive use of the term *agape*. It is not employed to denote the colourless and indefinite or 'weak and variable' kind of love which, as Stauffer has shown, is denoted by the pre-biblical use of the word;[7] rather, the Greek-speaking Christians employed the concept *agape* precisely because they were aware of the uniqueness of Jesus' love and sought to communicate it. They felt that neither *eros* nor *philia* sufficed to designate it and accordingly used the relatively rare and unknown word *agape*.[8]

Consequently, love in the Christian use of that term, is not love in some general sense but in a most particular and distinctive sense. Unlike *eros* and *philia*, which are general class names designating kinds of love exhibited by many different individual selves, *agape* in its definitive Christian use denotes the distinctive and unique *self-*

---

[6] *Life in Christ Jesus*, p. 21.

[7] See E. Stauffer, op. cit., pp. 36–7.

[8] J. Moffatt, op cit., 'When Christianity first began to think and speak in Greek, it took up ἀγάπη and its group of terms more freely, investing them with the new glow with which the NT writings make us familiar, a content which is invariably religious.' (p. 40) I do not think Anders Nygren in *Agape and Eros*, C. S. Lewis, *The Four Loves* or Gene Outka, *Agape*, do us a service when they speak of *agape* as though it were one general form of love to be contrasted with Eros (Nygren) or one of four general types (Lewis) or a human virtue (Outka). This generalized approach to the understanding of *agape* fails to recognize its definition in the life of the particular self to whom we refer as *Jesus*. However, other statements, especially of Nygren, correct this impression. See *Agape and Eros*, pp. 117 ff.

giving of *Jesus*. If *agape* is thought of as a class name, it must designate a unit class; it is the love that was known in the life of a single, unique individual.

Thus, Lindsay Dewar points out that if St Paul's famous hymn to love in 1 Cor. 13 is read by changing the tense of the verbs and substituting the proper-name 'Christ' for 'agape' the passage becomes a type of idealized description of what Jesus is remembered to have been during his life on earth.[9] *Agape* connotes the highly distinctive character of the love which was expressed in Jesus' life and lifted up in awful beauty on the cross. It was Jesus pre-eminently who was remembered to have been patient of suffering, kind, not jealous or boastful, arrogant or rude. It was Jesus the servant who did not insist on his own way and was not irritable or resentful; who did not rejoice at wrong but rejoiced in the right (see 1 Cor. 13: 4–6.).

The selfless love of Jesus, who in his concern for others 'did not please himself' (Romans 15: 3) is brought into focus in the image of Jesus the deacon (Romans 15: 8) who puts the interests of those whom he serves before his own self-interest. This same image of distinctive self-giving expressed through the humanity of Jesus is also summed up and celebrated in the ancient hymn preserved by Paul in Philippians 2: 5–11 where it is linked particularly to the cross. Here, in exhorting the Philippian Christians to 'have the same love' and to 'look not to your own interests, but the interests of others' (cf. vv. 1–4) Paul holds up what is in effect a verbal ikon or image of the character of Christ as a model for them to emulate: the character of the one who humbled himself and took the form of a servant and 'became obedient unto death, even death on a cross' (v. 8).

For the Christian Church the crucifixion of Jesus is so central a moment because it expresses in a single definitive episode something of the distinctive love that was remembered to have characterized the self-giving of Jesus throughout his life: St Paul speaks of the remembered Jesus as the Son of God 'who loved me and gave himself for me' (Galatians 2: 20). No wonder the cross has become

---

[9] L. Dewar, *An Outline of New Testament Ethics* p. 127. This idea is followed by G. Bornkamm in *Paul*, p. 217 and *Early Christian Experience* Ch. XI. A similar suggestion has been made by W. D. Davies with respect to Romans 1: 4. Davies follows P. Feine, J. Weiss, and others in noting that the name 'Jesus' could easily be substituted for the term 'love' to supply a description of his character; *Invitation to the New Testament*, p. 363.

such an important symbol for Christians: it sums up and expresses the distinctiveness of Jesus' loving character or self-giving.

Moreover, it is precisely this *agape* which, after the crucifixion of Jesus, was recognized as a powerful and living reality in the life of the Christian community. The particular kind of love or self-giving that was expressed in Jesus' life and symbolized by the cross was also released in mighty power at his resurrection and found as a concrete reality within the distinctiveness of the fellowship of the Church. '*Agape*', indeed, is a key concept in the identification of the living presence of Jesus himself. For the relationship of Jesus with his disciples was from the beginning remembered as one of love; at Calvary that love was brought to definitive focus as a love 'than which no greater could be conceived'. But at Easter, the primitive Church now knew the same distinctive kind, or quality, of love as the bond of unity and peace within its own life.[10] In this way, *agape*, as a concept denoting the specific quality of the remembered self-giving of Jesus, permits the Christian believer to recognize the Spirit of the Christian fellowship as the dynamic presence or self-giving of *Jesus*. In other words, the Spirit of the community may be identified as the Spirit or self-giving activity of Jesus because it is a Spirit which bears the distinctive Jesus-character.[11] As St Paul says, 'love has been poured out into our hearts by the Holy Spirit who has been given unto us' (Romans 5: 5). This is not love in some general sense, but the highly particular love that is remembered to have been exhibited by the historical Jesus and indeed, brought to clear and living focus in his life and death. To know that self-giving in the post-Easter period is to know Jesus, living still, for it is the distinctive *self*-giving of *Jesus*.

[10] See John Knox, *The Church and the Reality of Christ*, p. 56: 'the agape known in the Church, and known there as the Spirit of God, his very presence, could not have been recognized also as the Spirit of Christ if the same agape had not been remembered as the essential and distinctive quality of Jesus' own life.'

[11] Concerning the presentation by Paul of the character of Jesus, see Graham Stanton, *Jesus of Nazareth in New Testament Preaching* especially pp. 99 ff. On the relevance of Phil. 2: 6–11 as an image of the character of Christ, see p. 103: 'Whatever the original *Sitz im Leben* and meaning may have been, Paul uses the hymn as an exhortation to the Philippian Christians, setting before them the character of Christ.' Also see J. D. G. Dunn, *Jesus and the Spirit*, pp. 318 ff., especially p. 324: '*when Paul wants to find the distinctive mark of Spirit-given experience, he finds it not in the charismatic Spirit as such, nor in the eschatological Spirit as such, but in the Jesus Spirit, the Spirit whose characteristics are those of Christ.*' On the usefulness to systematic theology of the idea of the 'character of Christ' see S. W. Sykes, 'Th Essence of Christianity', *Religious Studies*, 7 (1971), pp. 291–305.

We noted in Chapter VI that Paul did not find it necessary to press the distinction between talk of the raised Christ and talk of the Spirit, but when the close identity between the use of these terms is set aside in order to draw a distinction, it is for the purpose of distinguishing the raised Christ 'as he is in himself' and the Spirit which is 'him in action' as it were. The Spirit of Jesus is Jesus in so far as he gives himself in love, to be known and experienced in human lives. Clearly, between self and self-giving there is a very fine notional line; in reality there is continuity for one is the dynamic or 'fluid extension' of the other: Christ is the Supernatural Rock from which the Spirit of which we drink flows (1 Cor. 12: 13; 10: 3–4). An emphasis on love as the particular self-giving of an individual self therefore militates against the drawing of any firm distinction between the *self-giving* of Jesus, on one hand, and Jesus as the *self who gives*, on the other, since to know Jesus in his dynamic self-giving is, at least partially, to know Jesus *himself*. Just as to remember Jesus is to remember, in particular, his self-giving on the cross, and to remember his cross is to remember Jesus himself,[12] so to know Jesus' self-giving is to know Jesus himself, giving.

Neill Hamilton, Eduard Schweizer, and Ernst Käsemann have all expressed this notion in slightly different words: 'Christ's gifts', says Hamilton, 'are inseparable from His person, the Spirit mediates the presence of the Lord'.[13] On the other hand, Schweizer draws attention to the fact that the identity of Christ and Spirit which is evident in Paul and John can also be detected in Luke in so far as *Jesus* sends the promised Spirit (Luke 24: 49). Luke's conviction that Jesus is the donor of the Spirit must explain, he says, 'the growth of the idea that the risen Lord himself is encountered in this his gift, so that either the Spirit or the risen Lord can be referred to interchangeably'.[14] Likewise, Ernst Käsemann notes that in the Lord's Supper 'food and drink . . . convey the πνεῦμα' (1 Cor. 10. 3 f) and that 'the gift takes on the character of the Giver and through the gift we become partakers of the Giver himself' (1 Cor. 12: 13).[15]

---

[12] See Chapter VII, pp. 286–7.
[13] Op. cit., p. 15.
[14] E. Schweizer, *op. cit.*, pp. 38–9. See Luke 24: 49, Acts 2: 33. Schweizer also draws attention to a comparison of Luke 12: 12 with Luke 21: 15 and Acts 10: 13–14 with Acts 10: 19 and 26: 17.
[15] E. Käsemann, 'The Pauline Doctrine of the Lord's Supper', p. 113.

In other words, the logical step from claiming an awareness of the Spirit, conceived of as the dynamic, self-expressive activity of Jesus, to the awareness of Jesus *himself*, *giving*, is a comparatively straightforward one. The Spirit, as we are given to know that Spirit in the life of the Church, is the Spirit which is remembered to have been in Jesus and in whose presence Jesus *himself* is present with us always, till the end of the Age. It is the promissory perception of the presence of Christ himself 'until he comes' in the glory of future fulfilment to be unequivocally revealed.[16] The Easter experience and faith of Christians consists therefore in apprehending the present Spirit of the religious fellowship and interpreting it by reference to the very same character that is remembered to have been placarded before men in clear and decisive form in the historical life and death of Jesus of Nazareth. After Easter the first Christians were able to speak of *agape* not just as the remembered reality of the Jesus-character but as an experienced reality in their own fellowship and thus as the presence or Spirit of Jesus in their own lives. We may therefore say that *agape* itself *is* the gracious activity of the Spirit, the medium of the presence of the raised Christ himself.

Moreover, in the vocabulary of the first Christians, the highly distinctive love that was remembered to have been expressed by Jesus both before and through his crucifixion and afterwards as a given reality in the fellowship of the Church, is also referred to as *God's love*; what the Church claims to remember is 'the love of God in Christ Jesus our Lord'. Apart from any significance the cross had for Paul as a symbol of the self-giving of *Jesus*, it, at the same time, derives its special significance because it is perceived as the place of the revelation of a love or self-giving which is Divine. Thus, the *agape* revealed in the life and death of Jesus is 'God's own *agape* towards us'.[17] In other words, Paul sees the Jesus-character as also the distinctive nature of Divinity revealed in the cross.[18] As Martin Kähler put it: 'The creed of the Church adds to the cross's superscription the interpretation, "Behold your God" '.[19] As a conse-

---

[16] Similarly, Jürgen Moltmann: 'To know God means to re-cognize him. But to re-cognize him is to know him in his historic faithfulness to his promises, to know him therein as the selfsame Self and therefore to know himself'; *Theology of Hope*, pp. 116 ff.

[17] See Romans 5: 6–10. On the central importance of the cross for the expression of the Divine Agape see Anders Nygren, op. cit., p. 117.

[18] E. Käsemann, *Perspectives on Paul*, p. 41.

[19] M. Kähler, *Das Kreuz: Grund und Mass für nostra theologia*, BFCT 15 (1911), p. 45. Cf. Karl Barth, CD, IV/2, pp. 105 ff. and 109 f.

quence, Paul can sometimes speak of Jesus' death as a divine sacrifice (as in Romans 4: 25; 8: 32) and proof and expression of God's love, whilst on other occasions he speaks (as in Galatians 1: 4; 2: 20; 2 Cor. 5: 14 f.) of the self-sacrificing love of Christ.[20] Bultmann's insistence on maintaining the closest of connections between the cross and what it reveals and the Resurrection and what it reveals is perfectly correct: the unifying factor is *agape*, the love which Jesus shows for us which at the same time is the expression of the love of God for us, remembered on the cross and known as a living reality in the ongoing life of the post-Easter community.

St John expresses a similar idea. His awareness of who the distinctive person Jesus was is summed up in the formula 'full of grace and truth' which reflects the definitive revelation of Yahweh himself in Exodus 33. A. T. Hanson has shown that the formula 'full of grace and truth' expresses the idea that the God who showed himself to Moses at the giving of the Law has now manifested himself in Jesus Christ and can be recognized by the same characteristics, which may more properly be interpreted as 'steadfast love and faithfulness'. The 'steadfast love and faithfulness' revealed in and through the human life of Jesus is the Johannine equivalent of the *agape* which in Paul's mind more than any other single term expressed what was really memorable about *Jesus*.[21] The word *agape* is thus no general brand-name for a kind of love or for the highest of human virtues, but God's love revealed in Christ in all its distinctiveness and uniqueness. For what has been said concerning the love of human individuals as their particular and unique self-giving may be said also of God's love. The 'love of God' is not merely a loving attitude of God towards his people; it is God himself, giving himself to his people. It follows that the *agape* that is remembered to have been in Jesus is not simply understood as Jesus' distinctive and indivdual *agape* but in some sense and at the same time, the Divine Agape, the particular or unique self-giving of God. Likewise, because the Spirit that was recognized in the Easter experience by virtue of the Jesus-character as *his* Spirit also made itself known as the exalted and heavenly reality of the Spirit of God himself, it is possible to say that the Spirit that is known in the life of the Church as the 'Spirit of Jesus' is also the active presence of God himself, 'the

[20] E. Käsemann, *Perspectives on Paul*, op. cit., p. 39.
[21] A. T. Hanson, *Grace and Truth*, pp. 5 ff.

Holy Spirit'. Whilst these terms bear slightly different meanings and thus connote differences within the Godhead, they in fact denote the one distinctive Divine reality in human experience. What is remembered to have been expressed uniquely and distinctively in the life and death of Jesus and known by acquaintance in the life of the Christian community after his death is a reality that, though variously described as the Spirit of Christ, the Spirit of God, or the Holy Spirit, is identified by virtue of the distinctive descriptive characteristic of *agape*.

In his treatment of the resurrection in *The Resurrection of the Dead*, Karl Barth perceived that there was a very close connection between what Paul had to say about *agape* in 1 Corinthians 13 and the eschatological discourse of 1 Corinthians 15; indeed, *agape* is not just a superior human virtue and not even one of the charisms mentioned in 1 Corinthians 12, precisely because whilst these will eventually pass away, *agape* as the self-giving of the raised Jesus and the eschatological reality of God's love 'never ceases'. In so far as this eternal reality is humanly experienced in time, it is the sign now of 'the eschatological "then" ' for it is the abiding love of God himself. It exists eternally when all else is done away.[22] *Agape* is the eschatological reality of the presence of the raised Christ himself, giving himself to his people, and signifying the eternal presence of God himself. It is 'the divine possibility in all human possibilities'.[23]

It is clear, therefore, that the reality that is remembered to have been expressed in Jesus' life is not a very general kind of love, but the particular self-giving of the remembered Jesus, which in turn may be understood as being identical with the particular self-giving of God.[24] It is not too much to say that *agape* is the eschatological

---

[22] K. Barth, *The Resurrection of the Dead*, p. 76.

[23] Ibid., p. 83. Bultmann agrees: 'Love (ἀγάπη) is not an ethical ideal but an eschatological event', *Faith and Understanding*, p. 78.

[24] See Jack Sanders, 'First Corinthians 13. Its Interpretation Since the First World War', *Interpretation*, 20 (1966), pp. 159–87, especially p. 180: 'agape is the presence of the transcendent in the sphere of the finite'. This follows the eschatological interpretation of *agape* outlined by Barth. See also H.-D. Wendland, *Die Briefe an die Korinther*, p. 1035. Of *agape* he writes, 'It is God himself among men, the authentic might and power and the "perfect" of the new eon'. See also James Moffatt, *The First Epistle of Paul to the Corinthians*, and Alfred Plummer, *International Critical Commentary* on *I Corinthians*, p. 300: 'Faith and Hope are purely human; . . . the virtues of creatures. Love is Divine'. Also, Jean Guitton. *Essay on Human Love*, p. 194–5: *Agape* alone 'has in essence, pure being, for, in its most exalted form, it is the character of God. God is Agape: that which is in no way changed by an object or an external interest, but is essentially a gift'.

reality of God himself acting in Christ and perceived, known, and celebrated in the faith and worship of the Christian community.

However, if it is admitted that the concept 'agape' can be employed to describe a unique and distinctive reality, we still want to know more precisely what the more detailed nature of this *agape* is. If it is going to be possible for the Christian to recognize the reality that is described by this term, it is necessary that he or she have some more information concerning its distinctive character. Here the Christian believer runs into some difficulty. For in the final analysis, if what is remembered to have been exhibited in the life of Jesus is a Divine Love, it cannot be expressed adequately in words; as God's love, *agape* by definition possesses a transcendent quality. If the love that is remembered to have been in Jesus is God's love, or God making himself known, it is an ineffable Reality. Accordingly, the cross, which, as we have already noted, is the symbol of the self-giving of Jesus, and the centre of the Church's memory of Jesus, is also the focus of the revelation of this ineffable Reality. One reason why the death of Christ has always been remembered as a strange and awful moment, significant beyond our understanding, is that it points us towards heights incalculably beyond our reach—the revelation of the Mystery of the Divine Love.

Now, this takes us one stage further in understanding the content of the Church's 'memory of Jesus himself' and, at the same time, helps to account for the elusiveness of any attempt to state that content. For, if what the Church remembers to have been uniquely and distinctively expressed in the life of Jesus is a transcendent reality, the Church's memory must be marked by a *necessary* elusiveness, the elusiveness that attaches to any attempt to describe the particularity of the Divine.

Abstract and Concrete

The problem of expressing and communicating what is essentially transcendent and incomprehensible may, once again, be understood by reference to the espistemological pattern of ordinary perceptual knowledge. For, the transcendence of the object of faith may be understood, at least in the first instance, in terms of a kind of transcendence that is encountered in the perception of ordinary things. Briefly put, the operative principle is that abstract and general concepts cannot fully and adequately describe the concrete richness of particular, empirically experienced realities: all descriptive language in some sense reduces the full richness of experience. For example, a hat and an autumn leaf may be described by the general word 'brown', but if one tries to define what is distinctive about the leaf's brownness in contrast to the hat's brownness, one may be confronted with considerable difficulties. A similar difficulty is encountered when one endeavours to distinguish Jesus' love from human love generally. The self-giving of Jesus may be judged to be unique because he was a unique individual self, but how is that uniqueness expressed in words? It is here that we encounter something of the difference also between scientific and religious discourse. Science moves in the realm of the abstract for its method involves the breaking down of the concrete and particular into abstract and general categories with a view to formulating general laws. It is concerned inductively to abstract from particular instances to general concepts and general laws, or statements of universal hypothetical form, and thereby to explain particular and concrete occurrences in terms that are abstract and general.

The abstractions of scientific language will be found to be particularly impoverished and unsuited to the communication of religiously significant truths, however, because religious language is not intended to 'explain' so much as to 'maintain' the ineffable particularity of its object. God's supreme revelation in Christ is *sui generis*; it is concerned with what is distinctive and historically particular for it is concerned with a concrete occurrence that is datable to a particular time and which involved Jesus, a concrete and particular individual. It is not adequately spoken of in terms that are abstract and general, for such terms do not exhaust nor even begin to communicate adequately the unique individuality of what is given. Because the concern of the Christian is to talk descriptively about the uniqueness of Jesus Christ and to capture at least something of his distinctive individuality, even the term *agape* must be understood as a code word signifying much more than could be clearly stated in a dictionary definition of its Christian use.

The 'scandal of particularity' and the difficulty of expressing the uniqueness of the particular is compounded when the unique and particular is understood also to be divine and therefore by definition ineffable. Jesus' love transcends our ability to express it not just because, though a human love, it is particular and unique and therefore defies attempts to describe it in a few precise words, but because this love is not, strictly speaking, a merely human love at all, but God's love. On one hand, therefore, the transcendence of Jesus' love is a kind of transcendence that attaches to all particular, concrete things; but on the other hand, the transcendence of his love is due to the fact that it is a uniquely divine love.

This leads us into the very heart of the Christological problem. Jesus was met as a man and his *agape* was first understood as a human self-giving. Through Jesus' career, as the apparently normal human career it was at first remembered to have been, Jesus was remembered to have been a man, a human person, the teacher and friend. However, after the crucifixion his love was known as the gift of a divinely exalted Spirit. In other words, though his love was first *remembered* as a *human* love, it was later *known* in the life of the Christian community as a *divine* Love: though remembered as 'Master' he was known as 'Lord'. Barth very cogently expresses the divine and human components of the experience of the post-Easter community: 'the particular content of the particular recollection of this particular time of the apostolic community consisted in the fact that in this time the *man* Jesus was manifested among them in the mode of *God*'.[25] After Easter the love remembered to have been in Jesus was experienced as a sovereign and divine love in the sense that it was now perceived without the constraints and limitations of space and time. The love of Jesus could now be experienced not just in Galilee, or wherever his physical and earthly body happened to be, but anywhere two or three gather in his name. And this is to be understood not in the sense of anywhere *two or three gather*, but *anywhere* two or three gather. Christ's love is experienced beyond the walls of any single place where he is met; like God himself, he, through the medium of his loving activity, is omnipresent. It is also a love which possesses the remembered steadfastness of enduring the cross and loving his brothers to the end which now goes on eternally, 'never to die again'. It is not determined by the worthiness or otherwise of its object to receive it but of its own nature it is changeless, constant, and reliable. It is rocklike and, thus, trustworthy—a legitimate object of faith as trust. It is also of infinite resource so that when all within the fold seek its succour and 'drink of the Spirit' there is still a complete supply for those who are still beyond the fold. These are the eternal and all-inclusive or catholic

---

[25] K. Barth, *Church Dogmatics*, III/2, p. 447 f.

dimensions of the love, now experienced as the Spirit of Christ, which together point to its *heavenly and divine* source: it is no mere human love but a love of cosmic, indeed infinite, proportions. In order to talk about it at all, as we shall see, it is necessary to engage not just in historical but in metaphorical or mythological talk. As a consequence of the resurrection the love remembered to have been defined in Jesus' life and death is now known, in the living experience of the Christian community, as a love that knows no bonds of time and place. Its source is infinite and eternal, in the heavens.

This means that strictly speaking, Jesus was remembered as a human person and the love that was remembered to have been expressed in his life was a human love. Later, that is to say, after Easter, it came to be experienced and known also as a divine Love. Yet this love had a transcendent quality from the beginning. It defied all efforts to describe it in a few literal statements, because of its distinctiveness as the particular *self*-giving of *Jesus*. Later, this transcendence came, in addition, to be apprehended as the transcendence of the Divine. Consequently, it is possible to speak of two kinds of transcendence involved in Jesus' *agape*—the transcendence of a particular and unique, though nevertheless *human* self-giving, and the transcendence of the *divine* self-giving. Thus, the *agape* that was remembered to have been in Jesus and later known as a living presence in the life of the Church involved both a human self-giving and a divine self-giving. It is the task of Christology to seek to understand how the human and the divine 'come together' in Christ and to determine whether Jesus' *agape* is best understood as being *numerically identical* with God's *agape*, or whether it is not so much identical with, but, rather, *coincides with* God's *agape*. In other words, we may say that Jesus' *agape* involved both a human self-giving *and* a divine self-giving, the divine known stereoscopically 'in and through' the human. To account for the relations between the two is precisely the Christological problem.[26]

[26] See J. Hick's notion of '*homoagape*' in 'Christology at the Crossroads', *Prospect for Theology: Essays in Honour of H. H. Farmer*, pp. 137–66. Hick's identification of Jesus *agape* simply as being *numerically identical* with God's *agape*, though it has met with the approval of E. L. Mascall, *Theology and the Future*, p. 111, seems to be open to the charge of Eutychianism. For, in Hick's Christology Jesus' human self-giving seems to be dissolved or replaced by the divine self-giving. Jesus' human body becomes the vehicle of a divine self-expressive activity, but apparently, not of human self-expressive activity. On the other hand, to say that Jesus' *agape* involves both a divine and a human self-giving suggests a broadly Nestorian position which is closer to the Christology of Norman Pittenger and J. A. T. Robinson. See

To complicate this matter further, in the New Testament we find Jesus as he was remembered to have been from the particular point of view of those who were affected by the impact of his love. As remembered in the Church, Jesus is not known in some utterly objective and abstract sense. Rather, because the content of the Church's memory of Jesus was originally formed from the point of view of those whose lives were transformed by his love, it includes something of the concrete effect of Jesus' love on those who experienced it. A consequence of this is that the awareness of God's revelatory activity in Christ also carries with it a subjective awareness, on the part of the believer, of his or her own transformation. Edward Schillebeeckx is perfectly right in insisting that the judgement of faith occurs within the broad context of an experience of conversion and reconciliation. To perceive the accepting love of Jesus is to experience the grace of Jesus' forgiving; he is in this way known not only as Lord but also as Saviour. On the other hand, to experience the love of Christ was to experience reconciliation with God; his love mediated the divine acceptance and forgiveness which dispersed all feelings of guilt and failure in order to replace them with the courage to be and to live anew. Moreover, because the Spirit which effects a reconciliation both with God and with fellow human beings in love and peace is the dynamic, outgoing activity of God himself, reaching men and women and possessing them in order to redeem them, Atonement with God is not a theory so much as a concrete experience. God's Spirit is thus appropriately described by Paul as the Spirit of adoption whereby we cry 'Abba! Father!' It is the gift of the Spirit that makes us sons and daughters of God. Revelation and salvation are therefore closely associated, for the revelatory act is also a 'saving act'. It is the saving act of God himself who is thus revealed in his saving action. This entails that in attempting to communicate the distinctive nature of the *agape* that is remembered to have been in Jesus, the early Christians also expressed something of what it meant to them.

In their attempt to express all this they resorted to the single term *agape*, but in order to unpack its meaning they inevitably had

W. Norman Pittenger, *The World Incarnate*, and *Christology Reconsidered*. Also, a very interesting article by Rowan A. Greer III, entitled 'The Image of God and the Prosopic Union in Nestorius' *Bazaar of Heracleides*' in *Lux in Lumine, Essays to Honor W. Norman Pittenger*, pp. 46–61. Also John Knox, *The Humanity and Divinity of Christ*, p. 113, and J. A. T. Robinson, *The Human Face of God*, Chapter 6.

recourse to the category of 'story'. Their own story indeed was continuous with the story of Jesus: both parts had to be told. Moreover, the rehearsal of all that Jesus said and did and of what was done to him is one way in which the Church avoids being drawn away from the concrete and particular reality of Christ to abstract and general categories and dessicated doctrinal formulas. The first Christians had recourse to the story of Jesus precisely because it was the most appropriate means of expressing at least something of the unique distinctiveness of the love they had encountered in Christ. It was a means of discourse that expressed the reality of their experience at a deeper level and with greater concrete richness than any philosophical, literal, and purely factual or scientific language could do. This is why, even to distil down to the single concept *agape* the quality of the self-giving discerned in the remembered episodes in which Jesus spoke and acted, listened and reacted—to say nothing of the succession of episodes which together form the climactic story of his passion and death—is already to use an inadequate code word for an incalculably profound and rich reality and thus to diminish its fullness. To unpack precisely what is meant by *agape*, the Jesus-story must be told and re-told, meditated and reflected upon, celebrated and cherished in precisely the way the Church does all these things.

It has already been said that when a person identifies another as a particular human person, he or she is normally in the position to justify such an identity judgement by citing the criteria upon which it is based. This also applies in the particular case of the judgement of faith. In our attempt to supply the content of the idea of the Church's 'memory of Jesus' we should, if asked, be able to cite some descriptive characteristics. In this case, we would be reducing the 'memory of Jesus' to a set of factual statements about him, a sub-set of which must at least be understood to be true for us to be able to continue to use the proper name either referringly or identifyingly (Chapter VII). But we must now be clear that a set of merely factual statements, though necessary, would not sufficiently express the rich, concrete fullness of the experienced quality of Christ's character and the impact of it upon human lives. A set of putatively factual statements of a historical kind is necessary to communicate *something* of what is meant by the 'memory of Jesus' but is not sufficient fully and adequately to define the uniqueness of the remembered One. In other words, the Christian claim is that those who had known Jesus came to appreciate and identify a reality which no bare summary statement of his words or life could convey. There is, indeed, a sense in which the distinctive quality of Jesus' self-giving defies our humanly feeble attempts to define it. To begin to appreciate its distinctiveness one must therefore begin to rehearse the entire Jesus-story.

The outcome is that the content of the Church's memory of Jesus is certainly not exhausted when certain historical facts of the kind that are normally established by scientific historians have been stated. Indeed, the Church must resist being lured into a one-sided preoccupation with a historical-critical attempt to establish factual propositions relating to Jesus. If what is remembered about Jesus is a love that possesses a divinely transcendent quality in its distinctiveness and uniqueness, it cannot be adequately handled with the categories of the natural and historical sciences and must have recourse to specifically theological motifs and conceptions. In addition to the telling of the earthly story of the life and death of Jesus it therefore became inevitable that the language should be taken behind the stage of history to speak of God's role in the story—namely, to speak of 'what God did in Christ'. Any 'story theology' must reckon with an implicit anthropomorphism as soon as God is spoken of as a character in the story and this means that the language of the story, which envisages the activity of God in an objectifying way on analogy with the activities of this world, will inevitably be mythological. In order to transmit the concrete and distinctive quality of the divine-human love that is remembered to have been in Jesus, and released in power after his crucifixion as a life-giving and life-enhancing presence within the community of faith, it became necessary to engage in, apart from certain assertions of historical fact and statements of a legendary kind, statements also of the specific kind that have come to be called mythological. The term 'myth' has been somewhat overworked since the Second World War as a result of the discussion of Bultmann's programme of demythologizing. If anything it is today rather out of fashion, for contemporary theologians show a preference for the category of 'story' or for a revived use of Barth's talk of 'saga'. It is probably more satisfactory to speak of 'story' or 'saga' in view of the fact that the historical existence of the human Jesus provides the central thread of episodes. The term 'myth' may then be used to denote those supra-historical parts of the story only, which seek to portray the divine activity in objectifying or analogical images. The mythological elements in the story told about Jesus may thus be understood to express the supra-historical elements of the early kerygma, including the pre-existence of Christ, God's decision to send his Son to redeem the world, his decision to come into this world as a man, his struggle with demonic powers and his triumph over them, and his ascension into heaven, where he reigns at God's right hand awaiting the time of his return. Though these elements of the kerygma are not to be regarded as themselves true in a literal or historically factual sense, they do express a theological truth. They express the truth of the infinite quality of the divine condescension and its cosmic implications. Thus, such statements contribute a fuller and richer content to the meaning of the term '*agape*'. The Christian story therefore represents the utmost effort of the primitive Christian community to express the realities of man's sin and God's grace: 'God proves his love for us in that while we were yet sinners Christ died for us'. Indeed, mythological conceptions are both indispensable and irreplaceable in the communication of the memory of Jesus himself. The mythological terms stand not primarily for abstract ideas, but for a concrete reality known within the experience of the community, and the significance of the Church's memory lies, not in its accuracy in preserving bare statements of historical fact, but in its effectiveness in preserving something of the concrete quality of the experienced impact of the event. If follows from all this that the statements of historical fact which we have been able to isolate as expressing part of the content of the Church's memory of Jesus (in Chapter VII), including the statements of the bare facts that there was a Jesus, that he was a man, that he died on the cross, that he exhibited (and his cross symbolized) a distinctive love called *agape*, must be supplemented by narrative stories as well as legendary and mythological statements if the full content of the Church's memory of Jesus' *agape* is to be adequately communicated. When these concepts and ideas are transmitted and shared within the life of the Christian community, they constitute the conceptual medium in which the essentially distinctive and ineffable faith of the community becomes communicable without ceasing to be ineffable and in a certain sense 'beyond words'. For this very reason not one simple categorical statement, nor a few straightforward historical assertions, but many statements of diverse kinds must be uttered before it will be possible to come anywhere near communicating it. The content of the Church's memory of Jesus is therefore bound to be elusive and mysterious.

Has Christianity a Revelation?

It is pertinent to note that it has been forcefully argued by F. Gerald Downing in an important though rather neglected book, that, precisely because the Church engages in *many* statements in order to express the alleged revelation of divinity in Jesus, Christianity has no revelation at all. At the beginning of his argument Downing concedes that it is traditionally held that ' "Christian revelation" is the manifesting of a "mystery", a manifesting of the imcomprehensible' and, as Paul Tillich says, 'Whatever is essentially mysterious cannot lose its mysteriousness even when it is revealed'.[27] Downing goes on to say that it is usually argued that, as God's revelation is not the revealing of something easy to understand, it is not fair to expect it to be expressed in a few words. But 'It is not because there are lots of facts to be known about him that God is "mysterious"; he is "incomprehensible" in the sense that three words "God is love", or three million are equally inadequate to tell the truth about him.'[28] This constitutes what Downing calls 'the problem of many words', for he believes that, if there has been a revelation of God, it should be possible to express it in a few, precise words. Many words could be justified, he says, 'if you were claiming that God had revealed himself as mysterious complexity: many books for many facts. But it is hard to justify them, if the claim is that God has revealed himself as one mysterious profundity'.[29] God has no 'body, parts or passions'; consequently Downing believes that it follows that, if God has revealed himself, Christians should be able to describe this revelation simply.

Downing therefore contends that it is not justifiable to speak of God's revelation where it is admitted that what is 'revealed' is 'obscure and . . . ambiguous'.[30] Thus, in a subsequent book, *The Church and Jesus*, he places a high premium on 'agreement',

---

[27] F. Gerald Downing, *Has Christianity a Revelation?*, p. 11. Cf. Paul Tillich, *Systematic Theology*, Vol. I, p. 121. See also K. Barth, *Church Dogmatics*, I/1, p. 188, I/2, p. 106, II/1 pp. 179–204, IV/2 p. 297 f.; also S. Bulgakoff in *Revelation*, ed. J. Baillie and H. Martin, p. 125; L. S. Thornton, *Revelation and the Modern World*, pp. 4–5.

[28] F. Gerald Downing, op. cit., pp. 11–12.

[29] Ibid., p. 12.

[30] Ibid., pp. 31, 208.

'unanimity', 'clarity and a firm consensus', and 'certainty',[31] and, since Jesus is said to remain a 'shadowy and insecure' figure,[32] he concludes that not 'only can we not reconstruct an objective development of Jesus as a man, nor even an objective character-sketch of him in his last days; but we cannot reconstruct with any real certainty the early Church's 'memory-image' either'.[33] Thus, Downing feels that the contention of his earlier book is justified: since clarity of expression eludes us God remains 'quite hidden in his saving activity, until the end'.[34]

The position I have outlined is, of course, quite the opposite. It is precisely the ineffable particularity of God's revelation that necessitates many words in order to come anywhere near communicating it. We can agree with Downing that there was a 'great deal of diversity among those who early on claimed some attachment to Jesus'.[35] Yet even today, it is possible to speak of the 'common faith' of Christians, for there is a wider area of agreement than is often at first supposed, an agreement deeper than our superficial diversities and hostilities. And though it is possible to point to diversities in early Christian belief, Downing must also demonstrate that it is utterly impossible or illegitimate to perceive some kind of purposive pattern or directionality within the diversity.[36]

Indeed, Downing's argument is open to criticism at numerous points, not least of which is his concluding affirmation that in place of revelation we must substitute a religion of obedience. For, we may ask, if nothing is revealed, if God remains 'quite hidden', what is the object of obedience? Can one be obedient to something about which one knows utterly nothing? Ludwig Wittgenstein says at one place in the *Philosophical Investigations* that 'a nothing would serve just as well as a something about which nothing could be said'.[37] This prompts the suggestion that it makes little more sense to call for obedience to a something about which nothing can be said, than

[31] *The Church and Jesus*, pp. 25, 49, 40, 187.
[32] Ibid., p. 187.
[33] Ibid., p. 188.
[34] *Has Christianity a Revelation?* p. 17.
[35] *The Church and Jesus*, p. 40.
[36] On the question of the diversity within the preaching of the early church see C. F. Evans, 'The Kerygma' in JTS, NS, 8 (1956), pp. 25–41. Concerning the fundamental agreement within the diversity of New Testament religion see Ernst Käsemann, 'The Problem of the Historical Jesus', pp. 30–4.
[37] *Philosophical Investigations*, I, para. 304. In its original context the remark does not refer to the knowledge of God.

to call for obedience to nothing at all. Must we not have some understanding of what the Divine Will for us is, before we can possibly talk of obeying it? Downing finds himself in the unhappy position of saying that, since nothing is revealed, we must be obedient to our own beliefs: 'the only "knowledge of God" yet possible is our obedience as sons to what are believed to be his demands'.[38] Or does this very statement imply that Downing himself has some inkling that God may be understood as, in some sense, a loving Father? Or that Downing has some inkling or justification for thinking that God desires obedience and righteousness of living?

But, if Downing's concluding thesis seems untenable, the premises from which he begins his argument are equally unacceptable. His fundamental contention that it should be possible to describe a simple reality, even a simple profundity, in a *few* words will not stand up to examination. For one thing, what is to count as simple and what as complex? Is the smell of hot bitumen simple or complex? Or is this a simple profundity? And, if it is simple, is Downing prepared to describe it in a few words?

Fortunately, we do not have to wait for answers to these questions in order to show that Downing's contention is unacceptable. At the same time it is possible to state the essential point, that it is impossible to describe the unique particularity of the *agape* that is remembered to have been in Jesus in a few precise words, in another way.

If the content of the Church's memory of Jesus hinges on the concept of *agape*, then the description of Jesus as a person who exhibited this distinctive and unique quality of character does not involve us in asserting the occurrence of any particular incidents or episodes, but in the making of a dispositional statement. We are asserting that, as he is remembered in the Church's continuing corporate memory, Jesus *tended* to act, or exhibited a *proneness* to act, in a particular kind of way in particular kinds of circumstances. The gospels' portrayal of Jesus evokes such an impression of his character that it is possible to anticipate and predict how he might have acted in this or that situation or even what he might have said.[39] The

---

[38] *Has Christianity a Revelation?*, p. 87. See also, p. 118: 'obedient love of the brethren' is said to be 'knowledge of God'.

[39] See M. Kähler, *The So-Called Historical Jesus and the Historic, Biblical Christ*, p. 78: 'all the biblical portrayals evoke the undeniable impression of the fullest reality, so that one might venture to predict how he might have acted in this or that situation, indeed, even what he might have said.'

statement of a disposition or its attribution to somebody gives us the ability, in other words, to anticipate what kind of actions and reactions are likely in given specific episodes, even thought the dispositional statement does not itself describe an episode.

Now, Gilbert Ryle has made a very useful distinction between single-track or specific dispositions and highly generic dispositions. Single-track dispositions are dispositions in which the verbs reporting occurrences which actualize the disposition are determinate, and correspond closely to the words which express the disposition itself. For example, to describe a man as a cigarette-smoker implies that there will be particular occasions when he will be found to be smoking cigarettes. To describe a man as a baker will entail that there will be particular occasions when he will be found to be baking. On the other hand, there are generic disposition-concepts whose actualization cannot be stated by employing only one verb, because they can take a wide variety of shapes. Their actualizations are not determinate but determinable. To describe a man as a grocer does not mean that on particular occasions he will be found to be 'grocing', but that on particular occasions he will be found to be doing a great variety of things—selling sugar, weighing butter, wrapping tea. Similarly, to describe a man as a solicitor does not mean that on particular occasions he will be 'solicitoring' but that on particular occasions he will be drafting wills, drawing up tenancy agreements, and representing clients in court.

Ryle observes, furthermore, that the higher-grade dispositions of people are, in general, not single-track dispositions but highly generic and determinable. Their actualizations, in other words, are heterogeneous. For example, when Jane Austen wished to show the specific pride which characterized the heroine of *Pride and Prejudice* she had to represent her actions, words, thoughts and feelings in a thousand different situations. In other words, the disposition of pride is a generic or determinable one which is actualized in an enormous variety of different situations and occurrences. 'There is no one standard type of action or reaction such that Jane Austen could say "My heroine's kind of pride was just the tendency to do this, whenever a situation of that sort arose".'[40]

Now, 'love' is also a highly generic or determinable disposition-concept. A wide range of actions and reactions are predictable from

[40] See Gilbert Ryle, *The Concept of Mind*, pp. 44 and 114.

the description of a person as 'supremely' or 'uniquely' loving. These include deeds, utterances, kindly glances, and expressions of concern, respect, care, and devotion. Similarly, the distinctive love referred to as *agape* signifies a proneness to do and say, not things of one kind, but things of many kinds. We are therefore perfectly justified in assuming that the *many* words which make up the Jesus-story in its various episodes are necessary in order to communicate something of the distinctive, concrete quality of Jesus' self-giving, even if it is understood as being a human self-giving.

This necessity becomes even more pressing when it is recognized that the love that is remembered to have been exhibited in Jesus' life is also (in some sense of 'is also') the transcendent love of God. For besides historical facts and legendary material, mythological statements are also necessary to communicate its particular quality. Moreover, Downing's basic presupposition that it is illegitimate to claim that revelation has occurred unless we can claim clarity of perception is tantamount to the requirement, as a necessary prerequisite of revelation, that the transcendent God surrender his transcendence. A necessary condition for revelation, in Downing's view, is that the transcendent should be describable in terms of the categories of finite mind with clarity; but the transcendent God would, in this eventuality, be reduced to the stature of an idol. This is what is unsatisfactory about the lives of Jesus of the nineteenth-century Jesus of history movement; Jesus was reduced to the dimensions of a man-made image. As Schweitzer put it, the authors of the nineteenth-century lives of Jesus 'were eager to picture Him as truly and purely human, to strip from Him the robes of splendour with which He had been apparelled, to clothe Him once more with the coarse garments in which He had walked in Galilee'.[41]

A basic aim of religious language is to try to say something about the transcendent, difficult though that may be, without requiring that it cease to be transcendent. The content of the Church's 'memory of Jesus himself' is, therefore, in the last analysis, subject to all the difficulties that arise with respect to talk of the transcendent generally. As a consequence, the Church's memory-image of Jesus is stamped with an in-built elusiveness.

---

[41] A. Schweitzer, *The Quest of the Historical Jesus*, p. 4.

Fact and Interpretation

We have seen that the unit of meaning for the transmission of the Church's memory and living experience of Jesus is not just the single word *agape*, nor a single categorical statement asserting a historical fact nor even a number of statements asserting bare historical facts, but a body of such statements plus many other statements expressing legendary and supra-historical elements. Together they form what we have called the Christian 'story'. It is an implication of this that, though the disinterested historian may rightly seek to discover the facts of Jesus' career by separating facts from Christological interpretation, that is, by distinguishing historical fact from Christological evaluation of fact, or by seeking to penetrate beyond or behind the fusion of historical fact and the Christological evaluation that is found in the New Testament documents, the transmission of the concrete fullness of the memory of Jesus involves a fusion of historical fact *and* Christological interpretation. In other words, there is a sense in which, in the rehearsal of the complex amalgam which comprises the Christian story, form and content are inseparable.[42] This is inevitable, for what is transmitted within the life of the Church, as distinct from what might be established by the critical researches of the disinterested historian, is that Jesus was a man who expressed the divine *agape*. Some element of mythological language must always remain as an integral part of the Church's proclamation so long as the Church proclaims the revelatory activity of the transcendent God in Jesus. For this reason, the memory of Jesus can never be communicated in a few literal and prosaic statements; his story is the story of the incredible self-giving of God and the concrete meaning of it can be represented and conveyed in no other or better way. When the scientific historian sets out to discover from the gospels what it was about Jesus that was so memorable, he inevitably comes to the conclusion that *qua* historian he cannot really answer this question. For the scientific historian it remains something of an unresolved mystery. The fragmentary details that can be established with certainty about the person of

[42] Paul S. Minear observes that in order to discover the facts about the circumstances of Jesus' death and the meaning of the approaching death to Jesus himself the historian must accomplish the *fission* of history and interpretation, showing how far were the original facts from the Christian understanding of them. But in order to discover the meaning of the death to the early Church the historian must achieve 'the *fusion* of history and interpretation'. *Religion in Life*, xxvii (1958), p. 610.

Jesus from the gospels are insufficient to explain the early Church's
response to Jesus as to a God, for the surpassing greatness of Jesus is
a greatness far beyond the historian's power either to describe or
explain. Though it is beyond the historian to account for the extra-
vagance of the response that Jesus evoked, the historian can go on to
say *how* early Christians came to account for Jesus' significance. He
can say how Paul, for example, sought to explain the significance of
Jesus in other-worldly, mythological terms of early Christology.

However, within the continuing life of the community of faith
the fullness of the memory of Jesus is transmitted not simply by
employing statements of historical fact that the historian could
establish, but by employing statements of historical fact *plus* the
primitive Church's interpretation or Christological evaluation of
the facts. Thus, the historian's task of trying to distinguish fact and
interpretation becomes, in a sense, irrelevant. It is at this point that
we can appreciate something of Barth's desire to avoid critical questions in the interests of preserving the literary integrity of what is
being communicated by the Scriptural texts as they stand.[43] The
amalgam of unharmonized stories, read more or less in a literary
sense, without too close a scrutiny or analysis of their detail, communicates the general impression of the distinctive divine disposition of Love which was revealed in Jesus; this is their intended
point.

D. F. Ford has observed that whilst Barth does not see the gospels
as biographies of Jesus, 'their protrayal of him by his words, acts
and sufferings and by the reaction of others to him is of great
importance for his theology'. Moreover, he points out that it was
just these elements which in the first century were accepted forms of
character-portrayal and that 'any simple separation of fact from fiction is especially difficult when it is a matter of conveying a vivid
character'.[44] The difference between a scientific historian's assessment of Jesus and the memory-impression of Jesus and of the dispositional reality of his distinct self-giving which is transmitted in
the life of the Church may be compared with the way in which a
portrait differs from a photograph. A portrait may not be an accurate and scientific likeness of physical features; indeed, some

[43] See D. F. Ford, 'Barth's Interpretation of the Bible' in *Karl Barth—Studies of his Theological Methods*, p. 81 asks: 'How important is the verification of details when they are being used as part of a complex synthesis to portray an individual?'
[44] Ibid., pp. 78, 81.

features may in fact be distorted in order to bring out a characteristic expression or a particular quality of character. The portrait may, however, be said to be true in so far as it is able to capture and express certain aspects of the character of the person concerned which are not physical in themselves but expressed in and through the physical and which are recognized to correspond to what is the case by those who remember the person *himself*.

Certainly, the fusion of history and Christological assessment and interpretation is not to be seen as an unfortunate entanglement of truth and error. The memory of Jesus himself and the memory of the distinctive quality of his love, is communicated by accounts of certain historical incidents, and, amongst these, his passion and death on the cross assume a central and important place. However, accounts of other incidents in Jesus' life are also important, together with apparently legendary and mythological material. The historicity of any particular incident is sometimes very difficult to judge, and there may be differences of opinion amongst historians about the truth or otherwise of *particular* propositions asserting the occurrence of historical happenings. Indeed, the line between statements of historical fact and legendary material may be drawn further to left or right by particular scholars. However, whether authentic or legendary, when read together in story form they nevertheless communicate something of the love that was remembered to have been in Jesus.

Consequently, the kerygma is not to be juxtaposed to historical information relating to the man of Nazareth; nor is it to be represented as a substitute for information about the historical Jesus, so that knowledge of the historical Jesus is utterly obliterated. Rather, Paul along with other anonymous early Christian preachers and writers developed the story in order to try to express an ineffable reality which had been experienced in and through Jesus' historical existence. This means that, though the factual stories and mythic elements of the New Testament originated in the practical life of the Church, they are the product not simply of a pragmatic desire to precipitate the decision of faith, conceived of in terms of self-understanding, but also of a desire to report something: it is *not* false to say that a herald is a reporter. The Church's proclamation as a whole, reports something concerning Jesus; it is thereby instrumental in the transmission of the memory of him and in the expression of the experienced nature of the Spirit of the community of faith.

Moreover, myth is not a substitute for statements of historical fact; it is a complementary attempt to interpret facts of religious experience. We start with the historically experienced facts; the myth neither creates nor in any way alters them but interprets them. Thus, mythology is complementary to history in the sense that it absorbs the historical career of Jesus as its central element. The story of Christ includes the account of an actual historical event as a part of itself. Moreover, details of the story, despite the fact that they are supra-historical, nevertheless express the dispositional reality of the Divine Love that was experienced in history. The meaning which the story as a whole sets forth is the meaning which was actually discovered in the event itself. Thus, the story grew inevitably out of history and out of human experience. In this respect, we may find that we hold more in common with Martin Kähler than with Kähler's successors—for example, Bultmann or Tillich.[45] Kähler did not drive a wedge between the kerygma and the historic figure of Jesus. The biblical Christ is not an invention of pure imagination, but a confession of the significance of Jesus, for the picture of Jesus which is set forth in the Church's preaching embodies the 'apostolic recollection': the 'apostolic recollection of Jesus can be shown to have been preserved for the sake of its religious significance'.[46] The Christ of faith and the historic Jesus are not diametrically opposed as abstract idea to concrete object, or appearance to reality. For Kähler the Christ of faith *is* the Jesus of

[45] Despite his notorious reputation to the contrary, in some of his statements Bultmann seems not to divorce the historic Jesus from the kerygma. For example he says: 'The content of the message is . . . an event, a historical fact: the appearance of Jesus of Nazareth, his birth, but at the same time his work, his death and his resurrection . . . Christian preaching . . . is the communication of a historical fact which is at the same time more than a historical fact, so that its communication is something more than mere communication.' R. Bultmann, 'Preaching: Genuine and Secularized', *Religion and Culture, Essays in Honor of Paul Tillich*, p. 240. This clearly suggests that the herald *is* also a reporter. See also, Paul Althaus *The So-Called Kerygma and the Historical Jesus*, p. 48: 'as well as being a message of salvation' the New Testament is said to embody 'at the same time a report about a historical event which happened'. Also, John Macquarrie, *The Scope of Demythologizing*, pp. 245 ff. However, many others of Bultmann's statements seem to justify the charge that he draws a drastic separation or antithesis between the kerygma and the historic Jesus. For example, Bultmann can say that an 'ancient mythology was transferred to a concrete historical figure so as to conceal his individual features almost completely'. See R. Bultmann, 'The Christology of the New Testament' in *Faith and Understanding*, p. 264.
[46] Martin Kähler, *The So-Called Historical Jesus and the Historic, Biblical Christ*, p. 93.

history: 'He is the Jesus whom the eyes of faith behold'.[47] Thus, contrary to Bultmann's assertion that the early Christians were only interested in the mere *Dass* of Jesus, Graham Stanton argues very forcefully in *Jesus of Nazareth in New Testament Preaching* that 'The resurrection faith of the Church did not obscure the past of Jesus. On the contrary, the resurrection acted as a catalyst which encouraged retention of traditions which told about the past of Jesus'.[48] This must be understood to include traditions of a kind which we would now classify as 'mythological'. The mythological elements of the kerygma were called upon precisely to disclose or express something of the ineffable particularity of the character of the historic figure and his impact on human lives; that is to say, the role of myth is not to conceal but to reveal. The mythology of the early preaching is not to be regarded in terms of 'disguises' which the Church had forced upon the original Jesus, but rather as the best possible means to express what was remembered to have been originally in him: the Divine Love. We can thus agree with C. F. D. Moule when he insists that rather than thinking of a Christological *evolution* away from the truth that was originally apprehended and expressed by the faith of the first Christians, the early Christological reflection must be understood as a legitimate *development* of it.[49]

Similarly, it is necessary to avoid speaking of the memory of Jesus in terms of a wholly ideal picture. It will not do to speak of 'the picture of Jesus as the Christ', as Tillich and others have done, unless we are also affirming an element of factual truth in the picture, that is, the actuality of the one pictured. The picture of Christ communicated within the life of the Church is the picture of an actual person for Jesus is primarily a person remembered.

Unlike the picture of the historical Jesus that is derived from the gospels by stripping away all Christologically evaluative statements, the Church's memory-image of Jesus is mediated through its full use of the gospels and the epistles. Once again, at this point, it is appropriate to recall the stance of Kähler. Kähler stressed that his aim was to explain 'how inadvisable and indeed impossible it is to reach a Christian understanding of Jesus when one deviates from the *total* biblical proclamation about him—his life as well as its sig-

---

[47] Ibid., p. 66.
[48] Op. cit. p. 191.
[49] *The Origin of Christology*, pp. 1–10.

nificance'.[50] Thus, he says: 'The recollection of the days of his flesh and the confession of his eternal significance and of what he offers to us are not separated in the New Testament, even if they are differently distributed between the two types of primitive Christian witness'.[51] These two types of proclamation 'combine to form the presupposition for faith's evaluation of the biblical picture of Christ'.[52] In similar vein, John Knox stresses that the picture of Jesus, as he is remembered in the Church, is greater than anything that can be derived from the gospels alone. The content of 'the "memory" of the Church goes far beyond anything a critical reading of the Gospels would alone justify'.[53] The scientific judgements of the critical historian reduce and distort the fullness of the image, an image that can be communicated only by employing the mythology which expresses the divine condescension, that is largely found in the Epistles. Thus, Knox believes that in one sense Paul tells us more about Jesus than the gospels, 'for he tells us at first-hand how he regarded Jesus'.[54]

It follows from this that it is not just the critical historian but the preacher who communicates the distinctive quality of the love that was originally remembered to have been in Jesus, for the preaching of the Church is designed to express and convey its concrete meaning. For this reason Kähler insists that the *'real Christ is the Christ who is preached'*.[55]

However, for all the importance of preaching in the communication of the memory of Jesus it does not, of course, stand alone in the life of the Church. Sacred art, hymns and prayers, and the liturgical practice of the entire tradition of the Church are also significant to it. Together these are all important bearers of the concrete content of the Church's memory and experience of the presence of Christ. Consequently, it is understandable that the use of the symbol of the cross and the symbolic liturgical acts of the Christian community are means of transmitting the memory of Jesus himself and the distinctive disposition of his self-giving. The Lord's Supper has always been in a pre-eminent sense an occasion for recalling Jesus:

---

[50] Op. cit., p. 68.
[51] Ibid., pp. 83–4.
[52] Ibid.
[53] *The Church and the Reality of Christ*, p. 57.
[54] *On the Meaning of Christ*, p. 87; *The Man Christ Jesus*, p. 10. Phil. 2: 6–11 is an obvious example.
[55] *The So-Called Historical Jesus and the Historic, Biblical Christ*, p. 66.

the breaking and sharing of bread has always been done 'in remembrance of him'. In other words, the unit of meaning for the transmission of the memory of Jesus is not only a fusion of fact and interpretation, found in different proportion in the gospels and epistles, but also the use of the symbol of the cross, the portrayal of Jesus in Christian art, and the symbolic acts of worship. It is the proclamation of the story, the rehearsal of historical facts and theologically interpretative myth, the use of the symbol of the cross, and the liturgical performance of symbolic acts, which *together*, in the life of the Church, preserves and communicates the memory of Jesus, and of the revelatory event of God's *agape* that occurred in and through his life. One of the glories of Anglicanism, perhaps *the* glory of Anglicanism, is its preference for liturgy as a way of expressing truth over the Latin proclivity for defining doctrines and dogmas. It is in the yearly rehearsal of the Jesus story in the liturgical round that the truth concerning the distinctiveness of the Jesus-character is most effectively communicated. We rightly spend more time in the production of our Prayer Books than in definitions of dogma and verbal formulas to which we may wisely choose to stand a little loosely: *Lex orandi, lex credendi*.

Unity in Diversity

It seems essential, however, that a multiplicity of statements and symbols calls for some kind of harmonizing if any one thing is to be communicated. In other words the diversity of the statements which have arisen in the life of the Church in witness to and celebration of the love of God that is remembered to have been in Jesus and known in its own ongoing life, poses a hermeneutical problem. How is the story to be heard and interpreted so as to distil the right truth out of it? Much that has been written in recent theology concerning the importance of the category of story does not take us very far in terms of the resolution of this matter. Story is said to be essential to the Christian dispensation and to theology; indeed, it is said that some truth may be expressed in story form and no other way; but how is it possible to hear the Jesus-story in such a way as not necessarily to have to acknowledge the literal truth of all its details in factual terms, but claim that it expresses a truth of a more general kind? How, in other words, is it possible for narrative story to be true whilst in another sense being fiction?

Karl Barth opts for what D. F. Ford calls a 'middle distance' read-

ing of the text of scripture, a reading which is suspicious of genera-
lizing of a kind which drifts so far away from the story as to blur its
particularities, but which does not become immersed in the minu-
tiae of technicalities.[56] In this way the story is said to convey its
essential point and meaning, 'the Word in the words.'

Whilst the 'general drift' of scripture and what it essentially communicates about the nature of God, particularly as revealed through
his activity in Christ, may certainly 'come across' in the way Barth
suggests, it is a rather too haphazard and perhaps too eirenic an
understanding of things to be allowed to stand alone: unfortunately
human ignorance and sin and rank psychological insecurity tend to
stand in the way as a kind of 'obex' which can distort what is heard.
Barth's tendency to suggest, against Bultmann, that Scripture may
be approached by an 'innocent' reader is mistaken, for 'that unlikely
belle sauvage, sans prejudice, ideology, commitment or stock
response' does not exist.[57] It is simply not possible for the Word of
God to speak freely through the words on the page, for a whole
world of presuppositions intervenes between us and the words of
scripture and shapes our response to them. Scripture must, therefore, be scientifically studied and expounded if we are to evade a
surface reading of scripture that results from treating it as nothing
more than a body of purely factual and detailed descriptive episodes. In other words, the story must be critically reflected upon
the theologically 'processed' with all the ingenuity and skill of
modern exegesis and with the most proficient techniques of textual
analysis at the Church's disposal, if historical, legendary, and mythological elements of the Jesus-story are to be recognized for what
they are.[58] This means that, as important as the kergyma and the
liturgical rehearsal of the story are in the life of the Church, we
must not overlook the complementary place of the trained theologian whose task is to distil truth from the multiplicity of biblical

[56] See D. F. Ford, op. cit., p. 78.

[57] Terence Hawkes, *Structuralism and Semiotics*, p. 153–4. It is not possible
simply to be confronted by the words on a page: 'A whole world of mediating presuppositions . . . intervenes between us and them and shapes our response: to deny
this is simply self-deceiving.'

[58] A. E. Harvey asks: 'If theological truth is to be expressed in the form of stories,
what room is left for any theological discipline?' See *God Incarnate: Story and Belief*,
p. 5. The theologian has a task in so far as he expands the meaning of the texts of
scripture and explains in precisely what sense the statements of scripture may be said
to communicate truth.

statements and to construct and articulate doctrines for the clarification of what would otherwise be a bewildering mass of evidence by revealing its theological purposiveness. The preacher as theologian has an important role to play in this process, as does the bishop in his teaching office. From time to time, the Church has seen fit to correct deviations from what it sees as the central thrust of the biblical witness by defining the fundamental divine meaning and significance that it discerns in it. In this way, the Church has evolved mechanisms of an ordinary or day-to-day, as well as of an extraordinary or more official, kind to direct its course: the believer is not just abandoned to a 'middle distance', 'liberal' or 'fundamentalist' reading of the texts, depending on how they strike the ear. The theologian in the Church and as servant of the Church, has a particularly important role to play with respect to the clarification and explanation of the essential meaning of the scriptural tradition.

Given the diversity of view found within the pages of the New Testament itself, it is unavoidable that there will be a large degree of diversity in the contemporary Church.[59] Theologians also bring their interests and presuppositions to the texts and it may not be possible to harmonize them into one neat overall summa. However, this is not to say that there are no common elements and that we must accept a bewildering chaos. Within the diversity of statements contained in the New Testament it is possible to discern the patterns of over-arching themes. The various episodes in which Jesus plays a part may therefore be 'summed up' in a phrase denoting a more inclusive episode: 'God was in Christ reconciling the world to himself'. Alternatively, the more general meaning of the sum of individual episodes may be expressed in one inclusive concept such as 'Incarnation' or 'Atonement' which may then be explained doctrinally. The theologians' doctrinal statements thereby seek to explain the meaning and significance which the stories are perceived to contain, by drawing general theological truths from the myriad episodic details of the scriptural stories, including their legendary and mythic components as well as the basic core of history.

Very importantly, the discernment of a pattern within a diverse set of episodes, when one is balanced against another, may be seen to express a directionality which points us towards the transcendent

[59] This is Ernst Käsemann's point in his very important essay 'The Canon of the New Testament and the Unity of Church' in *Essays on New Testament Themes*, pp. 95–107.

object of faith by communicating something of its distinctive quality. For the ultimate unity of the concepts and ideas generated by the Christian religion derives from their common referent—the divine love which is remembered to have been definitively revealed by Jesus and which as a consequence of Easter is now known as the distinctive Spirit of the Christian fellowship. The language arises out of experience and is evolved for the purpose of interpreting experience and not just for the purpose of articulating abstract doctrines, which are then offered to believers for their assent or otherwise. For this reason it is important to see that the pattern that is discerned within the myriad statements describing episodes of a historical and mythological kind, may be understood to point to a general truth, not itself of an over-arching episodic kind, but of a *dispositional* kind. The historical and, to some extent, legendary episodes relating to the life of Jesus from his birth to his death, reveal the character of Jesus. Because in and through him, the character of God is revealed, it is necessary to have recourse to the additional mythological elements of the story which give it an additional layer of meaning, a deeper dimension. The unity of the story is not therefore the false and strained harmony achieved by piecing together a surface reading of the texts in the manner of classical fundamentalism or the residual fundamentalism of much contemporary Christianity, or the attempt to 'homogenize' the New Testament by overlooking its diversity or neutralizing it. Nor is the truth of the story just a general impression of 'what happened' somewhat arbitrarily derived from a 'middle distance' reading of the story, despite some acknowledged problematic details. All this keeps it at an episodic level and leads to an understanding of faith as primarily an assent to propositional and abstract truths. Rather, the unity of the story is the truth of the disposition or character of Christ which is revealed in and through the myriad diverse episodes of the scriptural story to those who have an eye to see and an ear to hear. This involves an inductive reading of the text which allows the hearer to penetrate behind the specific episodes that first strike the ear in an initial reading of the narratives, in order to grasp the individual personality of the story's central character. The various and diverse aspects are to the communication of the truth concerning Jesus himself, as the variety of the colours of the spectrum are to white light. As we put what we discern of Jesus from various aspects together we begin to discern what it is about him that the Church finds so

memorable. Another way of understanding the method of discernment of the essential subject-matter would be to speak with Klappert of 'aspective integration':[60] it is a matter of holding various
aspects and perspectives on the character of Jesus as these are
revealed in the multitude of episodes in which he is said to have
been involved, in order to discern a particular purposiveness or directionality. We thus acquire, inductively, a single orientation on the
nature of the divinity revealed in and through his words and works.
Otherwise it will be impossible to see the dispositional wood from
the multitude of episodic trees, and thus impossible to interpret the
meaning of the story aright. Once this dispositional truth is grasped
it may once again be doctrinally unpacked and explained. Because
the disposition denoted by *agape* expresses both the character of the
remembered Jesus and of the eternal God, it may give rise, for
example, to a 'doctrine of the love of God' which seeks to explicate
all that is implicit in that phrase.

We may call the resultant statements which express something of
the divine disposition or character, as distinct from the episodic
statements of a historical and mythological kind which convey them
to us, ontological statements. Thus, statements concerning God's
act of condescension are mythological statements which express in
the details of an episode in the story, and thus report, an objective
ontological truth of a dispositional kind. The mythological details
indirectly communicate something of the nature of the love of God
that was actually remembered to have been in Jesus. Because historians do not normally draw out patterns in religious stories, nor postulate assertions about God of a mythological kind, this being the
work of the theologian, these statements are better called 'ontological' rather than 'historical', though this is not to deny that God's act
of love in Christ occurred in history. We may therefore speak of the
story, including its more clearly mythological elements, as the
appropriate medium for conveying theological truth. Clearly,
whilst all the details of the mythological episode are not literally

---

[60] B. Klappert, *Die Auferweckung*, p. 285: 'eines aspektivischen Ineinanders'. The
'integration of aspects' applies not just to the resurrection as such, but to the historical life and death of Jesus as well. The various incidents of his life may be held
together so as inductively to point to the nature of the particular self revealed in all of
them but in varied ways and with many nuances. 'It is not a question of explaining
the symbolic content and meaning, reducing it to logical, rational concepts,' but, as
R. C. Ware puts it, a 'matter of understanding—standing under' the influence of the
story and allowing it to work on us. R. C. Ware, op. cit., p. 188.

true, the 'ontological' judgements discerned through the details of the myth are for the Christian true: God is *in fact* our Redeemer from Sin and Death because he is in fact a God of steadfast love and faithfulness who does not abandon us but eternally cares. The mythological details of the stories thus express the ontological truth that God is a God of a particular kind. He who stands above and beyond history has acted in and through events of history, making himself known not just as the God and Father of our Lord Jesus Christ but as the God who raised Jesus from the Dead. Through the work of Christian theologians and preachers, then, a directionality is discernible within the variety of expressions that arose in the course of the early Church's preaching. In this way theological reflection, and the doctrinal definition which results from it, may be said to articulate the 'grammar of God' by explaining the sense in which theological terms are conventionally used within the linguistic community of the Church. In celebrating and commending their faith, those who comprise the Christian community thus depend upon the contribution of those who give precise definition to the Christian vocabulary. Doctrines or 'ontological truths' concerning God and man and how they 'go together' as a consequence of the complex of happenings that are narrated in the Jesus-story, may be said to be attempts to make explicit truths that are implicitly present within the story.

However true this may be, it is only half the story. For statements of doctrine are not ends in themselves, nor is faith a mere matter of assent to abstract propositional truths. The believer is not just the consumer of a ready-made doctrinal product. Indeed, we have already noted that there is a sense that it is impossible to distil the essential meaning out of the story in the form of a set of general propositions. That is impossible, for the referent, the raised and glorified and transformed Christ, is beyond words: theology therefore does its work, knowing that in the end it is a self-defeating exercise; by definition it is always transcended by its object. Doctrine explains faith: it is never itself the object of faith. Nevertheless it leads us towards such an object. In order to give an account of faith and to bring out the unity of meaning within the diversity of scriptural statements, we are obliged to endeavour to discern an intelligible pattern or directionality of meaning within them. This, however, keeps the ball game at the level of the abstract and cerebral, for, to use Kant's distinction, the concepts of theology are empty until 'filled' by actual experiences of religious discernment or intuition in which a given or revealed reality is actually identified by employing these conceptual tools *identifyingly*. In other words, the hearing of the Christian story which pre-eminently transmits and celebrates the memory of Jesus and God's revelatory deed in and through his life and death, should lead us beyond itself to a living encounter with the real presence of all that it celebrates and rehearses: him, whom by story we recall, we actually know as the living Spirit of the fellowship of faith. Apart from the story's being true (in some sense of true) it is important that it be religiously useful. The open character of the stories and our inability to distil a purified essential truth out of them, means that they remain somewhat nebulous until their chief point is discovered in their religious function. The Christian story, in other words, seeks to express a theological truth of a dispositional kind about what is memorable about Jesus, but its real point is not just theological but religious: it prepares us for and alerts us to the possibility of a living encounter with the Spirit of God, which we are at the same time able to identify as the Spirit of Jesus. The story is not true because it is religiously useful, but its usefulness lies in its ability to lead us to the perception of the reality of the *Christus praesens* in our lives, which we may declare to be really and truly present. It is not that the Holy Spirit whispers the right interpretation of the scriptural text in our ear so that we acquire the right meaning, the object of faith being the meaning of scripture itself. Rather, just the opposite, scripture and the rehearsal of the story equip us conceptually to discern the presence of the Spirit and to identify it not just with the term 'Spirit' and 'God' but the names 'Jesus' and 'Christ'. The Spirit leads us into all truth because what we know of it in the present is a down payment of more to come. The truth is Christ himself; in the revelation of the Day of the Lord, clarity of sight will be achieved, for then, we shall no longer see dimly, but face to face.

Theological reflection on the importance of the category of story and how it functions within the structure of belief is very important with respect to the particularity of resurrection belief. For one thing, the synthetic reading of the historical, legendary, and mythological components of the scriptural testimony in the Church's continuing life, entails that the stories of the discovery of the empty tomb and the narratives of the Easter appearances are integral to the kerygma. We cannot deny our human nature by refusing the historical reason the right, and even the responsibility, to investigate the evidence analytically in order to determine where the dividing line lies between statements of historical fact, theologically interpretative statements, and statements of an imaginative and apologetic kind that are designed to communicate and illustrate truths of faith: however, we have found in this particular case that the evidence at our disposal which is relevant to the determination of the question of historicity of the Easter traditions is in fact insufficient to achieve a final result. However, the historical inconclusiveness of such an exercise is not necessarily detrimental for faith or irrelevant to it. The fact that the appeal to the evidence of the empty tomb and the appearances does not succeed as historical proof of the resurrection does not mean that the stories do not have a role to play in the structure of faith or that they do not continue to be an integral element in the proclamation of the Easter message which precipitates faith. On the contrary, the ambiguity both of the empty tomb tradition and of the tradition of the visions which remains after a historical-critical examination of the evidence is itself dogmatically significant. The failure of the historical model, in other words, has an important positive impact upon our understanding of the structure of resurrection belief: it saves us from a purely past-centred approach to Easter faith which would allow us to conceive of it merely as a propositional attitude, relating us only to a set of statements asserting 'what happened' in the past. The failure of the attempt to 'prove' the occurrence of the resurrection by employing the historical model exclusively, also has the positive effect of preventing us from 'naturalizing' the resurrection, which, as we have seen, is an inexorable gravitational pull of any attempt to handle the mystery of the resurrection by this means alone. Such an approach must be complemented by alternative avenues of approach, that are not only more appropriate to its nature as an eschatological event, but also appropriate to the apprehension of a present reality and not just to the handling of an occurrence of the past. This means that we must incorporate an epistemology into our understanding of faith, as well as attempting to approach it in a purely retrospective, historical-theological way. Faith is the discernment of a present religious object. In so far as all this results from the failure of the historical model it is a positive gain. However, this does not mean that the stories of the empty tomb and the narratives of the appearances become irrelevant. Indeed, once it is seen that their usefulness in providing a historical proof is strictly limited, they may re-enter the arena for another purpose. Even if theologians have a desire to draw a dividing line between statements of historical fact and apologetic statements along with those which must be understood as being designed to communicate imaginatively a truth of a theologically meaningful kind, that was not a pre-occupation of the original authors who apparently designed the stories for another, more clearly religious purpose. The question of historicity does not seem to bulk very large in the mind of the evangelists, who could move freely between statements which we would today distinguish as statements of historical fact and statements of a more imaginative, legendary or mythological kind, without this being for them an issue. We in turn may find them less conclusive historically, but more religiously useful. This is because, in so far as they have a fact reporting function, it is not just to affirm the occurrence of a mere historical fact that is continuous with the natural events of human history, but the occurrence of the eschatological event of God's drawing near for our salvation. Because this event may be experienced in the present, apart from reporting something, they alert us to a possibility, irrespective of the fact that the question of historicity cannot be resolved. Indeed, precisely because the question of historicity cannot be resolved, the Easter stories constantly present themselves for our puzzlement. They do not just convey information. This is a positive function within the overall structure of resurrection belief. This points us to the religious usefulness of the Easter traditions despite their ambiguity from a historiographical point of view, in so far as they direct our attention to the reality of the raised Christ, whose presence may, even today, be known by acquaintance. As a consequence, the positive implication of the conclusion that the story of the empty tomb and the narratives of the appearances are insufficient to prove the occurrence of the resurrection as a historical event, is that we are released from bondage to this single model, in order to see the value of these same stories more clearly as signs of an eschatological and heavenly reality in our lives: they raise a perceptual possibility rather than pose as proofs. When that possibility towards which they point us is 'filled', as it were, by an actual experience of encounter with the living Spirit of the Christian fellowship, which, for other good and independent reasons may be identified as the Spirit of *Jesus*, we know in faith that the possibility which the story of the empty tomb and the appearance narratives opens up for us, is not an empty one. Our Easter faith is not vain. It is in this way that the stories of the tomb and appearances, inconclusive and ambiguous though they are at the point of the determination of their historicity, still have an essential and integral place in the Easter proclamation. They are not proofs but pointers. In this way the rehearsal of those stories and our present talk of the experience of the Spirit of Christ which we identify also as the 'presence of Jesus' 'hang together', in a purposive, synthetic unity.

Indeed, perhaps this is the most important implication of the narrative form of the traditions. The purpose of a story is not just to aim to convey the pure essence of a thing, like information or a report. If that were the case the value of stories would cease in the moment in which their baggage of information was conveyed to the hearer. Walter Benjamin saw this clearly: 'The value of information does not survive the moment in which it is new. It lives only in that moment; it has to surrender to it completely and explain itself to it without losing any time. A story is different. It does not expend itself. It preserves and concentrates its strength and is capable of releasing it even after a long time.'[61] The continuing value of the Easter traditions resides precisely in the capacity of their narrative form to arrest us and challenge us. They do not deliver a message in the form of information and then recede into unimportance. They do not attempt to explain themselves. Rather, in their ambiguity they raise a question and place before us a possibility. We must therefore be sensitive to the germinative power of the stories which prepare us for the momentous happening which we call 'conversion' or 'coming to faith'. The Easter stories are not for the purpose of reporting the Easter event in literal detail nor for the purpose of affirming the truth of a more general 'middle distance' reading of what happened, which may be distilled out of their more detailed form. Rather, they are told and re-told for the purpose of alerting the hearer to a possibility of present experience: their religious purpose lies in their ability to arouse astonishment and thoughtfulness, to turn us around and direct our attention to the eschatological reality of the presence of Christ in our midst.[62]

The Jesus-story, from his birth to his death on the cross, thus

---

[61] Walter Benjamin, 'The Storyteller' in *Illuminations*, p. 90.

[62] It is not, as Walter Benjamin says, that the 'storyteller is the figure in which the righteous man encounters himself'; in the religious stories of the Easter tradition, the righteous man is led to encounter the living Christ.

points us to the quality of the self-giving *remembered* to have been in his life; the Easter stories of the empty tomb and the first appearances in turn raise the possibility of *knowing* that same self-giving still, in the ongoing life and work of the Christian fellowship. It is impossible to distil the meaning of it down to a neat general statement or doctrinal formula, but once an intelligible pattern or theological purposiveness is discerned in the story it begins to point us towards the possibility of faith: when we do encounter the *Christus praesens*, the judgement of faith thus takes the form: 'Ah, *this* is what they were talking about! This is none other than the Spirit of the living Christ and I knew it not!' When this happens the immediate impulse is not to do theology in order to explain how this judgement is possible: that comes later as the believer reflects upon the experience of faith and seeks to understand it or when he or she begins to give an account of faith and hope. The more immediate response is to stand in his presence in the silent awe of worship: thanks be to God for the unspeakable gift of Christ himself, for Christ is risen: He is risen indeed.

·

BIBLIOGRAPHY

Alston, W., *Philosophy of Language*, Englewood Cliffs, NJ: Prentice-Hall, Inc., 1964.

Alsup, John E., *The Post-Resurrection Appearance Stories of the Gospel Tradition: A History-of-Tradition Analysis with Text-Synopsis*, Stuttgart: Calwer Verlag, 1975.

Althaus, P., *Die Wahrheit des kirchlichen Osterglaubens: Einspruch Gegen E. Hirsch*, Gütersloh: C. Bertelsmann, 1940.

—— *Fact and Faith in the Kerygma Today*, Philadelphia: Muhlenberg Press, 1959.

—— *The So-Called Kerygma and the Historical Jesus*, English trans. David Cairns, Edinburgh: Oliver & Boyd, 1959.

Aquinas, Thomas, *Summa Theologiae*, Vol. 55, *The Resurrection of the Lord*, Latin text, English trans., Intro., notes and glossary, C. Thomas Moore, OP, London: Blackfriars, 1976.

Badham, Paul and Linda, *Immortality or Extinction?*, London: SPCK, 1984.

Baker, J. A., Review of *Myth of God Incarnate* in *JTS*, 29, 1978, pp. 291–7.

Bammel, E., 'Herkunft und Funktion der Traditionselemente in 1 Kor. 15:1–11', *TZ*, 11, 1955, pp. 401–19.

Barrett, C. K., *A Commentary on the First Epistle to the Corinthians*, 2nd edn., London: A. & C. Black, 1983 (1st edn., 1968).

Barth, K., *Church Dogmatics*, ed. G. W. Bromiley and T. F. Torrance, Edinburgh: T. & T. Clark, 1936–74.

—— *The Epistle to the Romans*, English trans. E. C. Hoskyns, London: Oxford University Press, 1933.

—— *The Resurrection of the Dead*, English trans. H. J. Stenning, London: Hodder and Stoughton, 1933.

Barth, Karl and Bultmann, Rudolf, *Letters 1922–1966*, ed. B. Jaspert, English trans. and ed. Geoffrey W. Bromiley, Grand Rapids: Eerdmans, 1981.

Barthes, Roland, *Mythologies*, St Albans: Granada, 1973.

Bartsch, H.-W., *Das Auferstehungszeugnis*, Hamburg: Reich, 1965.

—— (ed.) *Kerygma and Myth*, English trans. London: SPCK, Vol. I, 1953; Vol. II, 1962.

Bater, R. R., 'Towards a More Biblical View of the Resurrection', *Interpretation*, 23, 1969, pp. 47–65.

Beare, F. W., 'Sayings of the Risen Jesus in the Synoptic Tradition: An Inquiry into their Origin and Significance', *Christian History and Interpretation: Studies Presented to John Knox*, ed. C. F. D. Moule, W. R. Farmer, and R. R. Niebuhr, Cambridge University Press, 1977.

Benjamin, Walter, *Illuminations*, ed. with intro. by Hannah Arendt, English trans. Harry Zohn, London: Collins (Fontana), 1983.

Bennett, Jonathan, *Kant's Analytic*, Cambridge University Press, 1966.

Benoit, P., 'Marie-Madeleine et les disciples au tombeau selon *John* 20: 1–18', W. Eltester (ed.) *Judentum, Urchristentum, Kirche, Festschrift für J. Jeremias, BZNW*, 26, Berlin, 1964, pp. 141–52.

—— *The Passion and Resurrection of Jesus Christ*, English trans. B. Weatherhead, London: Darton, Longman and Todd, 1969.

Bergson, Henri, *Matter and Memory*, English trans. N. M. Paul and W. S. Palmer, London: Allen and Unwin, 1962.

Berkhof, H., *The Doctrine of the Holy Spirit*, London: Epworth, 1965.

Berkouwer, G. C., *The Triumph of Grace in the Theology of Karl Barth*, trans. from the Dutch by Harry R. Boer, Grand Rapids: Eerdmans, 1956.

Bertocci, Peter A., 'An Analysis of Macintosh's Theory of Religious Knowledge', *Journal of Religion*, 24, 1944, pp. 42–55.

—— 'Macintosh's Theory of Natural Knowledge', *Journal of Religion*, 23, 1943, pp. 164–72.

Betz, H., 'The Concept of Apocalyptic in the Theology of the Pannenberg Group', *Journal for Theology and the Church*, 6, 1969, pp. 192–207.

Bickerman, E., 'Das leere Grab', *ZNW*, 23, 1924, pp. 281–92.

Billerbeck, P. and Strack, H. L., *Kommentar zum Neuen Testament aus Talmud und Midrasch*, Munich: Beck, 1922–8.

Blondel, M., *Lettres Philosophiques*, Paris: Aubier, 1961.

Bode, E. L., *The First Easter Morning: The Gospel Accounts of the Women's Visit to the Tomb of Jesus, Analecta Biblica*, 45, Rome: Biblical Institute Press, 1970.

Bornhäuser, K., *The Death and Resurrection of Jesus Christ*, English trans. A. Rumpus, Bangalore: CLS Press, 1958.

Bornkamm, G., *Jesus of Nazareth*, English trans. Irene and Fraser McLusky with J. M. Robinson, London: Hodder and Stoughton, 1960.

—— *Early Christian Experience*, London: SCM Press, 1969.

—— *Paul*, London: Hodder and Stoughton, 1971.

Braaten, C. E. and Harrisville, Roy A., *The Historical Jesus and the Kerygmatic Christ*, New York and Nashville: Abingdon Press, 1964.

Bradley, F. H., *The Presuppositions of Critical History*, ed. with intro. and commentary by L. Rubinoff, Ontario: Don Mills, 1968.

Broad, C. D., *The Mind and Its Place in Nature*, London: K. Paul, Trench, Trubner and Co., 1925.

Brown, Raymond E., 'The Resurrection and Biblical Criticism', *Commonweal*, 87, 1967, pp. 232–6.

—— *The Virginal Conception & Bodily Resurrection of Jesus*, London: Geoffrey Chapman, 1974.

Brunner, E., 'Die Grenzen der Humanität' (1922) in *Anfänge der dialektischen Theologie*, ed. J. Moltmann, Vol. I, Munich: Kaiser Verlag, 1962.

—— *The Mediator*, English trans. O. Wyon, London: Lutterworth, 1934.

—— *Dogmatics*, Vol. II, London: Lutterworth, 1952.

Bulgakoff, S., Untitled essay in *Revelation*, ed. J. Baillie and H. Martin, New York: Macmillan, 1937, pp. 125–80.

Bultmann, R., *Essays Philosophical and Theological*, (*Glauben und Verstehen* II) English trans. J. C. G. Greig, London: SCM Press, 1955.

—— *Faith and Understanding*, (*Glauben und Verstehen*, I) ed. with intro, by Robert W. Funk, English trans. Louise Pettibone Smith, London: SCM Press, 1969.

—— 'Preaching: Genuine and Secularized', *Religion and Culture, Essays in Honor of Paul Tillich*, ed. Walter Leibrecht, New York: Harper and Row, 1959.

—— *The History of the Synoptic Tradition*, Oxford: Blackwell, 1963.

—— 'The Primitive Christian Kerygma and the Historical Jesus', *The Historical Jesus and the Kerygmatic Christ*, trans. and ed. C. E. Braaten and Roy A. Harrisville, New York and Nashville: Abingdon Press, 1964.

—— 'The Quest for Meaning in History', *Listener*, 1 Sept. 1955, pp. 329–30.

—— *Theology of the New Testament*, English trans. K. Grobel, London: SCM Press, Vol I, 1952; Vol. II. 1955.

Buren, Paul van, *The Secular Meaning of the Gospel*, Harmondsworth, UK: Penguin, 1968.

Butler, Samuel, *Samuel Butler on the Resurrection*, ed. with intro. by Robert Johnstone, with an appendix by W. B. Primrose, Gerards Cross: Colin Smythe, 1980.

Campenhausen, H. von, 'The Events of Easter and the Empty Tomb', *Tradition and Life in the Church*, English trans. A. V. Littledale, London: Collins, 1968, pp. 42–89.

Carnley, Peter F., 'The Poverty of Historical Scepticism', *Christ Faith and History*, ed. S. W. Sykes and J. P. Clayton, Cambridge University Press, 1972.

Carpenter, W. B., 'The Fallacies of Testimony in Relation to the Supernatural', *Contemporary Review*, Jan. 1876, pp. 279–95.

Case, S. J., 'The Resurrection Faith of the First Disciples', *American Journal of Theology*, 13, 1909, pp. 169–92.

Cassels, W. R., *Supernatural Religion, An enquiry into the reality of divine revelation*, London: Longmans, Green, 1874–7.

—— 'The Christian "Conditions" ', *Fortnightly Review*, Feb. 1878, pp. 228–46.

—— 'The New Revelation', *Fortnightly Review*, March 1878, pp. 365–83.

Chamberlain, W. D., *An Exegetical Grammar of the Greek New Testament*, New York: Macmillan, 1941.

Cheek, John, 'The Historicity of the Markan Resurrection Narrative', *JBR*, 27, 1959, pp. 191–201.

Church, R. W., *Occasional Papers*, London: Macmillan, 1897.

Clayton, John P. (ed.), *Ernst Troeltsch and the Future of Theology*, Cambridge University Press, 1976.

Congar, Y., *Tradition and Traditions*, London: Burns & Oates, 1966.

Conzelmann, H., 'On the Analysis of the Confessional Formula in I Corinthians 15: 3–5', *Interpretation*, 20, 1966, pp. 15–25.

Coventry, J. 'The Myth and the Method', *Theology*, 81, 1978, pp. 252–6.

Crawford, P. G., 'The Resurrection of Christ', *Theology*, lxxv, (1972), pp. 170–6.

Cullman, Oscar, *Immortality of the Soul or Resurrection of the Dead?*, London: Epworth Press, 1958.

Cupitt, Don, *Christ and the Hiddenness of God*, London: Lutterworth, 1971.

—— *The Debate About Christ*, London: SCM Press, 1979.

—— 'The Resurrection: A Disagreement: A Correspondence with C. F. D. Moule', *Explorations in Theology*, No. 6, London: SCM Press, 1979, (originally published in *Theology*, lxxv, October 1972).

Davies, W. D., *Paul and Rabbinic Judaism*, 2nd edn., London: SPCK, 1965.

—— *Invitation to the New Testament*, London: Darton, Longman & Todd, 1967.

Delling, Gerhard, 'The Significance of the Resurrection of Jesus for Faith in Jesus Christ', *The Significance of the Message of the Resurrection for Faith in Jesus Christ*, ed. C. F. D. Moule, London: SCM Press, 1968.

Delorme, Jean, 'Résurrection et Tombeau de Jesus: *Marc* 16, 1–8 dans la tradition evangélique', *La Résurrection du Christ et l'exégèse moderne*, *Lectio Divina*, 50, Paris: Le Cerf, 1969, pp. 105–53.

Descamps, A. L., 'Compte Rendu', *Revue Théologique de Louvain*, 6, 1975, pp. 212–23.

de Vaux, Roland, *Ancient Israel*, London: Darton, Longman and Todd, 1961.

Dewar, Lindsay, *An Outline of New Testament Ethics*, London: Hodder and Stoughton, 1949.

Dodd, C. H., *The Apostolic Preaching and its Development*, London: Hodder and Stoughton, 1936.

—— 'The Appearances of the Risen Christ: An Essay in Form-Criticism of the Gospels', *Studies in the Gospels*, *Essays in Memory of R. H. Lightfoot*, ed. D. E. Nineham, Oxford: Blackwell, 1955, pp. 9–35.

Downing, F. Gerald, *The Church and Jesus*, London: SCM Press, 1968.

—— *Has Christianity a Revelation?*, London: SCM Press, 1964.

Dunn, J. D. G., 'Flesh and Spirit: An Exposition of Romans 1: 3–4', *JTS*, NS, 24, 1973, pp. 40–68.

—— *Jesus and the Spirit*, London: SCM Press, 1975.

—— 'I Corinthians 15: 45—Last Adam, Life-giving Spirit', *Christ and Spirit in the New Testament: Studies in Honour of C. F. D. Moule*, ed. B. Lindars and S. S. Smalley, Cambridge University Press, 1973, pp. 127–41.

—— '2 Corinthians 3: 17—"The Lord is the Spirit" ', *JTS*, NS, 21, 1970, pp. 309–20.

Durrwell, F. X., *The Resurrection*, London: Sheed and Ward, 1960.

Ebeling, G., *Word and Faith*, English trans. J. W. Leitch, London: SCM Press, 1963.

—— *The Word of God and Tradition*, London: Collins, 1968.

Edwards, Paul (ed.), *The Encyclopedia of Philosophy*, London: Collier-Macmillan; New York: Macmillan Co. & Free Press, 1967.

Elliott, J. K., 'The First Easter', *History Today*, 29, 1979, pp. 207–20.

Ellis, E. E., 'Christ and Spirit in I Corinthians', *Christ and Spirit in the New Testament, Studies in Honour of C. F. D. Moule*, ed. B. Lindars and S. S. Smalley, Cambridge University Press, 1973, pp. 269–77.

Evans, C. F., 'I will go before you into Galilee', *JTS*, NS, 5, 1954, pp. 3–18.

—— 'The Kerygma', *JTS*, NS, 8, 1956, pp. 25–41.

—— *Resurrection and the New Testament*, London: SCM Press, 1970.

Farmer, W. R. with Moule, C. F. D. and Niebuhr, R. R. (eds.), *Christian History and Interpretation: Studies Presented to John Knox*, Cambridge University Press, 1967.

Filson, Floyd V., *Jesus Christ the Risen Lord*, New York and Nashville: Abingdon Press, 1956.

Ford D. F., 'Barth's Interpretation of the Bible' in S. W. Sykes (ed.), *Karl Barth—Studies of His Theological Method*, Oxford University Press, 1979.

Frege, G., 'On Sense and Reference', *Translations from the Philosophical Writings of Gottlob Frege*, ed. Peter Geach and Max Black, Oxford: Blackwell, 1952.

Fuchs, E., 'The Quest of the Historical Jesus', *Studies of the Historical Jesus*, English trans. A. Scobie, London: SCM Press, 1964, pp. 11–31.

Fuller, D. P., *Easter Faith and History*, London: The Tyndale Press, 1968.

—— 'The Resurrection of Jesus Christ and the Historical Method', *JBR*, 34, 1966, pp. 18–24.

Fuller, Reginald H., *The Formation of the Resurrection Narratives*, London: SPCK, 1972.

Gardner-Smith, P., *The Narratives of the Resurrection: A Critical Study*. London: Methuen, 1926.

Geering, L., *Resurrection: A Symbol of Hope*, London: Hodder and Stoughton, 1971.

Geyer, Hans-Georg, 'The Resurrection of Jesus Christ: A Survey of the Debate in Present Day Theology', *The Significance of the Message of the Resurrection for Faith in Jesus Christ*, ed. C. F. D. Moule, London: SCM Press, 1968, pp. 105–35.

Gogarten, F., *Demythologizing and History*, English trans. N. H. Smith, London: SCM Press, 1955.

—— 'Die religiöse Entscheidung' (1921) in *Anfänge der dialektischen Theologie*, ed. J. Moltmann, Vol. 11, Munich: Kaiser Verlag, 1963.

Goguel, M., *La foi à la Résurrection de Jésus dans la christianisme primitif*, Paris: Leroux, 1933.

—— *The Birth of Christianity*, English trans. H. C. Snape, London: George Allen and Unwin, 1953.

Gooch, P. W. and Mosher, D. L., 'Divine Love and the Limits of Language', *JTS*, NS, 23, 1972, pp. 420–9.

Gore, Charles (ed.), *Lux Mundi* (12th edn.), London: John Murray, 1890.

Goulder, M. (ed.), *Incarnation and Myth*, London: SCM Press, 1979.

Grass, H., *Ostergeschehen und Osterberichte*, 2nd edn., Göttingen: Vandenhoeck and Ruprecht, 1962.

Green, M. (ed.), *The Truth of God Incarnate*, London: Hodder and Stoughton, 1977.

Greer, Rowan A., III, 'The Image of God and the Prosopic Union in Nestorius' *Bazaar of Heracleides*', *Lux in Lumine, Essays to Honor W. Norman Pittenger*, ed. R. A. Norris Jr., New York: Seabury Press, 1966.

Griffiths, D. R., 'The Lord is the Spirit', *Expository Times*, lv, 1943, pp. 81–3.

Grobel, Kendrick, 'Revelation and Resurrection', *New Frontiers in Theology*, Vol. III, *Theology as History*, eds. James M. Robinson and John B. Cobb, Jr., New York: Harper & Row, 1967, pp. 155–75.

Grundmann, W., 'δύναμαι/δύναμις', *TDNT*, Vol. II, pp. 284–317.

Guignebert, Charles, *Jesus*, English trans. S. H. Hooke, New York: Knopf, 1935.

Guitton, Jean, *Essay on Human Love*, London: Rockliff, 1951.

Hamilton, N. Q., *Jesus for a No-God World*, Philadelphia: Westminster Press, 1969.

—— 'Resurrection Tradition and the Composition of Mark', *JBL*, 84, 1965, pp. 415–21.

—— 'The Holy Spirit and Esclatology in Paul', *Scottish Journal of Theology*, Occasional Papers 6, Edinburgh, 1957.

Hanson, A. T., *Grace and Truth*, London: SPCK, 1975.

Harnack, A. von, *Die Verklärungsgeschichte Jesu, der Bericht des Paulus 1 Kor. 15: 3 ff und die beiden Christusvisionen des Petrus, SBA* phil.-hist. KE, Berlin, 1922.

Harvey, A. E. (ed.), *God Incarnate: Story and Belief*, London: SPCK, 1981.

—— *Jesus and the Constraints of History*, London: Duckworth, 1982.

Harvey, Van A., *The Historian and the Believer*, London: SCM Press, 1967.

Hawkes, Terence, *Structuralism and Semiotics*, London: Methuen, 1977.

Hebblethwaite, Brian, 'The Moral and Religious Value of the Incarnation', *Incarnation and Myth*, ed. M. Goulder, London: SCM Press, 1979.

Hebblethwaite, Peter, *A New Inquisition?*, London: Collins, Fount Paperback, 1980.

Hendry, George S., *The Holy Spirit in Christian Theology*, London: SCM Press, 1965.

Hengel, M., 'Maria Magdalena und die Frauen als Zeugen', *Abraham unser Vater: Festchrift für O. Michel*, hrsg, O. Betz, M. Hengel and P. Schmidt, Leiden: Brill, 1963.

Hermann, Ingo, *Kyrios und Pneuma: Studien zur Christologie der paulinischen Hauptbriefe*, Munich: Kösel-Verlag, 1961.

Herrmann, Wilhelm, *The Communion of the Christian with God*, English trans. J. Sandys Stanyon, revised by R. W. Stewart, London: Williams and Norgate, 1906.

Hick, John, 'Christology at the Crossroads', *Prospect for Theology, Essays in Honour of H. H. Farmer*, ed. F. G. Healey, London: Nisbet, 1966, pp. 137–66.

—— *Christianity at the Centre*, London: SCM Press, 1968 (revised as *The Centre of Christianity*, London: SCM Press, 1977).

—— *Faith and Knowledge*, 2nd edn., London: Macmillan, 1967.

—— (ed.), *The Myth of God Incarnate*, London: SCM Press, 1977.

Hodge, C., *An Exposition of the First Epistle to the Corinthians*, Grand Rapids: Eerdmans, 1953.

Holloway, David, *Where did Jesus Go?*, Basingstoke, Hants: Marshall, Morgan and Scott, 1983.

Holtzmann, H., *Lehrbuch der neutestamentlichen Theologie* (2 vols.), 2nd edn., Tübingen: J. C. B. Mohr (Paul Siebeck), 1911.

Hooke, S. H., *The Resurrection of Christ as History and Experience*, London: Darton, Longman & Todd, 1967.

Houlden, L., 'A Wider Framework', *Incarnation and Myth*, ed. M. Goulder, London: SCM Press, 1979.

James, M. R., *The Testament of Abraham*, Greek text with intro. and notes, Cambridge, 1892.

Jansen, John Frederick, *The Resurrection of Jesus Christ in New Testament Theology*, Philadelphia: Westminster Press, 1980.

Jeremias, J., 'Artikelloses Χριστός', *ZNW*, 57, 1956, pp. 211–15.

—— 'Flesh and Blood Cannot Inherit the Kingdom of God, (I Cor. 15: 50)', *NTS*, 2, 1955–6, pp. 151–9.

—— *Jerusalem in the Time of Jesus*, English trans. F. H. and C. H. Cave, Philadelphia: Fortress Press, 1969.

—— *New Testament Theology*, Pt.1, English trans. J. Bowden, London: SCM Press, 1971.

—— 'Nochmals: Artikelloses Χριστός in 1 *Cor* 15: 3', *ZNW*, 60, 1959, pp. 214–19.

—— *The Eucharistic Words of Jesus*, London: SCM Press, 1966.

Joest, W. and Pannenberg, W. (eds.), *Dogma und Denkstrukturen*, *Edmund Schlink Festschrift*, Göttingen: Vandenhoeck & Ruprecht, 1963.

Jung, C. G., 'Answer to Job' (1952), *Psychology and Religion: West and East*, *CW* 11, English trans. R. F. C. Hull, eds. Herbert Read, Michael Fordham, Gerhard Adler, London: Routledge & Kegan Paul, 1969.

Kähler, Martin, *The So-Called Historical Jesus and the Historic, Biblical Christ*, English trans. and ed. Carl E. Braaten, Philadelphia: Fortress Press, 1964.

—— *Das Kreuz: Grund und Mass für nostra theologia*, *BFCT*, 15, 1911.

Kant, I., *Critique of Pure Reason*, English trans. N. Kemp Smith, London: Macmillan, 1976.

Käsemann, E., *Perspectives on Paul*, London: SCM Press, 1971.

—— 'The Canon of the New Testament and the Unity of the Church', *Essays on New Testament Themes*, London: SCM Press, 1964, pp. 95–107.

—— 'The Pauline Doctrine of the Lord's Supper', *Essays on New Testament Themes*, London: SCM Press, 1964, pp. 108–35.

—— 'The Problem of the Historical Jesus', *Essays on New Testament Themes*, London: SCM Press, 1964, pp. 15–47; first published as 'Das Problem des historischen Jesus', *ZTK*, 51, 1954, pp. 125–53.

Kasper, W., *Jesus the Christ*, English trans. V. Green, London: Burns & Oates, 1976.

Kepler, Thomas S., *The Mystery of the Resurrection*, New York: Association Press, 1963.

Kilpatrick, G. D., 'Galatians 1: 18 "ΙΣΤΟΡΗΣΑΙ ΚΗΦΑΝ"', *New Testament Essays*, (T. W. Manson Memorial Volume), ed. A. J. B. Higgins, Manchester: University Press, 1955.

Klappert, B., *Die Auferweckung des Gekreuzigten. Der Ansatz der Christologie Karl Barths im Zusammenhang der Christologie der Gegenwart*, Neukirchen: Vluyn, 1971.

—— (ed.), *Diskussion um Kreuz und Auferstehung*, Wuppertal: Aussaat, 1967.

—— 'Zur Frage des semitischen oder griechischen Urtextes von *1 Kor* 15: 3–5', *NTS*, 13, 1967, pp. 168–73.

Klausner, Joseph, *Jesus of Nazareth; His Life, Times, and Teaching*, London: Allen & Unwin, 1925.

Knowles, David, *The Historian and Character*, Cambridge University Press, 1963.

Knox, J., *Chapters in a Life of Paul*, London: A. & C. Black, 1954 (Original American edition, 1950).

—— *Christ and the Hope of Glory*, New York and Nashville: Abingdon Press, 1960.

—— *Christ the Lord*, Chicago: Willett, Clark, 1945.

—— 'Christianity and the Christian', *The Christian Answer*, ed. Henry P. van Dusen, New York: Scribners, 1945, pp. 160–90.

—— *Criticism and Faith*, London: Hodder & Stoughton, 1953 (Original American edition, 1952).

—— *Jesus: Lord and Christ*, a trilogy comprising *The Man Christ Jesus* (1941), *Christ the Lord* (1945), and *On the Meaning of Christ* (1947), New York: Harper, 1958.

—— *Life in Christ Jesus: Reflections on Romans 5–8*, London: SPCK, 1963 (Original American edition, 1961).

—— *On the Meaning of Christ*, New York: Scribners, 1947.

—— 'Our Knowledge of Jesus', *Christendom*, 3, 1938, pp. 44–54.

—— *The Church and the Reality of Christ*, London: Collins, 1963 (Original American edition, 1962).

—— 'The Church *is* Christ's Body', *Religion in Life*, 27, 1957/8, pp. 54–62.

—— *The Death of Christ*, London: Collins, Fontana, 1967 (Original American edition, 1958).

—— *The Early Church and the Coming Great Church*, London: Epworth, 1957 (Original American edition, 1955).

—— 'The Epistle to the Romans: Introduction and Exegesis', *The Interpreters Bible*, ed. C. A. Butterick, Vol. IX, New York and Nashville: Abingdon Press, 1954, pp. 353–668.

—— *The Ethic of Jesus in the Teaching of the Church*, London: Epworth, 1962 (Original American edition, 1961).

—— 'The Hope of Glory: Ingersoll Lecture 1960', *Harvard Divinity Bulletin*, 24, 1960, pp. 9–19.

—— *The Humanity and Divinity of Christ*, Cambridge University Press, 1967.

—— *The Integrity of Preaching*, London: Epworth, 1965 (Original American edition, 1957).

—— 'The 'Prophet'' in New Testament Christology', *Lux in Lumine*:

Essays to Honor W. Norman Pittenger, ed. R. A. Norris, Jr., New York: Seabury, 1966.

Köhler, R., *Der Begriff a priori in der modernen Religionsphilosophie: Eine Untersuchnug zur religionsphilosophischen Methode*, Leipzig: J. C. Hinrichs, 1920.

Kremer. J., *Die Osterbotschaft der vier Evangelien*, Stuttgart: Katholisches Bibelwerk, 1968.

Kümmel, W., *Introduction to the New Testament*, English trans. A. J. Mattill, Jr., London: SCM Press, 1960.

Küng, Hans, *Eternal Life?*, English trans. Edward Quinn, London: Collins, 1984.

—— *On Being a Christian*, London: Collins, 1977.

Künneth, W., *Glauben an Jesus?*, Hamburg: Friedrich Wittig, 1962.

—— *The Theology of the Resurrection*, English trans. J. W. Leitch, London: SCM Press, 1965.

Laberthonnière, Lucien, *Annales de philosophie chrétienne*, 1907–8, vols. 154, 155: *Dogma et théologie*.

Ladd, G. E., *I Believe in the Resurrection of Jesus*, London: Hodder and Stoughton, 1975.

Lake, Kirsopp, *The Historical Evidence for the Resurrection of Jesus Christ*, London: Williams & Norgate, 1907.

Lampe, G. W. H., *God As Spirit*, Oxford: Clarendon Press, 1977.

—— 'Holy Spirit', *The Interpreter's Dictionary of the Bible*, Vol. II, ed. G. A. Buttrick, New York and Nashville: Abingdon Press, 1962, pp. 626–39.

—— 'The Holy Spirit in the Writings of St Luke', *Studies in the Gospels*, ed. D. E. Nineham, Oxford: Blackwell, 1955, pp. 159–200.

—— *The Resurrection, A Dialogue arising from Broadcasts* (with D. M. MacKinnon), ed. W. Purcell, London: Mowbrays, 1966.

Lapide, Pinchas, *Auferstehung: ein Jüdisches Glaubenserlebnis*, Stuttgart: Calwer Verlag, 1977.

Latham, Henry, *The Risen Master*, Cambridge University Press, 1901.

Lehmann, K., 'Die Erscheinungen des Herrn', *Auferweckt am dritten Tag nach der Schrift. Früheste Christologie, Bekenntnisbildung und Schriftauslegung im Lichte von 1 Kor 15: 3–5, Quaestiones Disputatae*, ed. K. Rahner and H. Schlier, Vol. 38, Freiburg: Herder, 1968.

Léon-Dufour, X., *Resurrection of Jesus and the Message of Easter*, English trans., London: Geoffrey Chapman, 1974.

Le Roy, E., *Dogme et critique*, Paris: Bloud et Cie, 1907.

Lewis, C. S., *The Four Loves*, London: Geoffrey Bles, 1960.

Leyden, W. von, *Remembering*, London: Duckworth, 1961.

Lightfoot, R. H., *Locality and Doctrine in the Gospels*, London: Hodder and Stoughton, 1938.

Lindars, Barnabas, *New Testament Apologetic*, London: SCM Press, 1961.
Lindars, B. and Smalley, S. S. (eds.), *Christ and Spirit in the New Testament, Studies in Honour of C. F. D. Moule*, Cambridge University Press, 1973.
Lindblom, J., *Geschichte und Offenbarungen*, Lund: Gleerup, 1968.
Lohmeyer, E., *Galiläa and Jerusalem, FRLANT*, 34: Gottingen, 1936.
Loisy, A., *L'Évangile selon Marc*, Paris: Nourny, 1912.
Longstaff, T. R. W., 'The Women at the Tomb: Matthew 28: 1 Re-examined', *NTS*, 27, 2, 1981, pp. 277–82.
Macan, R. W., *The Resurrection of Jesus Christ*, London: Williams & Norgate, 1877.
McCasland, Selby, 'The Scriptural Basis of "On the Third Day" ', *JBL*, 48, 1929, pp. 124–37.
—— 'The Origin of the Lord's Day', *JBL*, 49, 1930, pp. 65–82.
—— *The Resurrection of Jesus*, New York: Nelson, 1932.
Macintosh, D. C., *The Problem of Religious Knowledge*, New York: Harper, 1940.
—— 'Troeltsch's Theory of Religious Knowledge', *American Journal of Theology*, 23, 1919, pp. 274–89.
McIntyre, John, *On the Love of God*, London: Collins, 1962.
Mackey, James P., *Jesus the Man and the Myth*, London: SCM Press, 1979.
—— *The Christian Experience of God as Trinity*, London: SCM Press, 1983.
McLeman, James, *Resurrection Then and Now*, London: Hodder & Stoughton, 1965.
Macquarrie, John, *The Scope of Demythologizing*, London: SCM Press, 1960.
Malcolm, Norman, *Knowledge and Certainty*, Englewood Cliffs, NJ: Prentice-Hall Inc., 1965.
Mánek, Jindřich, 'The Apostle Paul and the Empty Tomb', *Novum Testamentum*, 2, 1957–8, pp. 276–280.
Mangenot, Eugène, *La Résurrection de Jésus*, Paris: Beauchesne, 1910.
Martelet, Gustave, *The Risen Christ and the Eucharistic World*, English trans. René Hague, London: Collins, 1976.
Marxsen, W., *Mark the Evangelist*, English trans. R. Harrisville, New York and Nashville: Abingdon Press, 1969.
—— 'The Resurrection of Jesus as a Historical and Theological Problem', *The Significance of the Message of the Resurrection for Faith in Jesus Christ*, ed. C. F. D. Moule, London: SCM Press, 1968.
—— *The Resurrection of Jesus of Nazareth*, London: SCM Press, 1970.
Mascall, E. L., *Theology and the Future*, London: Darton, Longman & Todd, 1968.
—— *Theology and the Gospel of Christ*, London: SPCK, 1977.

—— *The Secularisation of Christianity*, London: Darton, Longman & Todd, 1965.

Masson, C., 'Le tombeau vide: essai sur la formation d'une tradition', *Revue de Théologie et de Philosophie*, NS, 32, 1944, pp. 161–74.

Meyer, E., *Ursprung und Aufänge des Christentums*, Vol. 1: *Die Evangelien*, Stuttgart: Cotta, 1921.

Michaelis, W., 'ὁράω etc', *TDNT*, Vol. V, 1967, pp. 315–82.

Mill, J. S., *A System of Logic*, London: Longmans, Green, 1872.

—— *Essays on Ethics, Religion and Society*, ed. J. M. Robson, Toronto: University Press, 1969.

Minear, Paul S., Review of *The Death of Christ* by John Knox, *Religion in Life*, 27, 1958, pp. 610–1.

Moberly, R. C., 'The Incarnation as the Basis of Dogma', *Lux Mundi*, ed. C. Gore, London: John Murray, 1890, pp. 215–72.

Moffatt, J., *Love in the New Testament*, London: Hodder & Stoughton, 1929.

—— *The First Epistle of Paul to the Corinthians*, London: Hodder & Stoughton, no date.

Moltmann, J. (ed.), *Anfänge der dialektischen Theologie*, Vols. I & II, Munich: Kaiser Verlag, 1962–3.

—— 'God and Resurrection' in *Hope and Planning*, English trans. Margaret Clarkson, London: SCM Press, 1971, pp. 31–55.

—— *The Theology of Hope*, English trans. James W. Leitch, London: SCM Press, 1967.

Moore, G. E., *Philosophical Papers*, London: Allen & Unwin, 1959.

Morision, F., *Who Moved the Stone?*, London: Faber and Faber, 1968 (first published 1930).

Morrison, C. C., *What is Christianity?*, Chigaco: Willett, Clark, 1940.

Moule, C. F. D., 'St Mark 16: 8 Once More', *NTS*, 2, 1955, pp. 58–9.

—— 'St Paul and Dualism: The Pauline Conception of Resurrection', *NTS*, 12, 1965/6, pp. 106–123.

—— 'The Individualism of the Fourth Gospel', *Novum Testamentum*, 5, 1962, pp. 171–90.

—— *The Origin of Christology*, Cambridge University Press, 1977.

—— *The Phenomenon of the New Testament*, London: SCM Press, 1967.

—— 'The Post-Resurrection Appearances in the Light of Festival Pilgrimages', *NTS*, 4, 1957/58, pp. 58–61.

—— (ed.), *The Significance of the Message of the Resurrection for Faith in Jesus Christ*, London: SCM Press, 1968.

Nauck, W., 'Die Bedeutung des leeren Grabes für den Glauben an den Auferstandenen', *ZNW* 47, 1956, pp. 243–67.

Neill, Stephen, *The Interpretation of the New Testament*, Oxford University Press, 1964.

Niebuhr, R. R., *Resurrection and Historical Reason*, New York: Scribner's 1957.

Nineham, D. E. (ed.), *Studies in the Gospels, Essays in memory of R. H. Lightfoot*, Oxford: Blackwell, 1955.

Nygren, Anders, *Agape and Eros*, English trans. Philip S. Watson, London: SPCK, 1953 (first published 1932).

O'Collins, G., 'Karl Barth on Christ's Resurrection', *Scottish Journal of Theology*, 26, 1973, pp. 85–99.

—— *Foundations of Theology*, Chicago: Loyola University Press, 1966.

—— *Fundamental Theology*, New York: Paulist Press, 1981.

—— 'Is the Resurrection an "Historical Event"?', *Heythrop Journal*, 8, 1967, pp. 381–7.

—— 'Thomas Aquinas and Christ's Resurrection', *Theological Studies*, 31, 1970, pp. 512–22.

—— 'Revelation as History', *Heythrop Journal*, 7, 1966, pp. 394–406.

—— 'The Christology of Wolfhart Pannenberg', *Religious Studies*, 3, 1967, pp. 369–76.

—— *The Easter Jesus*, London: Darton, Longman and Todd, 1973.

—— *What Are They Saying About the Resurrection?*, New York: Paulist Press, 1978.

O'Neill, J. C., 'On the Resurrection as an Historical Question', *Christ Faith and History*, ed. S. W. Sykes and J. P. Clayton, Cambridge University Press, 1972, pp. 205–19.

Ott, Heinrich, 'The Historical Jesus and the Ontology of History', *The Historical Jesus and the Kerygmatic Christ*, English trans. and ed. C. E. Braaten and Roy A. Harrisville, New York and Nashville: Abingdon Press, 1964.

Outka, Gene Harold, *Agape; an ethical analysis*, New Haven: Yale University Press, 1972.

Pannenberg, W., 'Did Jesus Really Rise from the Dead?', *Dialog*, 4, 1965, pp. 128–35.

—— 'Dogmatische Erwägungen zur Auferstehung Jesu', *Kerygma und Dogma*, 14, 1968, pp. 105–18.

—— *Jesus—God and Man*, English trans. L. L. Wilkins and D. A. Priebe, London: SCM Press, 1968.

—— *Revelation as History*, ed., English trans. David Granskou, London: Collier-Macmillan, 1968.

—— 'The Revelation of God in Jesus of Nazareth', *New Frontiers in Theology*, Vol. III, *Theology as History*, ed. James M. Robinson and John B. Cobb, Jr., New York: Harper and Row, 1967, pp. 101–33.

Pelletier, A., 'Les apparitions du Ressuscité en termes de la Septante', *Biblica*, 51, 1970, pp. 76–9.

Perrin, N., *Jesus and the Language of the Kingdom*: *symbol and metaphor in N.T. interpretation*, Philadelphia: Fortress Press, 1976.
—— *The Resurrection Narratives*, London: SCM Press, 1977.
Perry, Michael C., *The Easter Enigma*, London: Faber & Faber, 1959.
Pesch, R., 'Zur Entstehung des Glaubens an die Auferstehung Jesu. Ein Vorschlag zur Diskussion', *TQ*, 153, 1973, pp. 201–28.
Pinnock, Clark H., 'On the Third Day' in Carl Henry (ed.) *Jesus of Nazareth*: *Saviour and Lord*, London: Tyndale Press, 1966, pp. 145–55.
Pittenger, W. N., *Christology Reconsidered*, London: SCM Press, 1970.
—— *The Word Incarnate*, London: Nisbet, 1959.
Plummer, A., *International Critical Commentary on I Corinthians*, Edinburgh: T. & T. Clark, 1914.
Price, H. H., *Thinking and Experience*, London: Hutchinson, 1953.
Rahner, K., 'Current Problems in Christology', *Theological Investigations*, Vol. 1, English trans. Cornelius Ernst, London: Darton, Longman and Todd, 1961.
—— 'Resurrection of Christ', *Sacramentum Mundi*, Vol. V, London: Burns and Oates, 1968.
Ramsey, A. M., *The Resurrection of Christ*, London: Geoffrey Bles, 1945.
Rawlinson, A. E. J., *The New Testament Doctrine of Christ*, London: Longmans, Green, 1926.
Reimarus, H. S., *Fragments*, ed. by C. H. Talbert; English trans. R. S. Fraser, London: SCM Press, 1971.
Reist, Benjamin A., *Toward a Theology of Involvement*: *The Thought of Ernst Troeltsch*, London: SCM Press, 1966.
Rénan, E., *Life of Jesus*, English trans., London: Trübner, 1864.
Rendtorff, R., 'The Concept of Revelation in Ancient Israel', *Revelation as History*, ed. W. Pannenberg, London: Collier-Macmillan, 1968.
Rengstorf, Karl H., *Die Auferstehung Jesu. Form, Art und Sinn der urchristlichen Osterbotschaft*, 2nd edn. Witten: Ruhr, 1954.
Richardson, A., *Introduction to the Theology of the New Testament*, London: SCM Press, 1958.
—— *History Sacred and Profane*, London: SCM Press, 1964.
—— *Science, History, and Faith*, London: Oxford University Press, 1950.
Richardson, Cyril C., 'Love: Greek and Christian', *Journal of Religion*, 23, 1943, pp. 173–85.
Robinson, J. A. T., *But that I can't believe!*, London: Collins, 1967.
—— 'Resurrection in the New Testament', *The Interpreter's Dictionary of the Bible*, Vol. IV, ed. G. A. Buttrick, New York & Nashville: Abingdon, Press, 1962, pp. 43–53.
—— *The Human Face of God*, London: SCM Press, 1973.
—— 'The Most Primitive Christology of All?', *JTS*, NS, 7, Part 2 (1956), pp. 177–89.

Robinson, J. M. and Cobb, J. B. Jr., (eds.) *New FrontierN in Theology*, Vol. 3, *Theology as History*, New York: Harper & Row, 1967.

Rowdon, H. H. (ed.), *Christ the Lord, Studies in Christology Presented to Donald Guthrie*, Leicester: Inter-Varsity Press, 1982.

Royce, Josiah, *The Problem of Christianity*, New York: Macmillan, 1913.

Russell, Bertrand, *The Analysis of Mind*, New York: Macmillan, 1921.

—— *The Problems of Philosophy*, London: Williams & Norgate, 1912.

Ryle, Gilbert, *The Concept of Mind*, Harmondsworth, UK: Penguin, 1966.

Sanders, Jack T., 'First Corinthians 13. Its Interpretation Since the First World War', *Interpretation*, 20, 1966, pp. 159–87.

Schenke, L., *Auferstehungsverkündigung und leeres Grab*, Stuttgart: Katholisches Bibelwerk, 1968.

Schep, J. A., *The Nature of the Resurrection Body*, Grand Rapids: Eerdmans, 1964.

Schille, Gottfried, 'Das Leiden des Herrn die evangelische Passionstradition und ihr "Sitz im Leben" ', *ZTK*, 52, 1955, pp. 161–205.

Schillebeeckx, E., *Christ*, English trans., London: SCM Press, 1980.

—— *Jesus: An Experiment in Christology*, English trans., London: Collins, 1979.

—— *Interim Report on the books* Jesus *and* Christ, London: SCM Press, 1980.

Schlette, H., *Epiphanie als Geschichte: ein Versuch*, Munich: Kösel, 1966.

Schmidt, Peter, 'The Interpretation of the Resurrection: Historical and Theological Truth', *Communio*, 11, 1984, pp. 75–88.

Schmithals, W., *An Introduction to the Theology of Rudolph Bultmann*, English trans. John Bowden, London: SCM Press, 1967.

Schonfield, Hugh J., *The Passover Plot*, London: Hutchinson, 1965.

—— *Those Incredible Christians*, London: Hutchinson, 1968.

Schoonenberg, P., 'Schillebeeckx en de exegese', *Tijdschrift voor Theologie*, 15, 1975, pp. 255–68.

Schweitzer, A., *The Quest of the Historical Jesus*, with an intro. by James M. Robinson, New York: Macmillan, 1968.

Schweizer, E., *Jesus*, English trans., London: SCM Press, 1971.

—— πνεῦμα, *TDNT*, Vol. VI, 1968, pp. 396–455.

—— *The Good News According to Mark*, London: SPCK, 1971.

Scott, C. A. A., *Christianity According to St Paul*, Cambridge University Press, 1927.

Scott, E. F., *The Spirit in the New Testament*, London: Hodder & Stoughton, 1923.

Searle, John R., 'Proper Names', *Philosophical Logic*, ed. P. F. Strawson, Oxford University Press, 1967, pp. 89–96.

—— 'Proper Names and Descriptions', *The Encyclopaedia of Philosophy*, ed. Paul Edwards, London: Collier-Macmillan; New York: Macmillan Co. & Free Press, 1967.

Seidensticker, P., *Die Auferstehung Jesu in der Botschaft der Evangelisten*, Stuttgart: Katholisches Bibelwerk, 1967.

Selby, Peter, *Look for Living*, London: SCM Press, 1976.

Shoemaker, Sydney, 'Memory', *The Encyclopaedia of Philosophy*, Vol. 5., ed. Paul Edwards, London: Collier-Macmillan; New York: Macmillan Co. & Free Press, 1967.

―― *Self-Knowledge and Self-Identity*, Ithaca, NY: Cornell University Press, 1963.

Sider, R. J., 'The Pauline Conception of the Resurrection Body in I Corinthians XV: 35–54', *NTS*, 21, 1974–5, pp. 428–39.

Smart, James D., *The Divided Mind of Modern Theology: Karl Barth and Rudolph Bultmann 1908–1933*, Philadelphia: Westminster Press, 1967.

Sparrow Simpson, W. J., *Our Lord's Resurrection*, London: Longmans, Green, 1905.

―― *The Resurrection and Modern Thought*, London: Longmans, Green, 1911.

Stählin, G., 'On the Third Day, The Easter Traditions of the Primitive Church', *Interpretation*, 10, 1956, pp. 282–99.

Stanton, G. N., *Jesus of Nazareth in the New Testament Preaching*, Cambridge University Press, 1974.

―― 'The Gospel Traditions and Early Christological Reflection', *Christ, Faith and History*, ed. S. W. Sykes and J. P. Clayton, Cambridge University Press, 1972, pp. 191–204.

Stauffer, E., 'ἀγαπάω, ἀγάπη, ἀγαπητός', *TDNT*, Vol. I, pp. 21–55.

Strachan, R. H., *The Second Epistle of Paul to the Corinthians*, London: Hodder & Stoughton, 1935.

Strack, H. L. and Billerbeck, P., *Kommentar zum Neuen Testament aus Talmud und Midrasch*, Munich: Beck, 1922–28.

Strathmann, H., 'Μάρτυς', *TDNT*, Vol. IV, pp. 474–514.

Strauss, D. F., *The Life of Jesus Critically Examined*, English trans. from the 4th German edition by George Eliot (1846), facsimile edn. with intro. by P. C. Hodgson, London: SCM Press, 1973.

―― *A New Life of Jesus*, 2 Vols., London and Edinburgh: Williams and Norgate, 1865. Originally published as *Das Leben Jesu, für das deutsche Volk bearbeitet*, 2 Vols., Leipzig, 1864.

Sykes, S. W. (ed.), *Karl Barth—Studies of His Theological Methods*, Oxford: Clarendon Press, 1979.

―― 'The Essence of Christianity', *Religious Studies*, 7, 1971, pp. 291–305.

Sykes, S. W. and Clayton, J. P. (eds.), *Christ Faith and History*, Cambridge University Press, 1972.

Tavard, G., *Holy Writ or Holy Church*, London: Burns & Oates, 1959.

Taylor, John V., *The Go-Between God*, London: SCM Press, 1972.

Taylor, Vincent, *The Life and Ministry of Jesus*, London: Macmillan, 1955.

Teeple, H. M., 'The Historical Beginnings of the Resurrection Faith', *Studies in the New Testament and Early Christian Literature, Essays in Honour of A. P. Wikgren, Novum Testamentum*, Supp. Vol. 33, ed. D. E. Aune. Leiden: Brill, 1972, pp. 107–20.

Tenney, Merrill, C., 'The Historicity of the Resurrection', *Jesus of Nazareth: Saviour and Lord*, Carl Henry (ed.), London: Tyndale Press, 1966.

—— *The Reality of the Resurrection*, New York: Harper & Row, 1963.

Thornton, L. S., *Revelation and the Modern World*, Philadelphia: Westminster Press, 1950.

Thurneysen, Eduard, 'Offenbarung in Religionsgeschichte und Bibel' (1928), in *Anfänge der dialektischen Theologie*, ed. J. Moltmann, Vol. 11, Munich: Kaiser Verlag, 1963.

Tillich, P., *Systemic Theology*, 3 Vols., Welwyn, Herts; Nisbet, 1953–64.

Timm, Hermann, *Geist der Liebe*, Gütersloh: Gerd Mohn, 1978.

Trites, A. A., *The New Testament Concept of Witness*, Cambridge University Press, 1977.

Troeltsch, E., 'Empiricism and Platonism in the Philosophy of Religion', *Harvard Theological Review*, 5, 1912, pp. 401–22.

—— *Gesammelte Schriften*, 4 Vols., Tübingen: J. C. B Mohr (Paul Siebeck), 1912–25.

—— 'Historiography', *Encyclopaedia of Religion and Ethics*, ed. J. Hastings, Vol. VI, Edinburgh: T. & T. Clark, 1913.

—— *The Absoluteness of Christianity and the History of Religions*, English trans. David Reid, with intro. by James L. Adams, Richmond (Virg.): John Knox Press, 1971; London: SCM Press, 1972.

—— *The Social Teaching of the Christian Churches*, English trans. Olive Wyon, London: Allen & Unwin, 1931.

Tupper, E. Frank, *The Theology of Wolfhart Pannenberg*, London: SCM Press, 1974.

Urmson, J. O., 'Recognition', *Proceedings of the Aristotelian Society*, 56, 1955–6, pp. 259–80.

Vermes, G., *Jesus the Jew*, London: Collins, 1973.

Ware, R. C., 'The Resurrection of Jesus', *Heythrop Journal*, 16, 1975, pp. 22–35 and 174–94.

Weeden, T. J., *Mark—Traditions in Conflict*, Philadelphia: Fortress Press, 1971.

Weiss, J., *Der erste Korintherbrief*, KEK, 1910.

Wellhausen, J., *Das Evangelium Marci*, Berlin: Reimer, 1902.

Wendland, H.-D., *Die Briefe an die Korinther*, Göttingen: Vandenhoeck & Ruprecht, (1936) 6th edn. 1954.

Wenham, J., *Easter Enigma*, Exeter: Paternoster Press, 1984.

Westcott, B. F., *The Gospel of the Resurrection*, London: Macmillan, 1879 (first published 1866).

—— 'The Resurrection of Christ—A New Revelation', *Contemporary Review*, Nov. 1877, pp. 1070–87.

—— *The Revelation of the Risen Lord*, London: Macmillan, 1881.

Whitaker, D., 'What Happened to the Body of Jesus?', *Expository Times*, 81, 1970, pp. 307–11.

Wicker, Brian, *The Story-shaped World. Fiction and Metaphysics: Some Variations on a Theme*, London: Athlone Press, 1975.

Wilckens, U., 'The Tradition-History of the Resurrection of Jesus', *The Significance of the Message of the Resurrection for Faith in Jesus Christ*, ed. C. F. D. Moule, London: SCM Press, 1968.

—— 'Der Ursprung der Überlieferung der Erscheinungen des Auferstandenen', *Dogma und Denkstrukturen*, ed. W. Joest and W. Pannenberg, Göttingen: Vandenhoeck & Ruprecht, 1963, pp. 56–95.

—— *Die Missionsreden der Apostelgeschichte*, Neukirchen: Neukirchner Verlag, 1960.

—— *Resurrection: Biblical Testimony to the Resurrection, An Historical Examination and Explanation*, English trans. A. M. Stewart, Atlanta: John Knox Press, 1978.

Wilder, A. N., 'Variant Traditions of the Resurrection in Acts', *JBL*, 62, 1943, pp. 307–18.

Wiles, M. 'A Survey of Issues in the Myth Debate' in *Incarnation and Myth*, ed. M. Goulder, London: SCM Press, pp. 1–12.

Williams, H. A., *Jesus and the Resurrection*, London: Mowbrays, 1960.

Williams, Rowan, *Resurrection*, London: Darton, Longman & Todd, 1982.

Winter, Paul, '1 Corinthians XV: 3b–7', *Novum Testamentum*, 2, 1957/8, pp. 142–50.

Wittgenstein, L., *Philosophical Investigations*, English trans. G. E. M. Anscombe, Oxford: Blackwell, 1967.

—— *The Blue and Brown Books*, Oxford: Blackwell, 1964.

—— *Zettel*, ed. G. E. M. Anscombe and G. H. von Wright, English trans. G. E. M. Anscombe, Oxford: Blackwell, 1967.

Yarnold, G. D., *Risen Indeed*, New York: Oxford University Press, 1959.

Zahrnt, Heinz, *The Historical Jesus*, English trans. J. S. Bowden, London: SCM Press, 1963.

—— *The Question of God*, English trans. R. A. Wilson, London: SCM Press, 1969.

INDEX

Abba 343
agape:
  divinity of 311, 336–9, 340–3, 346–7,
    350–3, 358, 362
  uniqueness of 286, 289, 292, 295,
    331–9, 349–51
agnosticism 306–7
Alexander the Great 192
Alston, W. 229
Alsup, J. E. 21, 23 n., 234–5, 241–2
Althaus, P. 54–5, 114 n., 355 n.
angels:
  at empty tomb 17, 49, 214–15
  in Luke 240
  St Michael 176
apocalyptic expectation 82, 92–4, 155–6,
    175, 231, 232
apologetic 32, 111, 142, 170, 190
apostles, *see* authority, apostolic
appearances:
  centrality to faith 113, 154–62, 172,
    212–13, 224–6, 364–8
  gospel narratives of 62, 109–10, 122,
    124, 188–9, 194, 202–4, 211, 224,
    234–49, 327
  kerygmatic tradition of 40, 47, 51–2,
    59–60, 62–72, 89, 92, 98, 110–11,
    113, 124–5, 160, 202–13, 216–17,
    221, 223–49
  as legitimation of apostolic status
    110–11, 209, 224, 238
Aquinas, Thomas 74, 98 n., 136, 190,
    193
Ascension 76–7, 80, 346
aspective integration 26, 362
atonement 4, 8, 99, 343, 360
Aune, D. E. 69 n., 153 n.
Austen, Jane 350
authority, apostolic 110–11, 209, 238

Babel 9
Baillie, J. 347 n.
Baker, J. A. 5, 9
Bammel, E. 141 n.
Barnabas, the Apostle 238
Barrett, C. K. 232 n.

Barth, K. 13, 23 n., 25, 96–147, 156, 157,
    159, 184, 186, 188, 198, 201, 203–5,
    210, 224
Baruch, Apocalypse of 53, 231
Bartsch, H.-W. 48 n., 99 n., 141 n.
Bater, R. R. 9 n., 55 n., 80 n.
Baur, F. C. 149–50, 167
Beare, F. W. 79 n.
beaten men argument 168–70
Benjamin, W. 367
Bennett, J. 317 n.
Benoit, P. 46 n.
Bergson, H. 281, 320, 323
Berkhof, H. 254
Bernadette, St 69, 176, 177
Bertocci, P. A. 314 n.
Betz, O. 48 n.
Bickermann, E. 49 n.
Bill, Alan 189 n.
Billerbeck, P. 53 n., 231 n.
Blondel, M. 192 n.
Bode, E. L. 48 n., 50 n., 60 n.
Bornkamm, G. 6 n., 38 n., 51 n., 133,
    329 n., 333 n.
Braaten, C. E. 132 n.
Bradley, F. G. 150 n.
Broad, C. D. 275–7, 279
Brunner, E. 17 n., 107 n., 108 n.
Buddhism 36, 175
Bulgakoff, S. 347 n.
Bultmann, R. 13, 14, 35, 48, 49, 52,
    96–147, 156, 157–8, 159, 184, 186,
    188, 191, 192, 193, 201, 203–5, 210,
    217, 224, 244, 255 n., 257 n., 272 n.,
    297, 303–4, 311–12, 328, 329 n.,
    337, 338 n., 345, 355, 356, 359
Buren, P. van 299–300
Buttrick, C. A. 268 n.

Caesar, Julius 192
Caiaphas 79
Calvinism 107
Campenhausen, H. von 48 n., 52–3,
    56 n., 57 n., 59–60, 62 n., 63, 155,
    218 n., 264, 274 n.
Carpenter, W. B. 153 n.

witness, NT concept of 137, 139–41
Wittgenstein, L. 295 n., 309, 317–18, 321 n., 322 n., 348
Wolfenbüttel Fragments 11, 149, 167
women:
  incompetent as witnesses 30, 59–60, 141
  omitted by Paul 17, 141

Word of God 96, 111–12, 116, 124, 128, 136–7, 139, 156–7, 210, 359
worship 27, 338–9, 358, 368

Yeti 174

Zahrnt, H. 103 n.